D1028892

With the compliments of

HAROLD VAGTBORG

President Emeritus
Southwest Research Institute
San Antonio, Texas

RESEARCH AND AMERICAN INDUSTRIAL DEVELOPMENT
A Bicentennial Look at the Contributions of Applied R&D

RESEARCH AND AMERICAN INDUSTRIAL DEVELOPMENT

A BICENTENNIAL LOOK AT THE CONTRIBUTIONS OF APPLIED R & D

By

HAROLD VAGTBORG

President Emeritus
Southwest Research Institute
San Antonio, Texas

Supplement
"Highlights of 50 Years in R&D Management"
by Maurice Holland

PERGAMON PRESS
NEW YORK / TORONTO / OXFORD / SYDNEY / BRAUNSCHWEIG / PARIS

Pergamon Press Offices:

U.S.A.   Pergamon Press Inc., Maxwell House, Fairview Park,
                 Elmsford, New York 10523, U.S.A.

U.K.   Pergamon Press Ltd., Headington Hill Hall, Oxford OX3 OBW,
                 England

CANADA   Pergamon of Canada, Ltd., 207 Queen's Quay West,
                 Toronto 1, Canada

AUSTRALIA   Pergamon Press (Aust.) Pty. Ltd., 19a Boundary Street,
                 Rushcutters Bay, N.S.W. 2011, Australia

FRANCE   Pergamon Press SARL, 24 rue des Ecoles,
                 75240 Paris, Cedex 05, France

WEST GERMANY   Pergamon Press GMbH, 3300 Braunschweig, Postfach 2923,
                 Burgplatz 1, West Germany

Library of Congress Cataloging in Publication Data

Vagtborg, Harold.
    Research and American industrial development.

    Includes index.
    1. Research, Industrial--United States--History.
I.   Title.
T176. V3   607'. 2' 73   75-14439
ISBN 0-08-019791-4

CONTENTS

FOREWORD

If this book were to be written single-handedly, its author, Harold Vagtborg, would probably be the best qualified individual in the country to write it. But as no one man is wise enough out of his own knowledge and experience to do full justice to so complex a subject as the history of applied science in the United States, without borrowing heavily from the impressions and work of others, Dr. Vagtborg has forthrightly enlisted a few contributors *who were there and saw it happen* to supplement his own work. This book then is neither a symposium nor a digest. It is one cohesive book which, like the product of a laboratory, results from the work of several creative minds with a high order of professional competence.

Vagtborg's qualifications for creating this book are unique. He was Director of Armour Research Foundation in the early days of R&D management, when scientific training was just starting to jump over the campus walls and infiltrate industry. He went on learning by teaching others the role of research in industry.

I think of Vagtborg in retrospect of 30 years of intimate association. I worked closely with him in the establishment of four research institutes—Armour in Chicago, Midwest in Kansas City, Southwest in San Antonio, and the Instituto de Investigaciones Industriales in Monterrey, N.L., Mexico. I visualize him as a "Missionary in Science and Education."

Like Junipero Serra, founder of Catholic Missions extending from one end of California to the other, spaced one day's journey apart, Vagtborg's institutes, which he established, extended north and south from Chicago to Kansas City and to San Antonio. They carried the "religion of research" to converts even in Mexican industry and business. My favorite name for Vagtborg is "Harold the Builder." Junipero Serra built missions which are standing today. They bring religion to millions, while Vagtborg's "Cathedrals of Science," called "Research Institutes," have the same basic foundation—"*Faith in Ultimate Results*." "There is no conflict between *Science and Religion*"—Robert Milliken, one of the first American Nobel laureates, used that phrase as the title of his book.

Unlike the specialized industrial scientist whose experience is limited by the walls of a single research institute located in one city, his work projected on the national scene. Vagtborg has given his whole working life to the establishment of the broad spectrum of the research institute movement.

His special talent is drawing management and research into a closer and more productive working relationship. Vagtborg has the rare ability and intuitive sense as a picker of men. No "palace guard" of "yes" men insulates him from the outside world. He has only one criterion for his management team that can be best summed up in a single word—performance!

It would be difficult to apportion the causes of the fantastic growth of research institutes in the 1930s and 1940s amongst the contributing factors; as I see it, they were:

- the crash programs during World War II;
- decentralizing of the concentration of power and policy in Washington;
- National Research Council was planning to open regional offices in four most densely populated industrial areas of USA;
- regional consciousness of the need for a local model of Mellon Institute or Battelle to serve their industry, with "research for hire" facilities;
- the blast of the atomic bomb over Hiroshima rattled the windows in every executive suite in American industry. That dramatic demonstration of applied science power blasted the theory of smug complacency in management circles and propelled American industry into world supremacy;
- top management became convinced that research was a paying investment. R&D was proved to be the most effective form of insurance for growth and development. R&D in a company or a nation is the offensive weapon of aggressive companies, to win wars and to beat off the enemy of competition; and
- management needs no longer to be sold on research. The greatest gamble for a company or a nation is to do no R&D at all.

But certainly Vagtborg has earned a distinguished place among many—through his untiring efforts and dedication to the cause of research. Through practical understanding of men and methods in industry and through his counsel, he has helped management to become the catalyst rather than merely the employer, the creative forces of man-built monuments of technology as enduring as the Pyramids of Egypt.

As management has accepted research at a high and fast mounting dollar price, it has found itself with a complex but indispensable asset that it does not yet know how to handle to best advantage. This volume is a greatly needed and long overdue synthesis of the problems common to the front office and the laboratory, as they work together toward a greater singleness of purpose.

Maurice Holland
July 1, 1974

ABOUT THE AUTHOR

Harold Vagtborg has spent almost forty years in the organization and administration of basic and applied research institutions. He was (1937-1945) director of Armour Research Foundation of Illinois Institute of Technology (now IITRI), director of the Institute of Gas Technology (1941-1943), both of Chicago, president of Midwest Research Institute in Kansas

City, Missouri (1945-1948). Early in 1947 he became consultant to Mr. Thomas Slick in establishing the several research institutions in San Antonio, Texas. In September 1948 he accepted the positions of president of the Southwest Foundation for Research and Education, the Southwest Research Institute, and the Institute of Inventive Research, as well as scientific advisor to the famed Essar Ranch. He was also made president of Southwest Agricultural Institute (San Antonio) when it was organized in 1957. Simultaneously with these appointments, he served as the first director of the Instituto de Investigaciones Industriales in Monterrey, Mexico, from 1951-1957.

He has been consultant to foreign governments and confederations in the organization of applied research institutions abroad and has assisted in the establishment of at least 40 research organizations in the United States that either operate under independent charters or are affiliated with colleges or universities.

Through the years, he has served his government in several advisory capacities and as head of missions to several European countries following

World War II that had the purpose of assisting to hasten economic recovery through the research process.

Dr. Vagtborg is the recipient of the Silver Medal from the Royal Swedish Academy of Technical Sciences, recipient of the Aristotle-Aquinas Award from the Catholic Foundation, honorary Doctor of Science degree from Missouri Valley College, and an honorary Doctor of Laws degree from Park College.

His professional societies include the American Association for the Advancement of Science, the American Chemical Society, American Physical Society, American Society of Civil Engineers, American Society of Mechanical Engineers, Scientific Research Society of America, Society of Chemical Industry of London, and the Chemical Society of London. He is listed in Who's Who in America and American Men of Science.

In this book the author has attempted to give an overall view of the history of technology from earliest times while presenting a definitive view of its rapid acceleration during the past two hundred years of American history. Of special importance is his account of the development and contributions of a type of scientific research institution that is unique to the United States and is in contrast to partially federally subsidized specific industry research and development laboratories in other countries—the private nonprofit applied research institution.

On January 18, 1976, shortly after returning the last galleys of this book, Harold Vagtborg died. Among the many tributes to him was this excerpt from a resolution by the board of one of the institutions with which he was closely associated:

Dr. Vagtborg was a dreamer and a doer. He was a maker of institutions, a builder whose works will live on to benefit the world of his grandchildren who gave him so much of his inspiration. Harold Vagtborg lived for the future and through his works he will continue to live.

PREFACE

To explore the circumstances that have caused the United States to become the strongest industrial nation in the world is an interesting challenge . . . and one that requires consideration of many factors relating to the phenomenal journey to such stature over the past 200 years.

As a colony of the British Empire, young America was expected to ship raw materials to the homeland and receive finished goods in return. Despite restrictions on home manufacture, the colonists had a will to become self-sufficient, and thus a strong sense of motivation was born, one that has existed for two centuries.

In this book, a brief account is given of the development of technology and its migration from the Mediterranean Sea to Europe to the United States, where it became the base for further invention and innovation, which reached amazing new heights. In general, this narrative is less concerned with details of products and processes and more with motivation, incentive, philosophy, methodology, organization, and reward.

Sufficient coverage is given to the beginnings and development of research activities in American industry and government so that the reader gains an understanding of the background and an appreciation of the importance of research in the development of our society. A scholar on this subject will find innumerable published works to supplement what has been written here. Ultimately, he will reach the same conclusion: namely, the realization that scientific research and the application of resultant new knowledge were slow to get started in this nation, but have yielded many rewards.

Special attention is given here to a type of organization that until recent years has been unique to this country—the not-for-profit applied research institute. American industry is highly fragmented, and only a relatively small percentage of the 250,000 manufacturing organizations in the country feel justified in maintaining their own research and development team. The British system of having numerous industrial research associations (48 in 1968) subsidized by the government for as much as 50 percent of the cost of operation is a plan that was never adopted in the United States. The independent applied research institutes with multidisciplinary staffs evolved largely to meet the research needs of small corporations and enhance the special projects of large ones. This evolvement of applied research institutions to serve industry and government was one of the important events that stimulated and supported industrial development in the United States in the last 50 years.

During the World War II era, probably as many as one hundred of these institutions were established. By far the largest number were closely related to universities, taking the form of departments or divisions formed to conduct applied research for government and industry. This applied research function was separate from the basic research activity traditionally associated with colleges and universities as a part of the educational process. After a few years of existence, many of these applied research activities in universities were discontinued for one reason or another. Only a very few have survived, and others continue to make their contributions, although at reduced levels of activity in many cases.

During even earlier times, however, a group of institutions known as the "independents" developed separately from these university-oriented organizations. They had remarkable success, and to this day, they continue to grow in size and scope of activity. Following this same pattern, other "independents" evolved in later years, and although less well known than the original group, they, too, are making important contributions to modern society.

As "independents," this original group of research organizations differed from the university-supported institutions in that they operated under corporate charters as nonprofit institutions with their own boards of trustees or directors and their own officers, staff, laboratories, and other facilities. Armour and Stanford were exceptions in this regard, however, because they had rather loose affiliations with universities as well. Cornell Aeronautical Laboratory (CAL) was also somewhat of an exception in that it was a stock corporation, wholly owned by Cornell University, and was granted a federal tax exemption. CAL did, however, operate in a manner very similar to that of other independents, under its own management and board of directors. Listed below are these "independent" institutions ranked in order of their year of beginning of operations:

Mellon Institute for Industrial Research, Pittsburgh, Pennsylvania	1911
Battelle Memorial Institute, Columbus, Ohio	1929
Armour Research Foundation, Chicago, Illinois	1937
Cornell Aeronautical Laboratory, Inc., Buffalo, New York	1945
Southern Research Institute, Birmingham, Alabama	1945
Midwest Research Institute, Kansas City, Missouri	1945
The Franklin Institute Laboratories, Philadelphia, Pennsylvania	1946
Stanford Research Institute, Menlo Park, California	1946
Southwest Research Institute, San Antonio, Texas	1947

Through their years of existence, the combined operating budgets of these nine "independent" institutions have never exceeded 1.5 percent of the total R&D expenditures of industry and government in any one year. Despite their small budgets, as a group, these institutions have probably contributed more to stimulate industrial research and its product, industrial growth, than any other single factor.

Thus, the purposes of this book begin to take form. Primarily, the intentions are (1) to review the character of the environment that has made American industry so strong (approximately 10 percent of the world's population produces 50 percent of the world's manufactured goods); (2) to relate the philosophies behind the successful research institutes, with regard to organization and development; (3) to demonstrate that this nation must expand its research appropriation and adopt drastic new research priorities; and (4) to guide people in developing countries who want to increase industrial growth and obtain the higher standard of living that such growth brings. With regard to the final objective, it is important to note that, as a rule, in developing countries, efforts toward this end are too involved with economists and flow diagrams of technology transfer. It is hoped that these countries will realize that economists and flow diagrams do not create new products and processes for industrial development. Instead, new industrial products evolve from the efforts of the scientist or engineer, who either develops new materials in his laboratory (if he has one) or interprets and applies worldwide dynamic technology as it relates to his country.

Finally, this book has been written for the purpose of relating the influence R & D has had on the phenomenal transformation of a British colony into a world power in the span of 200 years. It is a tribute to this nation's forthcoming 1976 Bicentennial Anniversary.

ACKNOWLEDGMENTS

I want to acknowledge the excellent cooperation I have had in the preparation of this book from personnel of the corporations that have assisted me in the preparation of Chapter III, the presidents of the research institutes that have contributed much of the material that is contained in the several chapters that relate to their organizations, and to the several individuals who have co-authored with me several sections of this work. In particular I wish to recognize Sherrie Gott who has again demonstrated her outstanding professional skill in editing the manuscript and counseling me on editorial content. Thanks also to Brenda Hedemann for her untiring efforts in typing and retyping the manuscript.

CHAPTER I

PROLOGUE

"Adams' inquisitiveness enabled man to escape from nature's trap of narrow specialization and to build a variety of civilizations out of the ideas in his head, as well as with the tools in his hands. Man, by science, can duplicate them all or discard them at will."

Dr. Loren Eiseley
University of Pennsylvania

Man's curiosity . . . his motivation to improve his environment—to fully develop his country's scientific potential—to contribute in a positive, tangible way toward the technological advancement of his world . . . this is the quality that opens the door to the wonder and excitement of scientific research and development. In this prologue, the reader will discover what transpired in the early stages of such R&D and thereby acquire the background information that is so essential if he is to understand the main theme of this book. Specifically, the topics of concern here are as follows: (1) the relationships of art, science, technology, and development; (2) the growth and migration of technology from earliest times; (3) the growth of industry in the United States from Colonial Times to World War I; and (4) man's involvement in science and technology.

RELATIONSHIPS OF ART, SCIENCE, TECHNOLOGY, AND DEVELOPMENT

In technology, art is an integral part, but art in the industrial or mechanical sense must be distinguished from art in the aesthetic sense. In the case of the former, art is a consideration in how a process is developed and followed . . . how a product is made. Thus, there are limitations (industrial or mechanical by nature) to Webster's definition of technology, to wit "technology is that branch of ethnology which treats the development of the arts."

Industrial art relates to something to be done . . . science to something to be known. Science per se evolved much later in time than technology. It represents the acquisition of knowledge—facts, laws, and proximate causes gained and verified by exact observation and correct thinking. In other words, it is knowledge reduced to law and embodied in systems. While the basic scientist is seeking new truths about natural phenomena, the applied scientist utilizes these new truths and converts them through practical application to new technologies. In turn, the development engineers transform these technologies into industrial activity. Then, in a very real sense, yesterday's basic science is today's applied science, tomorrow's engineering, and the next day's industry.

THE MIGRATION OF TECHNOLOGY FROM EARLY TIMES

It is interesting to note that the political history tracing the rise and fall of civilizations does not always parallel the development of technology. Since earliest days, there have been scattered examples of superior levels of technology in societies that have not received much historical attention, probably because they disappeared after a short life. With that in mind, the focus here is not on those fleeting elements of society but rather on the advancing technology of the great and long-lasting civilizations. History seems to support the fact that these enduring civilizations rose to new heights in technology and then ebbed in favor of another. Students of the history of technology appear to agree that there was a definite *pattern of migration* regarding technologies. Typically, technological advancement would soar to its highest level, sequentially, and then migrate from one area of the world, step by step, to another, in chronological order.

The popular belief that China was the point of origin of most early technologies is rapidly fading as archaeological discoveries are accelerating and are proving otherwise. The Chinese civilization evolved much later than that of Western Asia or Egypt; the popular impression that it is older is wholly incorrect. As of yet, in China, no piece of metal has been found dated earlier than about 1200 B.C., that is, at least three thousand years later than such concrete discoveries found in Egypt and very much later than those found in Western Asia. As for the written word, there is no surviving document written in Chinese which may be dated earlier than about the eleventh or, at the earliest, the twelfth century B.C., that is, over two thousand years later than such documentation in Egypt and Western Asia.*

Today, it is generally accepted that the ancient civilizations with their respectively developed technologies bordered on the southeastern and southern shores of the Mediterranean Sea. Briefly, the migration of early technologies was from such areas as Mesopotamia, Sumeria, Babylonia, Canaan, Egypt, Nubia, etc. A move upward then occurred to include Asia Minor and subsequently flourished into its main thrust in the Egyptian Empire where it reached its zenith in 1500 B.C. Technology then reached further heights in the growing prominence of the Assyrian Empire (zenith about 700 B.C.), and in the Median and Chaldean Empires (about 600 B.C.), followed by greater emergence in Greece (500 B.C.), Macedonia (about 325 B.C.—Alexander the Great), and Rome (200 B.C.).

To a degree, these rises and declines of civilizations and the corresponding alternating of the setting for technological development were limited to the lands that bordered or were located close to the Mediterranean to the south, southeast, east, and northeast. Since there was little space left in these areas for the nations' growth, the push was toward the northern and northwestern shores of the Mediterranean, toward which the barbarians from the north (present-day Europe) were likewise pushing. Through these movements and resulting contacts, a great deal of technology flowed into Europe until the continent sank into the ignorance of the Middle Ages. In the meantime, the Muhammadans, who had conquered the Eastern Roman Empire, established the Islam Empire around 700 A.D. Correspondingly, the Muslims conquered Spain and moved up into France; however, they were stopped at the Battle of Tours in 732 A.D. It was the Muslims who, during the Middle Ages, were the leading students of science, mathematics, grammar, and astronomy, building up a reservoir of knowledge made possible through contributions of the earlier civilizations as well as their own major efforts which flowed into Europe at the end of the Middle Ages. It was at this time that religious restrictions on free thinking and acting were lifted and people were stimulated to achieve a better way of life. Beginning about 1450 A.D., new and much-advanced technologies were developing throughout the European area, with more rapidly growing contributions from Britain. It was this resurgence that was to become the Industrial

---

*Breasted, J. H., *A History of the Early World*, 2nd ed., Ginn & Co., 1944.

Revolution, beginning in about 1750 A.D. and continuing until it was surpassed sometime in the early twentieth century by the American Industrial Revolution, which began in the United States about 1850 A.D.

For the reader who is interested to a greater extent in the development of technology, that is, on an almost year-to-year basis from ancient times, his attention is directed to the 36 pages of excellent charts appearing in the Appendix. This fascinating account, which is reproduced herein by permission of the Clarendon Press of Oxford University*, also gives parallels of historical events occurring at simultaneous points in time.

THE GROWTH OF INDUSTRY IN THE UNITED STATES
FROM COLONIAL TIMES TO WORLD WAR I by Herbert I. Hoffman†

The story of the U.S. research institutes should be told against the background of their forerunners—independent shops of artisans and innovators who helped to anchor and sustain the American colonies and to generate the Industrial Revolution. Research laboratories in the United States developed from a complex heritage of innovative drives, philosophical-scientific efforts, and capital structure. It is fitting that the prologue to this history of industrial developments examine not only the history of inventions but also the history of *innovation environments*, since the development of industrial laboratories can be traced through the environments in which they functioned. As a reference framework, an innovation environment may be envisioned as the incentives, stresses, and technical resources surrounding the innovators.

Most of the early colonial inventions were products of artful individuals seeking to improve their simple tools of livelihood. It is doubtful whether many of them generated their inventions in a technological atmosphere of academic interest and philosophical-scientific diversion. In contrast, some of the technically talented gentlemen of later times, including Benjamin Franklin, Thomas Jefferson, and others, appeared to be driven by intellectual curiosities to some of their clever adaptations and inventions. In the later periods, innovators knowingly drew upon theories and discoveries which provided added dimensions of growth potential to their new technologies. Finally, other innovation environments ranged from unsophisticated trial-

---

*Derry, T. K., and Trevor I. Williams, *A Short History of Technology*, Clarendon Press: Oxford, 1960.
†Manager, Central Proposal Office, Southwest Research Institute.

and-error searches to the application of scientific method and deliberate planning (as was developing in Europe) to achieve the objective of innovation.

In scanning the American innovative history, it is possible to recognize some classically diverse settings such as those of Thomas Edison and Benjamin Franklin. Driven by innovative compulsions, Edison tirelessly applied himself, through progressive experiments, to stunningly successful conclusions. Franklin, also self-taught (but widely educated), seemed to have theorized more completely before attempting an experiment. "Principles before practice" was apparently his view in founding the American Philosophical Society.

Historically, it seems fitting that the nonprofit research institutes were built on the broad heritage of Ben Franklin, while the industrial counterparts of the nation's R&D strength have descended from Edison's Menlo Park Laboratories and the electrically oriented laboratories of the utility industries which grew from Edison's work. With those classic and contrasting examples thus forming part of the aforementioned backdrop, it is plausible now to scan early U.S. technological history and attempt to understand the innovation settings. The sources of new technology as well as the personal, political, and economic motivations are all of interest. An added incentive was the patent law* of 1790 which recognized an inventor's right to a limited monopoly.

SETTLEMENT, SURVIVAL, AND LIVELIHOOD

The nation's industrial growth from colonial times is a human saga of settlement, survival, and livelihood in the new world. Early European settlements in North America depended upon trade, imported tools, and the primitive arts of survival. Many British colonial settlements, from which the mainstream of America's industrial growth developed, were outposts of private commercial ventures chartered by Parliament and operated under strict limitations designed to generate sources of raw materials and new markets for tools, provisions, and supplies in the developing colonies. British law banned the exportation of manufacturing machinery and manufacturing know-how to the new world. Despite this restriction, there was a persistent emigration of skills and manufacturing know-how to America. Additionally, as colonial skills and markets for finished materials grew, innovations in the colonies generated new spirals of technology and industrial nuclei.

---

*The Story of the United States Patent Office, January 1972. Superintendent of Documents, U.S. Government Printing Office, Washington, D.C. 20402. Price 35 cents, Stock No. 0304-0493.

The marketing opportunities for raw and finished agricultural products as well as for hardware of all kinds stirred the innovative skills among people of all backgrounds. The frontier and agricultural areas required improved tools for surveying, land clearing, hunting and trapping, and farming; cottage industries of all types were pressed for greater productivity; and mechanical inventions, even simple ones, were often phenomenal successes. In 1691, South Carolina passed a law permitting the granting of monopolies or patents to encourage mechanical innovations, and agricultural device patents were subsequently granted. The Massachusetts Colony granted a patent to Joseph Jenks in 1646 for improvements in sawmills and scythes. Perhaps the hope for a monopoly patent was a major incentive to *some* inventors, but few of the early colonial period inventions were patented.

By the early 1700s, the colonial governments were granting patents at increasing rates; the Industrial Revolution was becoming conspicuously important and the governments were anxious to protect and encourage new industrial enterprise.

Although the British Parliament restricted other manufacturing in the colonies, shipbuilding was encouraged and became well established. American entrepreneurs extended beyond shipbuilding into extensive shipping to Europe, the Mediterranean, and the Americas. Ultimately, the colonies' well-developed shipbuilding industry provided the background for the various innovations in American sailing ships, which served as trade route clippers to all parts of the world. The American shipbuilding industry, young and innovative, also encouraged the rapid adaptation of steam engines for marine and other transportation applications.

As evidenced, the colonial industrial growth rate and prevalence of independent spirit enjoyed a booming period, but, perhaps to a fault in the judgment of British government, for, in 1750 a law forbidding the American colonies to build steel furnaces or rolling and slitting mills was enacted by the British. In addition, under King George III, Parliament passed laws prohibiting the export of other new technology such as textile processing machinery, which was revolutionizing England. The colonial markets for manufactured products heightened the colonial innovative climate which, in turn, generated tightened protective laws by Parliament. The Stamp Act of 1765 was followed by the Townshend Act of 1767, which placed additional taxes upon manufactured materials as well as upon tea imported by the colonists. Although the Townshend Act was repealed in 1770, its basic philosophy remained; the Crown and Parliament had the right and the duty to levy taxes on the colonies in order to protect English commerce and industry. This philosophy was instrumental in advancing both political and technical independence in the American colonies.

THE EXPANSIONIST YEARS—TECHNOLOGY APPLIED

During the several decades before and after the American Revolution, Europe was rapidly becoming involved in the Industrial Revolution. The growing American towns and cities, while stifled by the British restrictions on manufacturing industries during the colonial period, nevertheless offered added dimensions to attract innovators and entrepreneurs. Primary factors were the demand for manufactured products and for methods of transporting them to the market centers. A special ingredient of the American innovative environment was the leveling effect of American culture and the expansionist viewpoints of its business and industrial people. In the young nation, cut-and-try inventors, entrepreneurs and businessmen, and a few philosophers were anxious to communicate and to participate in invention and industrial developments.

The raw land and the perpetual shortages of labor, money, and imported machinery continued to provide incentives for imaginative people to devise new ways to obtain and process goods for home consumption and for the vital trading. During the colonial period, the limited manufacturing of both hard and soft goods was carried out mainly in the individual cottage industries. Expanding local markets in many young cities, coupled with the poor transportation to distant markets, resulted in an innovation more entrepreneurial than technical: integrated, mass production systems converted farm products into packaged, edible products. This was a departure from previous European and American food processing, which was fractionated so that grain milling was, for example, independent from grain buying or biscuit baking. Nonetheless, this innovation dated back to a time before the Revolution when newer agricultural process plants were being built as integrated processing systems.

Independent ethnic settlements often developed products and machines that found favor beyond their domains when roads and canals made commerce a reality. The German settlers in Pennsylvania applied their imported manufacturing skills and produced small caliber long rifles designed for hunting. The barrels were bored and reamed on hand-powered machines, and small parts were made with hand-tools. These custom weapons for sharpshooters later proved to be a key factor in the personalized woodland warfare of the American Revolution.

Decades later, the weapon production mastery of Samuel Colt was dramatized when he dumped an assortment of mass-produced, identical pistol parts before a committee of the early U.S. Congress and invited the onlookers to assemble perfectly operable weapons from the interchangeable parts. Mass production of identical parts was driven home as the key to versatile production and maintenance. More than the invention involved in the pistol or in the machine tools, Colt's major innovation was the integration and management that provided interchangeable precision parts, thus demonstrating the importance of this concept.

During the colonial era, the industrial developments and pattern of innovations in the North grew quite differently from those in the South. The northern colonies, with terrain and climate which varied sharply from place to place, leaned toward the development of varied agriculture and hand processing for cottage industries. The northern lands were effectively used as small farms and as hunting and fishing grounds for game, which served both as food and as a source of fish and fur pelts for export. A shortage of skilled labor in the northern areas limited the growth of those cottage industries, and a similar labor shortage in the southern colonies restricted their production, which was largely single-crop agriculture. Seven colonies grew from British trading company grants which served their purposes through development of plantations for tobacco, indigo, and rice. These were the early major export crops of the South; the short-staple cotton that grew well on most southern farmlands was an important crop limited to colonial use in spinning and weaving for home markets. Long-staple cotton, which was much more economical to handpick in removing the cottonseed from the fiber, was shipped to English textile plants from the West Indies and from limited acreage along the southern colonial coastal lands. The American short-staple cotton, not as desirable as the easily processed long-staple cotton, was not a major export crop. The shortage of farm labor, in both northern and southern colonies alike, had been somewhat relieved by the practice of slavery, but slavery was beginning to diminish in the years following the Revolutionary War. To many Americans, slavery seemed in conflict with the intentions of the founding of the new nation, and slavery was not, by that time, a vital economic factor in most of the states.

Thus was the innovative environment in which Eli Whitney found himself when he left Connecticut and went to Georgia to serve as a private teacher on a large estate. Whitney had a liberal education and no doubt was acquainted with the textile machinery used at that time in his home state. When he became aware of the important need for removing seeds from short-staple cotton, he applied himself to the task with immediate deliberation and obvious talent. In a short time, Whitney produced a simple machine, which might be called a mechanical rotating comb; it served remarkably well for removing cottonseeds from the fiber and created considerable local interest in 1792. Certainly, even without Whitney's further business and entrepreneurial ventures, the cotton gin would have become a successful machine on its own right; however, Whitney struggled for several years with both patent and legal problems, especially with the task of raising capital with which to expand his business of manufacturing cotton gins. Ultimately, his efforts were successful and he went on to still greater renown with machine tools for the manufacture of muskets, thus becoming a champion of mass production and interchangeable parts.

It is noteworthy that the cotton gin made U.S. short-staple cotton a competitive fiber, very soon becoming king of the export crops—with the help of greatly expanded slave labor in the South!

By the end of the colonial period, changes in the marketing and political scenes were reflected by the innovation environment of the times. Major developments included an improved flatboat for inland rivers and a keel riverboat. Improvements in textile machinery were rapid in the colonies, and Benjamin Franklin's innovative spirit was evidently motivated more by the general human condition than by commercialism; his inventions include the famous Franklin stove, the lightning rod, and bifocal eyeglasses. The innovation environment of that period not only spurred commercial developments toward better transportation and better manufacturing but motivated developments of war machines. A hand-powered submarine attempted to mine ships of the British fleet in New York Harbor in 1776. Designed by David Bushnell, the screw-propelled submarine was probably the first working submarine and apparently the first American-developed war machine.

A significant step on the American industrial scene was made by Samuel Slater, who was responsible for establishing large-scale and practical spinning mills in America in the late 1700s. Slater learned his trade well under the innovator, Arkwright, in England. Evading British law, Slater secretly emigrated to America, ultimately to replicate Arkwright's machinery and factory system from memory. The result was perhaps the first significant factory in America. Slater's boldness was apparently in response to American prize offerings for workable spinning machinery. His larger impact on the

American scene came later, however, in response to the market demand for woolen cloth. By 1815, he began the manufacture of such cloth, a process that was an extension of his carpet milling operation begun by him a few years earlier. Slater's main contributions as a father of American industry were the organization of "borrowed" technology, available capital, and ready markets in order to develop and occupy an entire new community devoted to textiles.

By the end of the eighteenth century, the established textile industry was demanding more sophisticated machinery for spinning and weaving. The increased demand for new machinery, as well as the demand for repair parts and services, encouraged specialized machine shops and metalworking shops, particularly in the textile areas of Massachusetts. By the early 1800s, such metalworking shops had become very well established and widespread, beginning to branch out into production of various small metal parts and of steam engines, as steam technology was imported from England. New developments in textile machinery and in steam engines for various applications came about in these shops; they established themselves as the centers for American technical know-how. As the size and skills of custom machine shops grew, many of them specialized in large steam engines and in locomotive manufacture. Consequently, some of them grew from custom-job shops into manufacturers and designers of machine tools and, by the time of the Civil War, had become major machine tool industries.

The first generation of industrial America can be measured roughly from 1790, when Slater established major textile industries, to the period around 1837, when financial panic developed. The general environment for innovation in America during those years was something the world had never before seen. New frontiers of land, technology, and immigrant population had compound effects at this time. Steam as a power source was being attempted in many industries, particularly in mills and transportation. Shops and factories of many types were built; existing technologies were used in order to manufacture products for the rapidly expanding American markets and for export to Britain and other nations. From an engineering point of view, it was largely an era of consolidation and application. One major series of innovations took place during this period in the United States and in Europe; numerous rudimentary steam engines were developed and applied to various locomotive vehicles, sometimes with commercially successful results.

The expansion of American industry and agriculture through new machinery provided impetus for better transport of goods to market. The road system steadily improved along the eastern seaboard and to the major frontier cities such as Fort Pitt. Water routes became thoroughfares for commerce from Pennsylvania and Ohio to the Mississippi delta country and New Orleans. Although settlements, commerce, and military guardianship had also extended from Spanish and French strongholds in America, the industrial development extended from its nucleus in the original thirteen states. Construction machinery—scrapers, drills, pumps, etc.—became an area of development for steam power.

During the expansion following the War for Independence, the needs for the transport of goods and people resulted in considerable experiment, both in Europe and the United States, with steam powered transport for land and water.

Experiment—trial and error—was the brute force method used by most of the innovators of the early industrial age. Concerned with applications and generally without the means for traditional "scientific philosophizing," the innovators produced remarkable and valuable machinery.

Many of these organizations were operated by trained mechanic-engineers. The evolution and recognition of the mechanic as a skilled professional moved swiftly in the 1800s, and several industrial societies and schools were founded with hopes of strengthening the professionalism in that field. The Franklin Institute, founded in Philadelphia in 1824, served as a center of education and professionalism for mechanics. Other schools were founded in the northeast and in Ohio, and the Massachusetts Institute of Technology ultimately was founded as an industrial arts school based upon those early models.

The large machine shops specializing in steam engines for locomotives and naval vessels were centers for innovation. Steam engineering for naval ships grew rapidly as a science and provided a point of concentration for scientific and engineering growth.

For example, a classical theory of friction was shattered when an early locomotive proved successful even though it used smooth iron wheels rather than cogs under its heavy engine. That innovation showed the way for relatively simple traction engines and trains.

The first effective demonstration in the United States of a practical railroad was the circular track of Stevens in New Jersey. The commercialization was slow and expensive.

Early trains were limited mainly to the duty of coal hauling. By 1830,

South Carolina had a commercial railroad that grew by 1870 to a 50,000-mile system. The features which enhanced the railroads' early growth were the American "standard rail" and innovations in locomotive suspension. The durability of machines on long runs was assured.

Both John Stevens and his son Robert were instrumental on the American scene in the application and development of steam engines for boats and railroads. In the first several decades of the nineteenth century, the younger Stevens drew upon primitive British railroad technology and devised improved engines, trackage, and suspension systems similar to those still in use today. Credited with establishing the American railway system, Stevens built upon his heritage of engineering training, intellectual curiosity, and a history of family investments in the transportation business. His innovations included not only modern railway techniques but also the screw propeller applied with the steam engine for the propulsion of ships.

INDUSTRIAL MATURITY
The history of American technology in the second half of the nineteenth century is a story rich in individual innovations and inventions that appears even richer and perhaps more significant in its summary of industrial structuring, consolidation, and enterprise. During the decades following the Civil War, American technology grew mainly in the dimensions of organization and consolidation. During that same period, there was a sharpening awareness in the academic community, the industrial community, and even among the general civilian population, of the importance of science and the mechanic arts with regard to the nation's development. During this period, physical and chemical societies organized and became part of the mainstream of American technology. Industrial nations of the world were stretching themselves and displaying their scientific wares at exhibitions in major cities. For example, the London Exposition at the Crystal Palace in 1851 set an example for future major exhibitions of its kind. American inventions displayed there made tremendous impressions, not only because of their individual significance, but also because of the overall total quality of the wares, which served to convince the sophisticated technologists of the world that American industry was indeed a leader. McCormick's monstrous reaper outperformed every device against which it was pitted, and it was obvious that an agricultural technology boom was underway—a revolution as significant as that brought to the textile industry, 50 to 70 years before. Other American agricultural implements and plows carried away prizes in their categories.

Additionally, American exhibits revealed superior technology in firearm manufacturing machinery and techniques, in the sewing machine areas, and in mechanisms and machine tool areas in general. Many fine rubber items were displayed, and a major technological breakthrough was demonstrated by the vulcanization process developed by Charles Goodyear.

It has often been said, but must be reasserted, that American industry developed at an unusually rapid pace because of the advantages it had over competing international technologies. These advantages, at various times, were available land frontiers; new markets; and freedom of human relationships which did not fetter an American entrepreneur in the way that a counterpart might have felt himself restrained at the time in France, England, Germany, or Russia. The mentality of expansionism seemed to have existed in individual minds in America as well as in the national frame of mind; however, even a higher order of innovation environment appeared over the long pull of history. In each category—frontiers of land, technology, credit and business practice, public communication, and political innovation—the United States seemed to have been able to keep abreast or ahead of most other nations of the world; each of those frontiers of political-social evolutions provided a dimension of freedom of action for both enterprising individuals and opportunistic companies. It offered encouragement and hope for such groups and perhaps served always as the strong attraction and innovative environment for advancements in the United States with relation to the pace of advancements in other technological countries. The innovative and industrial world, as part of the total world, functioned in a sea of moving currents and various forces; the United States, during her first 100 years, seemed to have floated upon a more rigorous sea of forces than had her counterpart industrial nations. In many of the other countries, the calming effect of their national seas was *tradition* . . . at every level of life—political, personal, business, and religious. The United States, as the nation formed and grew, found herself moving in many directions, not bound by traditions nearly to the degree that other nations were bound. The relative weakness of tradition across the American scene can be rephrased in a more positive, perhaps euphemistic view, as the American innovative spirit. It is that spirit, then, that made the difference between the United States, as a colony, and the many other colonies around the globe that had performed from time immemorial in their *traditional* colonial manners.

The extent of American innovation and, even more emphatically, the extent of the American manufacturing activity was in evidence to the world at the Paris Exposition of 1867; however, the American industrial might of the period was even more dramatically demonstrated by the U.S. Centennial Exposition of 1876 in Philadelphia. Perhaps the dramatic highlight of that entire centennial exposition was the Corliss steam engine. This engine, designed to produce about 2500 horsepower, stood about 40 feet tall. Operating at the Centennial, it was distributing about 1500 horsepower through belts and shafts in a 14-acre building complex. The steam engine—conceived in antiquity and developed in Europe—was being demonstrated as a major industrial force at the American Centennial Exhibition.

Both the industrial and scientific worlds were literally aglow with new developments, and a number of international expositions attracted attention and exhibitors. In Chicago, at the Columbian Exposition in 1893, commercialized electrical lighting and power stole the show. From the 1860s, many different types of electrical arc lamps were operating in Europe and in the United States, and electric street lighting was applied on a considerable scale in Cleveland in 1879, the same year that Thomas Edison's carbonized cotton filament burned for 40 hours and proved the effectiveness of the incandescent lamp. Large-scale applications of electrical power then began in 1882 when Edison opened the Pearl Street Central Station and served over 200 customers with 5000 electric lamps.

During the final decades of the nineteenth century, every technological area in the United States as in Europe was undergoing great advancement and revolution. Basic development grew from scientific knowledge and from industrial momenta and enterprise in a melding of "philosophy" and industry. Steel, railroads, machine tools, textiles, transportation, communications, and the electric power industry—all developed into booming activities worldwide. There seemed to be no monopoly on innovation in the United States; the rapidity with which innovations moved into working commercial and industrial systems seemed phenomenal. International industrial statistics revealed that during the 1890s the United States equaled or surpassed the production of manufactured items, in all categories, of all the industrial nations of Europe.

NEW HORIZONS

During the score of years from about 1890 to 1910, the technological scene over the United States, as over the rest of the world, expressed itself through growth into new dimensions of technology. For example, telegraphy gave way to the advent and growth of radio voice communications. The electrical lighting industry enlarged rapidly into electrical power, which provided another major revolution in transportation and industry. Decades of experiment in all nations of the world culminated during this period into sudden advancements and acceptable competitive transportation methods for automobiles and for airplanes. It was as though the entire eighteenth and nineteenth centuries were devoted, through the Industrial Revolution, into plowing new ground and developing a technological base; at the beginning of the twentieth century, all these new technologies were like new seeds in that fertile soil. The innovation pattern in the United States continued: the "lack of tradition" which can be rephrased as "the strong innovative drive" was the major impetus that propelled U.S. technology more rapidly than that of Europe. The field of wireless telegraphy had advanced, in different nations, under the developments of Hertz, Maxwell, Bronly, Marconi, and DeForest. Although Marconi's commercial achievements were significant, the communication industry in the United States, following DeForest's developments, grew even more rapidly in the early 1900s. The audion tube of DeForest, which he developed in 1907, was a three-electrode vacuum tube which could serve as detector or amplifier. That scientific innovation from an American proved to be a key one for this era. Another innovation pattern, although not a fundamental type, was the application of demonstrated principles of mass production to the carriage or automobile industry. Although the Duryeas manufactured automobiles in the United States before 1900 and others in Europe followed the same technology, it was Henry Ford who introduced mass production techniques to automobile assemblying and parts manufacturing and, more specifically, who developed the "car for every man," the Model T Ford, which endured on the world scene from 1908 to 1928. It can be reasonably argued that Mr. Ford minimized the importance of the craftsman and maximized the importance of the laborer in the manufacture of automobiles; be that as it may, it apparently was the right approach for technological developments at that time and certainly set the pattern for industry today. Mr. Ford's main contribution was to break with tradition of manufacturing operations and the skilled machinist's viewpoint. This break with tradition, or innovation, turned out to be exactly what the transportation business needed at that time. Interestingly enough, mass production or division of labor had long been practiced in textile mills and meat processing plants, but it had not been translated into machine manufacturing.

The twentieth century brought into focus on the industrial scene in the

United States the coalescence and formalization of professional groups and industrial societies. One hundred years earlier, machine shops and small industry were recognizing the importance of the mechanic as a professional skill. Through the nineteenth century, engineering and supporting sciences—such as chemistry, physics, and electronics—became recognized as professional specialties needed to support industrial development. By the beginning of the twentieth century, professional engineers, mechanics, and recognized scientific groups were all part of the industrial scene. Most of the industrialists of this early period fell into the class of skilled mechanics, in contrast to the founders of industry 100 years earlier who were artisans in narrow specialties, but not generally well-trained mechanics; that art had not fully blossomed in 1800.

The major impact of the manufacturing output of U.S. industries around the turn of the century was made by the tremendous influx of immigrant population into the United States at that time. With machinery and production methods becoming established in industries ranging from the needle trades to the steel industry, immigrant laborers provided very cheap unskilled help at the proper time, that is, when American industries were ready and willing to meet the United States and the foreign markets with all types of goods. The greatest impacts made by the immigrant population were made in those U.S. areas where electricity, coal, steel, and water transportation were available and well developed. This technology belt, from New England to the Middle West, welcomed the new labor pool and proceeded to meet its national and international markets. With water and rail transportation well developed within the United States, new merchandising methods came into play, acting as catalysts for innovation in industry in its attempt to mass-produce. Innovative merchandising is illustrated well by the currently popular reprints of the 1902 edition of the Sears, Roebuck catalog.

On the American scene, the weakness of tradition—which is the strength called innovation—also expressed itself in the new dimension of personal mobility. An individual's mobility through geographical, social, and political streams has always been a part of the American background, and a multitude of anxious, hungry immigrants moved into those streams to accelerate American industry and business. The promises of cheap land or jobs were joint attractions on the American scene unmatched elsewhere in the world.

By the time that World War I galvanized American industry into maximum production, the technological scene in the United States had evolved into an organized structure including areas of science, engineering, and applied technology. The very complexity of technology, as well as the hierarchy of available specialists, served to push the ill-trained innovator and the simple artisan to the fringe areas of commercially fruitful innovative field. The most significant developments beyond this era came from organized technical laboratories. Numerous remarkable exceptions always arose, but this era seems to have marked the beginning of organized research as the primary source of innovation and industrial development.

MAN'S INVOLVEMENT IN SCIENCE AND TECHNOLOGY*

Mr. Henry Ellsworth, our country's first commissioner of patents, made the following statement in his 1844 annual report: "The advancement of the arts from year to year . . . tax [sic] our credulity and seems to presage the arrival of that period where human improvement must end." At the time, the government had issued less than 500,000 patents, and today, 130 years later, the number has grown to over 3 million. Why? Because of man and his intense inquisitiveness about the world around him. Even as early as the 1920s and 1930s learned men were offering omniscient words which professed the timelessness of scientific activity and the endlessness of man's improving his human condition.

Michael Pupin: "Science is simple. Science is man listening to nature and trying to understand her."

Dr. Stine of the DuPont Company: "Mother Nature had a rare sense of humor. She provided man with the materials with which to produce virtually anything his mind could conceive, but she omitted the labels. She scrambled, concealed, and disguised her gifts with diabolical cunning. She hid her secrets in the least obvious places and challenged man to fit together the colossal jigsaw puzzle she had created."

Man has been girded toward the *fait accompli* of that puzzle since the beginning of time. In the beginning, *survival* was of prime importance, and to survive, man had to use nature to his advantage to acquire food, shelter, and security. First came simple tools, then fire and the discovery of what it could do to other materials, let alone its obvious advantage of warming and com-

---

*Address presented by Vagtborg to the Torch Club in San Antonio, Texas, in which he explored the same topic that had been and was to be a favorite theme of his in speeches before a broad variety of audiences at many places, for many occasions, over a period of 25 years.

forting man. And yet, at some times, the tempo of invention and innovation was extremely slow, with only an occasional beat to mark a new discovery as thousands of years rolled by. The beats came at long intervals—suddenly and unknowingly—because discovery was generally accidental. Early man learned how to remove iron and copper from ore with heat, and the Phoenicians are said to have discovered glass accidentally through the use of long-burning, hot fires utilized on the seashores to signal to their boatmen.

In reality, all earthly beings *except man* are adapted to a specifically restricted environment and can survive nowhere else. Man, on the contrary, is adaptable and has learned to survive almost everywhere on earth. This adaptability has become his supreme instrument of survival, fighting off the fiercest of opponents—among them, superstition. How did he acquire this asset? Through inquisitiveness—for it is an unalterable fact that nature has not changed one iota since the beginning of time. The change has been in man, through his understanding of his environment, his mastery of the world of nature surrounding him.

Because of his innate inquisitiveness, man began to identify more and more of the materials of the earth, and his ability to reveal the secrets of nature increased; thus there came a gradual easing of his earthly lot through mastery of his natural environment. Aristotle commented on this quality of man when he called him, basically, an artist in that *he can have the conception of the result to be produced before its realization is material.*

The *wheel* was one of the greatest inventions of all time, and yet its origin is somewhat hazy. Most historians believe that it began as a potter's wheel, probably square, with the first record of it appearing in 3500 B.C. Strange that the American Indian never used the wheel. In another regard, some historians believe that the *bow and arrow* started with the caveman, who made it from antlers of a deer and used a strip of hide. Others believe that it began as a one-string musical instrument and evolved to a hunting device. Whatever the origin or the end result, one point rings clear from these examples: although the order of man's needs has changed from era to era, his inquisitiveness and resulting adaptability have served him well as a survival kit. He has learned to take advantage of the quickly observable things in nature that he can use to his advantage. What's more, this learning has been cumulative: man has greater knowledge today only because of the accumulated knowledge of previous generations. Of course, the knowledge alone is worthless; that's where man's reasoning and inventiveness come into prominence, for reasoning is to knowledge as motion is to rest.

MAN'S SENSE OF SUPERIORITY IMPROVES IN EVERY AGE

The caveman considered himself to be a very *superior* being . . . and a very *modern* being. In his mind, he had conquered nature: he had his tools, fire in his hearth, weapons for protection, and clothing that he could vary with the seasons. His descendant many generations later, the Roman, could stand on the threshold of his home and marvel at his accomplishments. He had a well-constructed home with a burning open fire in each of the main rooms, a chariot and team of horses that were the envy of some of his neighbors, clothing that was admired, and citizenship in a community which had conquered almost the entire known world through implements of war that he had designed. Truly, he was a superior being.

Each succeeding generation has likewise had a feeling of superiority over its predecessors, just as the Roman did over the caveman. Seventy-five years ago, a new generation sensed its improved status with the many modern conveniences of that era. The marvel of the age—*electricity*—was coming into use, and the newfangled automobile was beginning to appear. Nevertheless, a generation later, out of the same natural environment that surrounded the caveman and the Roman, there appeared such phenomena as radio, television, jet airplanes, automatic heat and cooking, as well as innumerable other material things for the comfort and pleasure of man. It is inevitable that, 50 years from now, out of this very same nature, will come innovations about which there is no concept today. This process of innovation and invention *could* have moved through the last millenniums without the encroachment of the word *science* or its processes; however, developments would have been much slower.

SCIENCE AND PHILOSOPHY

Science was born out of philosophy, but not until recent years. In the early days, philosophy was concerned with natural phenomena as evidenced by the records left by the Babylonians and Egyptians over 5000 years ago. These records demonstrate that they had knowledge of the movement of the planets and the relationship of the sun to the world, thus enabling them to determine seasons and seeding time. The Greek philosophers living in the few centuries before Christ had virtually insatiable curiosity about their natural environment. Their writings have come down to us in almost complete form, and, in addition to the famous Plato, Socrates, and Aristotle, there were numerous others who engaged in deep exercises of the mind based on reasoning, logic, and deduction. Practically all their conclusions were based on theory—hardly ever any experimentation—and yet their writings made an indelible impression on the population of the time. Even though many of their theorized beliefs were wrong, they were accepted. The climax of Greek advancement and what could be termed today as science came with Archimedes around the year 200 B.C. with the growth in importance of Alexandria. The Greeks, of course, differed from the Romans in that they theorized while the Romans used the results of their theories as real applied researchers in the construction of aqueducts, roads, bridges, stadiums, and implements of war that enabled them to conquer the entire known world. For each of these countrymen, the words of Dr. W. W. Campbell apply: "A scientist engaged in research work is looking for something that already exists. He does not invent the truth, he does not develop the truth, he does not do anything whatever to the truth except uncover it or discover it, and expose it to the comprehension of his fellowmen . . . " These exposures and discoveries endured long after the decline of the Roman Empire in 400 A.D.

MAN'S FALL INTO THE DEPTHS OF THE MIDDLE AGES
This decline plummeted Europe into a period of 1000 years—the Middle Ages—during which time the ancient classics were unknown to them.

A characteristic peculiar to this time was that any accidental discovery giving economic reward to its finder would be kept secret and passed on only from father to son over the generations. Others would try to imitate the discovery, but something was usually missing, and the secret was kept. These practices ultimately led to the Age of the Guilds in subsequent eras.

It was the Arabs and their colonies to the east and south who carried on the works of the Greeks and added many new discoveries. The Arabic culture fed back into Europe, largely through Spain, so that by the end of the eleventh century, a revival of scientific inquisitiveness was on the horizon.

A period of "cut-and-try" shed *some* light onto the dismal scientific scene. Man actually began looking for new secrets of nature rather than just stumbling onto them. Whiling away the hours on a long sea journey, Colt whittled the first revolver out of a piece of wood; Fulton's first steamboat was made in much the same way; and in many shops and laboratories, workers were mixing ingredients, unceasingly hoping that the desired result would occur. Frequently, something did happen, oftentimes a discovery that was entirely the opposite of the expected; nonetheless it contributed greatly to man's knowledge of nature. In later years, Edison was an inventor who cut and tried, and there were many others like him.

At the end of the twelfth century, a Spanish-Arab philosopher named Averrhoës published a commentary on Aristotle that had great influence at the University of Paris and at Oxford, among other educational institutions. Scholars again became familiar with the works of Aristotle and others, largely through Arabic and Latin translations. However, it was quickly recognized that Aristotle's teachings were in conflict with the church. It was Thomas Aquinas (1225-1274) who reconciled the differences, and so began the influence of the schoolmen—perhaps accurately termed a new generation of theoretical philosophers. This atmosphere, however, restricted free thinking and the progress of science.

Charles Kettering's admonition regarding research secrecy in industry is exceptionally applicable here: "A closed door keeps out more than it keeps in." Scientific progress was slow until the times changed with the beginning of the Renaissance and a revival of arts and letters. Prior to that fourteenth-century awakening, Roger Bacon was one of the first to revolt against scholastic restraints on the activity of the human mind. He also proclaimed the importance of experiment, and others followed quickly; yet, some of the most promising were imprisoned or murdered.

A REAWAKENING—A REBIRTH

The Renaissance began in Italy and spread throughout all of Europe where a rebirth of curiosity and spirit of discovery blossomed. In 1492, Columbus discovered America; Vasco da Gama found the sea route to India in 1497; and in 1519, Magellan sailed around the world. A long list of famous scientists and experimenters whose works are basic to modern science followed this bountiful time—Copernicus, Kepler, Galileo, da Vinci, Henry Cavendish, Antoine Lavoisier, Descartes, Newton, Boyle, Hook, Priestly, and others. Involvement in experimentation became very fashionable and, to a large degree, a rich man's activity. Kings, dukes, and princes dabbled in the business, mostly by supporting protégés who could not afford to maintain their own laboratories.

Prior to the nineteenth century, the issues concerning man most intensely were philosophy and religion; however, by 1850, science, philosophy, and religion became three distinct intellectual enterprises. Further, during the mid-nineteenth century, science, inventions, and innovations became intimately related. A keener understanding of the period can be gained by considering the fact that basic scientific effort was beginning to flourish in

European institutions, and applied research was being actively, yet secretly, carried on in European manufacturing cartels. This comparison, or distinction, of basic versus applied research had been visible since the early days of the Greeks and Romans. The goal in basic research is to increase scientific knowledge rather than practical application, whereas applied research is directed toward practical application of scientific knowledge, and development is the use of scientific knowledge for the production of devices, processes, or systems.

Contrastingly, the American scientific scene displayed only modest beginnings in this all-important realm of discovery and application. In 1863, at the instigation of Abraham Lincoln, the National Academy of Sciences was established to advise government departments on scientific matters. The first industrial research laboratory evolved in 1900, and in 1916, President Wilson instituted the National Research Council as a preparedness measure. The going was not easy—the sprouting of roots slow. It was a seemingly unending battle to convince American government and industry that, "Research is not an expense—it is an investment." The United States was apparently too young and her leaders too inexperienced to recognize the responsibility of the federal government in the interest of all the people to take firm action with sufficient appropriations to carry on research in the fields of national defense, human health, and utilization of natural resources. America relied on foreign countries for information in these areas and, at the time of the beginning of World War I, was paying European cartels $50 million a year as royalties for the use of industrial processes that had been developed by European basic science and technology. The United States was alarmingly dependent upon Europe, but the war was a great impetus toward self-sufficiency. With the coming of peace, the pressure was off, and universities found it easier to get funds for basic research, while large industries had less difficulty persuading stockholders to make at least modest appropriations for applied research.

AN INDEPENDENCE IN U.S. SCIENCE AND TECHNOLOGY

The belief that "All wealth comes from the processing of natural resources and research is the key to the method" began to take hold. One of many examples supporting this theory was the case of a Kansas chemical company that took $10 worth of natural gas and converted it into $120 worth of ammonium nitrate. This amount of ammonium nitrate put on 40 acres of land by the farmer increased the yield of grain by 560 bushels, which, at $2 per bushel, amounted to $1120 of new wealth gleaned from $10 of raw materials—an impressive lesson in multiplying natural resources.

A significant breakthrough in research funding came in 1930 when the federal government finally decided to give consideration to human health in an organized fashion and established the National Institute of Health.* As a method of fostering research in the physical sciences, the National Science Foundation was created in 1950. To illustrate the total federal budget for research and technology in 1939, the following distribution of the $60 million amount is given:

Public health	5%
Natural sciences	39%
Physical sciences	4%
Surveys	16%
Engineering	36%
Total	100%

Combined with the $190 million provided by industry for their own research projects, this $60 million figure was bolstered to a grand total of $250 million for R&D in the United States in 1939. That same year, there were only 100 corporations and 40 trade associations that made grants (and these were relatively small) to university research. By 1944, however, the R&D effort was up to a $720-million-operation, and the economic impact of research activities was felt not only in the resultant useful goods being fabricated but also in its contribution to increased employment.

> *"Man can fly or swim, roll with the wheel, bring light into the midnight darkness of his streets. All this he can do with the self-same body, while increasingly he spins the future out of the same mind that painted mammoths on the walls of ice-age caverns. Man is paradoxically the supreme generalized animal of a supremely specialized brain. It is his cities that are now his true specializations, his cities that lie vulnerable under the silent winging of the satellites."*
>
> Dr. Loren Eiseley
> introduction to *The Epic of Man*

---

*Through an act of Congress in April 1953, NIH became a part of the newly created Department of Health, Education, and Welfare.

CHAPTER II

THE ROOTS OF INDUSTRIAL RESEARCH†

Kendall Birr‡

Scientific research is big business today. According to one estimate, the United States spent about $8 billion in 1956 for scientific research and development. This is not surprising since American research laboratories perform virtually every imaginable scientific and technological operation. They are supported by the federal government, universities, foundations, and industrial concerns both large and small. And they play an important role in the economic life not only of the United States but also of other countries throughout the world.

A larger part of this research is carried on in industrial research laboratories—4834 of them according to a recent survey by the National Research Council. Books and articles on the subject of industrial research flow in endless streams from technical publishers. Several leading educational institutions hold regular conferences on the administration of industrial research and offer courses in the subject.

What is industrial research, this phenomenon of such importance in our present-day society? The term has suffered from a good deal of semantic confusion, and defining it has become a favorite pastime of the more thoughtful practitioners of scientific research. The "industrial" part of the term seems clear enough, but the word "research" has a variety of meanings. "Getting new knowledge, that is just what research is," one veteran of industrial research put it. An academician defined it in a somewhat more

*This chapter is very appropriate to this book. It provides a stepping-stone for very meager research appropriations in the 1920s and 1930s, which is brought to a research expenditure of $8 billion in 1956, to the 1974 level of research expenditures of over $25 billion. Reproduced by permission, Public Affairs Press.

†Chapter I from *Pioneering in Industrial Research—The Story of General Electric Research Laboratory*, published (1957) by Public Affairs Press, Washington, D.C.

‡Acting Chairman, Department of History, State University of New York at Albany.

sophisticated way; "research may be defined as the application of human intelligence in a systematic manner to a problem whose solution is not immediately available."

There can be little disagreement with such general definitions, but difficulties mount when one tries to distinguish various kinds of research. One common distinction between "fundamental" and "applied" research must be mentioned. The distinction lies not so much in "what" the researcher is doing as in "why" he does it. Fundamental research seeks to extend scientific knowledge, while applied research attempts to explore technology with scientific methods and principles. The former is motivated largely by curiosity, although the scientist may work in faith that his discoveries will at some time in the future have utilitarian value; the latter is more clearly motivated by considerations of usefulness. Fundamental research adds to understanding about the nature of the physical world; applied research uses this understanding to manipulate and control man's natural environment. Both varieties of research call for a high order of scientific competence, but the results are different. Industrial research laboratories have engaged in both kinds of investigations, but they are quite naturally concerned primarily with applied research.

The difficulties and follies of attempting to develop narrower definitions and make finer distinctions are soon apparent when one examines the kinds of activities research laboratories customarily engage in. So-called "research" laboratories have sponsored fundamental research, applied scientific principles to discover radically new processes or products, developed these processes and products to the point of commercial practicability, seen them through the pilot-plant stage, acted as troubleshooters for market or production difficulties, been responsible for quality control, and even, in a few cases, engaged in routine testing and production control. Obviously, the term "research" covers a wide spectrum of scientific activities. But equally obviously any attempt to distinguish fine gradations in a research hierarchy has little basis in reality since there is little or no agreement on the boundaries between the various types of research.

In the final analysis, industrial research as it developed in the late nineteenth and twentieth centuries involves at least four elements. First, it is nearly always organized research; the term generally does not include the individual inventor or the lone experimenter. Second, industrial research uses scientific methods and scientifically trained personnel. Third, industrial research is concerned with the natural sciences and technology and excludes such things as the social sciences or market research. Last, the investigations carried on in industrial research laboratories, whether they be fundamental or applied research, are connected in one way or another with industry and are directed primarily toward improving technology and maximizing economic satisfactions. Industrial research in the long run is utilitarian.

THE RISE OF INDUSTRIAL RESEARCH

In the age of the automobile, plastic chemistry, atomic energy, and modern medicine, it is difficult for the layman to realize that industrial research is a relatively recent development. Yet such is the case. This is not to say that human beings have only recently begun to apply intelligence to the solution of technical problems; technology in the sense of a systematic knowledge of the industrial arts is exceedingly old. However, the application of science to the solution of technical problems is something relatively new.

Historically, science and technology have occupied two separate and largely independent spheres of activity. Science devoted itself to the development of a fuller and more satisfactory philosophical understanding of the world of natural phenomena. Its cultivation was confined largely to members of the educated upper classes who pursued it out of curiosity. It is probably symbolic of its character that science was known as "natural philosophy" and "natural history" until the nineteenth century. By contrast, technology was concerned with the manipulation of things and the production of economic goods. It was essentially a traditional knowledge, handed down from one generation to the next, among eminently practical craftsmen. Innovation was the result of crude empiricism of the cut-and-try variety. Between the two branches of knowledge there was negligible interplay, in part because of the differing social statuses of the scientist and the craftsman, but largely because science had little or nothing to offer technology.

It would, of course, be an overstatement to say that there was no contact between the scientific and technological traditions in Western civilization. There were a number of notable exceptions. Archimedes, for example, mixed the two as he formulated the law of floating bodies and devised new and improved instruments of war. The medieval alchemists combined theorizing about the nature of materials with experimentation out of which grew primitive industrial chemistry. Medicine at various times in history combined the construction of elaborate theories of the nature and operation of the human body with practical information about its actual operation and techniques for combating at least a few of humanity's ailments.

The seventeenth and eighteenth centuries in particular brought some interesting contacts between science and technology. Huygens and Hooke utilized the scientific theories of mechanics in work on clocks and watches; astronomical discoveries had practical implications for navigation; and James Watt found that the theoretical work being done in the field of heat helped him to improve the steam engine. Yet it is fair to say that even in the seventeenth and eighteenth centuries, science was relatively helpless in the face of technological problems.

Despite these practical limitations on the actual contact between science and technology, the belief developed in the seventeenth and eighteenth centuries that science possessed great utilitarian possibilities. This belief found an outstanding exponent in the person of Francis Bacon, whose most recent biographer has dubbed him the "Philosopher of Industrial Science." Bacon not only argued for a greater amount of empirical research in science but also urged that science could be of practical importance and in his famous description of "Solomon's House" foresaw the cooperative approach which has been such a striking feature of modern scientific research. Robert Boyle, another prominent seventeenth century scientific figure, similarly claimed that practical inventions might well rise out of science. This view of the utilitarian possibilities of science was taken up and widely disseminated in the eighteenth century by the scientific societies which sprang up in Western Europe and began the popularization of scientific knowledge.

But before the marriage of science and technology could be consummated, three conditions had to be met. First, science had to develop to a point where there was no question about its usefulness to technology. Second, businessmen and those other people who made the basic decisions in economic life had to realize the importance of science to their economic welfare. Finally, some institutional arrangements had to be made for the conduct of industrial research. These conditions were finally met in the nineteenth century.

The development of science to a point where its principles had application in economic activity occurred at various times, depending on the science and the type of economic activity involved. The importance of science in agriculture was revealed relatively early in the nineteenth century. The work of the German chemist Justus von Liebig in the 1830s was the crucial development in this field, and eventually led to the modern agricultural revolution based on systematic scientific research in agriculture and vigorous efforts to disseminate new and better ideas among the practicing agriculturists. In the broad field of engineering, the convergence of science and technology came in the middle of the nineteenth century when it became apparent that close attention to scientific principles could work significant savings in the cost of construction.

More spectacular was evidence of the utility of science provided by individual industries. The synthetic dye industry is a good example. Although English chemist William Henry Perkin synthesized the first dye in 1865, German chemists soon seized the leadership of the industry, and by World War I they had completely ruined the formerly flourishing business of producing indigo. The scientific feats performed by the German dye-manufacturers and the profits they reaped as a result of their scientific prowess were often cited by the promoters of industrial research as evidence of the profitability of applying science to industry. Carl Zeiss' success in improving optical instruments through the use of scientific talent was another outstanding example of the way in which science could aid industry. The electrical industry, to be discussed in greater detail in subsequent chapters, was perhaps the prime example of the way in which the discovery of new scientific principles could create a whole new technology independent of any preexisting traditional craft techniques. By the end of the century, the petroleum industry, destined to become a leader in industrial research, had begun to realize that scientifically trained geologists could be of immense help in locating the eagerly sought pools of oil beneath the earth's surface.

Uneven progress in the various sciences meant, of course, that not all industries profited equally from the application of science. The nineteenth-century steel industry, for example, made little use of developments in physical metallurgy, in part at least because they seemed to offer little of practical importance, and C. E. Kenneth Mees, one of the most experienced industrial research directors in America and long-time head of research for Eastman Kodak has declared that "to this day the making of photographic materials is in advance of the understanding of the basic science of the subject." Such industries as textiles would provide further evidence for the generalization that in many industries traditional craft knowledge remained more important than systematic scientific knowledge until relatively recent times. This is not to say that these industries neglected research; it merely means that the research they did was based more on cut-and-try methods than on scientific principles.

The growing realization of the importance of science for industry can be seen in the increasing use of scientifically trained persons in nineteenth-century industry. Use of such men was sporadic and scattered, but from the little we know about the subject, it is clear that a growing number of industrialists called on the services of scientifically trained individuals. The French Revolutionary government, for example, mobilized French scientists in the 1790s in the defense of the fatherland. The scientists proved of considerable assistance developing new shells, a semaphore telegraphy system, captive observation balloons, and improved methods of producing gunpowder. A half century later, the noted German chemist, Robert Bunsen, was invited to use his knowledge in the study of blast-furnace operation. From 1858 to 1866, Sir William Thomson (later Lord Kelvin), one of England's outstanding physicists, devoted his talents to making a technical success out of the Atlantic cable.

In the United States the influx of scientifically trained men, especially chemists, into industry was steady and striking. In the first half of the nineteenth century Joseph Cloud became assay master at the Philadelphia Mint, while Samuel Luther Dana in a career lasting from 1834 to 1868 with the Merrimack Manufacturing Company of Lowell, Massachusetts, introduced numerous innovations into the textile industry. Shortly before the Civil War, pioneer oil men called on the noted American chemist, Benjamin Silliman, Jr., to analyze their oil samples. The use of scientifically trained men grew more rapidly after the Civil War as chemists moved into the iron and steel industry. By the end of the century, chemists were entering such industries as meat-packing, copper, paper, and others. Still, the prejudice against trained men remained strong, and many scientists reported resistance to their efforts to change traditional methods in the light of theoretical discoveries.

Of even greater importance than the individual scientist who entered industry to utilize his talents were the scientists who personally founded new industries as a result of outstanding inventions or discoveries. Many of the most important inventors of the nineteenth century—Eli Whitney, Oliver Evans, Robert Fulton, Samuel F. B. Morse, Alexander Graham Bell, and Charles Goodyear, to cite only some prominent American examples—were men of little scientific training, basically inventors whose ideas grew out of their knowledge of industrial arts rather than from science. But as the century advanced it became increasingly clear that inventions were flowing from the minds of scientifically trained men who proceeded to exploit their own ideas in business. In Europe, Perkin, the first scientist to synthesize a dye, went into the synthetic dye business himself, and gave practical training to other chemists who often left to found new firms. In the United States,

John Wesley Hyatt with the aid of Frank Vanderpoel, a trained chemist, developed celluloid in the 1870s. Chemist Charles M. Hall, experimenting at Oberlin, discovered a practicable method of producing aluminum in the 1880s and spent the rest of his life directing development work on the process. Leo H. Baekeland, a professor at a Belgian school, in the 1890s embarked on a career of independent inventing and promoting which produced a new type of photographic paper and one of the first important plastics, Bakelite. Such inventor-entrepreneurs, who combined technical training with a firm grasp of commercial necessities and possibilities, did much to convince industry in the usefulness of science and, as we shall see, were especially important in the electrical industry.

The final contribution of the nineteenth century to the growth of industrial research was the concept and practice of cooperative organized research. The historically minded scientist could find bases for such practice in the distant past in the researches pursued at the famous Museum in Hellenistic Alexandria, and the theorist could turn to the preachments of Francis Bacon for encouragement. But in the final analysis it was the developing practice of cooperative research that shaped the modern industrial research laboratory.

In part, cooperative research grew out of the techniques of graduate instruction in science in the nineteenth-century universities, particularly in Germany. The essential element in the Ph.D. degree was a piece of original research carried out by the candidate under the supervision of his instructor. The topics of research were generally dictated by the interests and knowledge of the instructor so that in effect, a kind of cooperative research system grew up with instructors acting as heads of research units and utilizing less-experienced students to assist in expanding the frontiers of science. Under the *Privatdocent* system, new Ph.D.s were often attached to the university in an unsalaried position where they were permitted to gain further teaching and research experience while eking out a living from student fees. The result was the development, particularly in Germany, of specialized research institutes which did a great deal of a kind of cooperative research. This variety of cooperative research received a further stimulus in the latter part of the nineteenth century with the formation of government-supported national laboratories designed to maintain physical standards and do additional research. The first was the German Physikalische Technische Reichsanstalt formed in 1870; the American counterpart, the Bureau of Standards, was organized in 1901.

Perhaps even more important than the example of the universities was the slow but steady establishment of organized laboratories within individual corporations or specific industries. In the United States, trained chemists set themselves up in consulting practice or organized laboratories which catered to the varied needs of different clients. Charles T. Jackson, the erratic discoverer of the anesthetic properties of ether, opened a laboratory in Boston, in 1836, where he conducted experiments on sorghum, cotton-seed, and other products. His contemporary, James C. Booth, studied in Europe with Wöhler and Magnus and then returned to Philadelphia in 1836 to open a laboratory which became not only a center of industrial investigations but also a leading training school for American chemists. C. M. Wetherill and Frederick A. Genth were other Philadelphians who operated analytical and consulting laboratories before the Civil War. Later in the century, Peter T. Austen, Henry C. Bolton, Thomas B. Stillman and Henry Wurtz operated such laboratories in New York, while James F. Babcock and Francis H. Storer were active in Boston.

Individual American corporations gradually set up separate laboratories during the nineteenth century, although much of their activity could hardly be considered research in any modern sense of the word. The Pennsylvania Railroad, for example, hired Charles B. Dudley in 1875 to set up testing and specification systems for the railroad; when he left, the Pennsylvania possessed a laboratory with 34 trained chemists. The iron and steel industry early founded laboratories of a kind. R. W. Hunt, a chemist trained in Booth's laboratory, in 1860 established an analytical laboratory at the Johnstown plant of the Cambria Iron Company, and one of the first successful Bessemer steel plants included a chemical laboratory when it was built at Wyandotte, Michigan, in 1863. But the transition from individual to organized scientific research in industry was perhaps best exemplified by Thomas A. Edison's laboratory. By 1876, Edison had already been so successful with his inventions that he was able to leave manufacturing and devote full time to inventing and experimenting. To assist him in his work he established a well-equipped and permanently staffed laboratory in Menlo Park, New Jersey. In 1878, when he began concentrated work on the electric lamp, he had a nucleus of about 20 men. Although Edison himself was more an inventor than a scientist and actually had few scientifically trained men in his laboratory, the fact that he had an *organized* laboratory probably enabled him to gain priority over his competitors in the invention of the incandescent electric lamp. He certainly demonstrated the profitability of organized research and development.

Industrial research burgeoned forth in its modern form in the late nineteenth and early twentieth centuries, primarily in Germany and the United States. In Germany the electrical, chemical, and optical industries made systematic use of scientific personnel and set up large-scale laboratories before World War I, while German industry as a whole supported the establishment in 1911 of the Kaiser Wilhelm Gesellschaft, a series of scientific institutes conducting both fundamental and applied research. In the United States, industrial research began to attract an increasing amount of attention in the technical press in the decade preceding World War I, and these years saw the organization of some of the most important industrial research laboratories, notably at General Electric, DuPont, Bell Telephone, Westinghouse, Eastman Kodak, and Standard Oil (Indiana). Rapid technical advancement in chemicals and electricity made the need for systematic research apparent, while the growth of large corporations provided economic organizations with sufficient capital to support research and exploit its results.

But it was World War I which really convinced Western Europe and the United States of the necessity for systematic industrial research. Both England and the United States found themselves cut off from German dyes, chemicals, medicines, and glass. The result was a vigorous effort to bring science to the aid of industry. In the United States existing industrial research laboratories turned toward the war effort, while the government set up the National Research Council to coordinate the activities of American scientists. The results were astounding. Applied research during the war gave a tremendous boost to the American chemical industry besides solving innumerable special wartime problems. It was a convincing display of the benefits of industrial research. In the United Kingdom the problems were similar, but the solution was different. There the government formed the Department of Scientific and Industrial Research (D.S.I.R.), an agency which has since played a leading role in encouraging cooperative British industrial research.

PATTERNS OF EUROPEAN DEVELOPMENT

Since World War I, research has been an established part of the industrial scene. But its exact character has depended so much on time and place that it is impossible to generalize with any degree of accuracy. The rate of expansion and the patterns of organization of industrial research have shown significant national variations. Similarly research activity has depended on technological and economic conditions which have varied widely from industry to industry. With such important national and industry differences existing it will be necessary to undertake a brief country-by-country survey. (No attempt is made here to discuss industrial research in the Soviet Union where administrative patterns have diverged sharply from Western practice.)

From about 1900 to 1930, Germany was quite clearly the leading industrial research country in the world. There were a number of reasons for this. German industry was relatively late developing, but when it did begin to flourish in the latter part of the nineteenth century, the application of science was unhindered by obsolescent methods or ideas. In addition, German universities of the nineteenth century were leaders in scientific work; Heidelberg, Berlin, Göttingen, Leipzig, and Giessen provided Germany with the best trained scientists of nineteenth-century Europe. Furthermore, industrial research in Germany did not suffer from the social stigma that was attached to it by the upper classes in England; instead it offered an outlet to talent in a country where it was increasingly difficult to acquire positions in the state, the university, or the clergy. Government offered its aid also by supporting the physikalische Technische Reichsanstalt and contributing to the Kaiser Wilhelm Gesselschaft. Finally, Germany had special stimuli for increased research in the 1920s. Industry turned to science for solutions to all kinds of economic problems in an attempt to recoup the losses of World War I.

The golden age of German industrial research in the 1920s gradually gave way to slow decline under the Nazis. While the Nazis made few structural changes in the conduct of German research, they did put ever increasing emphasis on immediate results and permitted long-range fundamental research to languish. Furthermore, the advent of politics into science helped disrupt many a research project while anti-Semitism hampered the flow of talent into the scientific field. The final blows came with the physical destruction of World War II, the invasion of Germany itself, and occupation by conquerors who all too soon fell to quarreling among themselves and thereby split Germany. Nonetheless, industrial research in West Germany has shown amazing recuperative powers. In the decade since the end of the war it has once again become an efficient auxiliary to reviving German industry.

Throughout the turbulent decades of its history German research has shown very persistent patterns of organization. A sizable part of industrial research has been concentrated in laboratories of the larger corporations. As early as 1900, the four leading German chemical manufacturers were employing over 500 chemists, while one particular company, the Badische Anilin und Soda Fabrik, supported Adolf Baeyer and a group of chemists for 15 years at a cost of $5 million while they developed a practicable synthesis of indigo from benzene via anilin. Chemical firms such as I. G. Farbenindustrie maintained this research lead in later years. Prominent electrical firms, such as Siemens and A.E.G., and leading steel companies, such as Vereinigte Stahlwerke and Krupp, had well-equipped laboratories and competent staffs. A good many of these managed to survive World War II in one way or another. Some were relatively undamaged. Others had a more difficult time. The Zeiss optical works, for example, had the misfortune to be located in the Russian zone, but 84 of Zeiss' ranking managers and scientists were able to escape west and begin anew.

Perhaps Germany's most significant contribution to the organization of industrial research was in the field of cooperative research. The most notable example of this was the Kaiser Wilhelm Gesellschaft. Founded in 1911, it drew support from both government and industry but remained independent of both as it set up a series of scientific institutes which conducted both fundamental and applied research. Germany also developed a good many cooperative research associations, especially in industries where plants were small or where cartels, trade associations or special societies existed. Textiles, automobiles, and railway cars provided pre-World War II examples of such cooperative research. In addition, German industry often sponsored work in the universities. While the specific organizations were often disrupted in the holocaust of 1944-1945, recent developments in Germany show a continued interest in the cooperative approach. The Kaiser Wilhelm Gesellschaft has been replaced by the Max Planck Society, and a whole new array of cooperative organizations has developed, most of them heavily supported by the government.

Germany's major European rival in the application of science to industry was Britain. While British industrial research has grown steadily since World War I, it has tended to lag behind Germany and the United States, at least until the temporary elimination of one of its rivals in 1945. Several factors have contributed to this situation. British industry, having gained a head start in the Industrial Revolution, has seemed reluctant to change with the times. Much of British industry has been dominated by small firms incapable of supporting very much scientific research. Moreover, British industry has too often been controlled by people with little scientific background or interest. Even the chemical and electrical industries, the chief backers of British industrial research, have had few men of scientific background or interest on their boards of directors. Some people have argued that the British educated classes have been prejudiced against industrial research, favoring instead the more rarified atmosphere of "pure" research in the university laboratory; but how important this has actually been is impossible to say.

The precise size of the British industrial research effort past or present is difficult to determine; most estimates have been little more than informed guesses. One observer in 1938 set research expenditures of British industry, apart from government assistance, at only about £2 million per year. A survey made in 1945-1946 found the situation somewhat improved. By that time British industry was employing about 10,000 scientific graduates and spending perhaps £30 million annually on research and development within its own establishments. The most recent figures reported by the D.S.I.R. reveal total British research expenditures of about £325 million with research being performed by 133,000 persons, 32,000 of whom were qualified in science or engineering. These figures for 1955 are substantial. Yet they are small when compared with American research and development outlay and are clearly inadequate for British needs.

A substantial proportion of British industrial research has been carried out in the laboratories of individual corporations. In 1955, over half of British research was carried out in privately owned industry, although the British government foots the bill for over 60 percent of British research. Estimates of the number and quality of these private laboratories have not been very accurate, but there were perhaps 500 of them doing some kind of research and development in 1950. Most of the important work has been concentrated in a relatively few laboratories of the most research-conscious corporations. Aircraft, chemicals, electrical manufacturing, and engineering and shipbuilding have been the British research leaders in recent years. Imperial Chemical Industries, for example, was one of the pioneers in British industrial research, and in recent years has possessed a highly developed system of laboratories working on every imaginable type of chemical problem. Within the electrical industry British Thomson Houston, the General Electric Company, Metropolitan-Vickers, and Philips Lamps all have had good-sized laboratories and spent substantial sums in industrial research.

One of Britain's more interesting contributions to the organization of industrial research has been the research association jointly sponsored by the government and a specific industry. Impressed by the virtues of industrial research during World War I, the government set up the Department of Scientific and Industrial Research (D.S.I.R.) with a fund of a million pounds to be spent over a period of years to encourage industrial research. The general plan was to set up cooperative research associations supported jointly by government and industry funds with the idea that the associations would eventually become self-supporting. Initial results were disappointing. Capital was at first inadequate, industry proved reluctant to provide money, and good scientists were dubious about joining an organization with such an uncertain future. Nonetheless, the government persisted and managed to organize over 20 associations in the 1920s. While the Depression of the 1930s inhibited expansion of the system, only one association failed, two more were added, and income grew slowly but steadily. There was a vast expansion during World War II, and by 1950 the number of associations had reached 42 and total income had risen sevenfold over 1939 to about £3.4 million.

Research associations have been formed to investigate everything from scientific instruments and refractories to laundry techniques and coil springs. Materials research and equipment design and development have been especially important fields of investigation. Much of the research has been fundamental, but there has also been some development work, a good deal of routine technical advice, and even some technical training. The scope of the operation varies widely; staff size may be under 20 or over 500, depending on the association. On the whole these cooperative research associations have proved to be workable and useful in stimulating industrial research, especially in those industries composed of firms too small to support extensive research in their own laboratories.

The government, in addition to its subsidies to the research associations, encourages research in other ways. The D.S.I.R. has operated the National Physical Laboratory since 1918 and the Geological Survey since 1919. It has set up research centers in several specific areas, notably fuels, food preservation, building, forest products, radio, high pressure and high temperature chemistry, water pollution, and road construction. Other government agencies conduct important work in telecommunications, agriculture, medicine, armaments, and atomic energy. In addition, the government pays for a substantial amount of research done in industrial laboratories, particularly in aircraft and armaments. To help exploit discoveries made in government laboratories, the Board of Trade established after World War II a National Research Development Corporation, provided with £5 million to develop to the marketable stage inventions resulting from government or government-sponsored research.

Other agencies have also participated in British industrial research. The universities have done their share. The D.S.I.R. administers a system of university science scholarships and research grants while private industry, notably Imperial Chemical Industries, has granted fellowships for university research in particular fields of interest. Some of the research sponsored by the D.S.I.R. research associations has actually been performed in university laboratories. Since World War II a new element has entered the industrial research scene. Two private research institutes, apparently modeled on American counterparts like the Mellon and Battelle institutes, have been founded. Such institutes may find a useful place in performing confidential research which the research associations have been reluctant to handle.

Any discussion of industrial research in France must inevitably revolve around the question of why there has been so little. In the early nineteenth century, France was the acknowledged scientific leader of Europe. Yet as the century advanced, France lost ground relative to Germany and England, and following World War I an absolute decline set in. There are a number of reasons for this. For one thing, a large segment of French society has always remained anti-scientific in temper. Furthermore, science has depended heavily on the state for support, and the state has at times been niggardly with its funds. The pitifully inadequate laboratories of great nineteenth-century French scientists such as Claude Bernard, Louis Pasteur, and the Curies bear eloquent witness to this. Furthermore, science has generally been considered primarily a part of man's cultural heritage rather than a tool of practical value. This tendency to shun practical applications of scientific knowledge, accentuated by the conservatism, passiveness and secretiveness of French business, has severely limited French contributions to industrial research.

The structure of French scientific research in the twentieth century has clearly been dominated by the state. Government laboratories and the laboratories of nationalized industries have been of great importance. Furthermore, French educational institutions, another important source of scientific research, have been closely under the control of the government. The state, in addition, in 1939 set up an elaborate organization, the National Center of Scientific Research, supported by state funds but controlled by leading scientists, which has since World War II supported a large staff of scientists, coordinated French scientific research, trained advanced investigators, and encouraged cooperative industrial research. While private industry has tended to lag behind the state, a good many of the more progressive firms have set up their own laboratories. If France has fallen far behind Germany, the United Kingdom and the United States in the twentieth century, some observers have been able to discern signs of a post-World War II scientific renaissance which may slowly bridge the gap.

Italian industrial research has followed a different pattern. Applied science has been steadily emphasized, in part because of the long years of Fascist rule with its emphasis on national self-sufficiency. Mussolini's 23-year regime also made the state a prominent element in the scientific scene, and even since World War II, government laboratories and the government-sponsored National Research Council have played an important role in industrial research. The state-supported universities, too, not only have done basic research but also have cooperated closely with industry. Most industrial firms have little time or money for research. True, Montecatini (chemicals), Fiat (mechanical engineering), Pirelli (rubber), and a few others support laboratories that are quite respectable by American standards, but these are exceptions. Small industry has been particularly neglected, for cooperative research has made less headway in Italy than in other parts of Europe.

While other European countries have not developed research organizations of a scope comparable with the four major powers already discussed, some excellent industrial research work is performed in the smaller countries. In many cases applied research is limited and specialized to meet the particular needs of the individual country. Sweden and Norway, for example, have done a good deal of research dealing with their particular raw material and power resources, while Denmark has concentrated on dairying and other aspects of agriculture. In most of the smaller countries cooperative research has played a very prominent role. Sweden, Norway, the Netherlands, and Belgium all have systems of cooperative research, the Belgian system having been inspired by the British D.S.I.R. The individualistic Swiss provide an exception. In most of these countries the state has contributed substantial support. Norwegian applied research is financed almost exclusively by the government; the Danish government supports agricultural research; Sweden aids research projects through a system of grants made by research councils; the Belgian government supports cooperative research in the same fashion as the British; while the Dutch government makes substantial grants through a national research organization. Again, the Swiss form a notable exception. In virtually all of the countries there are close relations between the universities and technical institutes and industry.

If most of the smaller countries have turned increasingly to state aid and various kinds of cooperative research, this has not prevented the establishment of some excellent private laboratories. In the Netherlands, for example, the Philips firm has performed outstanding research in the electrical field since the turn of the century, and Royal Dutch Shell has supported a sizable laboratory. In Switzerland, the prominent pharmaceutical firm CIBA spends close to $3 million per year on research. Nor are these merely exceptions. Many other Swiss firms support research, while a recent survey revealed over 50 good-sized industrial laboratories in Sweden.

Industrial research, like the Industrial Revolution, has tended to expand from the major centers of industry to the more peripheral areas. Most of the smaller countries of Western Europe tended to develop industrial research organizations at a later date than did countries like Germany and the United Kingdom. Thus, Austria and Ireland are only now beginning to encourage systematic industrial research. With the expansion of industrialism to other parts of the world has gone the idea of industrial research. Australia, for example, has since World War II copied the British system of governmental encouraged industrial research, while Canada has slowly broken away from its dependence on the United States and the United Kingdom and begun its own programs. More important, research has been seen by the so-called underdeveloped countries as a prime weapon in their struggle to industrialize and compete with the Western world in the economic realm. Japan, the earliest of the non-European powers to industrialize, developed an elaborate system of industrial research in the 1930s largely dominated by the government, but drawing partly on German, partly on American practice. Much of the work that was produced was of dubious value, but Japanese technology was making important strides before it was disrupted by World War II. Since the war, there has been a revival of scientific activity, largely sponsored by the government. India has similarly turned to research to assist its program of economic expansion. Inspired by the British D.S.I.R., the Indians have established a series of national laboratories and research institutes as well as cooperative research associations which have begun to attack the multitudinous scientific and technical problems of India's economic development. Even Burma has turned to research. Under a 1953 Point Four grant, American scientists from the Armour Research Institute have been assisting the Burmese to establish a technical institute which would do research in ceramics, metallurgy, and several other fields.

Thus, beginning in the late nineteenth century, scientific methods have been applied to industry and technology in Western Europe and its cultural appendages. The institutions for the promotion of industrial research and the vigor with which research has been prosecuted have varied from country to country. Clearly internal conditions—the state of scientific knowledge, the conditions of industry, political and social factors such as war, and the drive for self-sufficiency—have modified and conditioned industrial research. But by mid-century industrial research has become a clearly recognized aspect of science and an activity essential to economic and industrial advancement. Individual countries have had a wide area of choice in how they might utilize and administer industrial research; none could escape the consequences of neglecting it.

THE GROWTH OF AMERICAN INDUSTRIAL RESEARCH

Nowhere has industrial research been more assiduously cultivated than in the United States, and there is available a mass of statistical and descriptive material which presents a clear and reasonably precise picture of its growth and characteristics since World War I. The statistical material is of two types. First, the National Research Council since 1920 has periodically published directories of American industrial research laboratories and has estimated the number of personnel employed in them. Second, periodic attempts have been made to estimate American research expenditures. These figures are less satisfactory than the first, largely because of varying definitions of research, different accounting systems, a reluctance to publicize financial figures, and changes in the price level and the cost of research through the years. Nonetheless, the estimates that have been made are valuable in suggesting the general level and distribution of research efforts.

The picture that emerges from these statistics is one of steady growth during the 1920s, relative stagnation during the Depression of the 1930s, and a new and rapid increase in research during World War II and the subsequent Cold War. Indications are that the 1920s were the seedtime of most American industrial laboratories. Some of the more important ones had been founded before World War I, but interest in research was more widespread and active after that conflict than before. The first fairly comprehensive survey of the National Research Council in 1927 showed nearly 1000 laboratories; by 1931 the number had increased to over 1600. Total personnel had risen from 19,000 to 32,000 in the same interval. The best estimates available indicate that about $166 million were being spent annually for scientific research in 1930, 70 percent of this by industry, and indications are that most companies engaged in research had increased their expenditures steadily during the 1920s.

The advent of the Depression brought a minor setback to industrial research, although not as serious as one might have expected. Between 1931 and 1933 the number of laboratory workers declined by more than 5000, in part because 110 firms discontinued organized research. The smaller firms were apparently the hardest hit. Nonetheless, the setback was minor and temporary. By 1938, personnel employed in industrial research laboratories had risen above the 1931 level to total over 44,000, while industry research expenditures climbed over $200 million by 1940, encouraged by the profitability of research and by New Deal tax policies.

World War II brought important changes. There was a sharp increase in the total amount of research. The war effort mobilized scientists of every hue and description, and experience showed that scientists who had previously pursued scientific truth within the cloistered environs of the college campus could be of immense help in solving pressing technical problems. The war, too, emphasized the importance of the cooperative approach to research and brought new experience in the techniques of organized scientific endeavor. Above all, the success of Allied arms and the awesome results of the atomic research brought new prestige to science and a renewed confidence in its utilitarian potentialities.

The net result has been a marked increase in applied research in the United States since the war. The number of persons engaged in research is more than double the prewar level, and a shortage of trained personnel has become the limiting factor in research efforts and a matter of serious concern. Total research expenditures have risen even faster than the size of the research staff, in part because of the postwar inflation, and in part because of the growing cost and complexity of research. Indications are that we are spending as much or more relative to our gross national product as European nations. Above all, the war and the succeeding years have tremendously increased the role of the federal government in applied research. With the accent on atomic energy, aircraft, and missile development, the government has increasingly provided funds and shaped the character of research and development. The 1953 survey of science and engineering in American industry sponsored by the National Science Foundation revealed that the federal government paid for 37 percent of the research and development carried on in American industry besides spending substantial sums in its own scientific establishment.

Generalizations of this kind, however, cover a great many variations. Statistics on "research" encompass numerous activities. How much is basic research, how much advanced types of applied research, and how much simple production control or troubleshooting is difficult to say. What is clear is that the amount of basic research is relatively small. A 1952 study of 191 leading American corporations which account for perhaps a third of U.S. industrial research expenditures concluded that 50 percent of the research and development expenditures in these companies went for product improvement, 42 percent for new product development, and only 8 percent for basic research. The 1953 survey by the National Science Foundation found only 4 percent of total industry research and development expenditures going for basic research. Even allowing for a wide margin of error it is clear that it is unusual to find much fundamental research in an industrial laboratory.

General statistics of the numbers of people engaged in research also hide the precise character of the workers. The 1953 National Science Foundation survey showed, for example, that in corporations with more than 1000 employees, there were 180 supporting personnel—technicians, craftsmen, clerical help, and administrators—for every 100 scientists or engineers. Among the technically trained personnel, chemists have traditionally been the most numerous, although in recent years they have been overtaken and passed by engineers, a reflection of the growing importance of aircraft and armaments in the research picture. Physicists, metallurgists, mathematicians, and biological and earth scientists are also hired by industry, but in numbers they lag far behind chemists and engineers.

Industry is not the only agency competing for the services of scientifically trained men. Government and the universities require a share of the available manpower. As of 1954, the United States had around 850,000 persons with professional scientific or engineering training including about 650,000 engineers. Perhaps 192,000 scientists and engineers were engaged in research and development in 1953. Recent estimates indicate that colleges and universities hold around 42,000, some of them engaged full time in research work. The federal government employed around 80,000 people in scientific positions in 1951 according to the last available figures. Whether or not this is a proper distribution of available scientists is hard to say. There may be too few in colleges and universities considering that these institutions educate future scientists and carry on a large proportion of America's fundamental research.

Within industry, research workers are by no means evenly distributed. Geographically, research has been concentrated in the northeast and in the large urban centers. In 1950, 62 percent of the personnel employed in industrial research laboratories were located in New York, New Jersey, Pennsylvania, Ohio, Illinois, and Michigan, although the figure had been 73 percent in 1938 and the intervening twelve years had seen a marked expansion of research in states like California and Texas. The South, despite vigorous and highly publicized efforts to improve its economy through research, still accounted for only about 4 percent of U.S. industrial research in 1952.

More important, industrial research has tended to be dominated by big business and large laboratories. From the beginning, established industrial research laboratories tended to grow larger; 244 laboratories which reported in each of the National Research Council surveys from 1921 to 1938 showed a growth in the average number of employees from 32 to 70. This concentration of research in large laboratories is even more marked when one considers that in 1938, the 45 largest employers of research personnel employed half of the U.S. total with individual staffs ranging from 170 to 4000; these same corporations employed a third of the total in 1950, still a substantial percentage. The larger laboratories have been owned by the larger corporations. The aforementioned 45 companies included 36 owned and controlled by companies which were among the 200 leading nonfinancial corporations in the United States in the 1930s. The trend has not changed significantly since the war. A 1952 survey revealed that two out of three researchers were employed by companies with more than 5000 employees. This is not to say that small business has found research unprofitable and has not engaged in it; it merely points out that in the total picture, American big business has been the major backer of industrial research

The most startling variations in the pattern of industrial research appear when one examines the amount of research performed in specific industries. The differences from industry to industry have been and are enormous. Industrial research made its earliest start in the electrical and chemical industries and expanded into petroleum, rubber, and other fields. On the other hand, certain industries—textiles, primary metals, furniture, construction, and printing, for example—have never undertaken very much research. The validity of these generalizations has been upheld in virtually every study of American industrial research. In 1938, for example, the chemical, petroleum, rubber, and electrical industries employed about 57 percent of the researchers in American industry. By contrast, motor vehicles and agricultural machinery accounted for only 8½ percent and the metals industries for only a bit over 6 percent. Textiles employed less than 1 percent of the researchers at work in American industry in 1938. When industries were ranked on the basis of the ratio between research workers and wage earners in 1938, chemicals, petroleum, rubber, and electrical manufacturing again ranked at the top. Nor has World War II changed the situation significantly. A survey of 4800 companies in 1951 showed that a relatively large percentage of the companies in such fields as chemicals, scientific instruments, and electrical equipment maintained research organizations, while relatively few metal fabricators, wood product companies, or printers and publishers engaged in organized research. Of the industrial chemical firms responding to the survey, 68.4 percent maintained research organizations; only 7.8 percent of the firms dealing with lumber and wood products had laboratories.

Such generalizations as these can be further substantiated by examining briefly the history of research in specific industries. As we shall see shortly, the electrical industry, depending as it did on new scientific ideas for its founding and advancement, early engaged in organized technological improvement. Bell, Westinghouse, General Electric, and R.C.A. have become major research leaders. The chemical industry, like the electrical, was an almost wholly new industry based on the discoveries of nineteenth-century science rather than on the expansion of time-honored handicraft, cut-and-try techniques. The result has been that the chemical industry in Germany, the United Kingdom, and the United States has been one of the most important backers of research in each of these countries.

The leader of the American chemical industry, DuPont, used research as a method of expanding company interests. In the nineteenth century, DuPont was primarily an explosives manufacturer, but when it embarked on organized research shortly after the turn of the twentieth century it moved into dyes and general organic chemicals. By 1927, it was engaging in some fundamental research as well as a wide variety of more immediately profitable projects. By 1950, the company was carrying on about 1000 different research projects ranging from one-man laboratory work to pilot plant operations spread through 13 different departments and nearly 40 research laboratories manned by close to 2000 scientists and technicians. The research budget in 1950 was running around $35 million per year. In large part this was a reflection of the fact that research at DuPont had paid off spectacularly well; from the laboratories of the company had come dyes, synthetic rubbers, nitrocellulose lacquers, and most important, nylon and a wide range of other synthetic fibers. If DuPont has been the research giant of the chemical industry, other firms have followed closely. Union Carbide, American Cyanamid, Dow Chemical, Allied Chemical and Dye, and others have all developed substantial research programs.

Other industries closely related to basic chemicals have also engaged in extensive research. Eastman Kodak, for example, was a company founded on the inventions of George Eastman in the field of photographic film, and the company used professionally trained chemists almost from the beginning. The laboratory, established in 1912 as an independent unit, developed into one of the largest and best in the industry. Laboratory discoveries helped the firm branch out from photography into other fields of chemistry. The head of the laboratory, Dr. C. E. K. Mees, has become one of the most noted and articulate of American directors of industrial research.

Pharmaceutical firms also engaged in research at a relatively early date. Some firms employed trained chemists in the nineteenth century, and nearly all found it desirable to enlarge their scientific staffs with the passage of the federal Pure Food and Drugs Act in 1906. By mid-twentieth century such staffs had grown to very large size, and observers have estimated that the pharmaceutical industry spends more for research in relation to its sales than any other American industry. The reason is obvious. A 1947 survey indicated that 54 percent of the drugs then in use had been unknown 10 years before, and in the case of one leading firm, Abbott Laboratories, only 25 percent of its sales volume in 1951 was made up of items known a decade earlier.

The rubber industry was also an early and vigorous proponent of research. B. F. Goodrich entered the field as early as 1895, and U.S. Rubber began in 1913. While concentrating largely on tires and other rubber products, these companies have shown signs in recent years of branching out into new fields. This process of expansion of interests has characterized the growth of research in the petroleum industry as well. Research was slow to get started; as late as 1923 writers were pointing out the need for it in industry. It was the development of the cracking process in 1913 by Dr. William M. Burton of Standard Oil (Indiana) that really gave an impetus to research. Other companies were reluctant to depend on licenses from Standard and turned to research in an effort to get around the original patents. Some companies became interested in scientific investigation through their search for oil. Gulf Research and Development Corporation, for example, grew out of an interest in geophysical techniques in the discovery of petroleum. Research in turn has led to new fields, such as petrochemicals, as petroleum has become a source for a vast array of products in addition to the fuels and lubricants usually associated with the oil industry. As a result virtually all of the major oil companies have established sizable research laboratories. The Standard Oil Development Company was by far the largest in 1950 with 2600 technical and nontechnical employees, but Shell, Standard of Indiana, Gulf, and Texaco followed close behind with about 1700, while Socony-Vacuum, Standard of California, Phillips, Humble, Sinclair, Atlantic, and Sun each had more than 300.

The rapidity of the development of research as an organized activity in other fields has varied considerably. The American glass and optical industry, while lagging behind its German counterpart, had well-established laboratories in such firms as Corning Glass, and Bausch and Lomb before World War I. Producers of nonferrous metals similarly began research work at a relatively early date; New Jersey Zinc and American Brass both were engaged in research activities before World War I. On the other hand, the iron and steel industry was relatively slow. The major companies such as U.S. Steel, Jones and Laughlin, and Bethlehem, did not begin research in earnest until the 1920s, and then a large proportion of their effort was directed toward empirical improvement rather than the expansion of fundamental theory. The amount and character of research in the machinery field has varied a great deal. While such an industry as automobile manufacturing has always depended on engineering advancement and has had the benefit of research activities among its suppliers in, for example, the rubber and steel industries, it has never been a real leader in fundamental research in the same way as the electrical or chemical industries. The aircraft industry has, of course, always depended heavily on research. It has been somewhat unique, however, in that most of the fundamental research has been performed for it by the government. While most industrial research has been concentrated in manufacturing, food processing firms, most notably meatpackers, the large corporations such as General Mills, and important suppliers such as the Continental Can Company have also strongly supported industrial research.

Why have the variations in the amount of research performed in different industries been so great? There seem to be several reasons. In the first place, some industries have been pretty clearly "technologically based"; that is, from the beginning their prosperity has depended on a rapidly changing technology founded on scientific principles. The electrical and chemical industries have been such examples. By contrast, such a field as metallurgy has had to depend pretty largely on empirical research untied to any well-developed conceptual framework. While this situation has begun to change in the last two decades, it is probably fair to say that scientific knowledge has not been of central importance to practical metallurgy until quite recently. Scientific research is not particularly attractive when technological change is slow or when science seems to offer little hope of important technical improvements. In the second place, a good many industries have been so organized as to be unable to afford a substantial amount of scientific research. In industries dominated by small firms, effective research has been difficult to conduct. This has been a limiting factor in such fields as textiles and clothing, or in some branches of specialized manufacturing.

A small firm structure is certainly a handicap to research when carried on by individual firms, and research carried on in the laboratories of individual companies has clearly been the dominant form of industrial research in the United States. In the petroleum industry, for example, it has been estimated that 90 percent of the research is carried on in research laboratories of competitive companies. Estimates of this kind were confirmed by the 1953 National Science Foundation survey which found that only 4.5 percent of total industrial spending for research and development went for work performed by organizations other than the companies supplying the funds.

Yet the plight of the small businessman is not impossible. Cooperative research can do much to meet the scientific needs of small firms or to supplement the research activities of large companies. One of the most common forms of cooperative research is that carried on by trade associations. In 1953, some 543 cooperative organizations, most of them trade associations, spent over $20 million for research and development. Sixty-six of the organizations operated their own laboratories employing 696 scientists and engineers and spending just under $10 million. The earliest and largest of the separate laboratories was the Underwriters Laboratories (1894); by way of contrast the laboratory of the Association of American Railroads was organized only in 1940. Organizations which have not desired to support their own laboratories have turned to government laboratories, agricultural experiment stations, university research facilities, and research institutes. Association research has included investigations into canning, paper, tanning, meat, baking, fisheries, coffee, laundering, and petroleum. On the whole it is fair to say that cooperative research has been a useful supplement to individual corporation laboratories, but that it has not become a decisive influence on American research, nor has it reached the dimensions of some of the European efforts.

Perhaps the United States unique contribution to the organization of industrial research has been the semiprivate, nonprofit research institute. The earliest and one of the most successful of these was the Mellon Institute. The Mellon Institute grew out of the conception of Robert Kennedy Duncan, an American chemist, and the fortune of the Mellons. The scheme as it was developed shortly before World War I was to establish a well-equipped laboratory with a nucleus of trained personnel. Individual firms would then establish a fellowship for work on some specific problem. The laboratory administration would select the fellow and direct the research; the donor paid the salary of the fellow, the operating charges of the laboratory, and the cost of special equipment and at the same time received title to any results of the investigation. The Mellon Institute has been highly successful. Fellows have investigated everything from phenolic resins to sausage casings. In some cases fellowships have led to the organization of corporation research laboratories; in other cases the fellowships have become virtually permanent fixtures at Mellon.

In recent years the number of nonprofit research institutes has increased to 12. The largest, Battelle Memorial Institute, was founded in 1929, and has since expanded its operations as far as Europe. At Battelle the research project is carried out by the Institute as a whole rather than by a specially established fellowship. The 12 nonprofit institutes employed about 6400 persons and reported total research and development expenditures of just over $53 million in 1953.

Clearly related to the nonprofit research institutes are the independent commercial laboratories. There are several hundred such laboratories, most of them very small, but they did around $33 million worth of business in 1953 and employed over 9300 people. Some of these grew out of the nineteenth century firms of consulting chemists. Arthur D. Little, Inc., the outstanding example of this genre, did just that. A large proportion of the commercial laboratories have been established since World War II, in many cases to take advantage of government research contracts. Most such laboratories concern themselves with relatively specific and limited projects for which they have special skills, although a few like Arthur D. Little, Inc., are able to handle a surprising variety of problems.

Research organizations such as the nonprofit research institute and the commercial laboratory have performed an important function. They have served businesses unable to afford their own laboratories while at the same time they have provided large corporations with special facilities and talents which it would be uneconomical for the large company to provide itself. An increasingly large proportion of their research is paid for by the government —well over half in 1953. The largest industrial patronage comes from medium- and larger-sized firms who have more research funds to spend and who seem to be able to do a better job of formulating research problems and utilizing research results than very small firms. Very little of the research is basic; most of the institutes and commercial laboratories sell the kind of applied research services industry and the government seem to want. It is a small but important service.

To some degree the universities have become centers for industrial research. The original impetus came from industry which initiated a policy of contributing research fellowships to the universities, either for general research in a broad area or occasionally for the solution of fairly specific or well-defined problems. Some universities before World War II turned more and more to a campaign to attract industrial research problems, often carried out in semi-independent research institutes. This trend was accentuated by heavy government research contracts during and after World War II. Such extensive use of university facilities for applied research, however, has raised problems which suggest that this may not be a wholly desirable development. In part the problems are administrative; salary differentials easily develop between professors concerned largely with contract research and those carrying the normal program of the university, and this can harm university morale. More important, an excessive interest in applied research can easily divert the university from its major objectives of training scientists and carrying on fundamental research of a kind which is too seldom seen in industrial research laboratories.

While the prime responsibility for American industrial research has remained in the hands of private agencies, the federal government has expanded its role until at mid-twentieth century it is probably the single most important force shaping the direction and character of research. The federal government has become involved in research for several reasons. It became a major supporter of agricultural research largely because American farming has been so organized as to be incapable of supporting research through private agencies. The government similarly seemed to be the only organization capable of operating large-scale geological surveys or organizing a nationwide meteorological service. Most important, the government has become involved in research through national defense. World War II, the subsequent Cold War, and the development of atomic energy all contributed to the growing importance of the government in the research picture. Some of the research has been and is done in federal facilities, most notably in such establishments as the Bureau of Standards, the Department of Agriculture, or the Atomic Energy Commission. But a very large proportion—over half in 1955—has been done in industrial or other private laboratories under contract.

From this brief survey of the historical background of industrial research several generalizations emerge. In the first place, industrial research has had a substantial history. It has been the offspring of the marriage of science and industry in the nineteenth century. In the second place, industrial research has not been an isolated phenomenon. Nearly all of the industrially and scientifically advanced countries of the Western world have participated, and it is becoming apparent that the so-called "backward" countries of the world are becoming increasingly interested. In the third place, modern industrial research has been organized research. The increasing cost and complexity of research along with the growth of large-scale industrial organization made necessary and desirable an organized, cooperative approach. The lone investigator still plays an important role on the far frontiers of scientific knowledge, but applied research has generally been organized. In the fourth place, it must be noted that the characteristic forms of organization have varied considerably. Universities, private industry, the government, various kinds of cooperative agencies, private research laboratories, and consultants have all had their hands in research. Yet the particular pattern of research has varied from time to time and from place to place in accord with particular historical circumstances. Finally, it is clear that there have been immense variations in the amount of research performed in different industries. In part this has depended on the level of technical advancement in the industry, in part on the organization of the industry and its ability to support large-scale research. But whatever its character, it is clear that industrial research has come to play a major role in twentieth century society.

CHAPTER III

STIMULATING APPLIED RESEARCH IN THE UNITED STATES

In the previous chapters, the stage was set for further exploration into the phenomenal industrial activities that have propelled our country's standard of living and eventually brought to us the distinction of being the strongest nation in the world.

At the outbreak of World War I, we Americans were pathetically dependent upon European technology for much of the goods and processes that were utilized in the development of our economy. We were completely unprepared for war, and through the federal government administration, we did everything possible to avoid becoming involved. However, when involvement could no longer be averted, the American people rallied with much greater unanimity than even that exhibited in the Revolutionary War. By the time of World War I, American industry, by one process or another, was spending over $50 million (a huge sum at the time) for the use of and rights to European technology. With the demands of war, though, we were forced into becoming self-sufficient in many industrial areas where heretofore we had depended upon imports. The lesson that we learned from the war experience was one of self-sufficiency—American industry would have to depend upon its own resources and growth from within.

There were a few people at the time who recognized that *science and technology* had played an important part in the industrial and economic strength of some of the European countries. Several large industrial firms in Germany, in particular, were based upon the products from their scientific laboratories. On the whole, American industrialists were too inclined to feel that science had no benefits, that it was an activity of the university professor. They did not realize that this same attitude had been held by European industrialists many decades before; however, results of investigations by scientists and technologists had proven them wrong. Indeed, scientific advancement was responsible for the cartels in European countries

51

to which many American industries were subservient, paying fees and licenses for their use. During the First World War, this relationship had been severed, and American industry, of necessity, did a great deal of cutting and trying in the beginning as it sought the solutions to technological problems and the knowledge to become self-sufficient. There was practically no understanding of the fact that yesterday's basic science is today's applied science, tomorrow's engineering, and the next day's industry.

Eventually, a few of the larger corporations got the message and small research departments were initiated. These were staffed primarily by basic scientists who, in many cases, were given a relatively free hand to work in a company-supported laboratory on problems that were of general interest to the particular company. General Electric is a good example of this type of situation, for the scientists in the earliest laboratories at General Electric developed some very unique and original concepts that had much to do with the success of the corporation in following years. This lead was followed by others of the larger corporations, and the process began to show very specifically that, as Charles Kettering (of General Motors) once said, "Research is an investment—not an expense."

In 1920, the National Research Council (NRC) of the National Academy of Sciences made a comprehensive survey* of American industry to determine how many firms were doing testing or research. In response to questionnaires, many companies that employed technical personnel to work on product control listed themselves as having a research department. Very few people seemed to know the difference between basic research, applied research, development, and testing. Product control was classified as a research activity.

The publication of the NRC survey is of general historic interest. In the first few pages, it becomes clear how cautious the authors were to explain the difficulty American industrialists had at that time distinguishing between truly applied industrial research for a new product and process development and testing and evaluation programs they had underway merely for the purpose of maintaining a quality product.

---

*"Research Laboratories in Industrial Establishments of the United States of America," *Bulletin of the National Research Council*, vol. 1, (2), March 1920. This survey has become a rare document and may be obtained on microfilm from the Linda Hall Library, Kansas City, Mo.

As a step toward stimulating research in industry, the National Association of Manufacturers (NAM) entered into an agreement in 1937 with the American Institute of Physics to form a joint committee on scientific research. This committee was comprised of the following individuals:

Joint Committee of NAM on Scientific Research
(as of 1939)

Chairman—M. H. Eisenhart, President of Bausch & Lomb Optical Company

Members—

Dr. H. A. Barton, Director, American Inst. of Physics, New York, N.Y.

W. B. Bell, Pres., American Cyanamid Company, New York, N.Y.

R. Y. Bradshaw, Pres., Bradshaw-Praeger & Co., Chicago, Ill.

Frederick G. Brown, Treas., Apponaugh Co., Apponaugh, R.I.

G. S. Brown, Chrm., Alpha Portland Cement Co., Easton, Pa.

H. W. Butterworth, Jr., Pres., H. W. Butterworth & Sons Co., Philadelphia, Pa.

Arthur T. Cavey, Pres., Carthage Hills Inc., Carthage, Cincinnati, Ohio

Dexter D. Coffin, Pres., C. H. Dexter & Sons, Inc., Windsor Locks, Conn.

E. A. Fitch, Vice-Pres., Otis Elevator Company, New York, N.Y.

F. A. Hanlin, Vice-Pres., Weirton Steel Company, Weirton, West Virginia

Dr. Ross G. Harrison, Chrm., National Research Council, Washington, D.C.

M. W. Heinritz, Gen. Mgr., Battery Div., Philco Radio & Television Co., Philadelphia, Pa.

W. S. Landes, Pres., Celluloid Corp., Newark, N.J.

W. H. Loomis, Pres., The W. H. Loomis Talc Corp., Gouverneur, N.Y.

Arthur F. Manross, Gen. Mgr., F. N. Manross & Sons, Div. of Ass'd Spring Corp., Bristol, Conn.

Geo. A. Mattison, Jr., Pres., Woodstock Slag Corp., Birmingham, Ala.

Dr. F. B. Moulton, Permanent Secy., American Ass'n for the Advancement of Science, Washington, D.C.

Eugene Philip Pattberg, Pattberg Novelty Corp., Jersey City, N.J.

Wm. Rabkin, Pres., International Mutoscope Reel Co., New York, N.Y.

R. H. Rolfs, Pres., Amity Leather Pdts. Co., West Bend, Wisc.

Louis A. Rosett, Pres., Florasynth Laboratories, Bronx, N.Y.

F. L. Sagendorph, 2nd, Pres., Penn Metal Corp. of Penna., Philadelphia, Pa.

C. H. Shaver, Sec-Treas., United States Gypsum Co., Chicago, Ill.

Alfred L. Smith, Exec. Vice-Pres., C. G. Conn, Ltd., Elkhard, Ind.

C. H. Smith, Pres., The Steel Improvement & Forge Co., Cleveland, Ohio

Harold Vagtborg, Director, Research Foundation of Armour Institute of Technology, Chicago, Ill.

Lewis W. Waters, Vice-Pres., General Foods Corp., New York, N.Y.

Julius Weinberger, Radio Corporation of America, New York, N.Y.

Philip C. Wentworth, Treas., National Ring Traveler Co., Providence, R.I.

Geo. S. Whyte, Pres., MacWhyte Company, Kenosha, Wisc.

W. H. Worrilow, Pres., Labanon Steel Foundry, Lebanon, Pa.

Guest—

Maurice Holland, Director, Engineering Division, National Research Council,
    Washington, D.C.

On December 8, 1938, the NAM devoted its 43rd Annual Congress of American Industry to the subject, "Research: An Increased Asset for National Progress." Just prior to that date, on November 19, 1938, the NAM issued a science supplement to its newsletter. The lead article in this newsletter was written by Dr. Karl T. Compton, President, Massachusetts Institute of Technology. The following excerpts from the article give an interesting insight into the spirit of the times.

In a report to the stockholders a few years ago, the President of the General Electric Company pointed out that 60 percent of that year's business had been in products which were unknown 10 years earlier. Ninety-five percent of the chemical industry is built upon scientific discoveries made in university laboratories according to Roger Adams in his presidential address before the American Chemical Society. Ten percent of our population are supported by wages coming directly or indirectly from the automobile industry—a product of science, invention, and engineering.

Statistical studies made by the Division of Engineering and Industrial Research of the National Research Council show a strong positive correlation between the amount of research carried on by an industry and its financial health.

Witness the Congress appropriating billions of dollars under the National Industrial Recovery Act with no provision for research to develop new industries or new industrial products or improved public works. Witness the relative lack of attention to methods, organizations, support and results of research at meetings of manufacturers, bankers, and merchants.

About 1 percent of the 170,000 industrial establishments in the United States (1938) maintains research laboratories. The total value of the nation's annual manufactured products is on the order of $50 billion, whereas the total annual industrial expenditure for scientific and engineering research is about $100 million.

At the meeting of the committee held on October 19, 1939, in New York, the chairman "called attention to the importance of perpetuating the American system of private enterprise if free industrial research is to progress in the future as it has in the past. The essential part of this system," he said, "is the American patent system which in 1940 will be 150 years old."

It was decided to commemorate this anniversary by launching a National Modern Pioneer's Program by honoring inventors and research workers who had made outstanding contributions to the creation of new jobs, new industries, and higher standards of living. The nominees* for this award —qualified candidates from across the nation—were to be submitted by manufacturers, executives of trade associations, and professional, scientific, and engineering societies, and were to include qualified candidates from all over the United States. There were to be regional meetings in major cities throughout the country at which the selected local candidates would be given their awards. All nominees were to be judged by a committee of five eminent scientists headed by Dr. Karl T. Compton and including Forest R. Moulton, American Association for the Advancement of Science; George B. Pegram, Dean, Graduate Faculties of Columbia University; John T. Tate, Dean, College of Science, Literature and the Arts of the University of Minnesota; Edward R. Weidlein, Director, Mellon Institute; and Frank C. Whitmore, Dean, School of Chemistry and Physics of Pennsylvania State College.

The underlying motivation for these activities on the part of the National Association of Manufacturers to promote scientific research in these years was (1) the experience during World War I, (2) serious economic recession during the early 1930s, and (3) the further fact that Europe was already at war again and the general feeling was that the United States would shortly become involved.

In 1941, the completion of another task by the NAM committee was recognized. This was a survey of research expenditures by the members of the National Association of Manufacturers. In the frontispiece material of that survey the following statements are included:

---

*Requirements for Nomination—to be eligible for nomination for an award, an inventor or research worker must have discovered or invented "an art, machine, manufacture, or composition of matter, or useful improvement thereof" upon which the United States Patent Office has issued a patent within the last 25 years and which has been put into use by industry and through such use (a) increased employment, and/or (b) provided a new commodity or service, and/or (c) reduced the cost of a product already in use, and/or (d) improved quality of a product already in use.

All nominations must be made on the official form.

The closing date for submission of nominations is December 1, 1939.

In industrial research lies the great hope for re-employment, for productive application of savings and for the beneficial utilization of war production plants.

The tremendous sum being spent today for research is tangible evidence of industry's faith in America's future.

That so-called "tremendous sum" was the figure previously mentioned by Dr. Compton—an infinitesimal percentage of the research expenditures by industry and government in 1974.

The difficulty in stimulating research in American industry continued for many years, posing one of the many problems research institutes of the United States had to overcome in developing their relationship with American industry. The NAM committee, in an attempt to "spread the word" about research, spurred the publication of case histories of successful research efforts in the NAM Newsletter from time to time. Toward that same end some of the larger U.S. corporations that were actively and successfully engaged in research published books, pamphlets, and articles in professional and trade journals to identify themselves with activities that improved profits for their stockholders, but also to stimulate research in American industry in general.

Six examples of corporate case histories telling of success in research in the early days follow.

RESEARCH IN THE BELL SYSTEM*

Bell Laboratories is sometimes thought of as the pioneer among industrial laboratories. In fact, it must share the honors with somewhat similar laboratories which were organized by General Electric and DuPont a few years earlier (than Bell Labs). However, there is no doubt that among them the three laboratories blazed a new trail. Nowadays, of course, the country has thousands of industrial laboratories of various sizes, and the effectiveness of this kind of organization is seldom questioned.

The concept of the large multidisciplinary and, as it is sometimes called, mission-oriented laboratory received fresh support during and after World War II, through the success of many government laboratories, like Los

---

*Prepared in cooperation with the Bell Laboratories and based upon "A Statement Delivered to the Congressional Subcommittee on Science Research and Development," by James B. Fisk (1963), and "The Mission, Organization, and Management of Bell Laboratories," by Dean Gillette (1973).

Alamos and the Radiation Laboratory at MIT, which were organized roughly in this pattern . . . "Although this type of organization has not replaced the small specialty company or even the independent inventor as a source of innovation, it is to an increasing degree the source of basic technology both for public purposes and for industrial projects."*

463 West Street, New York City. Administrative headquarters of Bell Laboratories from the time of its organization in 1925 until 1941. It had been occupied by the Western Electric Engineering Department, one of the predecessor organizations from which Bell Labs was formed, since 1907. The building was sold in 1967.

Bell Laboratories was formally incorporated as a separate unit of the Bell System in 1925. It was, however, the immediate successor to a branch of Western Electric Company (WECo), which was itself organized in 1907. It thus represents a background of more than half a century of experience.

*Brooks, Harvey, "Applied Science and Technological Progress," a report to the House Committee on Science and Astronautics by the National Academy of Sciences, 1967, p. 44.

(There is in fact a line of continuity going back even from the 1907 organization to Alexander Graham Bell's original laboratory in the 1870s.)

The underlying principles of Bell Laboratories' work and organization are contained in some of the ideas behind this 1907 organization from the perspective of half a century. It is convenient to begin such an account by quoting a statement written by one of the executives of the AT&T Company some years later.*

> The reorganization in 1907 consisted of a consolidation [whose] purpose was to avoid duplication of facilities as well as to get the greater efficiency coming from a closer contact between the staff of the Western Electric Company and our own. [He means the AT&T Company.] It brought to one point scientific study and research, manufacturing experience, and operating experience . . . It simplified and expedited the work of the operating [telephone] companies in that it established one point where all statements of requirements, suggestions of improvements, or criticisms arising out of their operating experience could be considered and discussed from all points of view . . . It was helpful in the standardization of apparatus . . .
>
> We had at Bell Laboratories the scientists whose work involved laboratory facilities, the men conducting experiments, the shop design workers, and the inspectors with suitable equipment of laboratories and model shops available for all. The ideas of our research and development scientists and engineers, worked out on paper or in rough mechanical form, were there developed into a finished piece for shop manufacture and after manufacture the product was then subjected to all the tests necessary to satisfy our engineers that it was worthy of introduction into or continuation in the plant of the Bell System.

There are a number of aspects of this statement which deserve comment even from today's perspective. First is the fact that the formation of the new organization was, in itself, a tacit commitment that the Bell System would in fact supply its own technology. Second is the emphasis on the economy and efficiency to be brought about through centralization of engineering and standardization of apparatus. This acquires additional significance when it is realized that the Bell System had been formed by the

---

*Statement by Mr. H. B. Thayer in an article entitled "The Development of Development and Research," appearing in the January 1925 *Bell Telephone Quarterly*, vol. 4, no. 1, p. 2.

combination of literally hundreds of very small local units. Welding all these fragments into a coherent whole whose engineering and equipment needs could be satisfied economically was a major problem. It is equally true even today that the existence of many kinds of telephone equipment, designed and produced at various times and for special kinds of traffic, makes centralized engineering imperative to achieve technological advances with reasonable efficiency.

The simple mention of "scientific study and research" in the statement is also significant. The use of scientists to help solve industrial problems was not quite unprecedented in 1907. There had been a few scientists in the predecessor telephone laboratories, and use of the scientific method was well established, particularly in England and Germany, in such areas as the drug and dye industries. Nevertheless, technological progress had, on the whole, been a hit-or-miss process having very little contact with pure science. It was largely in the hands of the individual inventor or the "engineer" whose primary training was likely to have been in drafting and shop processes. As a result, technological progress often lagged advances in pure science by many decades. It was nearly half a century after Faraday first demonstrated simple generators and motors in his laboratory, for example, before anyone made a serious effort to design such equipment with practical goals in mind. At the turn of the century, the scientific population of the United States, in any case, was so small that large-scale use of scientists in industrial work would not have been feasible.

Dr. F. B. Jewett, first president of Bell Telephone Laboratories, and Dr. W. R. Whitney of the General Electric Company appear to have been the men who most clearly saw the advantages of the scientific method both in approaching industrial problems effectively and in capitalizing quickly on new scientific knowledge. Nowadays, of course, the country has thousands of industrial research laboratories of various sizes, and the question of the applicability of science, and even of very new science, has been learned very well indeed.

Another idea which appears very strongly in the quotation is that of the close cooperation among scientists, designers, shop people, manufacturing engineers, and the like in pursuing the final objective. This concept of the complete technological process as one involving close integration of a number of phases, from scientific research to final design for production, has been applied in amplified and developed form at Bell Laboratories ever since.

The integrated process also implies a close relationship between engineering design and actual manufacture. This has also been a continuing element of Bell System policy. The existence of the branch laboratories today is a recognition of the desirability of providing such a close tie.

One final concept of importance appears clearly in the extract. This is that the design engineer must be responsive to the needs of the final users—that is, the operating telephone companies who provide service to the public. There must be a final evaluation of the project to make certain that it will be satisfactory to the users, or, as the author says, "worthy of introduction into the Bell System." These principles are a reflection of the concept that the Bell System provides service rather than hardware to the ultimate consumer. They have meant that the ultimate yardstick of our engineers has always been the final effectiveness of the apparatus in actual service. Bell Laboratories has always retained design responsibility for all products Western Electric makes and certifies that they are made to design specifications.

A BASELINE OF RESEARCH, DEVELOPMENT, AND ENGINEERING POLICIES

AT&T's general policy is to support internal research, development, and engineering programs needed to invent, design, plan, manufacture, install, operate, and maintain the equipment that forms the physical base of the Bell System. Bell Labs is assigned the responsibility for research, development, and design of the telecommunications equipment used by the Bell System, and also has responsibilities in determining the performance and evolution of the network.

Throughout its history, AT&T's program of aggressive research and fundamental development (R&FD) has produced discoveries, like the transistor and the solar battery, that lie at the forefront of technology. Instead of keeping these discoveries as trade secrets, the company exchanges technical information with the scientific community and with outside industry as soon as proper patent protection has been obtained. Bell Labs freely and quickly publishes the results of its research and fundamental development for the benefit of the worldwide telecommunications industry.

Exploratory system development programs are also funded by AT&T. They are intended to test the feasibility of novel communications approaches for the Bell System. Bell Labs and AT&T Engineering work closely in carrying out these programs.

AT&T furnishes the funds for Bell Labs systems engineers who develop the technical information necessary for many Bell System activities. These engineers plan improvements in service and cost, the growth of the tele-communications network, and introduction of new facilities and services. They also carry the principal responsibility for assuring that the designs coming from Bell Labs specific development and design programs are compatible with existing Bell System equipment and with network performance objectives.

AT&T's Engineering organization, in supplying technical information to the Operating Companies, can call on the special expertise of scientists and engineers at Bell Labs. Bell Labs also has a program of two-year transfers to the Operating Companies to help design engineers gain a deeper understanding of technical conditions, opportunities, and limitations within the Operating Company environment.

The Bell Labs Quality Assurance organization is responsible for assuring that equipment designed or specified by Bell Laboratories is manufactured according to Bell Labs designs or specifications and to the stated quality. A particular benefit of this activity is to relieve the Operating Companies of acceptance testing on new equipment. The Quality Assurance organization also includes a group of field representatives—Bell Labs engineers who, by working on Operating Company premises, stay in close touch with company technological needs and problems and provide liaison with other engineers and scientists at Bell Labs locations.

As a natural consequence of its vigor in telecommunications research, development, and engineering, the Bell System in some technical areas is uniquely qualified to provide technical support for certain national programs. As government agencies request the Bell System to work in these areas, specific projects may be undertaken under contract. But, in contrast to aggressive R&FD efforts in telecommunications, there is no attempt to prepare the Bell System especially to acquire government contracts.

RESEARCH

At Bell Labs the research area is organized by scientific disciplines. The various divisions are responsible for physical research, materials research (including chemical research), mathematics and behavioral sciences, the communications sciences, and operations research.

Research organizations devoted to the physical and analytical sciences are based at Murray Hill, New Jersey. The intent is to enhance the full and open exchange of information among scientists in the various disciplines engaged in fundamental research. Most of the people in the Communications

Murray Hill, New Jersey. Administrative headquarters of Bell Laboratories since 1941. This view shows the building as it appeared in 1974.

Sciences Division work at the Holmdel, New Jersey, laboratory, along with most of the systems engineers and those engaged in exploratory phases of all system development activities.

Work in electronics technology embraces both fundamental investigation of the usefulness of new concepts and design for manufacture. Research physicists and materials people should interact closely with those in the electronics technology area who are investigating uses for new devices and circuits.

Bell Labs does not limit itself to applying new technology to development of brand-new products. There is constant alertness to opportunities for using new technology to improve old equipment. The 20-year history of the TD-2 microwave radio transmission system is a good example. The system originally carried 480 voice channels on each of six radio channels. Now, through continuous modification and upgrading, 1500 voice channels can be carried on each of 12 radio channels.

The mission of R&D is to discover and exploit technological opportunities in all aspects of telecommunications. It is hard to overemphasize this Bell System philosophy: innovative systems that are chosen for specific development are based on exploitation of discoveries in science and technology. The R&FD programs that produce these discoveries are dedicated to long-term needs and are not dictated by transient demands of the marketplace.

In reviewing the development selection process, we must first recognize the effects of basic corporate needs and policies. As reflected in its License Contract with the Bell Operating Companies, AT&T seeks to assure the supply of effective equipment for telephone customers. Throughout its history, the Bell System has supported internal resources to assure that this need is met with the very best that technology can offer. Bell Labs is expected to design the equipment required to meet these needs.

The Bell System's basic policy was stated by W. S. Gifford, president of AT&T in 1927: to provide continually improving telecommunication services with increasing performance standards, at as low a cost as is consistent with financial safety. When exploring ways of providing new service or meeting new performance standards, prudent management requires that adaptation of existing designs be investigated as an economic alternative to replacing older equipment by new kinds of facilities. These observations on policy provide us with several guideposts in selecting development programs:

- maintain a balance in development programs, to capitalize on new discoveries and opportunities for the advantage of all parts of the network;
- exploit opportunities that give increasing performance in the network; and
- exploit opportunities that reduce the cost of providing service.

The first guidepost suggests the reason for dividing system development among the various Bell Labs organizations, each dedicated to advancing the technology of a particular portion of the telecommunications network. The relative sizes of the development efforts are not static, and shifts have occurred over the years as opportunities and needs have changed. No portion of the plant has been abandoned, and none should be ignored for the benefit of another when opportunities for improvement occur.

Each of the three companies provides a particular type of contribution to the development program decision. AT&T and Bell Labs are responsible, with the Operating Companies, for assessing the needs for improvement or change. Bell Labs is responsible for generating technical possibilities, costs, and schedules for development. Bell Labs and WECo, working together, review manufacturing costs and prices to discover proper price/performance tradeoffs. AT&T provides the "market" information.

In the case of central office switching and transmission systems for the network, the Operating Telephone Companies are the customers. Here, planning for system growth and modernization is based on demand information provided by AT&T Engineering. In the case of customer products, such as telephone sets, data transmission services, PBX, and key telephone systems, AT&T's Marketing and Service Plans organization is responsible for estimating demand as an element of the tri-company decision.

For each candidate program, costs of development, manufacture, and introduction are computed, and the Operating Telephone Company demand is estimated. Many other factors enter the various reviews and, in various instances, different ones may be dominant. Such factors are savings in first cost, savings in annual charges, service improvement, flexibility in operation, installation cost, revenue-producing potential, and environmental impact. In carrying out these programs, systems and development engineers must examine the interaction between the existing network and newly introduced or modified equipment. Continuity and service integrity must be assured. Interfaces with the existing plant must be established (e.g., between frequency-division modulation and pulsecode modulation equipment). The need for electrical power and environmental controls such as air-conditioning must be determined. To compute all factors for all projects would be inefficient. Rather, it is a matter of experience and judgment to determine which quantitative measures should be made, and how much weight should be given to them.

Priorities among options are set in light of the economic and service benefits anticipated. Decisions are made on a tri-company basis by individuals who thoroughly understand the technical possibilities and the needs of the Bell System. It is particularly important to remember the backgrounds of the Bell System executives who make these final decisions. Most, if not all, of their careers have been spent in telecommunications.

The tri-company selection process has been in effect for decades. Currently, three "Councils" are formally responsible for reviewing development programs, one each for Transmission, Switching, and Customer Products. Members of these Councils either have or report to those who have authority to allocate funds. The Councils themselves have no operating budgets, but they depend for analysis and evaluation on task groups and committees whose members are selected from various organizations in the three companies.

There are additional mechanisms for informing those charged with making the final decisions. Each company has developed an internal reporting system to keep its management familiar with program status. In addition, Project Status Reviews are given regularly by Bell Laboratories. These reviews have the express purpose of giving AT&T and WECo the progress of continuing developments and describing the opportunities offered by new ones. Individuals from AT&T, Bell Labs, and WECo take part in preparing these Project Status Reviews.

The depth and continuity of technical interaction at all organizational levels among Bell Labs, WECo, and AT&T are direct results of corporate integration of the Bell System. An essential ingredient in maintaining our momentum of progress is that projects for advancing the telecommunications art are selected and resources allocated by well-informed, experienced, technical administrators who form the management of all three companies—AT&T, WECo, and Bell Labs.

A LOOK TO THE FUTURE

An added dimension to the territory ahead was given by W. O. Baker, president of Bell Laboratories, in a recent interview.*

> Our role is constantly evolving. I think that the era of having to demonstrate new technical communications functions is largely behind us. It's no longer necessary to show, for example, that all of the people of the world can be connected together, or that voice and video can be transmitted with fidelity and reliability.

> Now we have to concentrate on maximizing the efficiency, performance, and economy of all these facilities. This is a very exciting undertaking. It means that we will be at the core of satisfying the needs of the ultimate user of telecommunications services in the most efficient and economical way.

> Our first job is to model and understand the range of human needs and how to fulfill them—how to link the mind and the machine. This is a major new mission. All of the cables, terminals, switches, subscriber apparatus, and electronic devices are created by people, engineered by people, operated and used by people. We are beginning to understand how to connect these people with the hardware we create and how to help these people to decide on and to make optimum use of the hardware.

---

*"Bell Lab News," May 1973.

DuPONT'S SUCCESS STORY*

The origins of the DuPont Company go back to 1802 and the manufacturing of black powder. Eleuthère Irénée du Pont de Nemours, a student of the renowned French chemist Lavoisier, that year built a small mill on the banks of the Brandywine River in Delaware. The young French refugee had been urged by Thomas Jefferson to build an American mill to make gunpowder equal to that imported from Europe. The struggling United States lacked good powder for hunting, land clearance, mining, quarrying, and self-protection.

Until 1857, DuPont made only black powder, in various granulations, from three raw materials—potassium nitrate (saltpeter), sulfur, and charcoal. That year Lammot du Pont, a grandson of the company's founder, developed a new "soda powder," for blasting purposes. With a base of sodium nitrate, it was the first strictly industrial explosive.

The company made gunpowder for the young nation's fighters during the War of 1812 and the Mexican War and for the U.S. Government in the Civil War. But between 1802 and Appomattox, the great bulk of powder it milled was blasting powder employed in the development of farming and industry. In 1880, DuPont began to manufacture two high explosives—nitroglycerin and dynamite. These much more powerful commercial blasting agents were needed in ever-increasing quantities with the advent of steam railroads, discovery of new mines, introduction of steel in buildings, and growing use of machinery in shops and on farms. High explosives blasted out new roadbeds and tunnels and helped mine coal and metals and quarry rock. They gave new impetus to the industrial growth of the nation.

When Pierre S. du Pont, eldest son of Lammot, joined the company in 1890, he undertook as one of his first tasks the perfection of another new explosive smokeless powder based on nitrocellulose. This project presaged a turning point in the company's history because DuPont thus became interested in cellulose—the base for many products, especially cellophane and rayon, and a major part of DuPont's business for several decades.

PROMINENCE OF RESEARCH

DuPont's vigorous pursuit of excellence in research can be traced back to founder Eleuthère Irénée du Pont, for from the start, Eleuthère sought to

---

*Prepared in cooperation with the Public Affairs Department of E. I. duPont de Nemours and Company and based upon the 1972 and 1973 Annual Reports and information bulletins of 1973 and 1974.

improve both his process and his product—black powder. On November 23, 1804—only two years after he had finished building his first mill—he was issued a patent on a "machine for granulating gunpowder," evidence of his own powerfully inquisitive nature and his desire to improve methods of manufacturing. He was also ever mindful of the safety of his workmen and in that regard devoted himself to experiments that would reduce the danger of explosives. His investigations of more than 150 years ago, aimed at better quality and lower cost with greater safety, have remained an inspiration for the modern company.

For more than half a century, research has been a major factor in maintaining the DuPont Company's favorable position in the severely competitive climate of the chemical industry. The products of DuPont research have been the lifeblood of the company, approximately 20 percent of the sales resulting from products introduced within the last 15 years.

Prior to the establishment of formal research laboratories, DuPont research was carried out in works laboratories under the direction of the works superintendent. The Eastern Laboratory, built at Gibbstown, New Jersey, in 1902, was DuPont's first formal research venture. One of the first industrial research laboratories in this country, it is believed to represent the earliest organized research effort in the American chemical industry. In 1903, research activities were extended and broadened through the establishment of a new laboratory near Wilmington on the site of the present Experimental Station.

Most of the company's fundamental research is carried out at the Experimental Station, where a major expansion program was undertaken after World War II and still continues today. In addition, new facilities have been applied to other phases of DuPont research at plant and sales service laboratories throughout the company. For example, 9 technical service laboratories have been built at Chestnut Run, near Wilmington. In these laboratories, the operating departments are providing expanded sales and engineering services to their customers as well as increased development work on new materials and processes. All told, in 1974, DuPont was operating more than 100 research and development, sales service, and plant laboratories, with approximately 4500 scientists and engineers engaged directly in research, development, and closely related activities. Expenditures for research and development in 1973 totaled about $276 million.

DuPont's cumulative investment in pollution abatement facilities in the United States totaled $311 million at the end of 1973, including $113

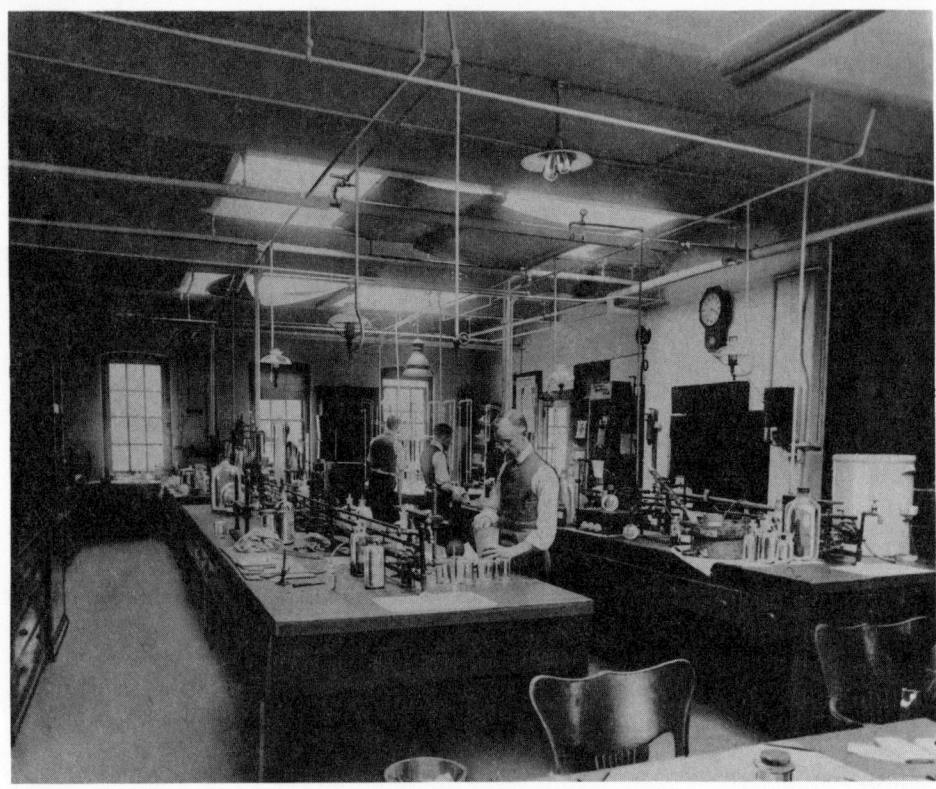

Interior of one of the first laboratories at the DuPont Company's Experimental Station, established in 1903 on the banks of the Brandywine, near Wilmington, Delaware. The assignment of the Station's small staff of chemists and engineers was significant to range over the entire chemical field, looking for new opportunities. This was the first step toward diversified manufacture. (The photo was taken in 1908.)

million in the facilities under construction or authorized. The company spent $92 million in 1973 to operate and maintain air and water pollution control facilities and to conduct environmental research and development activities. The equivalent of 2450 full-time employees are engaged in pollution control activities and antipollution research.

FRUITS OF RESEARCH LABORS

In 1904, DuPont began producing a special type of nitrocellulose for lacquers, belt cement, leather finishes, and other industrial uses, and in 1910, nitrocellulose-coated fabrics, then known as "artificial leather," were added. Pyroxylin or nitrocellulose plastics joined the new products groups in 1915, and rubber-coated textiles in 1916.

The following year, 1917, DuPont purchased Harrison Brothers & Company and several smaller concerns, thereby entering the acids, heavy chemicals, pigments, dry colors, mixed paints, and lithopone businesses. At about the same time, the company became interested in dyes, a commodity in great demand, as a step toward releasing American industry from dependence upon Germany in the broad field of coal-tar chemistry.

At the conclusion of World War I, during which DuPont supplied a major portion of the explosives used by the Allied forces, the company terminated all of its military activities except two small plants which were continued at the government's request for national security reasons. The Armistice of 1918 was a signal for accelerated expansion into new peacetime lines.

DIVERSIFICATION

In West Virginia, the Industrial Chemicals Department high-pressure synthesis plant for the fixation of atmospheric nitrogen was an outstanding development of this postwar period. It was one of the plants that helped relieve the nation of its prewar dependence upon Chilean nitrates for explosives and fertilizers, but it did more than that. New processes were developed there for manufacturing methanol, glycol, urea, higher alcohols, and other chemicals of great industrial importance.

Following an expenditure of $43 million before a dollar of profit was returned on the investment, dyes and other synthetic organic chemicals became major items on the DuPont sales lists. Cellophane was introduced into the American market and revolutionized retail packaging; "Duco" nitrocellulose lacquer effected equally sweeping changes in the finishing of automobiles and furniture. Another DuPont first, neoprene synthetic rubber, was announced in 1931, and, of course, nylon, presented in 1938, was hailed by scientists the world over as one of the great chemical inventions of the century.

In 1927, the DuPont Company launched a program of fundamental research in chemistry. Dr. Wallace H. Carothers, a brilliant young scientist, was chosen to direct the work in organic chemistry. Although immediate practical results were not expected, and not attained, Dr. Carothers nevertheless knew what course he wanted to pursue. He had long been eager to try synthesizing compounds of high molecular weight, for it was known that certain molecules combined to form "giant" molecules, characteristic of such substances as silk, cotton, and rubber.

Probably the most dramatic moment in DuPont research history is reenacted here—the birth of the first completely synthetic fiber, impractical for commercial use but true forerunner of nylon itself. Here chemist Julian Hill shows how he pulled molten sample of material from a laboratory test tube at the company's Experimental Station near Wilmington, Delaware. The molasseslike mass stuck to the glass stirring rod and was drawn out into a thin fiber.

The late Dr. Hale Charch, pioneer in the development of moistureproof cellophane, working in DuPont laboratory in 1924.

Development of the first successful moistureproof cellophane film is reenacted here at DuPont's Experimental Station near Wilmington, Delaware, by the inventor, the late Dr. Hale Charch. The new film was developed after 2500 formulas had been tried and hundreds of tests made. Large bag on right held water for weeks, while control bags of untreated film showed evaporation losses in a few days.

Dr. Wallace H. Carothers, shown here with neoprene, first commercially successful general purpose synthetic rubber, came to the DuPont Company the year after it launched its program of fundamental research in 1927. Dr. Carothers is remembered primarily for his direction of the program of fundamental research from which came neoprene and nylon, world's first synthetic fiber comparable to nature's fibers. Dr. Carothers died in 1937.

HINTS OF A NEW FIBER

In the course of subsequent studies, an associate of Dr. Carothers's one day drew from his laboratory test tube long strands of a syrupy moisture and noted that, even after cooling, they could be stretched several times their original length and retain their elasticity. Most important, these strands increased in strength after stretching, and became somewhat lustrous in appearance. This phenomenon observed in 1930 demonstrated, in Carothers's words, "for the first time the possibility of obtaining useful fibers from strictly synthetic materials." (Rayon, which had been known for many years, is derived from cellulose, a substance appearing abundantly in nature.)

The DuPont research chemists now had what they called a long-chain, or linear, polymer. The stretching process had aligned the molecules into long parallel bundles equivalent to those of natural fibers like silk or cotton. The chemist's drawing of the polymer resembled a chain of paper clips.

The first truly synthetic fiber, while a laboratory wonder, was not commercially feasible. It was comparatively weak and had a low melting point. For the next four years, Dr. Carothers and his associates tried several thousand chemical combinations and produced hundreds of fibers, none of which was satisfactory. Finally, one day in 1934, Dr. Carothers squeezed through a hypodermic needle a thread of the first fully practical synthetic fiber. It was made from Hexamethylene diamine and adipic acid and was known as Fiber 66 until 1938, when it was publicly announced and given the name of nylon.

FULL-SCALE PRODUCTION

This announcement could not be made until it was known with certainty that the new fiber could be brought from the laboratory to commercial production. Many difficulties were involved in doing this. Both the chemistry and the process were so new that new equipment had to be designed and new materials tested for use in much of the equipment. By the time the first plant, at Seaford, Delaware, began commercial production late in 1939, $27 million had been invested.

The year before, the new product appeared on public sale in the form of filaments for toothbrush bristles, but it was as a hosiery yarn that nylon scored its first real marketing triumphs. On May 15, 1940, the first nylon stockings went on sale and scored immediately with the consumer public. Other uses for the new fiber followed rapidly, and by the time nylon "went to war" in 1942, it was being used or proposed for scores of applications ranging from apparel to ropes and fish nets.

NYLON GOES TO WAR

In the absence of Japanese silk during World War II, the entire output of nylon was allocated to the United States Armed Forces. More than 3.8 million parachutes were made of nylon. Other important applications during the war years were in airplane tire cord, combat clothes, netting and hammocks for jungle service, life rafts, ropes, and literally hundreds of other uses.

Today, after many improvements in physical properties and appearance, nylon is shipped to the textile industry in three principal forms—monofilament, multifilament, and staple fiber.

In addition to man-made fibers, the DuPont Company also became involved in such diverse industries as paints, plastics, electrochemicals, and photographic film. DuPont also developed new insecticides, seed disinfectants, and other agricultural chemicals, including nutrition supplements for poultry and livestock feed.

As the company extended its activities into many market areas, the primary goal was to be the most inexpensive, innovative producer of quality products in each field. Other fundamental policies that have become part of the DuPont plan are (1) to provide opportunities for employees of vision and ability to enter management when they are still young, (2) to use ample venture capital for exploring and developing new chemical fields, and (3) to promote good employee relations.

ACTIVITIES FOR U.S. GOVERNMENT

During World War II, DuPont built 54 plants of various sizes for the government at 32 different locations. The largest undertaking was the design, construction, and operation of the Hanford Engineer Works near Pasco, Washington, for the manufacture of plutonium. The company withdrew from this operation in 1947.

Overall production from DuPont's own plants during the Second World War was increased to more than double prewar levels. Nylon and neoprene were of particular importance to the U.S. war effort, providing vital replacement for silk and natural rubber.

In 1950, the DuPont Company accepted an assignment from the U.S. Government to design, build, and operate new production facilities for atomic materials as part of the Atomic Energy Commission's support of national defense and security. The billion-dollar-plus Savannah River Plant in South Carolina ranks as one of the largest engineering projects of modern time. DuPont's contract with the Atomic Energy Commission to operate the Savannah River Plant and Laboratory has been extended yearly with the company receiving a token fee of one dollar.

The company accepted a contract in 1968 for process design and site responsibility for a government-owned TNT plant at Newport, Indiana. DuPont continues to have operating responsibility for the plant. In 1973, however, sales of DuPont products to the United States Government and its contractors amounted to less than 1 percent of the company's total sales.

NEW PROGRAMS

Today, DuPont's varied interests embrace chemistry, biology, solid-state physics, electronics, pharmaceuticals, and agricultural sciences. Product lines range from sulfuric acid to high-speed medical X-ray films; from fibers for the sheerest of garments to materials that insulate men from the temperature extremes of outer space; from paint to sophisticated analytical instruments; from polyethylene industrial pipe to photopolymer printing plants. An automatic clinical analyzer ("aca") developed by DuPont analyzes body fluids for diagnostic purposes. This sophisticated instrument has gained wide

Laboratory rooms and offices at DuPont's Experimental Station, Wilmington, Delaware, are designed to make a functional contribution to the research being conducted. Chemical laboratories are normally two-man units provided with spacious hoods built for versatility and safety. Physics and engineering laboratories are designed around basic types of physical and electrical equipment. Biological laboratories have low benches for easy sample manipulation and other special features, such as sterile transfer rooms. Shown here is a typical two-man laboratory.

acceptance in hospitals and medical laboratories. The disposable test packs for the "aca" also are manufactured and sold by DuPont.

Through its diverse 1600 products and product lines, DuPont supplies all major industries; however, the company is more than a creator and manufacturer of commercial products. It is also an inventor of new technologies. As such, DuPont serves broad economic and social functions—both as a community employer and a major technical resource. It is deeply involved in efforts to curb air and water pollution, to improve economic opportunities for the disadvantaged, and to increase world supplies of food and water.

The scope of new programs in the United States and abroad is impressive, with capital expenditures in 1973 totaling $736 million. To bring to the public the benefit of past and current research, several new plants are under construction, and substantial plant additions have been made and are currently underway.

In 1972, DuPont acquired Berg Electronics, Inc., manufacturers of precision electrical and electronic connectors; Ivan Sorvall, Inc., manufacturer of biomedical laboratory equipment, was acquired the following year. A new research and development laboratory and design center for automotive finish and refinish coatings was completed in 1973 at Troy, Michigan. The Brandywine Building, the company's third major office building in downtown Wilmington, Delaware, was dedicated in May 1972. The 19-story structure houses about 2000 DuPont employees and some commercial tenants. All in all, DuPont has more than 100 plants in 31 states and in excess of 118,000 employees in the United States and abroad—all of this having come from meager beginnings in the manufacture of black powder, a product which was discontinued when a government contract ran out in 1973.

ACTIVITIES ABROAD

In recent years, the DuPont Company has been expanding its activities and facilities abroad, particularly in Europe. The company has established 32 foreign subsidiaries and affiliated companies which make and sell DuPont products both to supply markets already built up by DuPont export business and to open new markets. In 1973, the company's total foreign business amounted to $1,616 million. DuPont's foreign operating investment at the end of 1972 was approximately $2,045 million.

Soon after the end of World War II, the company began a long-term program of plant expansion and improvement designed to provide facilities which had been deferred because of concentration on the war effort and government restrictions. The program included plant modernization and additional manufacturing capacity required to meet the expanded demand for certain prewar product lines as well as facilities necessary to commercialize new processes and products developed since the prewar years.

THE STORY OF GENERAL ELECTRIC RESEARCH*

The essential elements for the initial rise of the electrical industry were in existence by 1890. The arc lamp appeared at the Philadelphia Centennial Exposition in 1876. Edison produced his incandescent lamp in 1879, demonstrated his lighting system at Menlo Park in 1880, and put into operation his first central station in 1882. In 1886, William Stanley developed his transformer and exhibited his alternating-current system in successful operation at Great Barrington. The first commercial alternating-current system was installed at Buffalo, in 1887. Electric motors were available for industrial use. Sprague operated his first electric railway car at Richmond, in 1888.

The elements were there. But men were needed with the vision to perceive the great potentialities of systems composed of these elements, and with the ability and courage to make their visions come true.

There were such men. Prominent among them were the pioneers who, in 1892, founded the General Electric Company. That company was formed by the merger of two existing companies—the Edison General Electric Company (which had been organized to promote the incandescent lighting system developed by Edison) and the Thomson-Houston Company (which had been created by a group of businessmen in Lynn to exploit the arc-lighting system developed by Elihu Thomson). Charles A. Coffin, who had been president of the latter company, became president of the new corporation. By his sound judgment, business acumen, and resourcefulness, he brought the infant company through the Depression which assailed it almost immediately after its birth and placed it on the firm financial footing which it has enjoyed ever since.

The technical operations of the company were led by men of outstanding ability. Among them were Elihu Thomson, a prolific inventor and the

---

*Prepared in cooperation with the Research and Development Communication Branch of the General Electric Company and based on *The Story of General Electric Research* by Lawrence A. Hawkins.

first great American scientist to devote his talents to industry, and his right-hand man, E. W. Rice, Jr., a brilliant engineer and a sound judge of men. Rice was to become vice president and technical director and later president of General Electric.

Under such engineering leadership, the company's products rapidly grew in quality, in range of sizes, and in diversification. As new applications of electric power developed, they were met by sound engineering practice. So the company grew and prospered.

Gradually, however, it was perceived that one thing was lacking. Engineering is applied science. Scientific knowledge is the most important raw material for engineering development, and the source of scientific knowledge is research. The engineering progress of the 1890s was based on the researches of Faraday, Joseph Henry, and other scientists in the early part of the century. But unless new research produced new scientific facts, engineering development must inevitably slow down or halt.

There was little fundamental research in American universities or elsewhere in this country, so why should not General Electric itself engage in such research? Just as great steel companies find it advantageous to acquire ore fields of their own, why should not General Electric engineering possess a source of its most essential raw material? Why not a General Electric research laboratory? This question became explicitly asked, and was promptly answered by action.

It remained to find a competent director for the new undertaking. Obviously, success would depend on his capabilities. His selection must have caused some worry. No one in the country had demonstrated ability in industrial research, for there had been no organized industrial research. However, Thomson had met and admired a young professor at Massachusetts Institute of Technology and suggested that Rice interview him. The interview was held, and Rice was so favorably impressed that he at once made his proposal. The young professor was Dr. Willis R. Whitney.

Whitney showed some reluctance toward accepting Rice's offer. He was happy in his work at M.I.T. Industrial research was as new to him as to everybody else. He doubted whether he would find enough interesting problems in Schenectady to satisfy his active and eager mind.

Rice therefore proposed the experiment of a division of time between M.I.T. and General Electric. Experiments of all kinds have always had an irresistible lure for Whitney, so he swallowed Rice's bait and became a long-distance commuter. Thus, the General Electric Research Laboratory was

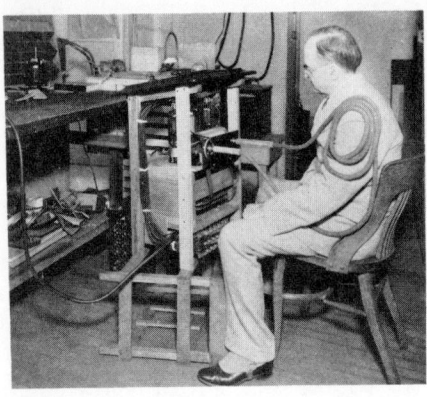

Dr. W. R. Whitney ready for experiment with high-frequency heating coil on his shoulder.

started in the fall of 1900, under the leadership of the man who was to remain its director for 32 years and is still contributing to its work through his experiments.

At its beginning, the Research Laboratory was Whitney, and Whitney was the Research Laboratory. In one very real sense that has been true throughout the laboratory's history, for it was he who designed, built, and launched it, charted its course, enlisted an able crew, and steered it for more than 30 years, through fair weather and foul, to a long series of ports of triumphant achievement. Above all, it was he who fired the crew with his own enthusiasm for the high adventure of research and by example created in it the spirit of wholehearted cooperation which has always characterized the laboratory.

For three years Whitney continued to commute between Boston and Schenectady, gradually increasing the laboratory staff. He proceeded cautiously at first, taking time to familiarize himself with the company's problems and gradually initiating a program of experiments that he believed would throw light on them. It was not long, however, before he perceived that there were enough fascinating problems fully to engage even his avid mind for a lifetime. So, convinced at last that he had found a task worthy of his best efforts and needing all his time, he ended his work at M.I.T., moved his family to Schenectady, and with a dozen assistants, began his real life's work of building up research in the General Electric Company.

The results were soon apparent. From the laboratory flowed a growing stream of new things—new devices for the company to sell, new materials and processes to improve its products, new facts and ideas to stimulate and help the engineers in their developments. The Research Laboratory gradually became recognized not only as an important but an essential part of the company, contributing largely to all engineering and manufacturing activities. Meanwhile, the laboratory moved into larger and better quarters—first, into the building now occupied by the Schenectady Works Laboratory and then into a new building.

Pride of authorship had no place in Dr. Whitney. Ideas coming from his staff always received the warmest welcome. A good idea was good whoever suggested it; a good experiment was even better. To his entire staff in all their experimental work, Whitney gave his enthusiastic support and encouragement. Such help as he gave came in the form of suggestion, not dictation. His attitude was that of a consultant, not of a boss.

With such leadership, it is no wonder that there grew up in the laboratory a strong spirit of loyalty, of mutual helpfulness, of enthusiasm for work, of pride in the laboratory, and of deep affection for its director.

In other ways, too, that director made the laboratory a worthy object of pride. He was a keen judge of men, and with the help of his magnetic personality he drew around himself a group of brilliantly productive minds and lovable characters, such as few if any other industrial laboratories have been able to attract. A new man joining the staff could not help feeling it a high privilege to become associated with such men.

INCANDESCENT LAMPS

In the 21 years which passed between the production of Edison's first successful lamp and the founding of the Research Laboratory, Edison and others had worked indefatigably to increase the life and efficiency of the lamps. The life was brought up to an average of 600 hours, and the efficiency was doubled. But in 1900, there seemed so little prospect for further progress that Edison is reported to have said in that year that the incandescent lamp was then so perfected it was unlikely that it would ever be materially improved.

In that same year, the Research Laboratory was started, and in the first 15 years of its existence, it quadrupled the efficiency of incandescent lamps, while nearly doubling the life. Later work in the Research and Lamp Development Laboratories increased the efficiency 50 percent.

Dr. William D. Coolidge (right) explains to Thomas A. Edison the process of working tungsten to make it ductile. (General Electric Research Laboratory, 1914)

PREWAR PERIOD

In those years preceding the First World War, the laboratory produced the magnetite electrode, with which the engineers of the company were enabled to design the best arc lamp for street lighting ever seen.

As the war in Europe became an increasingly direct menace to the United States, Josepheus Daniels, then Secretary of the Navy, conceived clearly the potential value of the application of science to military equipment and operations and organized the Naval Consulting Board, with Thomas A. Edison as chairman and Dr. Whitney as a member.

Upon declaration of war, E. W. Rice, then president of General Electric, telegraphed President Wilson placing all the facilities of the Research Laboratory and the services of all its personnel at the disposal of the government. But conditions in Washington were very different from those existing at the outbreak of World War II when the nation's research facilities were so quickly and effectively mobilized under the very able leadership of Dr. Vannevar Bush and with generous financial support by the government. In 1917, no one in Washington except Secretary Daniels seemed interested in mobilizing science in the national defense or even in taking advantage of proffered scientific aid. The laboratories which contributed to the war effort did so, for the most part, on their own initiative and at their own expense. Sometimes prolonged persuasion was needed to induce receptivity in the armed forces.

MANY ACTIVITIES

In the interval between the two world wars, the Research Laboratory staff was slowly but steadily expanding, except for a moderate retrenchment enforced by the Depression of the early 1930s. The laboratory activities were growing more varied as new fields were entered for research, but two laboratory sections were continuing to expand their old fields with new materials.

A CONGENIAL ATMOSPHERE

Dr. Whitney, while his staff was still small, began the practice of holding an informal weekly conference or colloquium, at which a selected topic was opened by one man, followed by a general discussion. As the staff grew, these colloquia, while inevitably losing a little of their original informality, continued through the years, except in wartime, when considerations of national security imposed on the laboratory the alien and distasteful policy of isolation and secrecy. In peacetime, each week some member of the research staff would tell of his recent work, his successes, and his problems, and would answer the questions asked in the ensuing discussion, thus not only informing others who might utilize his results, but also strengthening the solidarity of the laboratory and its spirit of teamwork.

Often some speaker from a university or another laboratory would bring the stimulus of the story of his researches in his own field—biological, astronomical, or whatever it might be. When available meeting places became overcrowded, Dr. Whitney insisted on the erection of an auditorium, seating 400, which was named "Rice Hall" in recognition of the leading part played by E. W. Rice in the founding of the Research Laboratory and the constant support he gave it in its early days. The auditorium was made available for meetings held by other departments, and its side corridors were used to install working exhibits of laboratory developments for demonstration to visitors. Once a year a Christmas party was held in Rice Hall for the entertainment of the families of the laboratory staff.

During a visit to the General Electric Research Laboratory in 1920, Guglielmo Marconi (right) is shown high-vacuum apparatus by Dr. Irving Langmuir. In 1932, for his work in surface chemistry, Dr. Langmuir became the first American industrial chemist to win a Nobel Prize.

In 1932, for his now classic researches in surface chemistry at the General Electric Research Laboratory, Dr. Irving Langmuir received the first Nobel Prize ever awarded an American industrial scientist. Making the presentation at the ceremony in Stockholm was King Gustavus V of Sweden.

WAR COMES AGAIN

World War II had a much more profound effect on the Research Laboratory than had World War I. Not only was the conversion of laboratory activities to war projects more complete, but the events of the war more greatly affected the postwar developments.

World War I brought home to our nation for the first time the realization that research is a vital force in the industrial economy and national security. World War II enormously broadened and deepened that realization, and like the earlier war powerfully stimulated the expansion of research endeavor.

Man-made snow has been created for first time by Vincent J. Schaeffer, scientist of G-E Research Laboratory. Here he waves his scientific wand through snow cloud produced in a cold chamber. Cloud was created by introducing moist air from the breath into -5 deg. Fahrenheit temperature of atmosphere in the chamber. The wand, cooled in liquid air to -70 deg. Fahrenheit, leaves tiny ice germs in the cloud which grow at expense of water droplets comprising the cloud. Result: man-made snow.

To the General Electric Company, war work revealed new fields inviting exploration and new leads to further developments in old fields. War developments demonstrated the possibility of breaking into and utilizing the awesome forces locked up in the nuclei of atoms, and both the fundamental phenomena of nuclear fission and the development of methods for applying the released energy clamored for intensive study. Radar extended the gamut of radio waves into new microwave ranges with the promise of yielding applications. Combustion problems in jet-propelled planes called for further study. New possibilities in the old fields of high-temperature insulations and alloys were revealed. The semiconducting elements had made an entree in the high-frequency rectifiers used in radar equipment. Nuclear research had come of age, and the exciting prospect of useful power from the atom had opened up. Moreover, the government desired extensive cooperation by General Electric in some of its own projects.

All this meant a great expansion of research activity. The laboratory staff needed to be much enlarged, new facilities created, and space provided to house both. In short, there was a need for a large new building.

It was realized that while success in the expanded and more varied activities would depend chiefly on the quality of the augumented research staff, facilities and space should be fully adequate to its needs if maximum results were to be achieved.

No suitable site affording the requisite space could be found in or adjacent to the Schenectady Works. After careful consideration of other possibilities, it was decided to build at a place known as "The Knolls" from an estate situated there. The site, five miles from the Schenactady Works, is on the Mohawk River and at the greatest elevation in the neighborhood. The river would provide cooling and process water, barge transportation, and a receptacle for purified wastes. A branch of the New York Central Railroad ran along the river bank through the property. Plenty of space was available for expansion and for auxiliary buildings as they might be needed. The scenic attractiveness of the location rounded out the advantages of the site.

KNOLLS ATOMIC POWER LABORATORY

With the close of World War II, one question was foremost in the minds of General Electric research men and engineers. Could those awe-inspiring forces, so devastatingly displayed at Hiroshima and Nagasaki, be harnessed economically to provide power for industrial uses? To seek the answer to this momentous question, the Research Laboratory recruited a number of leading scientists who were available from the break-up of some of the war-time projects, and with their help formulated an initial program.

For a time, progress was hampered by security regulations, but early in 1946 the "Manhattan District," which had developed the atomic bomb, proposed to General Electric that the company should take over the operation of the Hanford Works, which had been constructed and operated by the DuPont Company for the Manhattan District during the war for the production of plutonium.

General Electric was reluctant to undertake that operation, but a little later the Manhattan District proposed that the company should also design, construct, and operate a research and development laboratory at Schenectady for work on peacetime applications of nuclear energy, particularly the development of useful power. This proposal was directly in line with the company's own desire and was promptly accepted. Then, in view of the bearing of the work at Hanford on the problems of power production, the company agreed to take on its management.

The technical group which the Research Laboratory had engaged for nuclear work was at once organized as the atomic power division of the Research Laboratory and became the nucleus of the new activity.

EYES OF THE FUTURE

The laboratory has explored many and widely diverse fields. What has it brought back from those explorations? What did it find of value to the company that financed it? To the scientific world? To the general public?

As regards the value of the General Electric Company, an approximate estimate is not difficult. A very considerable number of its present products had their origin in the Research Laboratory. The modern incandescent lamp, with its drawn-tungsten filament and gas filling came from the laboratory. For many years it constituted the entire product of the Lamp Department, and still, in spite of the competition from fluorescent lamps, represents a major part of sales. All the products of the Electronics Department are based on electronic tubes, and most of the basic types of those tubes came from the laboratory. The entire product of the Apparatus Department benefits from the laboratory's work on insulations, silicon steel, permanent magnet material, hydrogen cooling, carbon brushes, vibrations, lubrication, arcs, fatigue of metals, and special alloys, while in the factory, production costs are lowered and quality improved by such laboratory developments as Carboloy cemented carbide tools, hydrogen brazing, and atomic hydrogen welding.

To the world of science, the Research Laboratory has made many diverse and substantial contributions. The 1700 papers it has published in technical journals have recorded new facts, new basic discoveries, and new theories. Many are recognized the world over as classics and are cited as authoritative references in their fields.

In all these ways the General Electric Research Laboratory has played a noteworthy part in the magnificent scientific advance in the past half century, but perhaps its most valuable service to science has been the proof it gave by its example that an industrial laboratory can conduct research in pure science, with profit to itself while promoting the advancement of knowledge. That proof served as a stimulus to fundamental researches in other industrial laboratories which have furthered scientific advance in many fields.

THE B. F. GOODRICH COMPANY*

Dr. Benjamin Franklin Goodrich was only 29 years old when he established his small rubber company in Akron, Ohio, in 1870. With the help of a $13,500 loan from local citizens, the former surgeon founded what was the first rubber company west of the Allegheny Mountains. Soon after Dr. Goodrich's arrival in Akron, which today is "The Rubber Capital of the World," articles of partnership were drawn up, and the city's first rubber company came into being under the name Goodrich, Tew and Company. One of the

Dr. B. F. Goodrich

partners was Dr. Goodrich's brother-in-law, Harvey W. Tew, whose son, James D. Tew, later was the company's fifth president, from 1928 to 1937.

Success came slowly. More than once, when faced with the probability of a shutdown, Dr. Goodrich packed his bags and went hunting for new business. His enthusiasm and strong belief in the quality of his products enabled him to obtain enough orders to keep his one-building factory in operation. When he returned from these trips, he would spend long hours supervising the making of products which were to make his name respected throughout the world. He told his co-workers, "Let's make goods destined for service."

For 18 years following the 1870 founding of the company in Akron, Dr. Goodrich ran it on a close, personal basis. According to those who were intimately associated with him, he was a man of foresight and strength of character. He was a hard, persistent fighter for honest dealing and justice—essential principles of business, he believed, were vital to the success of any enterprise.

Though he was frail physically, Dr. Goodrich did not spare himself in his work. He died in 1888 at the age of 46. By then, his company's annual sales had reached half a million dollars. Shortly before his death, he wrote a memorandum to his associates at BFG in which he said:

---

*Prepared in cooperation with B. F. Goodrich Corporate Communications.

The only anxiety that I have—the things that I can see that might break up this concern—are just what I talked about . . . whether the discipline of the concern is kept up, whether the repairs are kept to mark . . . but if it fails in either of these particulars, it will go to the devil in one-fourth the time it has taken to build it up.

The company's first product was a cotton-covered rubber fire hose, which was developed at Dr. Goodrich's insistence after he had watched a friend's home burn to the ground because a leather fire hose—the type commonly used in those days—had frozen and burst. Since then, the product range has been expanded to 30,000 different items for business, industry, and the consumer.

In the first 20 years of the company's existence—18 years of which Dr. Goodrich ran the company (until his death in 1888)—three significant developments set the pace for its rapid expansion. They were: the development of the first prestretched rubber transmission belt (1882), the first cord tire—a pneumatic bicycle tire—(1890), and the first clincher tire (1891). By 1890, the company's annual sales had grown to $1.145 million.

In 1895, Charles Cross Goodrich, one of the founder's two sons, established America's first rubber research laboratory in Akron. The laboratory that he founded has grown into the most highly regarded rubber research facilities in the world. These facilities have spawned many of the major advances in the rubber, plastics, and chemical fields. Among them are many "firsts" such as the following: organic accelerators to speed the vulcanization process (1906), carbon black for tires (use of carbon black changes the color of automobile tires from white to black) to add greatly to the abrasion resistance of tires (1911), synthetic rubber products (1931), and the first use of organic compounds to improve the aging properties of rubber (1921).

Many B. F. Goodrich firsts represent not only tremendous technical achievements but also proved to be giant steps in man's progress toward achieving a better life. One of these was the first commercial manufacture of butadiene-copolymer synthetic rubber in the United States in 1938. Two years later the company introduced passenger car tires containing man-made rubber—the first ever sold to the public.

B. F. Goodrich research also led to the birth of the nation's multi-million dollar vinyl industry in 1926 when one of its scientists discovered the first rubber-like polyvinyl material. Today, the company's vinyl materials, marketed under the well-known trade names of Koroseal and Geon, are used to make thousands of different plastic products for industrial and consumer use. More recently, BFG research has brought about development of the first space suit for American astronauts (1961); the first American-made, radial-belted passenger tires for American cars (1965); the first collapsible spare tire for automobiles (1966); and the Golden Lifesaver Radial, the world's only radial tire able to make its own permanent repairs of common punctures caused by objects up to ¼-inch in diameter (1973).

In 1910, the company marketed the first two-ply cord tire for automobiles, and tire sales accounted for the major part of the company's earnings. By 1914, annual sales had grown to $40 million. By that time, Dr. Goodrich's other son, Colonel David M. Goodrich, one of Theodore Roosevelt's "Rough Riders," had joined the company. He remained active as chairman of the board from 1927 until 1950 when he was elected honorary chairman.

Capitalizing on its development of the world's first cord aircraft tires in 1909, B. F. Goodrich led the rubber industry by the 1920s in developing and producing aircraft tires for American barnstormers, stunt pilots, and airmail pilots. When Charles A. Lindbergh soloed from New York to Paris in 1927, his aircraft *The Spirit of St. Louis* was equipped with B. F. Goodrich "Silvertowns." The first tubeless aircraft tire—also a B. F. Goodrich product—was approved for use by the U.S. Navy and placed into production in 1953, only six years after the company introduced the first commercial tubeless tire for automobiles in 1947.

Following 27 years of research, Goodrich began in 1937 the operation of the nation's first pilot plant for commercial man-made rubber. By 1939, the company was producing small quantities of man-made rubber in the first commercial unit of its kind in the United States.

John L. Collyer became president of B. F. Goodrich in 1939, and in 1940, the company introduced on the market the first passenger car tires containing man-made rubber. At the same time, Collyer recommended that the government build standby plants to make synthetic rubber in the event natural rubber supplies should be cut off by war. After the government followed this advice, B. F. Goodrich made available its patents and know-how in the field of synthetic rubber, thus aiding the American war effort tremendously.

Mr. Collyer functioned as chief executive officer for the B. F. Goodrich Company for 19 years, as president from 1939 to 1954 and as chairman from 1950 to 1958. Top officers of the B. F. Goodrich Company today are

O. Pendleton Thomas and John D. Ong. Mr. Thomas joined the company in 1971 as vice chairman of the board and chief executive officer, and was elected chairman of the board in 1972 and to the additional office of president in 1974. Mr. Ong has been vice chairman of the company since April 1974.

The four lots in Akron on which the company's original two-story manufacturing plant was constructed have grown to 60 acres dotted with 68 buildings. In addition, B. F. Goodrich now has 34 manufacturing plants across the United States and seven in Canada; a research and development center recognized as one of the world's foremost industrial laboratories; and interests in 30 foreign, subsidiary, and associate companies manufacturing rubber and chemical products. B. F. Goodrich also has 10,000 acres of natural rubber trees under cultivation in Liberia and 7500 more in the Philippines.

The company today is the world's largest producer of vinyl plastic raw materials, owner of the largest synthetic rubber producing facilities in the world, and a major factor in the retailing world with more than 30,000 dealers and outlets and about 400 company-owned or franchised stores. Indeed, B. F. Goodrich thrives as a lesson in innovation through research.

RESEARCH AT EASTMAN KODAK*

For the Eastman Kodak Company, a strong research and development program has been a tradition since its very early years. In 1912, Dr. C. E. Kenneth Mees founded the Research Laboratories in Rochester, New York, and thus formally established the Eastman Kodak research program. The basic underlying purpose of these facilities was to apply science to photography and advance the technology of the company. A logical result of technological advancement has been stimulated growth and diversification, and so the present-day success of Kodak owes a great deal to those 20 individuals who launched the company's research program in the early 1900s.

In 1956, Kodak's "father of research" Dr. Mees was afforded the opportunity to reflect publicly on his 44 years with Eastman Kodak and 54 years in the study of photography. The following selections from his presentation "Myself and My Journey Down the River of Time" afford a uniquely personal glimpse into research at Eastman Kodak.

*Prepared in cooperation with Corporate Information Department of Eastman Kodak Company and based on "Myself and My Journey Down the River of Time" by C. E. Kenneth Mees (1956).

44 YEARS SPENT WITH THE EASTMAN KODAK COMPANY AND
54 YEARS SPENT ON THE STUDY OF PHOTOGRAPHY

I started in England, the son of a Wesleyan minister. I had a very good education; my father was an educated man with a good library, and as soon as I could read I started to read his library through. I went to ordinary schools, and I was 10 when I first met in my schooling the thing that changed my life.

My schooling up to that time had been the usual schooling; little bits of history, little bits of grammar and English, a little arithmetic, and, as was usual in England at that time, quite a little Latin grammar. Then at the school I went to, which was founded by Queen Elizabeth I, a schoolmaster in the afternoon one day did something that I had never met before—he made a chemical experiment. What he did was to prepare chlorine, and it impressed itself enormously on me, because for the first time in my life somebody talked about something which was a fact instead of about something that somebody else had written. Chlorine was a greenish-yellow gas, he said, and I saw the greenish-yellow gas. He said it had an abominable smell, and I agreed with him. He showed how it was made, and that was most fascinating, and the first thing I wanted to do was to repeat it; I wanted to see if I could make chlorine, too. I went to him afterward and asked him if I could make chlorine, and he finally agreed that if I came back in the evening of the next day he would let me actually handle the apparatus and make some chlorine, which I did. By that time I had fallen in love, completely in love, with science. This was different from all the other stuff; it was about real things—things that you could touch and handle, that you could measure. I began to see at once, it seemed to me, what a marvelous thing science was . . .

So from the age of about 10 on, chemistry—the operation of chemical experiments, the handling of chemicals—was the thing that I was chiefly interested in and what I spent all my time on. This science became to me a sort of religion . . .

When I began to grow up, when I got to about 20, I began to see something else about science and that was its application to economics. I ought to explain that at this time I lived in London, and London was a place of very poor people. All the world was poor at that time. It was quite different from the world we are in today here—not different from the world as a whole probably, but different from the United States today . . .

At that time I read the writing of Francis Bacon who wrote some very interesting essays and who had some very interesting ideas, and I was much impressed by Bacon's ideas. Bacon was a very remarkable man, and one of the greatest intellects that ever lived. He had two great ideas. One is that knowledge comes from observation and experiment; we take that for granted nowadays, but it was quite a new idea in 1600. People thought that knowledge came from discussion and from reading the books of the ancients, and the idea of going and trying a thing was quite a new idea. There is a story which came to me somewhere—I always thought that Bacon wrote it but I have never been able to find it—about the time when in the monastery they were discussing the question of how many teeth there were in the mouth of a horse. The argument went on for a long time. They looked it up in the books, they read the ancients, they quoted the Fathers of the church and argued, and then there arose a young monk who suggested they should go out and look in the mouth of a horse and see how many teeth he had. They pointed out at once, of course, that that wasn't the orthodox way of obtaining knowledge; you didn't obtain knowledge that way—you did it by reference to the authorities, and they fell on the young monk and drove him out. Well, Bacon believed in looking in the mouth of the horse.

Bacon had another idea, which was less obvious and took longer for the world to learn. That was the science that people were acquiring, that was growing in the world, might be applied to increase the wealth of man. Perhaps, as we did more science and learned more about it, we could improve methods of production. If you could improve the methods of production, you could increase wealth. What Bacon thought of, in fact, was applied science, industrial science.

Those two ideas of Bacon's struck me very strongly indeed. I thought that the important thing was the acquisition of knowledge but that perhaps the next most important thing was the application of the knowledge to industry, so that we could relieve the poverty that was strangling my country. I could easily think of places where the production of wealth could be made easier, it would take less of man's time and more wealth could be produced. And I saw that in fact this was the road to wealth—to apply science to industry.

In 1900, I was a student in the Chemistry Department in the University College, London, under that very great teacher and investigator, Sir William Ramsay. I had to come to University College, London, from St. Dunstan's College, Catford, which was a technical school for senior boys, at the same time as another St. Dunstan's student, S. E. Sheppard. Sheppard was the son of a farmer at Catford and was a most brilliant student of not only science but of all the scholastic subjects. When Sheppard and I met Sir William Ramsay, he felt that both of us were well advanced in chemistry in our schoolwork and arranged for us to start at once carrying out some elementary research instead of doing the usual laboratory course.

Before going to University College, my chief interest in chemistry had been in organic chemistry, but Ramsay's students were expected to study physical chemistry, then a comparatively new subject, and Sheppard and I went to the lectures on physical chemistry and soon found ourselves greatly interested in all the work that was going on around us in the laboratory . . .

Sheppard and I, however, didn't join in the general work of the laboratory. We had become very interested in photography. Our curiosity was aroused by the fact that we could find no satisfactory explanation of the photographic process in any of the chemical textbooks nor, when we turned to the photographic literature, could we obtain much help. We read, for instance, Abney's *Instruction on Photography*, in which he writes equations that don't add up. We wanted to know what happened to silver bromide when it was exposed to light, what it was that made it developable, and particularly, being chemists, what the development reaction was and the factors that controlled the rate of development—what physical chemists call the "kinetics of the reaction."

Sheppard was a very good searcher of scientific literature, and before long he turned up a paper in the *Journal of the Society of Chemical Industry* which had been published in 1890—that's ten years before the time of which I'm talking—by a physical chemist who was in charge of the laboratory of the United Alkali Company, Ferdinand Hurter, and an associate of his in the company, W. C. Driffield. This paper, which we afterward found was quite well known and which was entitled "Photochemical Investigations and a New Method of Determination of the Sensitiveness of Photographic Plates," came as a revelation. Here were people who had really studied photography scientifically. They had found a way of measuring the amount of image produced by exposure to light followed by development and of measuring the rate of development of the exposed imate. So, in the work of Hurter and Driffield, we had a model for the attack on the nature of the photographic process.

The apparatus that Hurter and Driffield had used had been very primitive, and we believed that the advances in physical chemistry since 1890 would enable us to improve on their experimental methods . . .

We repeated a good deal of Hurter and Driffield's published work and, in 1903, submitted it in notebooks to the examiners. On that work the B.Sc. by Research of London was awarded to us and, incidentally, it was the only time it was ever awarded. I think that the senate decided that if we could get it so easily they had better not do it again . . .

Both Sheppard and I were by then intensely interested in the work on photography, and we were convinced that it would give us results of value. We were anxious to carry on work for another three years, which was the requirement of the University for the London degree of Doctor of Science . . .

At the end of our academic work, Sheppard was awarded one of the 1851 Exhibition scholarships for two years, which he spent at Marburg in Germany and in Paris. I discussed my future with Ramsay. I had no scholarship, and it was necessary for me to earn a living. He insisted that I should go into industrial research, which I was quite ready to do. I argued with him, of course, for an academic career, like most students, but Ramsay had a very clear vision of the part that science should play in industry, and he insisted that I had worked on photography and must go into the photographic industry. That wasn't so easy! After one or two of my approaches for a job were turned down by photographic manufacturers, I thought of a friend in Croydon, S. H. Wratten, who was the manager of the firm of Wratten and Wainwright, a small factory making dry plates. He had coated some of the special plates on flat glass that Sheppard and I had needed in our work. I went to him and asked for a job. He discussed the matter with his father who owned the business, and instead of a job they offered to incorporate into a company and give me a share in the business for a small sum and at the same time make me a joint managing director with Wratten. I think it was a most extraordinarily generous thing to do to a youngster who wanted a job; I have never heard of it being done by anybody else.

I was getting along quite nicely at Wratten and Wainwright; the company was growing and we were expanding our business steadily and making more profit. But I was still anxious to return to the study of the theory of photography. However, with the work I was doing at Wratten and Wainwright—I was largely running the company—I had no time to do much research. My time for research started at 7:00 in the evening, except for the weekend, when I could spend Sunday at it.

In 1909, I was invited to visit the United States as a special consultant to the American Bank Note Company. I was glad to do it for I could very well do with the money. Wratten and Wainwright was making money fast, but it was using money even faster, and it was in the usual state of a growing business. I went to New York to work with the Bank Note Company on methods which would make photographic counterfeiting of notes as difficult as possible. My wife and I spent two months in New York while I worked on their problems. I took the opportunity to write to Mr. Eastman, who, of course, I regarded as the greatest man in the photographic world, to ask whether I could visit Kodak Park and the Eastman Kodak Company. He was very nice about it and was very cordial when I came to Rochester. He talked to me for about half an hour about American football, which was something in which I had no interest whatever. He had me shown through the Kodak Park factory by Mr. Haste, who was the manager there. After I returned to England, in January 1912, at Wratten and Wainwright I received a telephone message from Mr. Thacher Clark of Kodak Limited. Mr. Clark was Mr. East-man's personal assistant and correspondent in Europe, and he told me that Mr. Eastman would like to repay the visit I had paid him; he would like to visit our factory in Croydon. That afternoon, Mr. Eastman came, and we showed him the factory, dwelling especially, of course, on our small laboratory and on the work we were doing on panchromatic plates and color filters.

After Mr. Eastman got back to London, he called me up on the telephone and asked me to come to see him in London the next day. I said that I couldn't go because I was going to Hungary to lecture; he asked when I was coming back, and I told him in two weeks. He said, "Well, that's too long, I'll be back in America. I think you had better come and see me—I want to ask you if you will go to Rochester." I replied that I thought that was more important than the lecture, and I sent a cable to Hungary. I still have the invitation card written in Hungarian for the lecture I didn't give. I went to see Mr. Eastman the next morning, and he greeted me with, "Well, will you come?" I said, "I will if you make it possible." He asked, "What have I got to do to make it possible?" I replied, "Buy Wratten and Wainwright." He said, "That's all right." And it was all right; we didn't have any difficulty in arranging terms.

So I came here in April 1912, primarily to work out the plans for the Laboratory . . .

The Laboratory was organized on the basis of a group of scientific divisions and a manufacturing division. We decided to make the Wratten plates and the Wratten filters, etc., in the new Research Laboratory. It was a very good thing to do because it gave us the opportunity of selling to the public anything new we worked out in the emulsion line. We could make it

Original Research Laboratory at Eastman Kodak—1912, Rochester, N.Y.

and sell it as a Wratten product, which didn't commit the Kodak Company very deeply if it went wrong, and if it went right we could rapidly expand it into our Kodak products. So, for a good many years, for the next 20 years or so, we used the Wratten Department largely for trying out things, and at the same time, of course, we sold a lot of plates and a lot of filters and, incidentally, made a good deal of money . . .

. . . We had no division for organic chemistry. It was one of my major errors not to provide for organic chemical work at that time, and it can only be explained by my obsession with physical chemistry . . . .

. . . I set up a form of organization which was based primarily on conferences. We had a conference practically every week on all the different sections of work. The conferences were extremely stimulating affairs and to

Interior view of original Kodak Research Laboratory, 1913

Interior view of original Kodak Research Laboratory, 1913

this day are, of course, a major factor in the Laboratory. Through the years we have changed the subjects of the conferences. Some of them have died and others have been started, but the conference system has persisted as the main factor, I think, in the organization of the work of the Laboratory—in planning what we do and in the discussion of the progress of the work.

Our finance was very simple. We spent what was necessary, and Mr. Eastman gave his approval. It wasn't until 1919 that we had a budget, but we did have, and this is interesting, the first budget in the Eastman Kodak Company. I'd had budgets at Wratten and Wainwright; I couldn't afford not to, for we hadn't any money and I had to see that we came out at the end of the year on the right side. When I came to Kodak, I found that there was no such thing as a formal budget of the kind that is standard now, and in 1919, I went to Mr. Eastman and told him that I would like to present a budget for the year 1920 from the Research Laboratory. He asked, "What for, don't you get enough money?" I said, "Yes." Then he asked, "Don't I always give you what you want to spend?" I said, "Yes." "Well," he said, "what do you want a budget for?" "Well," I said, "you might run into bad times or something and change your mind in the middle of the year and I don't want you to do that. I want you to make up your mind at the beginning of the year as to whether I can spend the money and then let me spend it."

I was very thankful because 1921 wasn't such a very good year. In 1921 Mr. Eastman asked me to cut my expenditures and I asked him if he wanted me to diminish the budget for the next year. "No," he said, "I want you to cut it down now." "Oh," I said, "we can't do that, Mr. Eastman, for we agreed to what we could spend this year." He said, "So we did." And that was the end of that. We have always had a budget since, and we have always kept inside our budget, and the budgets have grown tremendously and still look quite healthy.

Our early work was mostly photographic science. It was concerned with the theory of the photographic process. There was one thing that I had asked for when I had discussed the Laboratory with Mr. Eastman. I told him I wanted to publish the scientific work done in the Laboratory. He asked, "Well, what do you want to publish?" I said, "Everything that we do that is scientific." He said he would approve of that. I said, "If I can submit our papers to you that will be all right; anything you don't want me to publish I don't want to publish, but I don't want to submit our articles to anybody else, such as the Patent Department, Sales Department, Legal Department, etc. If I do that, they will be afraid that a paper they don't understand will do harm and they will say no." So Mr. Eastman agreed and we have always published our work. We adopted the principle of numbering our communications from the beginning. We left out all acknowledgments; we don't thank anybody in a scientific paper. We give our papers communication numbers, and we have published nearly 2000. We publish all our communications from French and English companies in the same series as those originating in Rochester.

At the end of the year, we publish a volume containing abridgments of the scientific publications. In 1915, I started to get out an abstract bulletin, and I think that among the things that we have done, our communication system has been a great success. Everybody respects our communications, and I am sure that you all appreciate the possibility of publishing your work as you do it, of getting credit for it in the scientific world, and of keeping in touch with the great stream of production of scientific knowledge . . .

In 1923, we made our first contribution of importance to the new products of the Company . . .

In 1918, we started to make synthetic organic chemicals to supply chemicals to all the research laboratories, universities, etc., in the country, so that people could get the chemicals that they had previously bought from Germany . . .

In 1930, we made the first supersensitive panchromatic film for motion picture work. In 1931, the new Emulsion Research Laboratory made the Verichrome film. We designed the Verichrome film and, with Mr. W. G. Stuber's assistance, we got it out on the market in very short time; of course, it has been one of our most successful developments . . .

When the Emulsion Research Laboratory was established, I was so impressed with the mistake I had made originally in not providing for work in organic chemistry that I decided that the head of the Emulsion Research Laboratory should be an organic chemist because I believe that organic chemists might have a good deal to add to the progress of photography. I think that the proper expression as regards that is: "Man, you said a mouthful!" because since then the organic chemists have developed the whole system of addition agents, and so forth, on which our present emulsion technology is based.

Through all these years, work continued on the theory of the photographic process and is still continuing. In 1942, I was able to put the whole thing together in a book, a very fat and heavy book, with the aid of a great of my associates in the company who wrote chapters and sections of the book, and we published *The Theory of the Photographic Process.* That achieved one of the two objectives I had when I started—the whole theory of the photographic process had been put into a form where it made a comprehensible whole. At the same time, the development of the Laboratory and its relation to the Eastman Kodak Company showed, in the photographic industry, that science could be applied to the technology of the business with advantages to all sides. Science has been applied to the photographic industry, and the Research Laboratories are now firmly established as a major department of the organization of the Eastman Kodak Company.

* * *

WESTINGHOUSE GREW WITH RESEARCH*

Research has been called the most powerful factor in the growth of an industrial enterprise. Certainly this has been demonstrated in the history of the Westinghouse Electric Corporation, where George Westinghouse established his first electrical research laboratory even before he founded the company.

This laboratory, inspired by Mr. Westinghouse's dream of widespread electric power, was housed in an abandoned rubber mill on the outskirts of Great Barrington, Massachusetts. Its research project was a new and untried device called a "converter," now universally known as a transformer.

The successful outcome of this project was a new and revolutionary system for generating and distributing electricity—the alternating-current system—first demonstrated at Great Barrington, on March 20, 1886.

Later that same year, the Westinghouse Electric Company moved into its first tiny plant in Garrison Alley in Pittsburgh, Pennsylvania. Three rooms on the second floor were set aside as the "electrical laboratory." Here, under the direction of Oliver B. Shallenberger, Chief Electrician of the company, Westinghouse gathered together its first handful of scientific talent.

In 1895, George Westinghouse moved his expanding company and his "laboratory men" to East Pittsburgh, Pennsylvania. There each department had its own laboratory to test materials and processes, set specifications, and help eliminate shop and field difficulties. In addition, early company records show that "two or three places" in the new plant were designated for specialized research.

---

*Prepared in cooperation with the Communications Department of Westinghouse Electric Corporation and based on the booklet, "Westinghouse Research . . . an Investment in Tomorrow," published in 1956.

The Westinghouse Van de Graaff generator, a four-million-volt "atom smasher" built in 1937, launched an intensive program of industrial nuclear research.

The Westinghouse Research Laboratories in suburban Pittsburgh, Pennsylvania, for the hub of the corporation's widespread research activities.

The growth of the electrical industry was so rapid that design engineers soon were utilizing all of the pertinent fundamental principles known. As the need for additional knowledge became apparent, it was decided to organize a group of research scientists unhampered by routine tasks. Freedom of thought and action would be guaranteed by a separate administration. The prime objective would be simply the acquisition of basic scientific knowledge. This was the company's first separate and distinct Research Department, headed by Charles E. Skinner, a pioneer in the field of electrical insulation.

The new East Pittsburgh laboratory, built and equipped for research and staffed with a half dozen scientists, began operation in 1904—marking it, by the modern definition of the term, as one of the earliest research laboratories in American industry.

A major Westinghouse development—the use of steam turbines in place of old-fashioned steam engines to drive electric generators—led to the expansion of these laboratory facilities. The metallurgy of turbine-blade materials became important, and a chemist was hired to be the "chemical and metallurgical research staff." This man's laboratory was an abandoned blacksmith shop.

Soon a high-voltage laboratory was established to investigate the multitude of problems arising from the need for higher and higher voltages on transmission lines.

The first building to be erected specifically for Westinghouse research, a two-story structure located at the East Pittsburgh plant, came in 1910.

Then, in 1916, came another building, which was to become the nucleus of Westinghouse research activities for nearly 40 years. It was one of the first major industrial research laboratories to be separated physically from a manufacturing location, thereby creating a scientific environment apart from plant activities—one geared solely to the pursuit of science. To this building, from time to time, were added several special-purpose laboratories, including a dome-shaped "atom smasher"—another first in industrial research.

In the early 1920s the Westinghouse Company organized a "research institute," within the framework of its factory operations, for the solution of scientific problems that were encountered in the design and development of electrical equipment. This was an early wedding of pure science and engineering applications, and it attracted many outstanding engineers and scientists. Under the direction of S. M. Kintner, Manager, Research Laboratory and Chief Mechanical Engineer Eaton, a number of foreign scientists were brought to the institute, and these men had a most important effect not only upon the Westinghouse Company but upon the entire country as well.

Many of these famous men—including S. P. Timoshenko, J. P. den Hartog, G. Karelitz, L. S. Jacosbon, A. Nadai, and C. R. Soderberg—later became professors and deans in the most important and prestigious engineering schools in the United States. Through their teaching and writing, as well as their direct relationships with individual students who themselves later became important engineering practitioners, this group of men had a most profound impact upon the development of engineering education.

Because the activities of the "research institute" within the Westinghouse Company concerned not only the solution of technical and scientific problems, but also the training of other Westinghouse engineers, the pedagogic activities not only led to the significant writings of these men, which played such an important role in their later success as teachers, but also greatly enhanced the importance of engineering as a profession through their active participation in the several engineering societies.

Thus, the vision and enthusiasm of the Westinghouse Company for infusing research-oriented people with the practical problems of design and production ultimately had an impact of great magnitude in the development of U.S. engineering. Many of these same characteristics are common in our research institutes of today.

In 1956, the Westinghouse Research Laboratories moved to its present location in the Westinghouse Research and Development Center, a 72-acre site in Churchill Borough, 10 miles east of downtown Pittsburgh. The Research Laboratories comprise the major portion of the R&D Center, which also houses the Product Transition Laboratory, the Manufacturing Development Laboratory, and the Patent Department.

Over the years, Westinghouse Research Laboratories have provided the scientific achievements that have helped build the corporation. A few highlights will illustrate the kind of contributions that an industrial research laboratory can make.

Magnetic materials are an essential ingredient to all electrical apparatus. In cooperation with the American Rolling Mill Company, Westinghouse research scientists pioneered one of the key improvements—silicon (or electrical) steel. Under the direction of Dr. Trygve Yensen, the Laboratories produced Hipersil—a vastly improved type of silicon steel, and Hipernik—

a unique magnetic alloy of nickel and iron used in special types of transformers.

Insulation is another essential ingredient in electrical equipment. George Westinghouse himself held the first patent for insulating large transformers with oil—still a standard practice. From the laboratories has come much fundamental knowledge of the physics of insulation and a distinguished list of insulating materials, including a family of solventless resins for impregnating electrical devices, improved high-voltage insulation for large electric generators, and superior enamels for copper wire.

Westinghouse research scientists long have investigated the multitude of problems posed by the flow of electricity in solid conductors. Among the most interesting and least understood phenomena associated with the flow of electricity through solids is superconductivity. Westinghouse scientists have made notable contributions to an understanding of this phenomenon.

No area of Westinghouse research demonstrates more dramatically the unforeseen applications that come from fundamental scientific investigation than research on the passage of electricity through gases. Among the earliest and most fruitful of these studies were those of Dr. Joseph Slepian, who discovered the principle of using glow discharges in air for lightning protection. In his studies on gas discharges, Dr. Slepian developed a better understanding of what goes on in an electric arc, knowledge that led to the development of better circuit breakers. Another Westinghouse development, the Ignitron rectifier, can be traced to Dr. Slepian's research with arcs.

One of the more glamorous and productive areas of research has been the investigation of matter as it behaves in near-perfect vacuums. In the early 1920s, the first mass-produced radio tube to have modern standards of tolerance and workmanship was devised at the Westinghouse Research Laboratories. In fact, the scientists themselves actually produced the first 10,000 tubes. The Laboratories also developed the first radio receiving tube to operate on alternating current, and as a result, the radio receiver became a standard plug-in appliance. From the Laboratories, too, came the large air-cooled and water-cooled transmitting tubes that made possible high-power broadcasting. One of them, a 200,000-watt giant, was the largest of its kind ever to be used commercially.

Closely interwoven with research on electronic tubes has been the application of these devices in radio communications. S. M. Kintner, a former manager of the Laboratories, motivated and guided many Westinghouse accomplishments in the field of commercial radio broadcasting.

The first all-electronic television system—the kind now in universal use —was a Westinghouse research development. Dr. Vladimir Zworykin invented the sealed-off cathode-ray tube and then adapted it to television scanning. In 1929, transmission of moving pictures by this system was demonstrated at the Laboratories and by the Westinghouse radio station, KDKA.

Dr. I. E. Mouromtseff of the Laboratories made some of the original experiments in transmitting ultra-short radio waves directionally in beams. The technique, forerunner of present-day radar, was publicly demonstrated at the Century of Progress Exposition at Chicago in 1933-1934.

Much of what a research laboratory does may never make headlines, but many of those developments are of major benefit to science itself. They mean new knowledge, new techniques, or new tools of research for the scientist.

The Westinghouse Laboratories pioneered the development and widespread use of the mass spectrometer for sorting out atoms according to their weight; of the scintillation counter, most versatile and widely used instrument for detection of atomic particles; of the quartz microbalance that weighs a single layer of atoms; of a helium bottle that permitted, for the first time in laboratory history, the long-time storage of liquids near absolute zero; of an ionization gauge for measuring gas pressures in a near-perfect vacuum; and literally dozens of other useful devices for scientific research.

While the Westinghouse Research Laboratories in Churchill Borough are today the heart of the company's research effort, many other company locations are conducting investigations of materials, processes, and products which, even by strict interpretation of the term, can be correctly classed as research. Major development laboratories are situated in the manufacturing locations for lamps, steam turbines, transformers, atomic power equipment, and other products.

Westinghouse pioneering in lamps for lighting dates back to the "stopper lamp," with which George Westinghouse so spectacularly lighted the Chicago World's Fair in 1893. Lamp research was separated from the main Research Laboratories when the Lamp Division Research Laboratory was organized in Bloomfield, New Jersey, at Lamp Division Headquarters in 1921, under the direction of Dr. H. C. Rentschler.

From that laboratory have come many significant achievements: the sodium vapor lamp; the fluorescent lamp introduced at the New York World's Fair in 1939-1940; the long-life krypton lamp; the fluorescent sun

From this lamp research laboratory setup came the first small pellets of pure uranium, which has now become one of the world's most sought after metals.

lamp; and a steady stream of developments for the improvement of incandescent and fluorescent lamps. Today, although most of the lamp research has been returned to the central research laboratories, a large advanced development effort is still located in the Lamp Division Laboratories in Bloomfield.

One of the most significant achievements of the Lamp Division Research Laboratories came somewhat by accident. As early as 1919, researchers there were investigating uranium as a possible lamp filament. It didn't work, but the scientists became proficient in making highly purified uranium, and for years the Lamp Division Laboratories were the only known source of supply.

Then, in 1942, they were asked to produce uranium—not in pounds—but in tons. It was a Herculean task, but they did it. That uranium went into the world's first atomic pile—the critical experiment that proved the feasibility of controlled nuclear fission.

The scope of many research projects has become so great today that they can only be financed by industry-government cooperation. A prime example is nuclear energy. Active development work by Westinghouse on nuclear energy for power production began in 1948, when the pressurized-water type of reactor was specified as the power plant for the USS *Nautilus*, the first nuclear-powered submarine. Westinghouse purchased a former airport site near Pittsburgh, and the U.S. Atomic Energy Commission built the Bettis Laboratory there. Westinghouse continues to operate this laboratory for the government. Work on the reactor for the Shippingport Atomic Power Station, the nation's first large-scale nuclear electric power plant, also began at the Bettis Laboratory when the PWR design contract was awarded to Westinghouse by the AEC in 1953.

Until 1964, the Hanford Engineering and Development Laboratory near Richland, Washington, was a key part of the nation's liquid-metal fast breeder reactor program. Management and operation of the fast breeder are by the Westinghouse Hanford Company, a subsidiary of Westinghouse Electric Corporation, under contract to the Energy Research and Development Agency.

The capability of industry comes in large part from industrial research, which has always been basic to Westinghouse, beginning with George Westinghouse's first electrical laboratory. The goals of industrial research coincide with the objectives of industry, and its value is determined by the contribution it makes to industry's overall profit and growth.

* * *

THE DISCIPLES

In addition to the promotional efforts by the NAM and NRC, there were many individuals who were stimulating research in industry by spreading "the gospel" at every opportunity. These were the people who were motivated by their conviction that the American public would be greatly benefited by a growing flow of new processes and products coming from a strengthening American industry . . . the key to which was research. The low level of technology in the United States at the time of World War I and the crises resulting therefrom motivated a number of individuals in corporation laboratories, universities, and other institutions to devote a great deal of their time to the stimulation of scientific research—basic research in the universities and applied research in industry. Those who were deeply devoted to this cause probably did not exceed 50 in number. Some were associated with the companies already experiencing research success, a few with universities, and a number with the research institutions—this last group increasing in numbers as new institutions were organized.

These people will be remembered not only for their stimulating addresses before public audiences, but also for catch phrases they coined for emphasis. A few of the latter follow.

- "If you wait until it is needed, it is too late to start research."
  —Charles F. Kettering, General Motors Corporation
- " 'Research' is a high-hat word that scares a lot of people. It needn't. It is rather simple. Essentially, it is nothing but a state of mind—a friendly, welcoming attitude toward change. Going out to look for a change instead of waiting for it to come. Research, for practical men, is an effort to do things better and not be caught asleep at the switch. The research state of mind can apply to anything: personal affairs or any kind of business, big or little. It is the problem solving mind as contrasted with let-well-enough-alone mind. It is the composer mind instead of the fiddler mind. It is the 'tomorrow' mind instead of the 'yesterday' mind."
  —Charles F. Kettering, General Motors Corporation
- "By research today we can assure prosperity tomorrow."
  —Karl Compton, Massachusetts Institute of Technology
- "Nothing on earth is so perishable as an established product."
  —C. J. Burnside, Westinghouse Electric Company
- "No matter how good a product is, it can be improved."
  —Harold Vagtborg, Armour Research Foundation
- "Large corporations do not hire technical men because they are large. Rather they are large because they hired technical men when they were small. Thereby industry profited greatly and the public profited enormously."
  —Charles F. Kettering, General Motors Corporation
- "In the test tubes of today are the industries of tomorrow."
  —Maurice Holland, National Research Council

- "Research is the department of a business which gives to the management the substance on which it grows."
  —Henry P. Kendall, Kendall Company
- "What is fundamental research today is applied research tomorrow."
  —Lammont duPont
- "The scientist engaging in research work is looking for something that already exists. He does not invent the truth, he does not develop the truth, he does not do anything whatever to the truth except to uncover it or discover it and expose it to the comprehension of his fellowmen . . . "
  —Dr. W. W. Campbell, President, University of California
- "Research creates markets."
  —A. D. Little
- "Technology is the only multiplier of our natural resources."
  —Harold Vagtborg, Midwest Research Institute
- "In a civilization making such full use of applied science, you have to run fast to stay where you are. If you want to move ahead, you have to run still faster."
  —E. C. Auchter, U.S. Department of Agriculture
- "We conduct research today to find out what we should be doing five years from now."
  —Charles F. Kettering, General Motors Corporation
- "Research is often a gamble, but the biggest gamble is no research."
  —Maurice Holland, National Research Council
- "Technology is both an opportunity and a threat—an opportunity to he who uses it and a threat to he who does not."
  —Roland Soule, Tri-Continental Corporation
- "Economic progress comes in waves paralleling new scientific discoveries."
  —Harold Vagtborg, Southwest Research Institute
- "Intelligent research is not merely digging for data, but also digging for dividends."
  —Harry R. Chapman, New England Confectionery Company
- "Research is the most valuable insurance policy a company can have."
  —Charles F. Kettering, General Motors Corporation
- "Applied research is the kind of research that rings up in the cash register."
  —Maurice Holland, National Research Council

And one from France that was often quoted:

- "Nothing in life is to be feared—it is only to be understood."
  —Marie Curie

Among the disciples, one of the most active was Maurice Holland, who devoted full time to the stimulation of research in American industry during the 20 years he was Director of Engineering and Industrial Research, National Research Council (1920-1940). During the 30 years that followed, while he was in private practice as a consultant to industry in research organization and management, he did much to raise the status of the research director from that of one usually reporting to the sales department to vice president for research and development with a voice in the highest councils of his company.

Following are two letters that indicate the kind of association he enjoyed while with the National Research Council.

For Mr. Holland

The progress of civilization, as all clearthinking historians recognize, depends in large degree upon "the increase and diffusion of knowledge among men." It is not merely a question of applying present-day science to the development of our industries, the reduction of the cost of living, the eradication of disease, and the multiplication of our harvests, or even the diffusion of knowledge. We must add to knowledge, both for the intellectual and spiritual satisfaction that comes from widening the range of human understanding, and for the direct practical utilization of these fundamental discoveries. A special study in an industrial laboratory, resulting in the improvement of some machine or process, is of great value to the world. But the discovery of a law of nature, applicable in thousands of instances and forming a permanent and ever available addition to knowledge, is a far greater advance.

—Herbert Hoover

Cable Address "Edison, New York"

From the Laboratory
of
Thomas A. Edison,
Orange, N.J.

November 7, 1928.

NATIONAL RESEAR...
DIVISION OF ENG...
AND INDUSTRIAL RESEARCH

Mr. Maurice Holland,
National Research Council,
29 West 39th St.,
New York City.

REC'D NOV - 9 1928
ANS'D _____
NOTE__ ____ ____ ___

Dear Mr. Holland:

I think you have chosen a most worthy subject in writing

a book on "Industrial Explorers." The striking ex-

amples you have named of industrial benefactors

should make a strong appeal to thoughtful young men.

If your book should be successful in its mission,- if

indeed it should prove to be the inspiration through

which even one more real industrial explorer is

given to the world, you would be entitled to be re-

garded as a public benefactor.

Yours very truly,

Thos A Edison

Ediphoned-C

Mr. Holland's extensive and intensive involvement in the stimulation of research and development are related in the Supplement. Typical of Mr. Holland's many publications is the one reproduced here from the *American Bankers Association Journal*, June 1927.

On the Frontier of Industry

By MAURICE HOLLAND
Director, Division of Engineering and Industrial Research,
National Research Council

Research Stakes Out the Claim and Capital Supplies the Means of Bringing Out the Pay Dirt. The Laboratories Forecast an Automobile with Dashboard Control of Carburetor, a Welded Skyscraper, Rubber by Casting and Shows by Television.

RESEARCH workers are prospectors on the frontier of industry. Years of toil on the borders of the unknown may be rewarded by a handful of glittering nuggets in the form of new facts. The discovery of new facts may shape the destiny of old industries or create new ones. The dividends of industry—the coin of the realm—are the minted winnings of pioneer efforts in research.

Banking takes a first line position also on the frontier of industry. The adventurous spirit of research opens up new territory; banking consolidates the new position. The enterprise of research stakes out the claim; banking supplies the capital to bring out the pay dirt. Research is a guarantee to the banker of invested capital, his insurance against loss in new enterprises. Research blazes a trail as the vanguard of industrial progress; banking builds a road to connect the frontier of industry with the main arteries of commerce.

Beyond the Earth

THE frontier marks the line of battle in the struggle of man with the forces of nature. The frontiers of science are further flung than those of industry—in one instance they have been extended to other planets. Dr. Hale, director of Mount Wilson Observatory, enchanted the directors of a great industrial corporation recently with a vivid description of his "laboratory on the sun!" He referred to the researches in the field of pure science, which resulted in the discovery of helium in the gases around the sun. Less academic-minded workers in applied science brought the discovery down to earth in the utilitarian application of this rare gas to the building of non-inflammable dirigibles which were to span continents and seas in a flight over the top of the world. More recently this rare gas, first discovered by men gazing at the stars, has been used as a cure for "bends," a temporary paralysis caused by men working at great pressures, boring a tunnel under the North River, which will soon connect New York and New Jersey. The occasion of this meeting of eminent scientists and men who sit in the high councils of big business was the presentation of the case of the vital need of the support of research in the field of pure science by American industry. These men of vision recognized the fact that our national progress in the future will depend in large measure upon scientific research. This instance is but a single effort which is being made by a committee of distinguished men of science, industry and public

Welding steel with atoms of hydrogen. This may foreshadow a noiselessly built skyscraper

affairs, led by Secretary Hoover in a campaign to raise a National Research Endowment of $20,000,000 or more for the support of research in pure science.

In regard to the importance of this movement to the future of American science and industry, which Dr. Pupin called "the most significant in a century," Secretary Hoover declared: "We must add to knowledge, both for the intellectual and spiritual satisfaction that comes from widening the range of human understanding, and for the direct practical utilization of these fundamental discoveries. A special study in an industrial laboratory, resulting in the improvement of some machine or process, is of great value to the world. But the discovery of a law of nature, applicable in thousands of instances and forming a permanent and ever-available addition to knowledge, is a far greater advance."

Anticipating New Competition

ON these frontiers new empires are being built, new industries being created, and new products being developed on a foundation of research. Three elements are essential in all these undertakings. They are men, money, and management. The interests of men—the research workers—and the interests of money—the investors and bankers—are intimately interwoven and mutually dependent.

Consider a banker in New England. He may have extensive loans in the textile industry. He may be intimately acquainted with the representative concerns in that in-

dustry, may have considerable knowledge of manufacturing processes and trade practices, and he may keep posted on the general state of the industry by reading its trade journals. As long as the natural conditions, the old order of competition, continues, there appears to be no cause for concern, for was it not the moisture of New England air, with its exact natural humidity, that fixed the center of the textile industry?

As long as nature withholds her secrets from man, the old order prevails. Then along comes science and wrests another secret from nature and the center of industries—yes, of worlds—is changed. A single discovery from the laboratory may mean a new competitive industry, or expansion for one and losses for another.

For a long time it was the climate that prevented us from locating textile mills in the South, in the area of raw materials. Engineers and chemists then tackled the problem of manufacturing suitable weather indoors with mechanical aids, and nature's deficiencies were supplied by science. Recently the enterprising Chamber of Commerce of Los Angeles made a bid for the fine cotton goods industry of the East, and these "home industry" boosters promised a local supply of raw material in the form of "native" long staple cotton grown in the Imperial Valley.

Out of a test tube of chemicals science created the rayon industry, and another triumph of research produced weather "on order." Rayon factories are now erected in the region of cheap power—Buffalo, for instance. With the advantage of economic power, plants are located in favorable labor markets and strategically placed to take advantage of raw materials produced locally. With production costs reduced by research the rayon industry is today selling half hose on the counters of the Five and Ten Cent Stores at ten cents "a half," and attractive stockings have been placed within reach of more millions of women, once customers of the cotton industry. The cotton textile industry is now making a belated effort to organize for research.

Older Industries Last to Adopt Research

THE experience of our division in promoting research in specific industries has demonstrated the truth of the statement that the older industries are the last to adopt research. Compare the relative position, the rate of development and growth of technical or semi-technical industries, such as radio,

Reprinted from the American Bankers Association Journal, June, 1927

Marconi, inventor of radio telegraphy, being shown newest developments by Dr. Langmuir, perfector of vacuum tubes

This testing machine at the Bureau of Standards, in Washington, can exert a pressure of 5000 tons. It can break steel girders or brick walls

machine is completed it may cut down operations from three to one. The history of industrial progress before the latter half of the nineteenth century was largely a record of natural evolution. Knowledge was accumulated by the cut and try method of experience. Twentieth century research is accelerated experience.

Research, nevertheless, is handicapped by inherent limitations when an attempt is made to dramatize the stages in its development. Progress from test tube or laboratory experiments through semi-commercial scale development, and finally the transition to full-scale operation, seems to be only of academic interest. The cycle of research from test tubes to earnings paid out of commercial operation is written in laboratory note books or buried in the financial pages of the newspapers.

Movements by Groups

RESEARCH has proved a formidable weapon in the new competition—the competition between industries. Ten thousand trade associations are now operating in the United States. Their group activities, organized in the interest of the industry as a whole, include cooperative buying, advertising, publicity, research, and a host of other activities. A recent survey shows some ninety trade associations actively engaged in cooperative research. Less than half of these publish the amount of their annual expenditures for research, yet those reporting present an imposing total of $15,000,000 spent in this division of their activities.

Most of the basic industries and practically all of the commodities in general use are included in the list of cooperative or associated research groups. There is iron and steel, copper and brass, lumber and wood, brick and clay, cement, glass and paint, and varnish as well as silk, cotton, paper, leather, to name but a few in the single field of materials.

The importance of research as a valued tool in building up the general industrial structure of the United States is clearly demonstrated by the findings of a recent survey which reported that we are spending approximately $200,000,000 annually for re-

electric illumination, telephone, automobile, and electrochemistry—five industries which have taken important places in our industrial structure within the last fifty years—with older industries, such as textiles, fisheries, and iron and steel. The first group of industries have developed during the age of industrial research. The second group, having their beginnings in the earliest recorded history of man, are steeped in tradition and handicapped by prejudice.

A comparison of the rate of development and growth of the two groups of industries will furnish proof that the first group have developed with the aid of research in decades to a position which has been attained by the second group in centuries. The second group of industries, until comparatively recent times, were arts as distinguished from scientific industries, dependent upon skill rather than technical knowledge, employing artisans rather than technicians. Textile, fisheries, iron and steel, in fact all the older industries, have been retarded in their development by the excessive use of hand labor and traditional technology handed down from generation to generation. At no point, except within very recent years, has applied science touched the course of their evolution. Their basic processes and tools are the inventions of practical mechanics and skilled artisans.

In the older industries, textile, for example, there has been an over-emphasis on evolution by improvement in machinery design and refinement of process, and too little emphasis on revolution by research. The redesign of machinery or refinement of process has an advantage over research in obtaining financial support, because here you can see the wheels go round and progress is visibly reported. At first there are pencil sketches, then blue prints follow, next a small model appears. At various stages of the development new mechanical motions are added or subtracted. Finally a full-scale model is demonstrated, and when the new

search. Of that amount the government is spending one-third, while industry is matching the government appropriations two dollars for one for research. There are over a thousand research laboratories, exclusive of government and university research agencies, representing practically every field of industry at present. The universities and technical colleges spent $1,250,000 last year for engineering, technical, and industrial research.

The National Bank of Commerce in New York, recently, in analyzing basic factors in the present era of prosperity, had this to say of the importance and value of science in American industry: "Not only are we freely utilizing the processes being developed elsewhere, but individual industries and groups of industries are making great expenditures for research of a type to be directly productive, and a few are doing remarkable work in theory."

Of the ten great industrial corporations which led the income tax list in 1926, seven have research laboratories as integral units of their manufacturing plants. The United States Steel Corporation, which heads the list, recently added a research laboratory as a "technical asset" behind the balance sheet.

Where Is Industry Going?

THE record of development of American industry and commercial achievement is written in the income tax returns. As to how long the present era of prosperity will continue, there is great diversity of opinion. Analysts are busy searching out the basic factors; statisticians present formidable arrays of factual data as proof of their theories, and bankers keep daily tab on the shifting currents; they watch the surface ripples for a sign as to which way the wind is blowing.

Statistics, barometer charts, market letters, business cycles, car loadings, as indicators of the state of industry or trade, are accessories after the fact. They are based on past performance.

A great roll of rayon—the silk of research

We all know industry is on its way, but the important thing to learn is where is it going?

Research is an industrial X-ray revealing basic causes and conditions. Research activities forecast future trends. The work of the research laboratory today is the commercial product of 1929 or 1930.

New developments in welding will eliminate the noise of riveting, reduce fabrication costs, and save steel in future building operations. By 1930 we may have dashboard control of carburetors, with a reduction of operating costs, a cut in gasoline consumption, and a visible reminder of the most economical running speed. This is at least one automotive research laboratory's promise of a new accessory for the drivers of the 1930 models.

Laboratory demonstrations of television forecast a future of feature pictures, prize fights, and the latest Broadway hit brought to the home of every telephone subscriber.

Experiments under way at the Eastman Kodak laboratory in electroplating rubber will encourage some enterprising manufacturers to go into the business of "casting" hot-water bottles, rubber aprons and bath-ing caps. The process is cheaper and better control is possible than methods used in present practice.

Corrosion fatigue tests being run in the research laboratory at Annapolis for the Navy already show that moving metal parts grow tired and break down under the strain of working in sea water much faster than their land brothers working in air. In fact, it looks as though they die a premature death, their's is only 60 per cent of the life of metals in air. Perhaps we'll have to revert to war-time practice and build reinforced concrete dreadnoughts in the future.

The Lag Before Introduction

THE "time lag," the period represented by time elapsed from research laboratory discovery to industrial application, is unavoidable. A product in the test tube stage of development cannot be released for commercial production until the mechanical difficulties of the process have been perfected. In order to maintain scientific control during the development of the process, small units of equipment and small scale volume of product are first tested in what is known as semi-commercial scale operation. A test tube of viscose converted into lustrous strands of thread is a long way from full-scale production of rayon stockings.

Great industrial companies with millions of dollars tied up in present model stock on the shelves cannot afford to release a new process or product for production until the development costs and a profit has been made from the sale of current models. The research laboratory has been geared up and integrated in the whole machine of industrial progress to focus on futures, and secure the present position of the industry or company which supports it.

Nevertheless, the research worker is blazing a trail which leads to the broad highway of commerce. Here in the laboratory the first stakes are driven which mark out the frontier of industry. The general direction of the advance is unmistakable. The signboards on the road to industrial progress are painted in the laboratory. Built by research, new industrial skyscrapers are anchored in the bed rock of pure science; the flexible steel frame is fashioned by applied science; and the stone and mortar are fitted in place by practical experience—the technology of the industry.

RESEARCH-THE PRIME MOVER

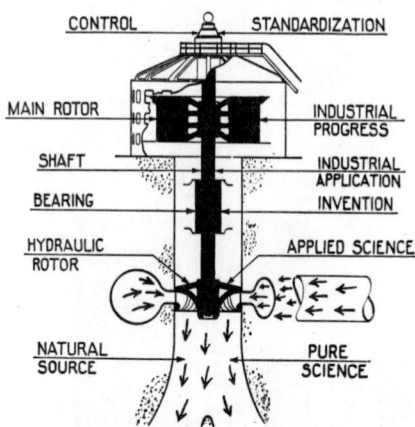

CONTROL   STANDARDIZATION

MAIN ROTOR   INDUSTRIAL PROGRESS

SHAFT   INDUSTRIAL APPLICATION

BEARING   INVENTION

HYDRAULIC ROTOR   APPLIED SCIENCE

NATURAL SOURCE   PURE SCIENCE

EFFORTS BY THE RESEARCH INSTITUTES

Without exception, the founders of the 9 independent research institutions were all motivated by the strong belief that research was the key to a stable industrial and agricultural economy. Directors of these institutions in the early days were selected because they, too, were likewise motivated. They were all faced with the challenge of convincing the thousands of disinterested industrial firm managements of the value of research—the kind as Dr. Kettering said, "will let you know what to do five years from now when you cannot do what you are doing now." The first wave of these individuals were Edward Weidlein (Mellon), Clyde Williams (Battelle), Harold Vagtborg (Armour, Midwest, Southwest), C. C. Furnas (Cornell), Wilbur Lazier (Southern), Nicol Smith (Franklin), and Jesse Hobson (Stanford).

These were the practical people. Their laboratories were operating between the university environment and the corporation laboratory in the research organization spectrum. The seeds of thousands of industrial laboratories that were created as the years went by were first planted here. It is interesting to study the utterances of these people before public groups in the early days of their institutions. Their emphasis was on "doing research," no matter where. Of course, their laboratories were ideal places to get a "taste of it" before deciding on in-house programs.

Duncan, and then Weidlein—both of Mellon—were the forerunners of this group of "research salesmen," followed by Williams of Battelle; Vagtborg of Armour (now IITRI), Midwest, and Southwest; Lazier of Southern; Furnass of Cornell; Smith of Franklin; and Hobson of Stanford. Their successors followed through in these efforts but were not forced to put as much emphasis on the need for research and could thus stress to a greater degree what their own institutions offered. Over two decades, the initial group appeared before thousands of audiences throughout the country in the 1920s, 1930s, and 1940s. The following capsules of addresses and publications by Vagtborg are representative of the variety of approaches suitable to diverse audiences. Although each of these early "disciples" had his own style of presentation, the objectives were the same.

WHY RESEARCH*

Exceptional is the trade journal which does not announce the development of new or improved industrial products in each issue, and exceptional is the

*Delivered before the Chicago Manufacturing Association and published in the February 1939 issue of *Manufacturing News*.

executive who does not feel a pang of regret if a newly announced product related to his industry was not produced by his company. He realizes that a discovery which may seem relatively unimportant today may grow into a great industry tomorrow. It may force him to completely alter his production methods and it may even shift the desire for his product to an entirely new one.

To successfully guide the destinies of his company, the industrial executive must not only be prepared to meet these situations as they arise, but he must also anticipate them far in advance. It is unnecessary to say that financial stability is a prerequisite for the success of any business enterprise. Financial stability, however, comes largely from having a product which is a little better than a competing one. The better product is certainly the result of industrial research.

Unfortunately, when the subject of research comes up, too many of our industrial executives excuse themselves from the discussion to become absorbed in operating statements or the details of an advertising campaign. This is unfortunate because in spite of the importance of operating statements and promotional activities, research is still the lifeblood of our competitive system. He who falls behind the advancing front of industrial development through scientific research finds sales going to those in the frontline.

RESEARCH IN INDUSTRY*

The progressive American manufacturer no longer considers research as a frill in his industry. He has learned from repeated observations that the sum total ultimate results of a well-directed and sustained research project make it the best of all investments for future profits and the best insurance against decadence.

Whether his interest is with a small or large industrial organization, he knows from a rapidly increasing mass of evidence that scientific research, having industrial application, creates jobs and profits. However, the majority of manufacturers have been slow to make use of the opportunities afforded by research in their own individual companies.

RESEARCH FOR THE GAS INDUSTRY†

Anyone who will take the time to carefully analyze the great advancements that research has brought about in other industries cannot help but be

---

*Published in the February 1939 issue of *Central Manufacturing District Magazine.*
†Published in the April 1942 issue of *The New England Gas News.*

enthusiastic about the opportunities in your industry. In coal and gas, nature gave us materials which are potent in dividend-producing possibilities if we will be heed "the hammering on the door."

There are a number of economic factors characteristic of gas which are the foundation of your industry. These can be named again and again. We must always remember that where heat is required, some two to three times the amount of useful energy can be made available to a customer in the form of gas from a given amount of coal as can be made available in the form of electricity. . . . The use of gas affords better control of atmosphere and temperature, particularly important in industrial heat uses. Gas is a material substance not merely a difference in potential. Gas can be stored. It is a basic raw material for the entire petrochemical industry and the substances used and produced are potent in industrial and domestic possibilities yet untouched.

The question of how much to spend on research is a difficult one. The gas industry has never been willing to invest in research anything near the proportion of its income that other industries have insisted upon investing as an insurance for their future prosperity.

It has been reported that the 1941 gross income of natural and manufactured gas operations and related appliance and equipment manufacturers was approximately $1 billion. Even though the chemical industry, which is an isolated case as far as American industry is concerned but has many relationships to the gas industry, spends 4 percent a year. We had better look at the 2 percent of gross income that the large successful industries are currently averaging on their expenditures for research. If this figure is taken, then this industry should be spending $20 million across the board in the entire industry instead of the $600,000 which is the figure if all aspects in the industry are totaled.

TECHNOLOGY FOR INDUSTRY*

Technology is the common heritage of all American people. It involves a procedure for revealing the secrets of nature and the application of these to the comforts of mankind. This research procedure should, in the broader sense, be made available to everyone and should not be a tool by which monopolistic systems can be developed.

We, therefore, have before us a long-range program which involves to

*Paper presented before Small War Plants Corporation meeting, Washington, D.C., May 26, 1944.

a large extent a carefully thought-out program of education for the smaller manufacturer, who in general needs to know more of the true function of research in his business. In such a program, a thoroughly organized educational department with group demonstrations of research by actual tours of laboratories and similar means of dissemination of the facts can readily become the greatest contribution of a government agency to the manufacturer's problem. With adequate facilities and personnel on hand, which should be the case after the war, and with a properly educated smaller manufacturer's group throughout the country, there will be no problem in initiating research institutional services to these organizations that need them so badly.

TECHNOLOGY AND THE MILLING INDUSTRY*

Through recent years we have seen the milling industry develop from an art to an industry, making greater and greater use of science. It must be admitted that similarly with all of the older industries, the transaction is taking place very slowly. There still exists too generally a resistance to the trying of the scientific approach to its problems.

The research problems of the milling industry are exceedingly difficult as compared with those of most other industries. This industry deals with a very highly complex substance, one that not only has physical and chemical characteristics, but one that is rarely at equilibrium. It is almost a living substance, changing in characteristics from day to day. Involving a suitable food for mankind, it is also a food for all types of insects and thereby is created a number of problems not inherent in some of the other industries.

NONFUEL USES OF NATURAL GAS†

Nature gave man two general types of resources—the kind that are reproducible each year in the form of crops from our forests and fields, and the kind that are not reproducible and take the form of products from our mines and wells.

Although we have understood for some years the amazing degree to which we can interchange most forms of our natural resources as raw materials in the production of new chemicals, it is only in more recent years that we are beginning to realize the necessity of conservative use of those non-replaceable natural resources—petroleum and natural gas—that took nature

---

*Published in the *Association of Operative Millers*, June 1945.
†Presented before the Inter-State Oil Compact Commission in Tulsa, Oklahoma, April 13, 1946 and published in the *Proceedings of the Inter-State Oil Compact Commission* of that year.

millions of years to create.

Conservation does not mean saving the material by not using it; rather, it means the continued best use of the material, thereby securing the very optimum of its potentials.

It is sometimes difficult for the owner of the land from which our petroleum and natural gas are derivable to realize that different uses of these resources may mean greater return to him and his heirs. However, the increasing realization on the part of the general public of the relative value of our natural nonreplaceable resources is surely resulting in a trend that will give us optimum uses of these materials in time.

The chemical elements with which we are here dealing are carbon and hydrogen, and in coal, natural gas, and petroleum, these elements exist in various combinations forming a whole family of hydrocarbons. The chemical use of hydrocarbons began many years ago with attempts to utilize the by-products resulting from the production of coke from coal for the iron and steel industry. These by-products were in the form of gases, liquids, and residues produced in the coking process. These early attempts met with almost immediate success, and many of our large industries today are founded on the background of this development. However, when research on nonfuel uses of petroleum and natural gas were advanced, it was found that chemical products or synthetics could be produced from these with greater ease and to a greater and more varied extent than from coal or coal tar through the coking process. Thus we find the beginning of a new industry.

It is well, then, that we are concerned with extending the life of usefulness of these extremely important natural resources—petroleum and natural gas—for the supply is limited and we cannot add to it. The day is undoubtedly coming when we will have expended our petroleum and natural gas resources and can then turn only to coal deposits to meet hydrocarbon needs. That may be a matter for contemplation and study of our children and their children, but we do owe it to ourselves and those who will follow us to do the very best with what we have and make the supply go as far as possible. Technology and free enterprise alone will meet these problems.

TODAY'S RESEARCH—TOMORROW' INDUSTRY*

In 1844, Henry L. Ellsworth, our first Commissioner of Patents, stated in his annual report that, "The advancement of the arts from year to year—

*Presented before the Public Affairs Luncheon, sponsored by the Omaha Chapter of Commerce in Omaha, Nebraska, April 23, 1946.

tax our credulity and seem to presage the arrival of that period when human improvements must end." At that time the government had issued less than 500,000 patents, and today just 100 years later 2.5 million patents have been issued with each year seeing a substantial increase in the rate of issuance. New industries that have been created through research and technological development since 1900 alone, just 45 years ago, today employ 15 million people. Through an increasingly better knowledge of our natural resources and a growth of the technical skills of our people, we have seen the growth and development of the automobile, the airplane, and the radio to mention just a few of the industries employing millions. (Note to the reader—no reference in this 1946 paper was made to television, the space program, atomic energy power generation, or the many other advancements in the last 25 years.)

* * *

CHEMICAL AND ENGINEERING
NEWS

"NEWS EDITION"

of the

American Chemical Society

VOLUME 23, 1945

Published by the

AMERICAN CHEMICAL SOCIETY

1155 Sixteenth Street, N. W., Washington 6, D. C.

Industrial Research Pattern
of the United States

HAROLD VAGTBORG, President, Midwest Research Institute, Kansas City, Mo.

RESEARCH—possibly not as such in name—began with Adam. The tempo was extremely slow in the early days with only an occasional beat to mark a new discovery as the thousands of years rolled by. First came fire and then the discoveries of what fire could do to the the simpler materials. The beats came at long intervals, suddenly and unforeseen, because discoveries were generally accidental. Early man learned how to remove iron and copper from ore with heat. He began to identify more and more of the materials of the earth and his ability to reveal the secrets of nature increased. Research began to take a more definite form. Many discoveries were kept secret and passed on from father to son. Others tried to imitate, but often something was missing. These early beginnings led to the age of artisanship and craftsmanship. But the research tempo quickened and science marched on. The period of "cut and try" opened and man began to look for new secrets of nature rather than just to stumble onto them. Colt whittled the first revolver out of a piece of wood, whiling away the long hours on a sea journey. Fulton's first steamboat model was made in much the same way. At the same time, in many shops and laboratories, workers were mixing ingredients unceasingly hoping each time for the desired result. Very often something happened that was entirely different from what was expected and a discovery of great importance was added to our knowledge of science.

Today the research approach is basically more sound. A problem is analyzed carefully and then segregated into its component parts for study. As missing links are supplied a complex picture becomes clear and a new discovery is added to our store of knowledge. This procedure has greatly increased the research tempo and its productiveness is accelerating. Today the world is research-conscious and an activity which began in the laboratories of our educational institutions in a small way many years ago has become the pilot of industry. The tempo is fast and ever on the increase. Many prefer to think of research as an industry in itself—one employing almost 70,000 workers in 2,350 research laboratories in 1940 at an approximate investment of $345,000,000.

But what of the research incentive? It certainly must exist and must take a variety of forms to engage a host of miscellaneous types of workers in both institutions and in industry. The incentives are many, but the more obvious will include the following:

Success of past developments. The over-all success of research activities during the past 50 years is a great stimulation to probe further the mysteries of nature.

Rapid growth in recent years of new industries. Radio, television, the airplane, plastics, synthetic rubber, the wire recorder, and new electronic applications in general spur us on to find new discoveries of the same importance.

Appreciation of future possibilities by use of newly available scientific tools. X-ray diffraction, electron microscopy, atom structure investigating equipment, ultra-speed photography are just a few of these. What will they produce in the way of new and amazing development?

Research may hold the answer to the conservation of existing materials and certainly does for the development of new products. How can we prevent great annual loss due to oxidation of iron and steel structures? What can be done to enable us to get more than 10% of the power effectiveness of gasoline?

Social aspects of research. Principles of economics state that there are three frontiers of development of employment and a prosperous economy—land, population increase, and new industries. It becomes increasingly important to create new industries through research if our prosperity is to continue.

Research is the life blood of our free competitive system. Industry is dependent for its continued growth and success on its ability to produce new and better products at lower cost.

Research offers not only monetary reward but professional advancement and recognition. Of these two it is believed that the research workers in our educational institutions put much greater stress on the latter than the former.

Organization of Effort

That, briefly, is the background of research. In considering the system under which it operates we shall limit ourselves to research in the physical sciences.

Individuals. It is true that practically every research development or discovery is the product of individual effort. This classification, however, refers to the scientist working in a private laboratory operated by his own resources. Most of the significant early developments in transportation, communication, and manufacturing processes came about in this manner.

These laboratories are contemporary with those of past decades and their workers are urged on by enthusiasm for their work and their desire to serve their fellowmen. Edison, Marconi, Fulton, Newton, and Franklin are typical of these and many of our great industries are the outcome of their efforts. The same kind of men are at work today contributing much to our research progress but in general are associated with industrial organizations or educational institutions where they have found advantages in having co-workers and extensive facilities.

Companies. In normal years and certainly in the war years (1940–45) by far the largest proportion of industrial research was done by company laboratories. The research expenditure of these grew eightfold from $29,000,000 in 1920 to $234,000,000 in 1940, the latter expenditure representing about two thirds of total expenditures for scientific research in the United States in that year. A survey by the National Association of Manufacturers revealed that in 1940 181 member companies spent a minimum of 2% of sales income each year on industrial research. A recent survey of American industry indicates that generally speaking postwar research activity will be doubled as soon as personnel and facilities become available.

Taking a reasonably normal prewar year, it is noted that the steel and the automotive industries each spent about $10,000,000 in research in 1939, and in the same year the chemical industry alone spent $20,000,000, which is equivalent to $4.30 per $100 of income. Numerous individual companies expend over $1,000,000 per year, and the fact that appropriations for research are increased indicates lucrative returns.

New corporation laboratory projects are being announced regularly. Very recent ones of magnitude are a $20,000,000 research plant for General Motors, Inc., and a $6,000,000 unit for General Electric Co. A substantial proportion of corporate research expenditures covers projects which are "farmed out" to colleges and universities and to research institutes. Many of these projects are of a long-term fundamental or special nature and are ideally suited to investigation in laboratories remote from the numerous interruptions caused by pressing production problems in corporation laboratories.

Scientific research has opened new fields for the employment of thousands through the development of new products and consequent new industries. Fifteen major industries of today have been developed since 1880. It has been estimated that these have created, directly or indirectly, 15 million new jobs. In other words, one out of every four persons gainfully employed today owes his job to an industry which grew out of a research development since 1880.

Someone might say, however, that scientific research has also crippled other industries and thereby reduced employment. A good example of the unsoundness of this argument is that when the horse and buggy industry was at its height in 1900 it gave employment to approximately one million persons, whereas the automotive industry in 1939, which replaced it, employed over six million.

At any rate, the industries have found that scientific research is essential to the improvement of existing products and the development of new ones. Industry's big problem today is the securing of proper personnel and naturally it is concerned about the serious effect the war has had on the training of young scientists. American industry will contribute much to the inevitable solution of this problem.

Associations and Industry Cooperatives. A number of trade associations have actively participated in research through the years and follow the pattern of utilizing the laboratories of their associations, member companies or outside laboratories for the development of scientific information of value to their manufacturing operations. Ventilating fan manufacturers, for example, have conducted extensive cooperative investigations of standardization of capacities of their equipment. The Portland Cement Association conducts a great deal of research in advancing the quality and uses of portland cement. The American Meat Institute and the American Petroleum Institute are organizations of an association nature operated to a large degree for the purpose of developing scientific information on the industry's products.

The industry cooperative is a type of research and industry education organization which has been developing particularly in recent years. The Institute of Paper Chemistry at Appleton, Wis., initiated the movement and was created for the purpose of not only conducting re-

search of a basic nature on the problems of the paper and pulp industry, but also to train technologists for the industry. The training of men is considered one of the most important features of the industry cooperative plan. In 1941 members of the gas industry created the Institute of Gas Technology, affiliated with the Illinois Institute of Technology. This institute, as in the previously-mentioned case, has an educational program paralleling a scientific research program for the gas industry. An institute of glass technology is in process of development and the Textile Research Institute has been under way for a short time.

Commercial Testing Laboratories. It has been estimated that about 250 of these organizations are in operation in this country today. They are performing an important day by day service to industry primarily in the handling of physical tests and analyses requiring special facilities and personnel. A great number of the smaller industrial corporations not justified in maintaining their own testing laboratories have found such organizations of great value. There are numerous instances where corporations have their routine analyses and testing problems handled by commercial testing laboratories and turn their long-term projects over to universities or research institutes.

Consulting Laboratories. Consulting research laboratories have always been an important factor in the American industrial research scene. These laboratories are operated as service organizations, charging a fee for their services to their clientele in accordance with the program undertaken. These organizations are extensive throughout the United States and are typified by such well known ones as Arthur D. Little, Inc., and Foster D. Snell, in the East, Kansas City Testing Laboratory in Kansas City, and Miner Laboratories in Chicago. In addition, a number of consulting organizations actually do no research work but are skilled in the application of science and technology to industry, and render consulting services.

Research Institutes. Research institutes are generally endowed, nonprofit organizations operated primarily to serve industry on long-term applied research projects. Typical of these is the Mellon Institute of Industrial Research at Pittsburgh and the Battelle Memorial Institute at Columbus, both of which were founded and endowed in the interest of research service to industry by the individuals, after whom such institutions are named.

Within very recent years a modification of this plan of research organization has been developed where the support comes not from the endowment created by an individual but by contributions from a large number of people who have the same objective in mind as the creators of the previously-mentioned institutions. These latter organizations take on the aspects of not only being industrial, but

also regional research institutes. In other words, they are dedicated not only to service to the industries but to the development through scientific research of the resources of the areas in which they operate.

The Midwest Research Institute located at Kansas City, Mo., and operating since January of this year is not only serving industrial organizations on their research problems but has undertaken a number of research projects in the interests of the development of industry in the midwest area of the country. Similarly, the Southern Research Institute located at Birmingham, Ala., was recently created to serve the South. Both of these organizations were established by rather substantial contributions coming from large numbers of people who were interested in the betterment of standards of living in the areas involved. In this way it is expected that as years go on endowments will be developed from broad support of people of all walks of life who have a regional interest. A third institution of this character is just being established in California and is known as the Pacific Research Foundation and one is being planned for the Pacific Northwest. The geographical location of these organizations and their extensiveness of operations are dependent upon common natural resources and area economy and trade conditions.

There is a migration of industrial research from the great industries of the East to the Midwest and to other sections of our country. It is significant that research, which always is the forerunner of industrial development, is moving nearer to the sources of our country's raw materials. Obviously, this is one of the first steps in the decentralization of industry.

Not being tax-supported, all research institutes can enter into agreements with sponsors which provide for outright patent protection and keeping the results confidential where these features are desired. In the case of regional research projects patent rights are expected to belong to the institute sponsoring the program for licensing to interested manufacturers.

The research foundations of educational institutions have much in common with the research institute. For purposes of clarity, however, these are discussed under "Universities and Colleges".

Foundations and Councils. The foundations of this classification refer to the numerous endowed or industry-supported organizations which sponsor research. Typical of the endowed foundations working in public interest are Rockefeller Foundation, Carnegie Corp., Carnegie Institution, the Engineering Foundation, and the Research Corp. of New York. The industry-supported foundations and councils are increasing year by year and are typified by such organizations as the Nutrition Foundation, the Tanners' Council, Lithograph Research Institute, National Cotton Council, Sugar Foundation, and the Iodine Foundation. Companies within the industry involved in each case make annual contributions to the program which in turn support research projects conducted at outside laboratories under the general supervision of the council or foundation involved. It is significant that expenditures in some cases reach a million dollars or more annually.

The National Research Council is included in this classification although its activities are much broader, for it operates in many fields of which engineering is one. Not only is it the recognized national research clearing house but it also makes grants to various research agencies including universities and colleges. The National Research Council publishes from time to time an important directory under the title, "Industrial Research Laboratories in the United States", and has recently published a listing of research grants by industrial corporations to universities and colleges as well as to other research agencies. The council also sponsored the organization of the Industrial Research Institute which is a national organization of industrial research directors and executives.

Professional Societies. Most of our national scientific and engineering societies have funds which are granted usually through a research committee, to institutions equipped to do research of basic importance to the society. Such committees may also serve in correlating national and international research activities having a bearing on the functions of the society. In many instances a committee of one society will work jointly with a committee of one or more societies in sponsoring research of mutual-interest. Much of our engineering progress in past years has been made possible by the activities of this group.

Universities and Colleges. The very idea of research comes from our universities and colleges which mothered it long before American industry had much interest in it. Research has been in the past and is today a primary factor in higher education, thereby enabling the universities to furnish industry with men possessing knowledge not only of the underlying scientific facts and theories but of the methods and techniques of research. From the universities also flows much of the basic knowledge of science on which modern technical industry has been built and will build in the future.

Research work in our educational institutions today is carried on in one or two ways: either as individual activity in a field in which the worker is interested and urged on by his enthusiasm for his particular subject, or as part of a sponsored plan. In any event the reputation of an institution seems to depend to a large extent upon its research productiveness and most institutions encourage research by their faculties and graduate students, some even

tending to make it a prerequisite for appointment.

There exist several plans for sponsored research in our educational institutions. The worker or faculty member may be given a grant, either by the institution or by an outside agency. It is generally conceded that most of the research grants that go to our universities and colleges today are given not because of the standing of the institution entirely but because of the reputation of a particular faculty member who has unusual capabilities and facilities for carrying on research in the particular field in which the outside agency making the grant is interested.

Institutions may receive support from governmental agencies for work in specific fields. These are mainly state or tax-supported institutions which function partly to render research services in agriculture and the mechanical arts to their communities through grants from the state or government.

A third instance of a sponsored plan is organized research in educational institutions, often taking the form of an experimental engineering station. Typical is the Engineering Experiment Station, University of Illinois. Organized research programs of this kind offer numerous incentives for industrial participation, proved by the fact that many receive substantial research support from individuals, corporations, associations, and other research agencies.

Universities and colleges usually prefer to carry on research under circumstances where patents are not involved and the publication of results is desired by all parties. This is usually the case in all fundamental research, certain industrial research sponsored by manufacturing associations, and research made possible by grants from societies and other agencies. However, complications have arisen under this system when a sponsor wants patent protection and the results kept confidential. To meet this situation many of our universities are creating affiliated non-profit research corporations operated under the administration of the university. Typical of these organizations is the Research Foundation of Ohio State University, the Research Foundation of the University of Wisconsin, the Purdue Research Foundation, and the Institute of Research of Lehigh University. Generally speaking, these foundations are placed under a director who establishes contacts with industry and other grant-giving research agencies, and, through faculty co-ordination, research projects are undertaken by agreements which cover patent policies and publication rights.

Armour Research Foundation of Illinois Institute of Technology comes under this classification with the modification that its staff comprises primarily full-time personnel engaged to work on research projects exclusively. Further it gives full patent rights to its sponsors, whereas

most of the others give varying degrees of patent protection.

The increased tendency to organize research activities in educational institutions during the past decade has been brought about by the necessity for adopting well-defined policies in regard to inventions made by faculty members. An excellent treatise of this subject is given in "University Patent Policies" by Richard Spencer, lecturer on patents, Northwestern University Law School, and published in 1939.

Before passing from the subject of patents it seems desirable to state that several educational institutions such as Massachusetts Institute of Technology and Princeton University have working arrangement with the Research Corp. of New York whereby the inventions of their faculties are generally turned over to that corporation and any proceeds from commercialization accrue in a fixed manner to the principals who are involved.

Federal Government. Prior to the war years (1940–45) the Federal Government held a very secondary place to industry in research activity. If it had not been for the war the discussion of this classification could have been dispensed with simply with the following few comments which give the picture for 1940:

"A basic activity of any government is to carry on research which has a bearing on the general welfare of its people. The budget for research by our national government agencies during the year 1940 was approximately $69,000,000 and was distributed about as follows:

	%
Engineering	36
Surveys	16
Physical sciences	4
Natural sciences	39
Public health	5
Total	100

"Government research generally covers those fields which private industry either has no incentive or no reason to enter on a broad scale. It is the kind of research that is carried on to improve health, increase our national security, and conserve our natural resources. Typical of these fields are national defense, mining, and agriculture. The bureaus most widely known are the National Bureau of Standards and the Bureau of Mines. The United States Department of Agriculture recently created four regional research laboratories to work on the agricultural problems of their respective regions."

Out of the war years there arose a very complex and even revolutionary situation as far as research is concerned. Almost overnight peaceful pursuits were dropped and with almost no exception scientific personnel and research facilities were geared to the war program. The government research budget of $69,000,000 in 1940 grew to approximately $720,000,000

CONTINUED ON PAGE 2055

Industrial Research Pattern of the U. S.

(CONTINUED FROM PAGE 1945)

in 1944 and a total of approximately $1,800,000,000 for the 5 years. Only a small portion of these funds was spent in government laboratories, the large portion going to the laboratories of industry, universities and colleges, research institutes, and private consultants in the form of underwritings of specific war research projects. In these arrangements 'the government was represented by several federal war research agencies created for that purpose.

The results have been most gratifying. A major lesson learned is that highly efficient research productivity results from the use by the government of private, industrial, and institutional laboratories throughout the country.

The experience has also taught us the real need for increased activity in fundamental or pure research and for expanded

PRESENTED before the Mexican-American Conference on Industrial Research, Chicago, Ill., Oct. 1, 1945.

means of fostering scientific education for American youth having proper qualifications. It is not believed that these objectives can be accomplished by prewar methods and that government support is necessary. Industry gladly will expand fundamental research knowledge into industrial applications for the comfort of man and will take the young people trained in our colleges and universities and mold them into a great scientific force geared to the betterment of the world in which we live. Several proposals for the promotion of basic scientific research and education are now in Congress, the two most noteworthy being one providing for a "National Research Foundation" and based on the proposals of Vannevar Bush, Director of Office of Scientific Research and Development, in his report to the President entitled "Science—The Endless Frontier", and one providing for a "National Science Foundation" containing principles that the Subcommittee on War Mobilization of the Senate Military Affairs Committee deems desirable. It is not the purpose of this discussion to cover their relative merits. In some respects they are similar but in others they are in direct conflict. Strong controversial phases of the bills are methods of administration and patent rights. In any case they represent a trend—a trend which will bring very substantial financial aid to the American research scene through all types of laboratories throughout the land.

Research in the United States is destined to become a billion dollar a year industry and today is limited only by the shortage of personnel and facilities.

CHAPTER IV

THE ENDOWED RESEARCH INSTITUTES—MELLON AND BATTELLE

AN IDEA . . . MAKES OTHERS AWARE

Prior to 1900, pure research in the United States was usually performed only in the larger universities. In such an academic environment, a professor was able to choose his area of research with little regard for any concrete results. Thus, he frequently chose to study a particular problem because it interested him, and, as a result, it often happened that the only outcome, after years of exhaustive research, would be a theory of a natural law. Nonetheless, the formation of this theory qualified as part of science's responsibility to man, according to the professor's understanding—i.e., to construct a systematic and useful body of fact and theory. To work on a research project in a deliberate attempt to apply the results toward creating a new or better product or process for industry was considered beneath a self-respecting scientist who would not want to be accused of "commercializing science." One individual who resisted this trend as early as 1906 was Dr. Robert Kennedy Duncan, a professor who developed the idea that the resources and methods of physical science could and should be applied to the problems of industry. Duncan conceived this idea while he was attending the Sixth International Congress of Applied Chemistry in Rome, Italy, in 1906. After returning to his home at the University of Kansas, he put his idea to work.

Dr. Duncan, a man of great personal magnetism and persuasion, convinced a laundering company of Boston, Massachusetts, to fund a totally new research program that would establish an Industrial Fellowship at the University of Kansas. This event, on January 1, 1907, marked the first time that any American industry had ever established a research program in a university to study its specific problems. In this program, the scientist chosen for the fellowship devoted his research efforts toward solving a major scientific problem faced by the laundering industry. Dr. Fred Faragher was

Dr. Robert Kennedy Duncan

Edward R. Weidlein,
Director of Mellon Institute since 1921

the man chosen for this task. He was so successful in his research efforts that a new organization—the American Institute of Laundering—was created to expand the research into other problem areas.

Encouraged by his success with the laundering industry, Dr. Duncan continued with the program, persuading other industries with technical problems to establish a fellowship. To spread his ideas, Dr. Duncan spared no effort: he gave talks, presented lectures, visited interested company officials, and wrote books. It was one of his books, *The Chemistry of Commerce*, that marked his second great milestone. Two brothers, successful Pittsburgh businessmen, read the book and realized the value of the fellowship system in coupling science to technology as an aid to industry.

Andrew William Mellon and his brother Richard Beatty Mellon were enthralled with the possibilities of this still new—and in some circles unpopular—concept. They wasted no time in persuading Dr. Duncan to come to Pittsburgh to discuss the possibilities of this type of program at the university there. The Mellon brothers understood what Duncan had in mind with his program. They visualized it; they had seen it applied; and they were supporting research in aluminum, carborundum, and other industries. Dr. Duncan's fellow scientists, however, were not as enthusiastic as the Mellons. In fact, he was receiving a great amount of criticism from his cohorts. Even the American Chemical Society had an editorial condemning such a system to "commercialize" science. At that time, the professors dominated the American Chemical Society; however, dedicated scientist Duncan did not let this censure prevent his enlarging the program. He organized a program similar to his Kansas operation at the University of Pittsburgh.

At first, Dr. Duncan continued to direct both organizations, making frequent trips to Kansas. His headquarters, however, were in his new Pittsburgh institute. Late in 1912, he decided to close out his activities in Kansas and recommended his 24-year-old protégé Edward Ray Weidlein to head the Kansas organization. When university officials refused to advance this young man to the same rank and salary as the heads of all the other established departments, Duncan moved the entire department to Pittsburgh. The addition of the Kansas operation to the Pittsburgh branch as well as enlarged activities convinced the Mellon brothers that this institute was the proper way to advance exact knowledge by discovery through research.

As a result, Andrew and Richard Mellon established the Mellon Institute of Industrial Research and School of Specific Industries on March 1, 1913. In addition to their name, the Mellon brothers gave the institute their promise to provide its first permanent home and to give financial support for a period of five years. Unfortunately, Dr. Duncan died in 1914, one year before the new six-floor research laboratory—at the time the most modern research laboratory in the country, if not the world—was completed. The structure was dedicated to him and to Judge Thomas Mellon, the father of the two brothers. Duncan's innovative spirit continued to inspire his co-workers, however, for over the doorway of the new building was the following inscription in bronze:

> *This building is dedicated to the service of American Industry, to young men who destine their lifework to the Industries, the goal being Ideal Industry, which will give to all broader opportunities for purposeful lives.*

This inscription exemplifies the purpose for which the building had been constructed.

Because of World War I, the brothers extended their financial support to 1921, a year in which another significant event occurred. Although a part of the University of Pittsburgh, the lusty institute had a loose operating arrangement with its sponsoring host. In 1921, the Mellons gave the institute to the university. At the time, Dr. John G. Bowman was chancellor, and he understood that the best administration was the least administration. As a result, he never quite accepted the institute as a real gift, and it continued to operate, with his support, but very much on its own.

A strong source of impetus for the growing institute was Dr. Edward Weidlein, Dr. Duncan's young cohort who made the move from Kansas to Pittsburgh in 1912. In July 1921, he was made acting director, and as such, he placed a 20-percent overhead on the fellowships. Thus, between July 1 and October 1, 1921, the institute became self-supporting. This convinced Andrew and Richard Mellon that the institute had a firm foundation and was of great value to industry by carrying out its two paramount functions—namely, the betterment of manufacturing practice and the advancement of both pure and applied science.

By 1927, the institute's unusual progress caused the Mellons to decide that it should have a separate charter. That same year it was incorporated as the Mellon Institute of Industrial Research by a charter from the state of Pennsylvania. Also, a board of trustees was established with Dr. Bowman as a charter member, and Dr. Weidlein was officially made the director. This operating structure proved ideal for the businessman who wanted the advantages of the extensive facilities offered by the research institute, while

*Chemistry building at the University of Kansas, home of the Industrial Fellowship
System, wholly 1907-1911, in part 1911-1913.*

*The new building of the Mellon Institute of Industrial Research and School of Specific Industries
(1915)*

still retaining control of the results. The procedure that was followed usually involved these steps: (1) a problem requiring investigation was proposed by an individual, company, or association of manufacturers; (2) if the problem was of such scope as to require the services of at least one man for a period not less than one year, a contract covering the establishment of a fellowship was arranged between the donor and Mellon Institute, provided that no other research was already in progress on the same problem and that the institute could give the necessary accommodations for the satisfactory conduct of the investigation; and (3) the area of research had to pertain to those realms of science important to human welfare—mainly the fields of health, biology, chemistry, physics, and technology. In return, the donor had control over the research results, including matters pertaining to patents and publication. In general, however, publication was approved after a one-year period.

Because of multiple research programs, the overhead expenses not chargeable to a particular donor and the costs of long-term equipment could be defrayed among many organizations. Thus, each donor had the benefit of comprehensive facilities for research projects, which, if conducted singularly, would be much more costly. In addition, the physical separation of the institute and its laboratories from production plants was regarded as an advantage to broaden company research.

Time after time the institute proved its mettle to the patron companies, and the fellowships continued to come. As the institute grew, it seemed to the founders that researchers were needed in the sciences that had more direct relationships to human welfare, and thereby man's basic knowledge would be advanced. Dr. Duncan's original concept included fundamental research to supplement applied research, and so, such fundamental work was initiated. A special fellowship on pure research began in 1922, and in 1927, the Department of Research in Pure Chemistry was formally established with Dr. Leonard H. Cretcher as head of the fledgling group. This program of basic science continued to be supported by grants from the Mellon family, whose policy had been to increase emphasis on basic research.

EXCELLENCE OF PERSONNEL

In his annual report to the trustees in 1927, Institute Director Edward Weidlein made the following statement regarding the quality of "Fellows" under Mellon's employ:

> The ideals which from the first have actuated the fellows of the institute have led to the solidarity of the institution. No guild has a sounder code of ethics; no professional group stronger ties of cooperation and brotherhood. There are other driving motives, besides the constraint of contractual obligations, which keep the fellows to their task, and promote the well-being of the fellowship. The utility of their work, the craving for results, the fascination of what to them is a very interesting sport, move all the fellows more effectively than the articles of agreement governing the operation of their fellowships.

According to Weidlein, "There has never been an organization that has such a strong alumni group as Mellon Institute. It is our people who have emphasized the high character of the institution." This display of pride in personnel is understandable as well as justifiable . . . perhaps also traceable to the character of those first men, the pioneers in Mellon's industrial research adventure. Weidlein has said, "Men came in and did not ask if they would have an office, what kind of pension plan was offered, the number of vacation days, the type of health program, etc. They were interested in the research program and wanted to get to work. It was a wonderful spirit which produced a large number of outstanding men." They have become presidents, vice presidents, and research directors of organizations, as well as professors and department heads in universities.

In this same vein, by 1962, over 650 novel processes and products had been invented or developed by Fellows of Mellon Institute. In a number of cases, new industries had evolved from such inventions/developments, among them Visking Corporation, Plaskon Company, Inc., and Dow-Corning Corporation. In other instances, new branches were added to existing manufacturers—the chemicals division (now Union Carbide Chemicals Company) of the Union Carbide Corporation and the extensive research facilities of the Gulf Oil Corporation. Contributions too numerous to itemize have also been made to scientific literature through the vast number of publications authored by Mellon staff members. These individuals have also taken a very active part in many scientific and engineering societies. They have been presidents, directors, editors of journals, and members of innumerable committees.

EXPANSION IN FACILITIES

One of the most significant and beneficent acts of the founders of Mellon Institute was their gift, in 1937, of the 8-story structure which today houses the research institution. As expressed by Dr. Weidlein, "In the minds of the institute's founders this massive building, designed in the classic Greek style with its majestic columns, was the culminating step toward the dream they held—the vision of a greater institute, beautifully and efficiently housed in keeping with the character of its contributions to science and humanity." The magnificent structure has more than 200 laboratories and is located in Oakland, the civic center of Pittsburgh, approximately three miles east of the city's business district and in close proximity to the University of Pittsburgh, the Carnegie Institute of Technology, and the Carnegie Institute.

Andrew Mellon, in his address at the dedication of the present Mellon Institute building in 1937, said of Dr. Duncan's book, the piece of writing that started the whole research endeavor of the Mellons: "The part which particularly enlisted my attention was the last chapter in which Dr. Duncan described his plan for industrial fellowships, by means of which industry could utilize the services of qualified scientists to solve its problems, in much the same way as is being done here today. It seemed to me that an institution based on Dr. Duncan's ideas could help in this advance movement; and, as my brother was keenly interested in this project, we lost no time in persuading Dr. Duncan to come to Pittsburgh and organize for us, here at our University of Pittsburgh, this Institute of Research."

Under Weidlein, new departments were created and new projects were funded: the Department of Research in Organic Chemistry was largely concerned with the synthesis of new drugs; the personnel in the Departments of Research in Chemical Physics and Physical Chemistry applied their methods and discoveries to aid fellowships and to engage in basic studies of their own choice. Expertise in technique, as first brought out in analytical chemistry, has always been a goal of the research scientist's work. Great skill in that elaborate thinking, understanding, and performing process has been tremendously increased by developments in physical chemistry and chemical physics as well as in their comprehensive instrumentation. Obviously, then, a well-equipped department of instrumentation plays an integral part in institute research. In time, this type of department and others were created as necessary to carry out a number of specific projects for the benefit of the people, all of these expansion activities being predicated on the Mellon brothers' belief that worthwhile utilization of the wonders of natural science

Headquarters of Mellon Institute, 1915-1937.

The home of Mellon Institute, dedicated in 1937, is one of Pittsburgh's great structures, with the largest monolithic column installation in the world. Each of its 62 columns surrounding the edifice weighs 60 tons. Three of the six floors are below ground level, and there are four interior courts for natural lighting. Rooms for the great scientific investigational work carried on at the institute total about 450, in addition to the extensive library, offices, lecture and social rooms, and shops.

would expand and refine man's niche in God's world.

The results of these projects were published and widely distributed. They usually treated subjects on public health and included studies on smoke abatement; industrial and urban pollution, both air and water; investigations into the cause and prevention of dental caries; nutrition, sleep, and tension; better ways to diagnose tuberculosis in its early stages; and searches for new compounds of value in treating pneumonia and cancer. One of the first investigations on smoke began in 1911, while the infant institute still resided in its original two-story wooden building. From this three-year program came information of such value that the research was recognized internationally as being of utmost importance to every industrial center. And this was over 50 years before the ecologists began to lament the damage to our atmosphere caused by NO_x emissions. These early studies, in addition to others carried out in the 1920s and 1930s, are the direct forerunners of the clean air programs which are now in effect in Pittsburgh and other American cities.

Richard Mellon was most enthusiastic about this particular program, and as a result, the Air Pollution Control Association, headquartered in the institute, named its most distinguished award "The Richard Beatty Mellon Award." Each year this honor is presented to an outstanding individual, "In recognition of high motive of public service, fruitful accomplishments, and distinguished achievement in the field of air pollution control." This work also led to the creation of a separate organization in the field of industrial hygiene. The Industrial Hygiene Foundation, also located in the institute, carried on broad research, especially in the control of air pollutants in industry.

Through cooperation with the University of Pittsburgh and the Carnegie Institute of Technology, hundreds of men and women have received their advanced degrees while employed in scientific research at the institute. The institute policy of close cooperation with these universities, and others throughout the world, is based on a firm belief that the university is and always will be the natural breeding ground for scientific interests. In an article in the *Journal of Chemical Education** this belief was expressed as follows.

Our teachers must be relied upon to furnish the scholars, both in their own persons and in the pupils to whom they impart their spirit

---

*Hamor, William A., and Lawrence W. Bass, *Journal of Chemical Education*, vol. 7, no. 1, January 1930.

and methods. To train new personnel for research would leave the teaching profession as overburdened as ever, and would take away one of the main hopes of relief. Encouragement of further division between teaching and research would be equally bad for the mere teacher and for the mere man of research. The teacher would lose in freedom and incentive and in the power to impart the spirit of creative inquiry. The researcher would lose his contacts with the great intellectual tradition, with his colleagues in allied branches of knowledge, and with students who furnish both criticism and discipleship. It cannot be gainsaid that the university is the proper center of scholar endeavor; in it are focused the influences of history and culture; and therein the achievements of maturity are constantly being renewed by the enthusiasm and forward look of youth.

ENDOWMENT FOR FUNDAMENTAL RESEARCH

With the retirement of Dr. Weidlein in 1955, General Matthew B. Ridgeway was brought in as chairman of the board of trustees and chief executive officer. Many far-reaching changes were thereupon instituted. The Mellon families contributed $20 million—$2 million of which was for completion of additional laboratories and $18 million for a fundamental research trust fund. General Ridgeway employed Dr. Paul J. Flory as director of research, and a group of persons was brought in to establish a program patterned somewhat after the Rockefeller Institute in New York.

A major development under Ridgeway was the establishment of the Busby Run Laboratory on a 230-acre tract, 22 miles east of the Oakland Laboratory. This included facilities for the toxicological investigations of the Union Carbide Corporation and a high energy Van der Graff accelerator coupled to electron spin resonance equipment as the major facility for the Radiation Research Laboratory.

When General Ridgeway retired in 1960, Mr. Paul Mellon assumed the chairmanship of the board and engaged Mr. Jonathan Raymond to preside over the affairs of the institute. In the meantime, the board of trustees had been enlarged to include new members from outside of the Pittsburgh area. Of these, doctors James R. Killian and William O. Baker exerted major influence on institute policies. For nearly a year after Ridgeway's retirement, exhaustive studies were made of the possibility of merging the institute with the Carnegie Institute of Technology. This plan was eventually abandoned because of opposition from loyal supporters of the University of Pittsburgh, with which the institute had had a long and usually satisfactory association.

In 1961, Dr. Paul C. Cross was brought in as president and chief executive officer, and the Mellon families added another $10 million to the endowment to create what was envisioned as a fifty-fifty operation between fundamental research and industrially sponsored applied research. It was hoped that the fundamental research would somehow benefit the workers in applied fields.

THE MERGER, CARNEGIE-MELLON UNIVERSITY

By 1966, the University of Pittsburgh was in dire financial straits, with a deficit of over $20 million. The Ford Foundation financed a study of the Pitt situation, which also included consideration of the Oakland cultural center (including Mellon Institute), Carnegie Institute of Technology, and the Carnegie Museum-Library complex. When the University of Pittsburgh became "state related," the objection to the contemplated merger between Mellon Institute and Carnegie Institute of Technology seemingly disappeared. Resumption of negotiations between the two institutes led to the announcement in the fall of 1966 that such a merger was scheduled for July 1, 1967. The originally designated survivor institution was "Carnegie University." Contrary to most prevalent opinions, some members of the Mellon families were reluctant to have their name associated with the new university. Eventually, however, they agreed, and on August 10, 1967, Carnegie-Mellon University was chartered. Subsequently, after a period of neglect regarding industrial contracts, there arose an awareness of the value of such relations, and the administrators of the university launched an attempt to revive some of the Mellon Institute tradition of cooperation with industries. Only time will tell whether or not this will be successful.

* * *

BATTELLE—THE BIGGEST OF THE INDEPENDENTS

The academic atmosphere of a state university is not the only environment conducive to the birth and growth of an applied research institution. Battelle Memorial Institute (BMI) is a "living," thriving example of such an institution, conceived and nurtured not only by an academician but by a businessman who dreamed of better things through creative research. Gordon Battelle shared *that* particular characteristic with the benefactors of Mellon Institute.

IT IS MY WILL . . .

The only son of John Gordon and Annie Norton Battelle, Gordon was born to wealth and trained to inherit and manage his father's vast holdings. After his schooling, which culminated in his studying metallurgy at the Sheffield Scientific School of Yale University, he struck out on his own and invested in prominent mining and smelting operations in the Joplin, Missouri, area. While there he became interested in the research a former university professor W. George Waring was engaged in—the development of a process for recovering valuable chemicals from waste products. So intense was his interest, Gordon set up a small laboratory for the professor's research, and eventually a commercial process was perfected. Parallels between this experience of Gordon Battelle and the Duncan-Mellon relationship are obvious and, likewise, Gordon was ahead of his time with his deep interest— which was to become an obsession—in the application of science to industry. In 1915, industrial research was still an undeveloped field, and, of course, the number of interested parties was so slight as to make this enterprise advantageously uncrowded. There were only about 100 industrial research laboratories in the entire United States; the first permanent laboratory of this type—that of General Electric—was only 15 years old; and Mellon Institute had just dedicated its first real laboratory building; so *that* institution was still too young to be well known.

To learn more about how research was being organized in the new laboratories, Battelle visited many of them. During this period of several years, which was probably the most formative period in Gordon Battelle's life, his father died. That event catapulted him into a new role as the young heir to one of Ohio's great industrial fortunes.

During the next five years, he fulfilled his obligations of "carrying on" the family business, but according to friends who talked with him during those days, he was not truly interested in nor dedicated to financial success. He still wanted to do something on his own, and that "something" was a scientific research center. He must have sensed that the only lasting way to use his wealth would be to "foster some mechanism whereby the bounties resulting from man's efforts could be increased. In science, he saw great hope for improvement of the common lot."*

On September 21, 1923, Gordon Battelle died suddenly and unexpectedly at the age of 40 following an appendectomy. In his will, he left a sizable endowment for the creation of "a Battelle Memorial Institute . . . for the encouragement of creative research . . . the making of discoveries and inventions . . . the education of men," and "the discovery, license, and disposal" of new technology. Implicit in the institute's establishment was the fundamental concept that modern man exists in an industrial society—that his material welfare can, and should, be improved by science and technology.

Exactly what kind of institution Gordon Battelle had in mind can only be presumed. He was well aware of the many research laboratories, as well as of Mellon Institute, and yet the likelihood was that he was trying to create something totally new, something that did not exist at the time. Before his death, during his period of visitation and investigation into the field of industrial research, he may very well have sensed that industry, especially smaller companies, had a need for research help that was not then available from universities, laboratories, or the existing research organizations.

Gordon Battelle's endowment fund was left in trust to a board of trustees that included Bishop John W. Hamilton, a relative and the then president of American University in Washington, D.C.; Warren G. Harding, a friend of Gordon and the then President of the United States; Annie Norton Battelle, his mother; Earle Clark Derby, a Columbus industrialist; Joseph H. Frantz, a close business associate of Gordon's father; and Harry M. Runkle, a lawyer and business associate of Gordon Battelle. All of these people were impressive in their own right, yet none had any notable knowledge of science nor any particular experience with or appreciation of its applications to industry. Of these designated trustees, several were unable to serve: the most famous member, Warren G. Harding, died the same year as Battelle, and Gordon's mother, Annie Norton Battelle, died two years after her son. She thought so highly of the idea of a research institute, however, that she left the balance of the Battelle family fortune to the same purpose, bringing the total endowment to a sum in excess of $3.5 million.

CORNERSTONES AND OFFICERS
Battelle Memorial Institute was formally established by the board of trustees

*"The Battelle Family," in the March and May 1953 issue of *Battelle News.*

in 1925 under the laws of the state of Ohio, providing for the incorporation of charitable trusts, as a not-for-profit corporation. The expression "not-for-profit" meant that all the income of the institute had to be used or reserved for the stated purposes of the charitable trust that forms the basis for the corporation. This reservation was important because some of the discoveries and inventions proved to be quite profitable, and monies gained from these discoveries made possible the further extension of the institute's work.

The trustees were active in the years following incorporation. They acquired about 10 acres on King Avenue, formulated plans for a laboratory, and built that laboratory by late summer of 1929. Bishop John Hamilton, one of the charter trustees, laid the cornerstone in October of the same year. Although the remaining group of trustees was weak in scientific judgment, they had keen business minds and made some excellent staff choices, notably, Horace Gillett to serve as director. Gillett, who had held the position of Chief of the Metallurgical Division of the National Bureau of Standards and had also once worked with Thomas Edison, established the initial character of the institute. He himself was a pipe-smoking, wiry, wisp of a man who usually wore a baggy sweater and enjoyed the outdoors, his English Setters, and a summer camp in Canada. So humble in nature and unkempt in appearance, he was once mistaken for the janitor by a new secretary who scorned him for not emptying her wastebasket regularly—whereupon he dutifully performed the task.

Many people may have believed he had little regard for the amenities, but he had a sharp mind, instantaneous perception, and the ability to detect the slightest deviation from intellectual integrity. In addition, he had a phenomenal reading rate combined with the talent to spot typographical and orthographical errors without fail. Considered by his fellow scientists as "The Dean of American Metallurgy," Gillett was a prolific writer, editor, and abstractor, and he was generous and unselfish, going beyond the normal expectations in helping younger scientists establish a firm foothold in the academic world.

With adept Horace Gillett at the helm, Battelle Institute was "off and running," but two awesome obstacles that had existed as shadows before began to garner some of the spotlight. They were: the world's worst economic situation ever—The Great Depression—and industry's indifference to research. The only way that these obstacles were surmounted was by the truly remarkable concentration of talent that Gillett was able to attract. Among the more notable personnel were Clyde Williams, who came from the U.S. Bureau of Mines and who ultimately took the reins at Battelle after Gillett; Howard Russell, a dominating personality trained as a physicist and firmly entrenched in the belief that the long-range future of metallurgy lay in explaining phenomena such as hardness and tensile strength in terms of basic physical principles—indeed, the very nature of modern metallurgy; John Sullivan, one of the first chemists who helped to establish Battelle as a center for research in ceramics; Bert Thomas, later director and president; and Oscar Harder, an invaluable inspiration to the younger, less-experienced men on the job.

In its first year of operation, the institute's total expenditures on research amounted to $71,000. Although a substantial amount at the time, it is less than the institute spent in one *day* in 1973. By 1934, this sum jumped to $175,000, and the staff was nearing 100. The man directing the course at that time was Clyde Williams. Gillett had asked to be relieved from the onerous chores of chief administrator in order that he could devote his full time to his first love, science. He did so until his death in 1950. Williams had acquired a reputation as one of the most promising metallurgists in the steelmaking industry and had been persuaded by Gillett to enter the research world, whereupon he began working for the institute in 1930. He showed a talent for the administrative tasks that Gillett disliked, and the director asked the board of trustees to appoint Williams as his replacement. Williams accepted the challenge. And indeed it was just that.

When Williams accepted his appointment as director, he probably saw more clearly than anyone else the challenge offered by a new approach to the problem of transforming scientific discoveries into applications for practical use. He recognized that the principal obstacle preventing revolutionary change in the world of technology was the attitude of industry toward science, an attitude caused by the deadweight of the Depression, a lack of understanding, and sometimes indifference and ignorance of what science can do! Nevertheless, by 1934, when Williams took over, Battelle was almost in the black. The key to this success and to the bountiful years to come was the concept of contract research—work undertaken for a specific sponsor on a break-even financial basis. Williams was a great proponent of this concept and even had a hand in drawing up the first contract blanks. In short, the contract arrangement was and is handled according to the following provisions:

Battelle agrees to undertake a specific research project, whose goals are carefully described. The starting and finishing dates are inserted. The sponsor is committed to pay for staff costs, materials, equipment, travel, and overhead, with the total not to exceed a stipulated amount. The information to be developed or found, including patentable discoveries, belongs to the sponsor. The Institute is not allowed to disclose results of the research without the sponsor's consent. On the other hand, the sponsor agrees not to exploit Battelle's name and reputation in advertising, sales promotion, or publicity without the Institute's permission. Battelle does not guarantee success; it just promises to do its level best.*

AN INNOVATIVE APPROACH

For the Battelle staff member, the contract research approach provided him a means by which to exploit his own ideas. All he had to do was generate an idea that a sponsor was willing to support, and usually the director's approval would follow. By this means, Battelle made even further advancements in its specialty of metallurgy—concentration of low-grade ores to be used in iron; specialization in nonferrous metals; development of low-alloy, corrosion-resistant steel; utilization of aluminum by the steel industry, etc. It was during the first stages of the Depression when Battelle undertook a project that was to be responsible for the institute's subsequent diversification of research activities. A trade association of copper producers contracted with Battelle to discover new uses for copper. The results ranged from the agriculture realm—copper was found to be important as a trace element in soil—to that of graphic arts—improvements in copper printing plates were developed. As a result, by the end of the 1930s, lateral as well as vertical expansion was so great that it was difficult to keep up with all the varied directions in which Battelle was heading. During this time, the Department of Chemistry was formed . . . with the "standard" orientation toward metallurgy. Also, process metallurgy became important, and emphasis on the engineering properties widened to include studies on the workability and machinability of metals, electrochemistry, and electroplating. At this time, Charles Faust developed the method of electropolishing, an important standard process for finishing metals. Other fields were opened that would play an important part in the history of the institute—and the world.

---

*Boehm, George A. W., and Alex Groner, *Science in the Service of Mankind*, Lexington Books, D. C. Heath and Company, 1972.

In this same segment of time, the institute pioneered some of the work in the use of radioactive tracer techniques. Battelle scientists were the first to use radioactive materials to study an industrial problem—specifically, that of wear in bearings. It was also during these years that Battelle began the development of *methods* of research. The team approach, as opposed to Mellon's one-man/one-project concept, came into use, requiring the speedy formation and sometimes speedy dissolution of groups of research workers cooperating toward a common objective. This multidisciplinary approach was to play a significant role in the war efforts that were beginning to crank up.

The year 1939 was significant for Battelle—it marked the first contract for research for the federal government. The U.S. Army project concerned the improvement of armor plate. As part of its public service activities, the institute staff performed the work at cost, without the usual markup for overhead. Other government contracts were performed on the same basis, but the flood of military research requests soon made the continuation of this practice infeasible. The usual markup had to be charged. When Japan attacked Pearl Harbor in December 1941 and the United States entered the war, Battelle, like the rest of the nation, gave the government its complete support. Director Clyde Williams went to Washington to head the newly created War Metallurgy Committee, and he, backed up by his Battelle staff, made significant contributions to the war effort. Undoubtedly, he, more than any other one individual, "spread the word" for Battelle, using every conceivable opportunity to sell its product—applied research. It is an understatement to say that his 23 years at the helm were anything short of extraordinary in the area of making the world aware of Battelle, aware to the point that industrialists were finally beginning to think of research as an essential part of their budgeted activities. The tables were starting to reverse themselves . . . with the industrialist now beating a path to the scientist. Much credit for this reversal must be given to Clyde Williams—the scientific research salesman *extraordinaire*.

Battelle was prepared and equipped to lead the search for the new materials needed in the conduct of the war. The institute had acquired a reputation during its early history of having certain expertise in the field of rare metals, one of which was uranium. The managers of a top secret research project recognized this superior knowledge and assigned to the institute the task of working and handling alloys of the metal. After the war, it was disclosed that 400 institute staff members had worked in the Manhattan District of the U.S. Army Corps of Engineers, as the atomic bomb program was then known. In 1943, the institute extruded the uranium fuel elements used for the first full-scale nuclear reactor at Oak Ridge, Tennessee. Projects involving this metal continued and, in 1949, Battelle developed the prototypes of the fuel elements in the *Nautilus*, the first nuclear-powered submarine and, in that same year, Battelle invented and developed the ion-exchange process for extracting uranium from its ores. Today more than 50 percent of the world's uranium supply is recovered by procedures based on this process.

THE POSTWAR ERA . . . AND A BRILLIANT DISCOVERY

The war ended in 1945 with the dropping of the atomic bomb, but an expected postwar slump never materialized at Battelle. The war had produced many changes—political, technological, and sociological—and there was a subtle change in attitude toward science as well. The people of the world began to recognize that civilization was truly dependent on science. Electronics, transportation, and communication had radically altered the relations among individuals, communities, and nations. Obviously, the world would never be the same as it was before the war. Many new wartime discoveries had opened additional avenues of research that, of necessity, had to be ignored during the frantic war years. The end of the war reopened those avenues, and new peacetime inventions were created. One of the most remarkable of these discoveries was electrostatic printing or photography. The process, which evolved into xerography, went almost unnoticed during the tumultuous war years, but about a decade later, its successful development and perfection were to make it the most momentous project Battelle ever undertook. The monetary rewards the institute and the inventor were to reap from this unspectacular success proved to be phenomenal.

The discovery itself was not an overnight success. It was the creation of one man, Chester F. Carlson, who, with many years of personal effort and much aid from a Battelle subsidiary, developed a method of photoreproduction which combined obscure and neglected phenomena into a dry-copying process. The complete story of this great scientific breakthrough is told in Chapter IX of this book, but for narrative purposes now, it is significant to know that by 1969, Xerox® Corporation had unmistakably joined the ranks of the industrial giants, with its worldwide revenues reaching $1.48 billion. Battelle, for its share in the development of xerography, received over a 10-year period cash and stock valued at $40.2 million at the time of receipt.

The stock, of course, eventually split a number of times and grew dramatically in market value. And for Chester Carlson, who as a young attorney was very "conscious of the tedious and time-consuming processes of copying contracts, pleadings, and briefs and of sending out drawings to be photocopied,"* (thus recognizing the need for a fast, inexpensive means of copying), there were monies to put a permanent end to his years of privation and struggle.

BDC, SAI, AND BATTELLE "INTERNATIONAL"

The concept behind the establishment of the Battelle Development Corporation (BDC) in 1935 was basically the belief of Battelle president Clyde Williams that "ideas should make money." Battelle scientists were fruitfully bearing the ideas, but many times the notions would not progress beyond that embryonic stage. Williams established BDC as the vehicle by which patentable ideas could be further developed and refined to the point of being salable to industry. Indeed, if BDC had not existed, xerography probably would not have come through Battelle at all.

Other successes of the corporation have included a process for waterproofing leather and a typewriter correction fluid Snopake®. In the early stages, all projects came to BDC from Battelle, but later, outside sources began to supply a goodly percentage of the projects undertaken (Xerox® being a notable example). Today, BDC officials consider approximately 600 inventions that are submitted annually, narrowing the field to about a dozen for funding by the corporation. The selection criteria include patentability; technical feasibility; and the nature, size, and penetrability of markets. Of that original 600, only three or four ideas ever reach the market. This low percentage unfortunately exists because of the undaunted unwillingness of private industry to accept some new development. In the history of BDC, not more than 12 of its marketed products have ever paid their own way. And yet this subsidiary performs a vital, essential function for Battelle Memorial Institute and continues to be allocated sufficient funds for its operation. Who can tell when another Xerox® innovation will gravitate toward Columbus, Ohio?

To deal with the aforementioned unwillingness of industry to accept new developments, in 1962, Battelle instituted Scientific Advances, Inc.

---

*Ibid., p. 37.

(SAI), an operation designed to take the high-risk products shunned by industry and market them. This mission has involved forming new companies to market the products once they have been developed to that point and then going public with the company or disposing of it after continuing profitability has been assured. Recently, Sensotec, Inc., a company formulated in this manner, traveled the complete cycle and was spun-off by SAI. UNIRAD, a company concerned with ultrasonic medical diagnostics, is now experiencing rapid growth. Another venture of SAIs is Holotron—a joint endeavor with DuPont (on a fifty-fifty basis) to seek out commercial uses for holography, the use of laser light to create three-dimensional pictures. Together then, BDC and SAI have provided two more avenues by which scientific advancement can become of practical use to industry and to society in general. Of course it is hoped that Battelle's willingness to go "out on the proverbial limb" for a particular product or process will encourage industrial concerns to modernize their thinking and actively make R&D a more important part of their operations.

Battelle's interests in scientific research outside the United States go back to early times and the days of Horace Gillett, who conscientiously kept abreast of research progress across the seas, particularly in Germany and her advances in the field of metallurgy. Ironically, after the war, intense survey and study revealed to Battelle that Germany was the European country most conducive to the advent of contract research. It turned out that this postwar interest on the part of Battelle occurred at just the right time, because the German industrial revival was just getting started, and many firms needed all the help they could get. Frankfurt was subsequently chosen as Battelle's German site, opening its doors in the summer of 1953. Concentration at first was on those "growing" industries of the period, for the major market for contract research was there—in physics, electronics, and chemistry. In only five years, Frankfurt was self-supporting, but not before weathering a storm of allegations, including: (1) Battelle-Frankfurt was a new tool of the U.S. State Department; (2) it was established to spy for U.S. industry; (3) the activities engaged in there were so assigned to get research done at cut rates; and (4) native scientists were being proselyted off to America. Actually, the "brain drain" to the United States was just starting, but it would have happened regardless of Battelle's presence in Germany. In answer to the other alleged offenses, European nationals primarily were used as directors and staff members; no recruitment of Europeans for Columbus Laboratories was engaged in; and projects were placed in either America   or Europe on the basis of where the work could be best executed and not as a means of exploiting economic advantages in Germany.

Battelle's other European branch was located in Geneva, where its laboratory was more international in concept, as opposed to Frankfurt, which was originally Germany oriented only. The choice of the Geneva site was based on the international flavor of Switzerland and the fact that the Swiss franc was convertible, an economic consideration that was all important during the uncertain postwar period. Battelle-Geneva differed from Frankfurt in another way—the environment there was not noisy with industrial revitalization, and the basic Battelle approach of contract research was simply not applicable. Instead, this laboratory had to generate ideas, products, processes from within and then develop the salable items to completion, or close thereto, before presenting them to potential sponsors. The original geographic philosophy regarding the "territory" of Battelle-Geneva was that it would take care of all of Europe except Germany, which was the domain of Battelle-Frankfurt. This scheme soon changed as Frankfurt began to get projects from other countries and Geneva from the "Roman" countries, primarily. Another rather obvious division resulted because of the location of, and more importantly, the leadership of the two laboratories, and that was the trend toward Geneva getting the basic research and Frankfurt the applied. This difference was perceptively expressed by one of the early "Battelle International" employees: "Germany needed Battelle; Switzerland tolerated it."

The real significance of Battelle's European laboratories was the proof that American science and technology could be successfully transported abroad, even into industrial nations. In 1970, Sherwood Fawcett, president of Battelle since 1968, prepared a white paper projecting Europe's economy in the future. The interesting conclusion he reached was that it would be wise for Battelle to expand its overseas activities in Europe and in Asia as well, since in 1970, Geneva and Frankfurt with their combined staffs of over 1500 operated in the black, while American laboratories slipped into the red.

STABILIZING, LOOKING AHEAD, DIVERSIFYING, AND MATURING

BATTELLE INSTITUTE

From a pragmatic point of view, a successful business must eventually reach a point of economic stability so that the administrators can predict future

The Columbus Laboratories of Battelle Memorial Institute, Columbus, Ohio.

growth and indulge in long-range planning. Such a point was not reached at Battelle until the end of the 1950s, at which time Xerox® money was steadily coming in and the European laboratories had become self-sustaining. Once this enviable state was reached, President Bert Thomas was eager to have the trustees consider the funding of $1 million per year to an effort to be called Battelle Institute (BI). This was not to be a new laboratory but a fund through which fields not yet ripe for contract research could be further explored and developed. That amount has since grown to over $7 million per year.

Bert Thomas succeeded Clyde Williams as president of BMI in 1957, being the natural choice since he had served as acting director when Williams was away during the war. Thomas showed much greater interest in staff matters than his predecessors: he encouraged staff-community functions, seminars, talks, symposia, etc., for which purpose he had an auditorium and conference rooms built at Columbus. Other innovations for which he was responsible include the Battelle laboratories and projects abroad and Battelle-Northwest. He combined a rather fundamental belief that science owed a debt to society with a knack for originating the right idea at the appropriate time. As for the selling of research, he sort of "let that take care of itself." The business/sales world of Clyde Williams was as foreign to Thomas as it was to Gillett.

Battelle Northwest Laboratories, Richland, Washington.

ENTRY INTO SOFT SCIENCES

This security of economic soundness, the vehicle of BI, and the new Thomas regime characterized by intellect and inventiveness allowed Battelle to enter into areas theretofore unencroached upon; that is, there was not merely diversification in well-established fields or disciplines but rather a branching out into new domains—education, medical care, oceanology, regional planning, desert ecology, pollution control, urban problems. Until Thomas's regime, of course, the interest and diversification had been in the *hard* sciences, but his guided penetration into the *soft* science world eventually accounted for 12 percent of the Columbus Laboratories' work. The economists were among the first of the "soft" groups to gainfully establish themselves and offer undeniably valuable assistance in the advancement of the hard science program. They were responsible for the establishment of Aids to Corporate Thinking, "a large group research project to which many companies subscribe in order to learn Battelle's analysis of technical and business trends five to 15 years in the future."*

In the early 1960s, Battelle contributed to the field of education through application of its staff of psychologists to the innovative programed instruction, and in 1966, it entered into its first public educational research project. This was a study of 90 Ohio school districts, from which the Center

---

*Ibid., p. 72.

for Improved Education evolved. This organization applied its expertise to a variety of problems in education, including student health services, minority group problems, and land acquisition for new facilities. The penetration of applied research into the field of education has, of necessity, been cautious as have applications of science to pressing urban problems.

BATTELLE-NORTHWEST

The most significant diversification activity for Battelle was the acquisition in 1964 of the management contract for the Atomic Energy Commission's Hanford Laboratory in Richland, Washington. Through this venture, Battelle gained 1800 staff members and a fourth major research center—renamed the Pacific Northwest Laboratories—as well as the accrued experience of the personnel there in monitoring nuclear wastes.

Sherwood Fawcett, a nuclear physicist who excelled during the empire-building days of Clyde Williams, came to Battelle in 1950 and immediately set about to create his own empire in nuclear physics, increasing a nucleus of 27 people into an impressive group of 83 quality personnel in only two years. Thoroughly competent, Fawcett was a natural for taking on the Hanford Laboratory when Battelle pulled off that coup. His belief that every new venture needs a "fanatic" could not be more clearly evidenced than by these two accomplishments of his—the Department of Metallurgy and Physics at Columbus and the Pacific Northwest Laboratories. Sherwood Fawcett was one of two men in the final running for the job of BMI president upon Bert Thomas's retirement, and since he had displayed his worth in competently handling the Battelle-Northwest venture, he was the eventual choice.

The quest for a closer relationship, an intermingling, of Battelle professionals with outstanding individuals in the academic world was another diversification venture which Bert Thomas pursued . . . with great gusto. Early in his presidency, Thomas initiated the endowment of professorships at The Ohio State University and actively encouraged the interchanging of ideas between staffs. With the establishment of Battelle-Northwest, there came an opportunity to create an even closer bond between Battelle employees there and those of the University of Washington. The creation was the Seattle Research Center, opened in 1967 and comprised of several long-term fellows—the nucleus—and varying numbers of visiting fellows who stay for periods ranging from a few weeks to a year to work on projects of special importance, write books, polish theories, etc. This center has succeeded remarkably in enhancing Battelle's image and with its fine reputation has attracted some of the world's most illustrious scientists with whom Battelle personnel have had the advantage to associate in an almost retreat-like atmosphere.

BATTELLE AND THE FUTURE

To say that Battelle has reached its peak would be as preposterous as the remark of the commissioner of patents in 1844 when he quipped that the number of patents could hardly go any higher. The limits of scientific re-search are as nebulous as man's own limitations as a living, inquisitive, mo-tivated human being. Currently, new projects unimaginable 20 years ago are being approached at Battelle: a study for NASA of man's nutritional needs in space; a plan to better route passengers and baggage at large airports; renewed interest in magnetohydrodynamics (MHD), a way of generating electric power by blowing streams of gas and charged particles between pairs of electrodes; an attack on the zooming costs of health care; and greater utilization of our country's ores (long a specialty of Battelle) to alleviate somewhat the paralyzing energy crunch. An exciting reaffirmation of Battelle's interest in education has occurred as recently as 1971 when the institute announced plans for an Academy for Contemporary Problems to be funded by Battelle and to do research on public problems of all kinds, promote the application of knowledge, and provide advanced training. The venture is being funded on a fifty-fifty basis by an argeement between Battelle and Ohio State.

Growing pains, of course, are associated with diversification, as they are with vertical growth, and the pain most keenly felt by Battelle has been that in the area of personnel. In the era of Clyde Williams, the rise to division chief was possible for an individual by his bringing in a certain amount of revenue in contracts. The fear is that too many chiefs will surface and there-after see no further growth. Battelle has always prided itself in the offering of advancement to whomever earns it. The institute does not want able and bright youngsters to rise rapidly to a point and then stagnate because the higher levels of the organization have little room for them. Perhaps the solution is the addition of European, and perhaps Asian, laboratories sug-gested in Fawcett's 1970 white paper. At the present, however, there is no dead end in sight for dedicated, deserving employees just as there is no foreseeable plateau or decline in the activities of Battelle itself.

For many years Battelle has been engaged in a discussion with the IRS regarding the tax exempt status of its contract research operations; finally, in late 1974, Battelle decided to relinquish its tax exempt status so as to preserve its ability to conduct contract research to meet its objectives as outlined in the Battelle Will. This was done at a cost of $46.8 million in taxes and interest; however, Battelle continues as a not-for-profit corporation under the laws of the state of Ohio, and it is anticipated that its contract research operations will continue and expand in substantially the same manner as in the past.

Battelle has also been engaged in a court case with the Attorney General of the state of Ohio concerning the interpretation of the Battelle Will, including amounts distributable to other charities. The case is still pending at the time of publication of this book.

Distributions from the Battelle portfolio resulting from the above will represent a major reduction in funds available to Battelle, and will place a premium on the development of innovative concepts for future growth. Fawcett obviously intends that Battelle shall continue and grow, and this is possible only through outstanding people with dedication to research and its utilization. His plans envision this combination.

CHAPTER V

THE FIRST NONENDOWED RESEARCH INSTITUTE*

THE ORIGIN OF ARMOUR

Patronage and endowments by a Gordon Battelle or an Andrew or Richard Mellon were not essential elements in the formation of the not-for-profit, independent research institutes listed in the Preface of this book: The first *nonendowed* research institution to emerge on the American industrial scene was the Research Foundation of Armour Institute of Technology, organized in September 1936. The name was to undergo a period of metamorphosis during which time it was changed to the Armour Research Foundation, affiliated with the university (Armour Institute of Technology or Armour Tech), and finally to the present name of the Illinois Institute of Technology Research Institute (IITRI), which is affiliated with the Illinois Institute of Technology.

An interesting historical note regarding Illinois Tech is the fact that its predecessor Armour Institute of Technology was founded by Phillip D. Armour in 1892. This man, who himself had a spectacular rise from lowly beginnings to great wealth and prominence, had no difficulty in understanding the aspirations of young men who were to reach upward in search of academic advancement from the less prosperous strata of society. In the year prior to the founding of the educational institution of Armour Tech, Mr. Armour had heard a sermon in his church in Chicago by the pastor the Reverend Dr. Frank W. Gunsaulus in which he emphasized the need for educational facilities to assist "poor boys in the Chicago area that deserved a college education." Following this sermon, Mr. Armour asked questions of the minister and learned that about $1.5 million would start such an institution. Mr. Armour made an immediate commitment to donate just that amount, providing the minister would become its president. An agreement

---

*The author's intimate involvement necessitates the use of the first person point of view in this chapter.

151

Armour

Gunsaulus

between the gentlemen was reached, and subsequently, two main buildings were constructed for the college, which was to emphasize engineering. In addition, Armour constructed 150 apartments in the immediate neighborhood, the rental income from which became the endowment for the educational institution.

In the early years, these apartments were considered to be the finest in Chicago; however, as time passed, they lost this prestige and began to depreciate, eventually into a very blighted neighborhood. The result was the loss of practically all income generated therefrom, and so the endowment for the institute was lost. This necessitated an annual pilgrimage by Mr. George Allison, treasurer of the institute, to members of the Armour family, who upon request, obligingly wrote a check to cover that year's deficit. Phillip Armour's son J. Ogden Armour carried on this family tradition through the years until about 1924, when reverses in his financial situation became so severe that he had to give up the support of the institution. However, this unfortunate event did not forebode the closing of Armour Tech because in 1926, the alumni and friends of the college raised $1 million which provided for seven years' continued operation. In 1933, when this fund had been depleted and the deep depression of the early 1930s threatened the liquidation of the institution, a number of Armour alumni rose to the occasion. These individuals, who had become very successful businessmen in the Chicago area, did not want to see their institution extinguished, and so they decided to have a series of studies made to determine exactly how a college like Armour Tech could best serve the industrial needs of Chicago. From these studies, the following needs were identified: (1) a substantially expanded evening school program so that advanced degrees could be afforded to deserving students; (2) a cooperative course in mechanical engineering whereby companies could engage the services of a pair of young male students to accomplish a year-round job effort; that is, one student would work for a semester while the other was in school and vice versa; and (3) a research facility for industrial concerns. This final project was the initial mention of the applied research institution that was to become the Research Foundation of Armour Institute of Technology, later the Armour Research Foundation, and finally IITRI. All three activities were initiated by 1936, and the board of trustees of Armour Tech was expanded from a very few to over 50 of the leading industrialists and professional people in Chicago.

During 1935, Dr. Phillips, the professor of municipal and sanitary engineering at the institute, passed away, and since I was trained in this field (at the time a partner in the firm of Allen and Vagtborg, Inc., Municipal Consulting Engineers of Chicago), I was asked by Henry T. Heald, then dean of the college, to take over the two courses Professor Phillips had been conducting. I accepted, and thus began my association with Armour Tech. Incidentally, Dean Heald was later to serve as president of three organizations— Armour Tech, New York University, and the Ford Foundation. As time went on, I became more involved with Armour Tech and at the same time disenchanted with municipal engineering because of some of the practices of that era involving, in my opinion, unethical relationships with city councils.

By 1937, the research foundation had been formed, with Dr. Thomas Poulter as scientific director. I had been named its executive director and a year or two later was made director, with Dr. Poulter, a very distinguished scientist, continuing as scientific director. He had been senior scientist and second in command of the recent Byrd expedition to the Antarctic. Together we teamed up to do what we could with no endowment, building the Foundation strictly by the so-called "bootstrap" method. In fact, the entire operation at Armour was of the bootstrap type, and several of us had to wear many hats. For example, in 1938, I was not only director of the research foundation, but also executive secretary of the board of trustees of Armour Institute, executive assistant to its president, professor of municipal and sanitary engineering, chief of the maintenance department for the entire institution, and public relations officer for the complete program—all at a salary of $6000 per year.

From the beginning of time, it has been a policy of most institutions of higher learning in the United States to permit faculty members to supplement their salaries by doing consulting work for industrial and governmental clients. At the present time, these institutions place a limit on the amount of time that a faculty member can devote to such activities. Conversely, years ago there was virtually no policy across the board in the United States. In the case of Armour Institute personnel, who earned relatively meager salaries, even for those times, there were no limitations or restrictions at all on consulting-type work. As a matter of fact, many of the faculty members engaged in testing work and used the laboratories of the institute. In a few instances, these laboratories were used to such an extent for this type of outside work that students found it difficult to utilize them. It was also allowable then for faculty members to give expert testimony in court cases. All in all, the spectrum of such activities led to conflicts of interest that often became very embarrassing to the institution. Over the past 40 or 50 years, problems such as these, which exist primarily in engineering and scientific schools, have grown in complexity and difficulty in almost direct relationship to the industrialization of this country. The same situation could arise in developing countries throughout the world, thus making the knowledge of a viable solution advantageous. In the cases of the larger educational institutions that have been bothered by the problem, the procedure has been to organize a separate entity that is, at the same time, related to the institution and under its control; all questionable activities engaged in by faculty members are cleared through this organization.

INDEPENDENCE FROM UNIVERSITY CONTROL

In the last 30 years, at least 60 research foundations or institutions closely associated with an educational institution and under its control have been organized; however, Armour Research Foundation has always been considered an independent because it has had its own charter, board of trustees, and in the early years, its own officers to conduct all business transactions, the director being the chief executive officer. This organizational structure was later changed so that the president of Illinois Tech (the educational institution) is today also the president of the research foundation. Such action was taken so that the offspring could be brought closer to the mother, thus causing a very close coordination of all activities. Although a closer bond exists today, the creation of the research foundation at Armour Tech has in no way ever interfered with the basic research work done in the graduate school. This was and is as it should be. A testimony to the success of the coexistence and mutual stimulation provided by the two activities is represented by the Technology Center in Chicago, as these institutions and others associated with them are called, a center recognized for greatness in both basic sciences and technology.

With these concepts serving as bases at the time the research foundation was created, the president of Armour Tech proclaimed to the entire faculty of the school that, henceforth, all testing and research activities would be handled through the newly created organization, which thereby served Armour as the aforementioned "separate entity"; that all fees would be paid to the organization; and that, by volunteering to engage in such activities, each faculty member could become a staff member of the organization with a fixed salary adjustment as an offset to the compensation he had been receiving for work he had been doing on his own.

* * *

THE ART OF SELLING RESEARCH

CONTRACTS FROM A TO Z

In my capacity as executive director of the research foundation, I quickly learned that, although many of the industries of Chicago did physical testing and chemical analysis as product control measures, there was hardly anything in the way of applied research underway in these organizations. A revelation, an education for these firms regarding the invaluable contribution of applied research was necessary. I determined that the best procedure would be to have a face-to-face discussion with the chief executive officer of each corporation that I contacted. Toward this end, I prepared an alphabetical list of 100 of the leading industrial corporations in Chicago, and by using that as a base as well as various other means, I made contacts, one by one, from company A to Z, oftentimes utilizing the offices of some of the institute's trustees. Before each of my discussions, I prepared myself with the knowledge of a number of case histories that related to that particular company and then left with each officer a brochure outlining our staff and facilities. Since the primary objective of these talks was to stimulate each company executive to look further into the possibilities of utilizing our services, the brochure was intended to provide such stimulation after he had taken the time to give the proposition some thought and make some investigations of his own. Though my intention was to run the gamut from A to Z, I never got beyond the letter "L" because by that time, the A, B, and C corporations were coming in with modest research programs. This is reflected in the records that show, at Armour in the early days, the largest number of sponsors were corporations that had names occurring in the first half of the alphabet, with very few coming in the latter part. However, a "W" did appear along with the first half grouping. It represented the Whiting Corporation, the president of which, General Hammond, was also president of the research foundation board of trustees.

MULTIDISCIPLINARY APPROACH

From the very beginning at Armour, we emphasized the group or inter-disciplinary approach to each research problem as opposed to the Mellon Plan. In early Armour studies to determine just how we could best contrib-ute to the research needs of the industry in the area, we had noted that the few companies that did have internal research activities had their R&D concentrated in a single scientific discipline. In other words, if the industry were a chemical manufacturer, the few people engaged in research were all chemists, and, likewise, if the firm happened to be a metals manufacturing organization, the researchers were primarily metallurgists. It was, therefore, our goal at Armour to develop our staff to incorporate as many and diverse scientific disciplines as possible. In that way, we would be able to serve even the largest corporations having in-house research departments in good fashion. This approach became standard at Armour, thus exemplifying our endorse-ment of the concept of a group approach to the special problems of industry. To present this concept to potential sponsors, we prepared a brochure, which is reproduced hereafter (pp. 157-166) entitled "Searchlights," considered at the time to be very novel.

CONCENTRATION ON PHYSICS AND MECHANICAL ENGINEERING

As indicated earlier in the book, any survey of research activity throughout American industry in the thirties reflected that, by far, the greatest activity was in the chemical industry. For this reason, at Armour, we decided to concentrate on the "untapped resources," emphasizing staff development in the fields of physics and mechanical engineering, with secondary emphasis given to metallurgy, mineralogy, chemistry, and chemical engineering. This strategy proved to be wise, and from the very beginning, we were able to undertake programs (for example, for chemical companies) into which we could interject additional disciplines, thus adding increasing dimensions and chances for success to problem-solving efforts.

Searchlights

RMOUR RESEARCH FOUNDATION

Founded to Render
a Research and Engineering Service to
Industry

THE
ARMOUR PLAN
FOR
INDUSTRIAL
RESEARCH

ARMOUR RESEARCH FOUNDATION

An Industrial Research Institute Not for Profit,
Affiliated with Illinois Institute of Technology

THIRTY-THIRD, FEDERAL AND DEARBORN STS.

CHICAGO, ILLINOIS

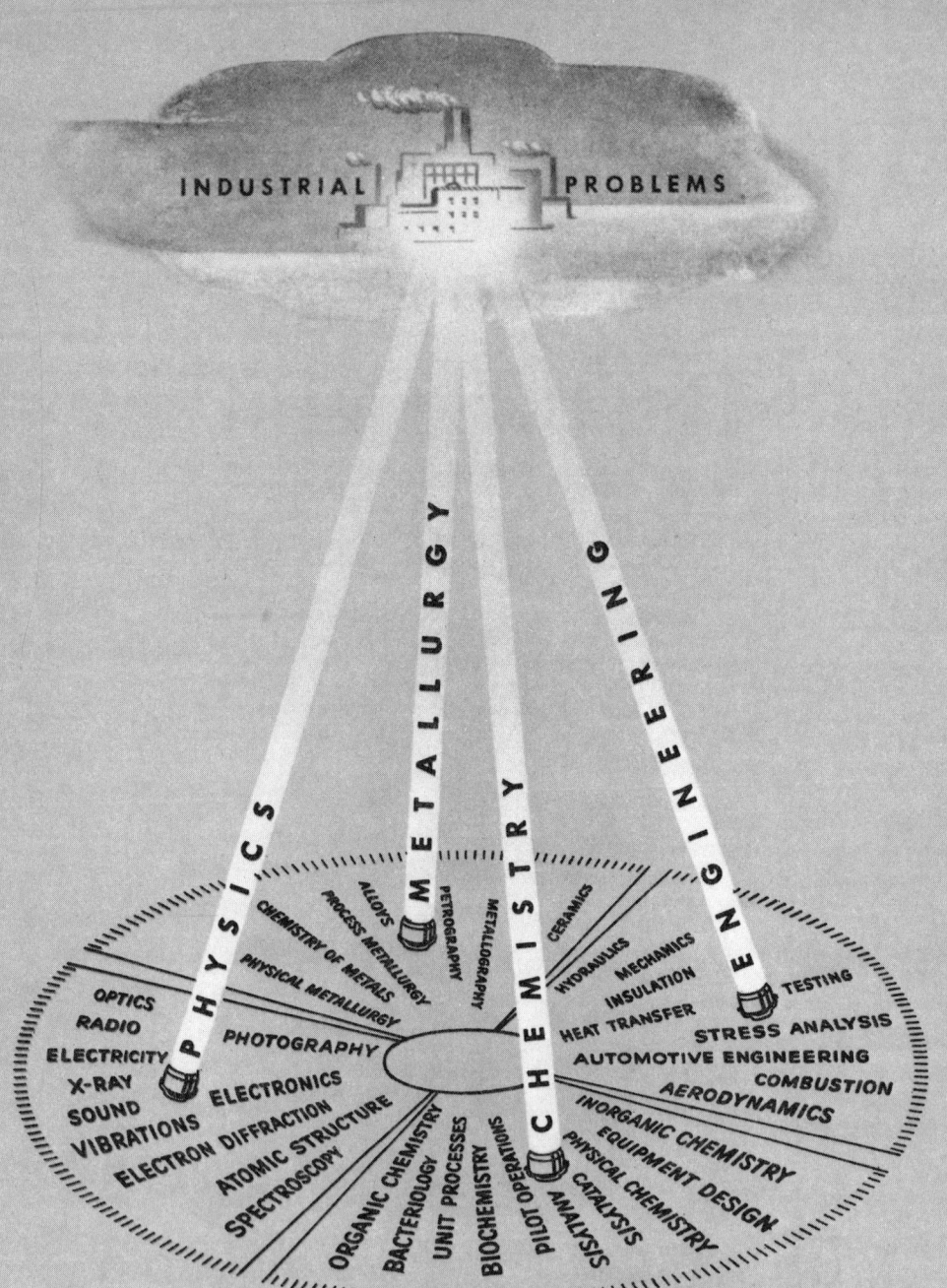

INDUSTRIAL PROBLEMS

PHYSICS

METALLURGY

CHEMISTRY

ENGINEERING

CHEMISTRY OF METALS
PROCESS METALLURGY
PHYSICAL METALLURGY
ALLOYS
PETROGRAPHY
METALLOGRAPHY
CERAMICS
HYDRAULICS
MECHANICS
INSULATION
HEAT TRANSFER
TESTING
STRESS ANALYSIS
AUTOMOTIVE ENGINEERING
COMBUSTION
AERODYNAMICS
INORGANIC CHEMISTRY
EQUIPMENT DESIGN
PHYSICAL CHEMISTRY
CATALYSIS
ANALYSIS
PILOT OPERATIONS
BIOCHEMISTRY
UNIT PROCESSES
BACTERIOLOGY
ORGANIC CHEMISTRY
SPECTROSCOPY
ATOMIC STRUCTURE
ELECTRON DIFFRACTION
VIBRATIONS
SOUND
X-RAY
ELECTRICITY
RADIO
OPTICS
PHOTOGRAPHY
ELECTRONICS

THE ARMOUR PLAN FOR INDUSTRIAL RESEARCH

SEARCHLIGHTS PROBE the sky. Slowly their great swing narrows. Now they converge, in unerring focus, upon the object of their search. Once more, scientific achievement mounts guard over a nation.

From the four quarters of the compass these searchlight beams shoot upward . . . but with a single purpose. Theirs it is to locate the objective more quickly and to reveal it more clearly than any single beam could reasonably be expected to do.

Similar co-ordination of its own scientific resources for discovery is fundamental to the ARMOUR PLAN for INDUSTRIAL RESEARCH, developed by Armour Research Foundation in Chicago.

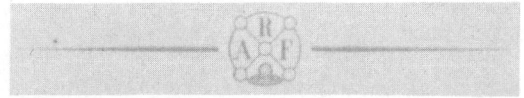

Experience has shown that any given industrial problem will be found to require particular scrutiny within a specific field of scientific activity . . . but the process of solution almost inevitably involves the bringing to bear upon it of resources from other fields, the relationship of which may not be immediately apparent.

The "searchlights" which the ARMOUR PLAN is prepared to focus upon industry's research problems represent the co-ordinated resources from the four broad fields of scientific endeavor . . . Chemistry, Physics, Metallurgy and Research Engineering. These are the quadrants of Armour Research Foundation service.

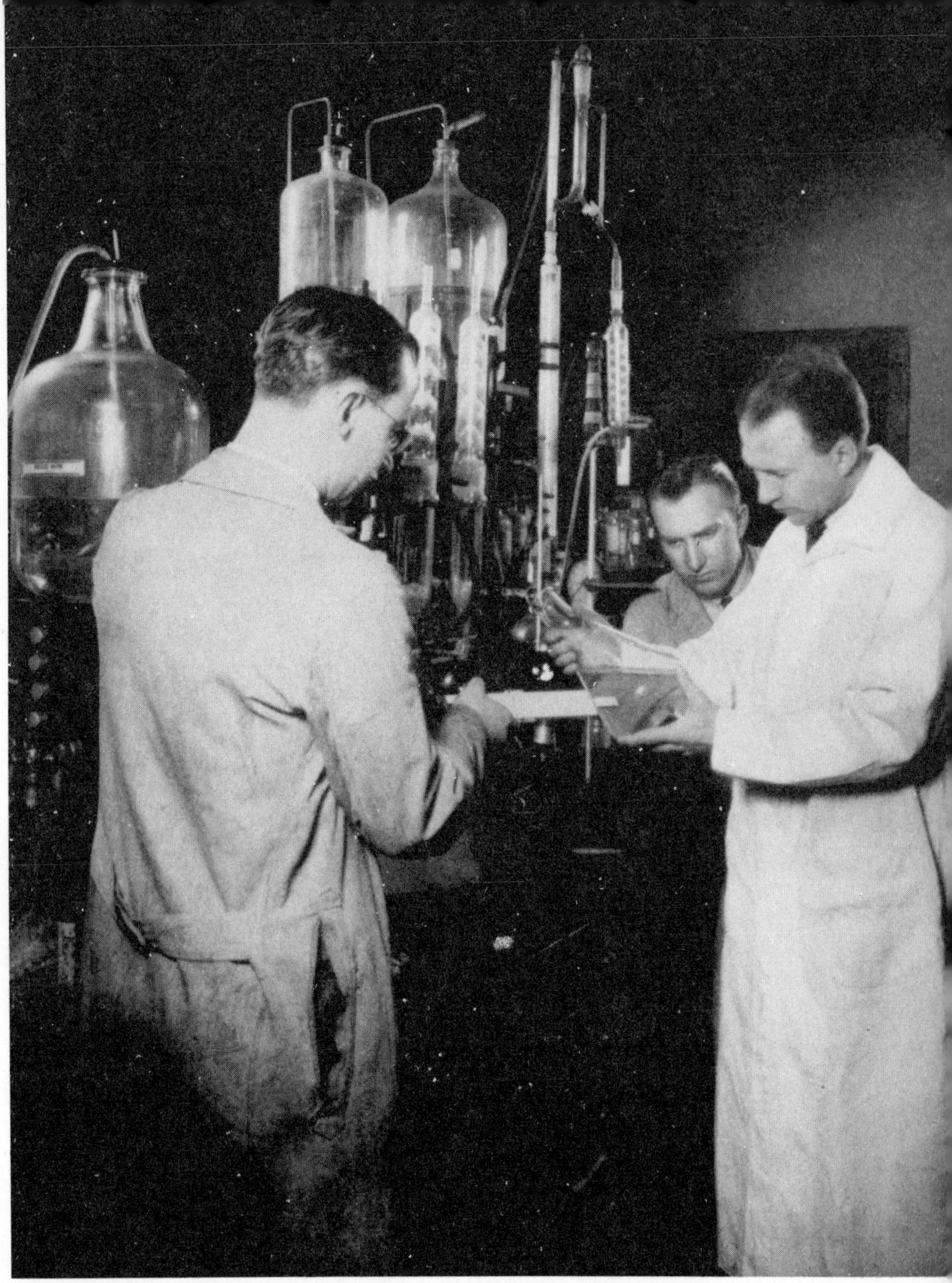

CHEMISTRY

Discussion of an experimental distillation product

UPON ACCEPTANCE, each project becomes the direct responsibility of the Foundation itself. Supervision and guidance are assumed by one of the Foundation's four section chairmen. The latter, in turn, assigns it to one or more of the Foundation's competent full-time research specialists, selected from existing staff, if available, or drawn from outside and added to the staff on the basis of qualifications and achievement.

The bulk of the work on each project is done by the man or men to whom it is assigned . . . but the PLAN developed by Armour Research Foundation provides that whenever the study leads temporarily into another scientific field, a staff specialist from that field is attached to the project.

As the project progresses, its pertinent developments and major problems become the subject of weekly presentation before the Foundation's Scientific Advisory Council, made up of 40 or more selected representatives from all four sections. Here ideas are pooled, for subsequent organization into plans of approach by a Steering Committee, which includes sponsor representation as well as Foundation staff members.

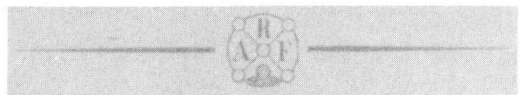

Under the ARMOUR PLAN, therefore, the creation of thought and ideas bearing upon a specific project involves not one but many minds . . . each approaching the problems as they develop, from a different angle.

THE PLAN permits no conflict of competitive interests. The Foundation does not undertake a specific research assignment for more than one sponsor. Agreements covering industrial research projects provide for patent rights, monthly and final reports, and the execution of the investigation and treatment of findings in strict confidence.

A particular project may, after careful study, be classified as constituting a problem in metallurgy. In this event it will be turned over to the Foundation's section of Metallurgy, and one or more staff members of that section assigned to it.

As the investigation proceeds, it may appear necessary to focus the resources of other sections upon the problem. Help may be required from allied sub-divisions in the metallurgical field, and also in chemistry, electricity, acoustics, mechanical engineering, and from similar sub-divisions of other sections.

Under the ARMOUR PLAN, the resources of all four sections of the Research Foundation are completely co-ordinated and geared for co-operative effort. All of their individual functions can be brought to bear at once, if necessary, toward the early solution of the entire problem. In such focus, responsibility for the sponsor's project is that of the entire cooperating staff.

PHYSICS

Consultation on the structure of an alloy specimen.

MEETING FREQUENTLY during the course of a project, the Steering Committee keeps the advancing work on the selected path, and decides the advisability of pursuing study in connection with incidental discoveries.

One man, with the collaboration of such assistants as he may require, then takes charge of the rapid prosecution of laboratory work and the organization of data. Uninterrupted progress is made possible by frequent and free consultation with the staff specialists in other fields. To conserve his time, the Foundation's photographers, draftsmen, machinists, carpenters and other craftsmen are at his disposal.

This in brief, is the ARMOUR PLAN for INDUSTRIAL RESEARCH, whereby the Foundation brings to each project competent analysis by research scientists representing distinct fields of endeavor. Thus the Foundation centralizes control of each project in its indicated field of research activity . . . at the same time making available the thought and effort of a full-time staff representing all other fields to which the project's problems may reveal a relationship.

The service involved is equally adaptable to the needs of larger corporations in the handling of specific "farmed-out" projects, and of smaller companies in connection with general research projects and "short-term" problems.

A project typical of those generated by our decision to emphasize physics and mechanical engineering in order to serve industries in disciplines auxiliary to their own was one for the Caterpillar Tractor Company. This project was undertaken in 1941 at the request of Caterpillar's director of research, Mr. Arthur Rosen. It serves to reflect how unprepared we were with regard to facilities and equipment in our attempts to service industrial concerns. Mr. Rosen was interested in having us undertake a project using physics to study the products of combustion at various positions in the piston stroke of diesel engines by utilization of spectroscopy in combination with a stroboscope. The program entailed use of a rather large single-cylinder diesel engine which was too heavy for the carrying capacity of the apartment units that we were occupying; therefore, I took Rosen down into the basement of the three-story building where he saw a dirty, dark, coal-dusted space, with no lighting, three coal bins, and three gravity-type hot-air furnaces that served the three apartments immediately above. He reacted by laughing and saying, "If you've got the nerve to show this to me as suitable space for this project, I've got the nerve to help you put it into shape. How much do you think it will cost?" I replied that for $500 we could tear out the partitions and old furnaces, clean up the place, put on a coat of white paint, and build an engine mounting. His reply was, "I'll tell you what I'll do; I'll make it $700 to give you a little leeway." This program got us started in very solid research in engine operations and the study of the products of combustion. A few years later, the scientist who was in charge of the program became a senior member on the staff of the Caterpillar Tractor Company's research department in Peoria, Illinois.

THE ARMOUR PLAN

This multidisciplinary concept, together with others that we developed to engender a feeling in industry that we could best serve as a corporation's research department, resulted in what became known as the "Armour Plan." Under this plan, an interdisciplinary steering committee was established to activate and guide each project, and provisions were made so that all patentable developments belonged to the sponsor, with the work being conducted with the same degree of confidence that would be expected from a corporation's own laboratory, if one existed. Another aspect of this plan concerned charges for services. They were based on the simple formula of the professional salaries involved, puls a 100 percent surcharge on such salaries. Also, it was a precept of Armour's that no program would be undertaken if it in any way conflicted with an earlier program that was already underway; further, it was our policy that a year must elapse before a program that had any relationship to a previous discontinued one would be undertaken.

The simple charging system came about in a rather interesting way. After two or three years of operation, we noted that our professional salaries represented approximately 50 percent of the total cost of operation. Thus, a surcharge of 100 percent on these salaries should then balance the budget. The scope of the surcharge included all items other than the professional salaries of those involved in the conduct of the project. There was no charge for the people on the steering committees because these costs were considered washouts since these people, acting in the capacity of advisors, were helping each other to a rather equal extent. In other words, the charge covered the cost of laboratory technicians, utilities, general administrative expenses of all types, depreciation, and the writing of reports. In time, this formula came to be used by institutions throughout the country, with a modification on the surcharge percentage depending upon the local situation and the development of fringe benefits that gradually became a rather major factor, especially in recent times.

Even though the institution had a deficit of $47,000 during its first year of operation, the plan really worked very well. The deficit resulted largely because of the acquisition of equipment. By the end of the third and fourth years, it became obvious that the 100 percent surcharge was more than adequate. By that time, we at Armour had reached the level of $1 million a year in research support and showed an income over expenses of $200,000. Upon the occurrence of this situation, I called together the chief officers of a number of sponsors that were involved in supporting this work and advised them of our financial status. I explained that two avenues were open to us: (1) to reduce our surcharge, or (2) to direct the income back into better facilities, equipment, and staff. Frankly I was surprised at their enthusiastic acceptance of the second avenue, namely the concept of self-improvement so that we could do a still better job for them as time went on. I also found that another suggestion of ours was entirely satisfactory to them, i.e., that they leave us "better off than they found us." Since we were exceedingly short of equipment, one of the charges made in addition to the surcharge formula— the only other charge—was for special equipment required on a sponsor's particular project. This equipment remained the property of the sponsor, but, at the conclusion of the project, more often than not the sponsor usually chose to "leave us better off" and donated the equipment to us. In this way, we were able to rapidly develop our assets and do a better job for subsequent sponsors, progress that was highly endorsed by our early sponsors.

Even though our third and fourth years showed such good fiscal results, we nevertheless had severe difficulties during the first three years. This resulted because salary monies or any other financial assistance by Armour Tech was terminated at the end of the first year. I vividly recall the necessity of having to go around to individual staff members on payday and ask each, "How much can you get by with?" This was the amount paid until we got in some receipts. In this way, we were able to stay afloat, and the staff members were able to meet their most pressing financial obligations.

AN AID THROUGH PUBLICITY

We felt that, in addition to our program of face-to-face discussions with industrial leaders on the matter of doing research, we needed some kind of a publication that would accomplish several goals: (1) a broader base of approach to solving a problem, (2) partial preparation for the people we contacted on a face-to-face basis, and (3) an excellent reminder to those contacts afterwards; however, we had no funds for such a project. When this problem was discussed with Mr. Robert Wishnick, president of Witco Corporation of New York, a graduate and trustee of Armour Institute and a chemical manufacturer, he not only agreed that the idea was excellent but was willing to fund it fully for the first year, 75 percent for the second, 50 percent for the third, and 25 percent for the fourth, with expectations that we could maintain it by the fifth year. Further, he provided outstanding public relations assistance and advertising counsel from the city of New York to develop an editorial policy that would make the concept successful. We decided to call this quarterly journal *The Frontier* for it represented a publication concerned with discussions of frontiers in science and technology. The editorial policy included such decisions as opting to have almost the entire journal written by outside authors who, in prosperous corporations, had had success through research in the development of new processes or products. These successes were related as case histories. Further, a portion of the publication's space was to be utilized to indicate newly discovered scientific information that might be of value to industry, and finally, one page, but only one page, was to be comprised of discussions of work at Armour. The first issue appeared in February 1938, and the journal has been published every year since, with some changes in editorial policy from time to time as circumstances justified.

At about the end of five years of operation at Armour, we had a survey made by a New York organization for the purpose of determining what people thought about us, who knew us, etc. We hoped to have other questions of this nature answered in order for us to further develop our relationships with the public in general and with industry in particular. The survey organization made contacts on a face-to-face basis with some 400 U.S. corporations throughout the country by a process of mixing our name with those of four other institutions, two of which were universities heavily oriented in research and the remainder, Mellon and Battelle. This study was very revealing, but of particular note here is that, even though our *Frontier* had only been published for two years, it was considered to be the second-best publication of its kind in the United States at the time. It must be remembered that there were no textbooks on the selling or managing of research or on the techniques of operating a successful research department. Consequently, industry was actually hungering for information of this kind, and as the years went by we were consistently told how valuable this device had been to American corporations in stimulating their thinking regarding research activities.

Publications at Armour also came to involve, as expected, annual reports. For some time, the *News Edition* of the American Chemical Society had been printing the annual report of Mellon Institute. When I had an occasion to see Mr. Walter Murphy, who was editor of this publication, I asked him if he could do likewise for us. He immediately said that he would be delighted to do so because he was beginning to get some criticism for having an annual report of only a single institution during the year; he reasoned that, with two, there would be less criticism. Thereupon, our third annual report to the board of directors, a total of four pages, appeared in the October 10, 1939, issue of the *News Edition*. By 1944, the annual report had grown to 14 pages in the *News Edition*, whereupon Walter Murphy found it necessary to discontinue the whole idea of printing annual reports of research institutions because several others had been asking him to do likewise for them. Nevertheless, the American Chemical Society did us a great service by following this practice for six full years. Even though progress was being made in "spreading the Armour word," we concluded as late as 1944 that something different was necessary. We decided to publish a sponsor's manual, which first appeared in early 1945, for the purpose of explaining to a sponsor how to get involved in research activity as a benefit to his company and how to conduct himself in relationships with his program at Armour. The

Foreword to this booklet was written by Dr. Francis Godwin and is reproduced here to show the "spirit of the times."

Foreword

For those of us who engage in it as a profession, scientific research on any subject is the most absorbing of occupations. To us research is a state of mind, and at any given moment the particular object of our study is of less importance than the fact that something needs to be found out about it.

But, remembering the traditional shoemaker's children, we have been prompted to wonder whether enough study has been given to the subject of *research itself*. As a matter of fact, we began wondering this in September 1936, the day the Armour Research Foundation was born. Since then Research Project A-1, best described as a search for improved methods for conducting research, has been of greater interest to us than any other single study. The project is not finished, and it never will be. Even at this stage, however, we are able to see some basic principles.

One of the first observations from our notes is that successful industrial research depends upon executive understanding. Therefore this booklet has been written to dispel some of the mystery with which a few persons have surrounded research; to define some terms, methods, reasonable expectations and limitations in research as we see them now; to answer some of the questions which are asked of us most frequently; and to aid the industrial executive in crystallizing the plans and decisions which he must make in connection with research and his organization's future. The emphasis here is upon the What, When, and How of research, rather than the Why, for it is assumed that those who do not already know Why in all probability will not be in business for many years and will have little use for this material.

Introduction to Research is given to all those who wish to use the research services of the Armour Research Foundation, to be read as a preamble to further discussion of projected work on the basis of mutual understanding. Copies are available to all interested persons upon request. The Foundation invites comment and discussion on the content of the booklet, in the interest of whatever public service future editions may render, for we have a sincere desire to make research as useful as possible to industry.

It must be remembered that during this period of industrial development in the United States, there were no seminars being held anywhere in the country with relationship to the benefits of research, how to establish a research department, how to judge how much money to spend on research, and all the other aspects of utilizing applied research as a tool for growth and profit. There were no textbooks on this subject; there were no courses given at our educational institutions; and Mellon, Battelle, and Armour were following uncharted courses, but their sound philosophies prevailed, and they were thereby able to accomplish their mutual purpose.

* * *

THE SNOW CRUISER

In 1939, Armour embarked on a tremendous project for a research institute as new and small as ours. It resulted because of our scientific director, Dr. Thomas Poulter, who had been senior scientist on the Byrd expedition to the Antarctic in 1936 and in 1938. Admiral Richard E. Byrd asked Dr. Poulter if he could suggest any type of program that should be included in a forthcoming Byrd expedition to the Antarctic (1939-1940). From his previous experience, Tom had felt that one of the most important developments that was needed for exploration in the area was a vehicle that could cross crevasses, carry an airplane on its back to make surveys of the entire continent, and provide such facilities that would enable the scientific staff to move about rather readily in warm quarters. His idea resulted in the snow cruiser program at Armour, and although the institution was young and almost starving, we decided that this opportunity to create a very significant scientific and engineering development was too promising to pass up. The vehicle would have great public interest and thereby reflect favorably upon our institution as we sought a position in scientific, engineering, and industrial activity. The brochure that is reproduced herein sets forth the many interesting details of this project.

Through the generosity of American industry, we were able to finance the snow cruiser project in its entirety from contributions of money or materials that organizations made to the program. I distinctly recall approaching Walter Beech of the Beechcraft organization to help us in getting a Beechcraft plane, which would enable the necessary surveys of the continent, using the snow cruiser as a base. Mr. Beech was very much interested in the project and stated that, if I would get together all the necessary materials for the building of the plane, then he would provide the labor to

THE SNOW CRUISER

PROJECT No. 1-69

ANTARCTIC EXPEDITION · RESEARCH FOUNDATION OF ARMOUR INSTITUTE OF TECHNOLOGY ·

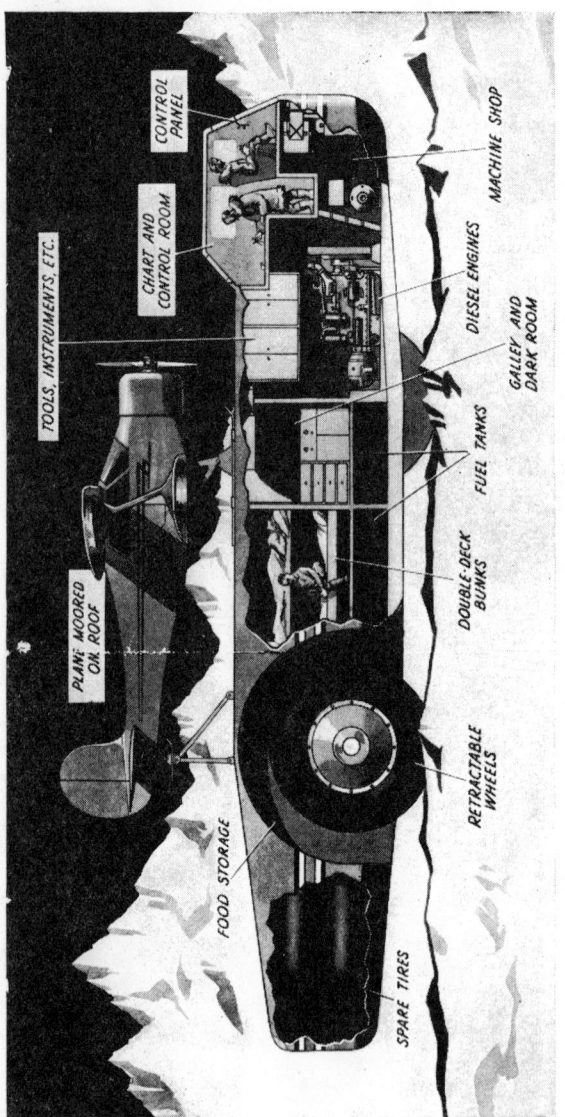

TOOLS, INSTRUMENTS, ETC.

CONTROL PANEL

CHART AND CONTROL ROOM

MACHINE SHOP

DIESEL ENGINES

GALLEY AND DARK ROOM

FUEL TANKS

DOUBLE-DECK BUNKS

PLANE MOORED ON ROOF

RETRACTABLE WHEELS

FOOD STORAGE

SPARE TIRES

The Story of the Snow Cruiser

PROJECT No. 1-69, RESEARCH FOUNDATION OF ARMOUR INSTITUTE OF TECHNOLOGY

HAROLD VAGTBORG, DIRECTOR

● Five years ago, while serving as second in command of the second Byrd Antarctic Expedition, Dr. Thomas C. Poulter, Scientific Director of the Research Foundation of Armour Institute of Technology, visualized what he considered the perfect exploration unit for use at the South Pole. He proceeded to plan a unit that would be a complete world of its own. . . . It would be mobile . . . equipped to span large crevasses in the ice and to cruise thousands of miles from its base or source of supplies; it would accommodate four or five men and provide them with living quarters and complete facilities for the pursuance of their scientific investigations . . . a radio station with which to maintain contact with stationary bases and the outside world.

During the past four months, Dr. Poulter has watched the product of his imagination develop into a monster of iron and steel and rubber and glass called the Snow Cruiser. Resembling a huge trans-continental bus of ultra-futuristic design, the Snow Cruiser is 55′ long, approximately 20′ wide and 15′ high, weighing — completely equipped — approximately 75,000 pounds. Shortly after November 1, the Snow Cruiser will be shipped from Boston. Two months later it will be unloaded on the Great Ice Barrier—where the Antarctic begins. There it will serve for three years as the mobile research and survey unit of the United States Antarctic Service.

The Snow Cruiser is a project of the Research Foundation of Armour Institute of Technology. It was designed by the staff of the Research Foundation under Dr. Poulter's direction. Its cost of $150,000 was defrayed by friends of the Foundation and more than seventy co-operating manufacturers. The Snow Cruiser is merely loaned to the government for the forthcoming expedition to the South Pole.

Both motive and auxiliary power for the Snow Cruiser is supplied by two 150 hp. diesel engines, each directly connected to a traction-type generator. A 75 hp. traction motor is affixed to each wheel and power may be directed to any one wheel or to any combination of one, two, three, or four wheels.

One of the most interesting features of the Snow Cruiser is the ingenious arrangement which will enable it to cross 15-foot crevasses in the ice. Each of the wheels is equipped with a hydraulic lift, making it possible to raise any one—or any combination—of the 10-foot, rubber-tired wheels a distance of four feet. When the Snow Cruiser reaches a crevasse, power is directed to the rear wheels, the front wheels are withdrawn and the back wheels push the nose across the crevasse. When the rear wheels reach the crevasse, the front wheels are lowered, power is diverted to them, the back wheels are drawn up and the tail of the Cruiser is pulled across the opening. Once across, the back wheels are lowered into normal position and the Cruiser proceeds under four-wheel drive.

The Snow Cruiser, which can turn around in its own length, move sidewise at a 25 degree angle or climb 37 per cent grades, has a cruising range of 5,000 miles and a maximum speed of 30 miles per hour. In the Antarctic, it will carry a year's supply of food for the four or five-man crew of scientists and technicians, two spare tires, 2,500 gallons of diesel fuel oil, and 1,000 gallons of gasoline for the five-passenger, ski-mounted cabin plane which will be moored on the top deck. The Snow Cruiser contains living quarters, combination galley and dark room, two-way radio station, engine room, $50,000 scientific laboratory, a machine shop and control room.

The plane will be equipped as a laboratory and will also carry special aerial cameras. It will operate within a 300-mile radius of its moving base, enabling the crew to photograph and map large unexplored areas of

Antarctica. It is hoped that the Snow Cruiser and its plane, together, will be able to accomplish more in the way of exploration and survey during its first three months in the Antarctic than have all previous expeditions combined.

Dr. Poulter will command the Snow Cruiser during its first three months in the South Pole region. When it returns for supplies to one of the two stationary bases to be established at strategic points, he will return to the United States, remaining in touch with the Snow Cruiser by means of radio. Dr. F. A. Wade, Chief Scientist of the United States Antarctic Expedition, will then become commander of the Snow Cruiser. Other members of the crew will include Corporal Felix Ferranto, radio operator, Theodore A. Petras, airplane pilot, both of the United States Marine Corps; Charles Meyer, chief machinist's mate, U. S. Navy; and "Navy," Dr. Wade's pet Labrador huskie, like his master, a veteran of the last Byrd expedition.

DR. F. A. WADE   DR. THOMAS C. POULTER

Stamp collectors will be interested to learn that the Snow Cruiser will carry special covers to the South Pole. These will be given a special cachet of historic significance, franked to the most currently available commemorative and dated on the day, hour and minute of arrival at the South Pole. These covers, individually to each collector, are being handled through the Fidelity Stamp Co., 945 Pennsylvania Ave., N W., Washington, D. C., at 50c per cover, or 12 for $5.00.

*The Research Foundation of Armour Institute of Technology expresses its appreciation for the cooperation of the following firms:

*The Research Foundation of Armour Institute of Technology is a corporate organization under the state laws of Illinois, established in 1936 to "render a research and experimental engineering service to industry; to conduct fundamental research for the purpose of improving our comforts of life and knowledge of science."

Allegheny Ludlum Steel Corp., Pittsburgh, Pa.
American Brass Company, Chicago, Ill.
American Chain & Cable Co., Inc., New York, N. Y.
American Flange & Mfg. Co., Inc., New York, N. Y.
Arens Controls, Inc., Chicago, Ill.
Armstrong Paint & Varnish Works, Chicago, Ill.
Bausch & Lomb Optical Co., Rochester, N. Y.
Graybar Electric Co., Inc., Chicago, Ill.
Grimes Manufacturing Company, Urbana, Ohio
The Hallicrafters, Inc., Chicago, Ill.
Ilg Electric Ventilating Company, Chicago, Ill.
Hamilton Standard Propellers Div.,
   United Aircraft Corporation, East Hartford, Conn.
Harbor Plywood Corporation, Chicago, Ill.
Hunter Sash Company, Inc., Flushing, N. Y.
Hydraulic Controls, Inc., Chicago, Ill.
Illinois Auto Electric Co., Chicago, Ill.
Inland Steel Company, Chicago, Ill.
S. Karpen and Brothers, Chicago, Ill.
Kem Plastic Playing Cards, Inc., New York, N. Y.
Kilborn-Sauer Corporation, Fairfield, Conn.
Lasker Boiler Works, Chicago, Ill.
De Vilbiss Company, Toledo, Ohio
The Dumore Company, Racine, Wis.
Eclipse Aviation, Bendix, N. J.
Electric Hose and Rubber Company, Chicago, Ill.
Electric Storage Battery Company, Philadelphia, Pa.
Fairbanks, Morse & Company, Chicago, Ill.
Foote Bros. Gear and Machine Corp., Chicago, Ill.
Gatke Corporation, Chicago, Ill.
General Electric Company, Schenectady, N. Y.
Goodwillie Green Box Company, Rockford, Ill.
Goodyear Tire & Rubber Company, Akron, Ohio
Protectoseal Company, Chicago, Ill.
Pyle National Company, Chicago, Ill.
Peabody Coal Company, Chicago, Ill.
Pioneer Instrument Company, Brooklyn, N. Y.
Polar Hardware Company, Chicago, Ill.
Pullman-Standard Car Mfg. Company, Chicago, Ill.
Pyrene Manufacturing Co., Chicago, Ill.
Standard Oil of Indiana, Chicago, Ill.

Sears, Roebuck & Company, Chicago, Ill.
Shepherd Chair Company, Chicago, Ill.
James H. Smith & Sons, Inc., Griffith, Ind.
Smith Welding Company, Minneapolis, Minn.
South Bend Lathe Works, South Bend, Ind.
Summerill Tubing Company, Bridgeport, Pa.
Suncook Mills, New York, N. Y.
Lincoln Electric Company, Cleveland, Ohio
Linde Air Products Company, New York, N. Y.
Link-Belt Company, Chicago, Ill.
Lord Manufacturing Company, Chicago, Ill.
Marshalltown Manufacturing Co., Marshalltown, Iowa
National Carbon Company, Inc., New York, N. Y.
D. W. Onan & Sons, Minneapolis, Minn.
Owen-Corning Fibre Glass Company, Toledo, Ohio
Pennsylvania Flexible Metallic Tubing Co. Chicago, Ill.
Pioneer Gen-E-Motor Corporation, Chicago, Ill.
Beech Aircraft Corporation, Wichita, Kans.
Blackmer Pump Company, Grand Rapids, Mich.
Borg and Beck Company, Chicago, Ill.
Braden Winch Company, Tulsa, Okla.
Bredouw Aeromotive Corporation, Kansas City, Mo.
Chase Brass & Copper Company, Chicago, Ill.
Chicago Belting Company, Chicago, Ill.
Chicago Metal Hose Corporation, Maywood, Ill.
Chicago Metal Manufacturing Company, Chicago, Ill.
Chicago Rawhide Manufacturing Company, Chicago, Ill.
Colin Products Company, Chicago, Ill.
Crane Company, Chicago, Ill.
Cummins Engine Company, Columbus, Ind.
Underwood-Elliott-Fisher Company, Chicago, Ill.
Timken Roller Bearing Company, Canton, Ohio
Vacuum Can Company, Chicago, Ill.
Vapor Car Heating Company, Inc., Chicago, Ill.
Westinghouse Air Brake Company, Chicago, Ill.
Weston Electrical Instrument Company, Newark, N. J.
Whiting Corporation, Harvey, Ill.
W. & L. E. Gurley, Troy, N. Y.
Wright Aeronautical Corporation, Patterson, N. J.
Young Radiator Company, Racine, Wis.

assemble it. He also supplied me with a list of people to contact for the needed parts—a group of companies numbering 117. I made all these contacts with most satisfactory results: all necessary parts for the plane were contributed, with the exception of the engine and propeller which were given to us on assignment.

The most predominant technical problem that faced us from the beginning with respect to the design and future functioning of the snow cruiser was the relationship of the tires to the character of the snow and ice in the Antarctic. The best information we were able to get was that the snow there is so crystalline that it behaves much like fine sand. For this reason, we knew that we would have to have a large contact area of tire on snow, and since no one was positively sure that the tires needed treads, we concluded to use the smooth tire. At Goodyear Tire & Rubber Company, the molds for these tires were available in a size that we required and that had likewise been used on very large marsh buggies. Upon completion, the monster was driven from Chicago to Boston Harbor over the national highways by prearrangement with the commissioner of highways in Washington. In the course of this shakedown cruise, the snow cruiser was seen by at least 11 million people. This number was derived because that quantity of leaflets describing the device and the activities of the research foundation were distributed to people along the highways. As the craft moved further to the east, the crowds became larger, and traffic jams were the mode of the day. A Boston newspaper printed large headlines—**SNOW CRUISER ARRIVES**—in the same type that was used when word came that **WORLD WAR I IS OVER!!!** A following headline stated, "The Biggest Traffic Snarl in History, 70,000 Automobiles All Bogged Up on Every Highway," and yet, the interesting thing was we never heard any criticism at all about those traffic jams. People had been warned in advance of the coming of the snow cruiser and its effect on traffic flow, but nevertheless, the desire on the part of the American people was so great to witness such a feat that it seemed to be a day of fun.

When we got to the Antarctic, we found that the tire problem was of no significance, but we were troubled and eventually defeated instead by the gear ratios between each of the 75-horsepower series-type traction motors and the gears in each of the wheels themselves. The pitfall was that, in driving in the snow, we were unable to get the motor up to the critical speed needed to keep the necessary cool temperature. For this reason, the snow cruiser actually traveled only seven miles in the Antarctic and then only a short distance at a time. Nonetheless, even as a nonmobile unit, it rendered great service in the Antarctic because of the many facilities it contained, and it was of particular importance in the tremendous work that the Beechcraft plane was able to do in almost completely surveying the Antarctic continent. Surveying snow and ice areas is always difficult because there is little contrast of the terrain to enable the development of a matrix which covers a large area of the continent. This problem was overcome by the dropping of bags of carbon black, each of which took a different configuration when spread out over the area where it hit the ground. In this way, a very accurate map was developed.

MAGNETIC RECORDING AND LIMITLESS IMPROVEMENT

Another triumph for the foundation in 1939 was the beginning of the revolutionary discovery of magnetic recording. It was in that year that Armour staff member Marvin Camras was given two very solid patents by the U.S. Patent Office that sparked the exploding field of magnetic recording throughout the world. This is a success story all its own and is told in Chapter IX of this book.

1943—Early wire recorder for military operations.

Five years later, in the April 1944 issue of *The Reader's Digest*, there appeared an article about our foundation entitled "We Can Improve Anything." A draft of this article (title not included) had been sent to me by the author who had interviewed me, toured our laboratories, and talked to various scientists on our staff some time before the publication of the article. At the time of his visit to Armour, rather than saying, "We can improve anything," I had made the statement that anything can be improved. I was amazed when I saw the distorted title in the printed magazine and had to withstand the kidding of many of my friends and associates; nevertheless, the title as used certainly expressed the enthusiasm of our staff, and the article itself generated a great deal of interest in our institution. All in all much good came from it. A unique sequel to this story and the article is the fact that when Mr. Tom Slick of San Antonio, Texas, was in the South Pacific in the navy, he was attracted by the title "We Can Improve Anything" and decided right there and then, as he told me later, that he wanted the man that made that statement to be president of the research institutions that he would found in San Antonio, Texas, when the war was over. A few years later when I had moved to San Antonio, I told him that I had come under false pretenses.

THE WAR ERUPTS . . . AND ARMOUR,
AS WELL AS THE UNITED STATES, GETS INVOLVED

Almost the day after the Japanese attacked Pearl Harbor, we at Armour were practically enveloped by government agencies that were most anxious to have immediate work done on a large variety of programs. Initially, these projects related primarily to protection of the citizens, since there seemed to be a fear of airplane attack from the Japanese as well as from the Germans. Early programs at Armour show almost around-the-clock efforts in developing black-out techniques, warning systems for the citizens, fire control methods, rescue, and safety techniques and devices.

One of the first activities that the government negotiated with Armour was to establish with us its Precise Gage Laboratory for the Chicago Ordnance District, which included all of the area surrounding the industries of that neighborhood. This laboratory was staffed by experts from ordnance as well as from the foundation who had skills in calibrating the measuring devices of industrial concerns against the standards of this laboratory. After some months, this defensive type of work turned to more offensive-type research activities.

* * *

A SUMMATION OF SUCCESS

The research underwritings and staff growth of the Armour Research Foundation in the early days are rather interesting. The four charts that follow reflect strength as well as diversity, and specialization as well as growth.

Obviously, the Armour Plan was working. What's more, the growth pattern at Armour was much more rapid than what was experienced by its two predecessor institutions—Mellon and Battelle—and they were endowed. On the other hand, it must be recognized that both Mellon and Battelle aided Armour by initially demonstrating the value of institutional research, and Armour was able to capitalize on their efforts. Most importantly, the Armour Plan demonstrated that substantial endowment was not necessary, even though such funding made the job much easier. Its success also demonstrated to research-inclined people all over the United States, especially those in educational institutions, that research institutions could be established even with limitations of very little capital and relatively small provisions for operating expenses in the early years.

My involvement with Armour terminated on January 1, 1945, when I resigned my position as director of the Armour Research Foundation to become president and director of Midwest Research Institute in Kansas City. I saw in this change a challenging opportunity to establish a successful applied research institute in Mid-America, where the economy was almost exclusively agricultural but where there was a strong desire to create a balance with industry.

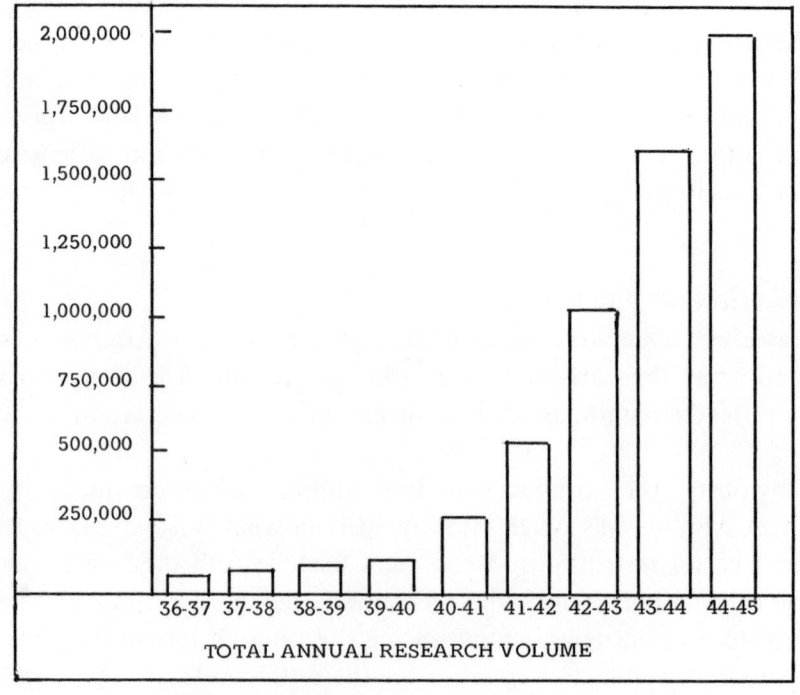

ARMOUR RESEARCH FOUNDATION (NOW IITRI)

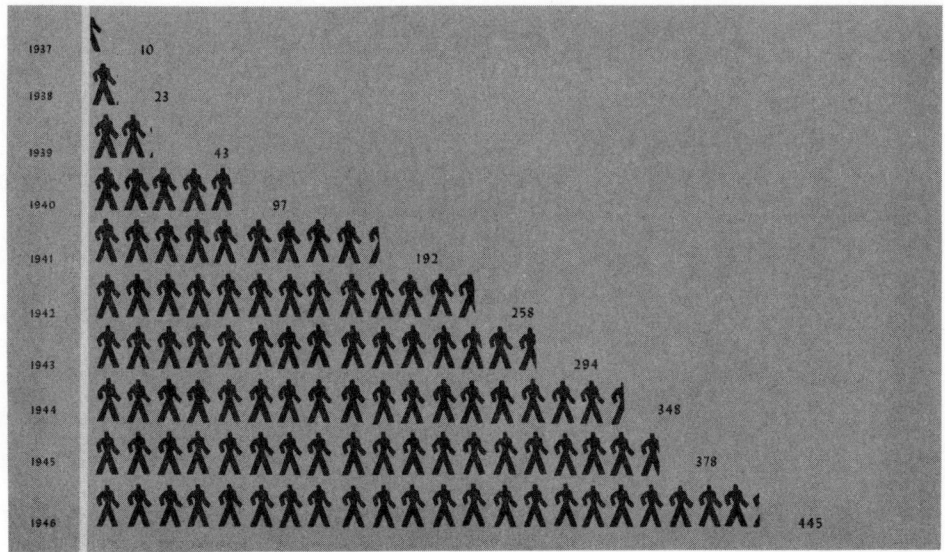

Personnel at Armour Research Foundation 1936-1946.

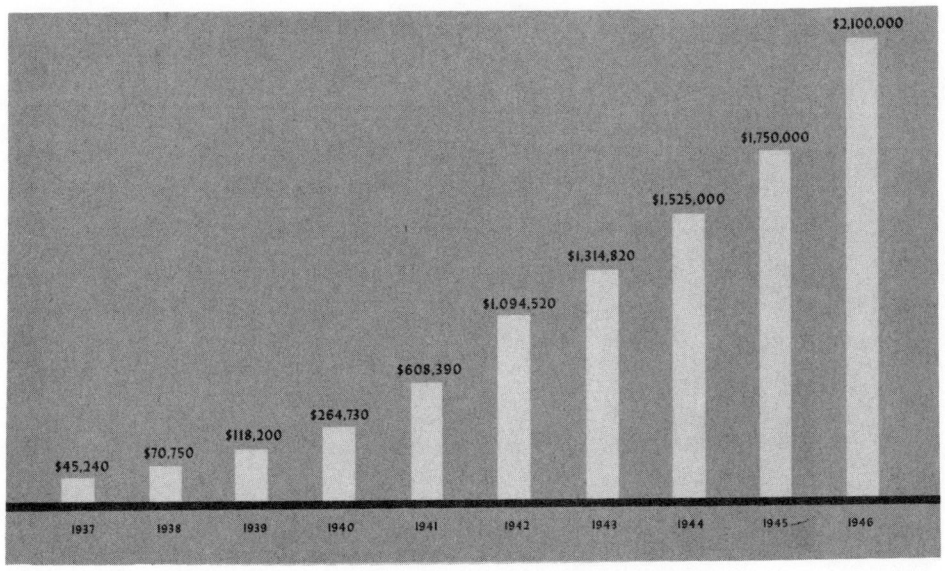

Research Volume at Armour Research Foundation 1936-1946.

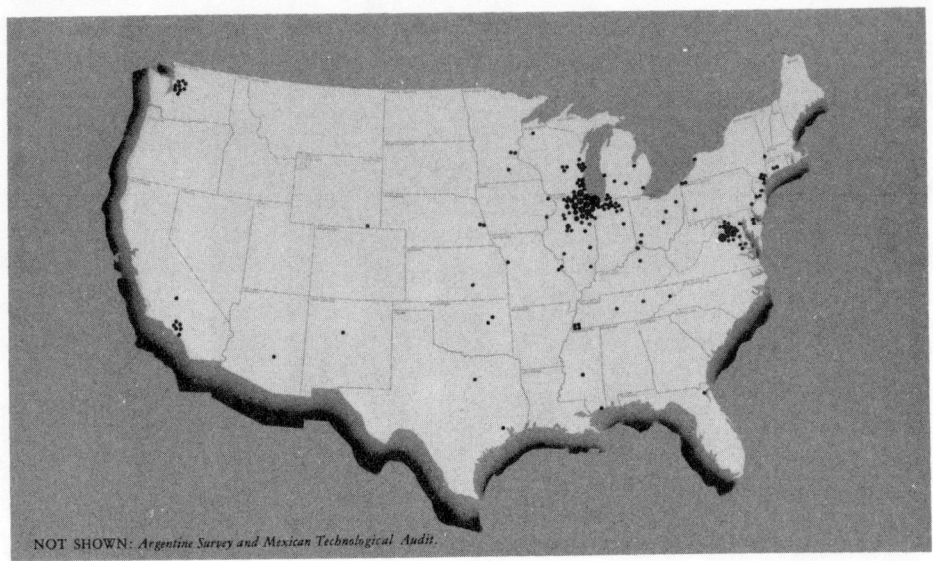

NOT SHOWN: *Argentine Survey and Mexican Technological Audit.*

Distribution of companies sponsoring research activities.

CHAPTER VI

THE WORLD WAR YEARS (1940-1945) AND NEW INSTITUTES

THE FOUR REGIONAL RESEARCH INSTITUTES
by Hugh Buhrman*, 1950

INTRODUCTION

Behind the prosaic title of this review, there is an inspiring story of how unselfish men banded together to give of their time, their knowledge, and their money . . . to the end that present and future generations might enjoy greater prosperity, health, happiness, and security within the framework of the American free enterprise system . . . a new way of life which already had brought this nation from a virtual wilderness to being the world's strongest and wealthiest within the short span of less than 200 years.

On July 4, 1776, our Declaration of Independence was proclaimed to the world. It was signed by 56 representatives of our then 13 struggling, newly born states. By profession, those patriots were lawyers, merchants, farmers, and jurists with a lesser number of physician-lawyers, lawyer-farmers, lawyer-soldiers, soldiers, merchant-judges, and merchant-jurists. One was a college president, and only three were from industry as we would classify industry today—one brewer, one printer and publisher, and one iron manufacturer—but the signers constituted a representative cross-section of the economic structure of those colonial times.

The important point is that those signers of our Declaration of Independence constituted a cross-section of American life as it then prevailed, and thereby established a lasting pattern which has become an American tradition whenever any problem of regional and national interest must be solved.

The purpose and objective now is to review the charters of the four not-for-profit regional scientific research institutions which have been founded

---

*Institution Development Counsel. New York City. Deceased 1960.

within the last 10 years and objectively determine whether they are being operated in full accord with the unselfish, public-spirited, regional-betterment goals of their respective Founders, and if they are in full compliance with federal laws and regulations which grant them complete tax-exemption under the Internal Revenue Code on the grounds that they are operated exclusively for scientific and educational purposes.

The four institutions, in the order of their founding, are the Midwest Research Institute based at Kansas City, Missouri, which is dedicated to the economic upbuilding of the Midwestern states; the Southern Research Institute based at Birmingham, Alabama, for like service in behalf of the South; Stanford Research Institute to serve and advance the overall welfare of the West; and Southwest Research Institute for the benefit of all the people, present and future, who live and work in the states adjacent to the western Gulf Coast of the United States. Stanford Research Institute is based at San Francisco (Stanford, California) and at Los Angeles, California. Southwest Research Institute is based at San Antonio, Texas. These are the only four such regionally minded and regionally dedicated scientific research institutions in the United States.

Let us review the reasons for their origin, their founding, and their operation.

MIDWEST RESEARCH INSTITUTE

The history and birth of Midwest Research Institute goes back to comparatively recent national preparedness days prior to World War II . . . when our federal government was seeking sites and manpower for defense plants which would be fully adequate for the emergency then on our national horizons.

Patriotic, totally unselfish civic leaders of Mid-America were gravely conscious that the mechanization of farming had vastly reduced the manpower requirements necessary for the Middlewest's basic agricultural economy. They were also acutely aware that their region did not possess sufficient industry as a balance to absorb the excess labor supply created by this condition, and that as a result, their region was not only failing to keep pace with our nation's growth, but that three of their six states had actually suffered a loss of population during the 10-year period between the official United States census of 1930 and 1940.

During that 10-year period, the population in the United States had increased from 122,775,046 to 133,669,275, a national gain of 10,894,229 representing a national average gain of more than 8.8 percent, whereas the six states of Mid-America collectively had a gain of less than 1 percent.

State	1930 Population	1940 Population
Arkansas	1,854,482	1,949,837
Iowa	2,470,939	2,538,268
Kansas	1,880,999	1,801,028
Missouri	3,629,367	3,784,664
Nebraska	1,377,963	1,315,834
Oklahoma	2,396,040	2,336,434
Total	13,609,790	13,726,065

In Washington, D.C., these civic leaders at their own time and expense pointed out to top-level federal authorities the advantages of their mid-continental geographic location; the availability of plant sites removed from close proximity to overly large centers of population; the availability of and willingness of their population to encourage industrial production; their very high percentage of native born citizenry; and the fact that the location of some of such plants in the Midwest would serve to strengthen the economy of the entire nation.

The federal government officials were understandingly skeptical but impressed with the sincerity of the men who had left their own businesses, and at their own expense were advancing a plan whereby the people of their region could help their government in its objectives and at the same time at least get a start toward the larger industrial base so vitally needed as a balance to the region's agricultural economy.

One major obstacle cited by the government was the region's almost total lack of scientific research facilities so vital to industry and government alike, but friendly persistence prevailed. Large plants were built in the region. Men and women, boys and girls came in from the farms ... were trained ... and it is a matter of official record that the efficiency and production of such new plants in Mid-America were second to none in the entire United States.

While the foregoing was being accomplished, the same civic leaders at their own expense toured all major research laboratories of the country seeking information as to how they might establish a not-for-profit research institute or foundation to spearhead the development of the Midwestern United States, serve existing industries, help small industries to become large through research, and to give birth to as yet unborn industries which would be based upon the natural resources of the region.

These civic leaders did not want just another industrial research laboratory. They wanted strictly nonprofit facilities which would be dedicated to the fundamental problem of regional betterment. They wanted to cure the need of their sons and daughters and large segments of their population to migrate to other sections of the country in order to gain employment and career opportunities.

In the summer of 1943 they called their own "Continental Congress." Bankers, lawyers, businessmen, railroad men, college presidents, farmers, merchants, insurance men—in fact, a representative cross-section of the economic and cultural strata of their entire six-state region. Unselfishly, leaders from research institutions in other sections of the country came to the Midwest and gave freely to the representatives of Mid-America from their experience, advice, and counsel. They pointed out the difficulties and expense of establishing new research facilities but emphasized the necessity of having them if Mid-America was to build an industrial economy sufficient to balance her predominant agricultural economy.

It was determined that a minimum of $500,000 would be necessary for even a modest start. Scientific research was new to the region but a small group of volunteers undertook the responsibility of soliciting contributions and within one year had cash and pledges slightly in excess of that goal.

Concurrently, volunteer attorneys were conferring with federal and Missouri State tax and legal authorities . . . and on June 17, 1944, Midwest Research Institute came into legal being. Article III of its Charter contains six paragraphs, three of which are pertinent to this review.

• **Paragraph 1.** The association is formed for the following scientific and educational purposes: Subject to the laws of Missouri, to receive, acquire, and maintain funds and other property, real, personal, and mixed, and apply the income and principal thereof

(a)   to promote pure and applied science;

(b)   to improve and assist industry, agriculture, and livestock production by the application of science;

(c)   to conduct scientific investigations and industrial research for industry and agriculture;

(d)   to foster the exchange of technical experience and research results among producers, manufacturers, agriculturists, and all others who may be benefited by the application of pure science;

(e)   to assist manufacturers, farmers, and all others in the development of more efficient and scientific methods of production;

(f)   by the application of science and research, to advance the use of natural resources;

(g)   to grant scholarships and studentships and otherwise aid in the advancement of scientific education;

(h)   to carry out and perform experiments, economic and scientific research, and do any and all other things which may be necessary or advisable in carrying out the general purposes hereinbefore mentioned, including the acquisition and dissemination of knowledge in relation thereto;

(i)   to assist the universities and educational institutions in the states of Arkansas, Iowa, Kansas, Missouri, Nebraska, Oklahoma, and in other states, in the coordination and development of experimental scientific and industrial research;

(j)   in connection with universities and educational institutions as well as independently thereof, to foster and encourage education and learning in science, agriculture, and mechanic arts, and to promote the liberal and practical education of the industrial classes in the several pursuits and professions of life.

• **Paragraph 5** specifically provides that, "No part of the net earnings shall be distributed to, used for, or inure to the benefit of any private shareholder or individual. No part of the money of the corporation shall be spent and none of the property of the corporation shall be used outside of the continental United States. The corporation shall not carry on propaganda or otherwise attempt to influence legislation."

• **Paragraph 6** specifically provides that "Should the corporation cease to do business and be dissolved, all property and funds remaining after the payment of the debts of the corporation shall be distributed to a corporation trust, or community chest, fund or foundation which would then qualify under the provisions of Section 23 (o) and (q) of the Internal Revenue Code, as they now exist or as they may hereafter be amended, provided that if said sections are repealed or materially changed, such funds shall be paid and distributed to the University of Kansas City, Kansas City, Missouri, or to its successor."

The nine men who were the original incorporators of this pioneer movement, the first of its kind whereby a scientific research institute was created specifically to benefit a region and its people, were: Mr. Robert L. Mehornay, who was a merchant; Mr. J. C. Nichols, who was a realtor; Dr. Roy Cross, president of The Kansas City Testing Laboratory; Mr. Kenneth A. Spencer, an industrialist; Mr. B. C. Adams, a public utility president; Mr. C. T. Thompson, an industrialist; Mr. J. F. Stephens, also an industrialist; Mr. C. J. Patterson, industrialist; and Mr. Paul D. Bartlett, grain merchant. The gentlemen named were serving as the representatives of approximately 100 other leaders devoted to civic and regional betterment in the states of Mid-America. In this original group there were the presidents of 12 midwestern colleges and universities; six state geologists; eight newspaper editors or publishers; 24 industrialists; four public utility presidents; the three owners of three commercial testing laboratories; six bank presidents; five grain merchants; three petroleum executives; three department store presidents; with mine operators, lawyers, farmers, railroad presidents, realtors, and scientists, together with one United States Senator.

On January 1, 1945, Midwest Research Institute opened the doors of its modest rented quarters, consisting of one office and two small laboratories staffed by the president-director, his secretary, and one scientist. Word of the start of this pioneer effort to better an entire region seemed to capture the imagination of brilliant young scientists. Hundreds of applications were received, many of them from native sons who had been educated and trained in the universities of the region, only to have to migrate elsewhere upon graduation because of the lack of scientific openings in their native region. They were carefully screened, and as needed the best were selected, and more often than not, were glad to return "home" at a financial sacrifice to start so that they might have a part in the first regional research movement designed and planned solely for the economic upbuilding of all Mid-America . . . for the benefit of all her people.

On May 6, 1945, Germany signed terms of unconditional surrender. Cutbacks on war contracts in both new and old plants in Mid-America, as well as elsewhere in the nation, were rumored and soon became realities.

The Board of Governors of Midwest Research Institute met and decided the program of the institute should be accelerated, that every effort possible should be made to retain the industrial employment gains which had been achieved by reason of defense contracts and later war production contracts in both new and old plants of the six-state region. Particular emphasis was placed on helping small business and infant industries. The board authorized an appeal for $2 million; one-half to develop opportunities through research to promote peacetime industry and thereby create jobs for the people; one-half for equipment facilities essential to those objectives.

The governors of the six states joined in the proclamation given on the following pages.

All over the Midwest, towns and cities have been awakened and encouraged through the recent development of industry, and with it, have come greater incomes and a higher standard of living. This new-found prosperity is now being threatened.

It is essential to the well-being of the Midwestern states that this new industrial growth be maintained by making use of the abundant natural resources found right here in our own home states. The Midwest Research Institute, a non-profit organization, has established as its aim the development and encouragement of industry in this general area through research in agriculture, minerals, and industrial processes.

WE, THE GOVERNORS of these six Midwestern states comprising the geographical center of our nation, sincerely support such a program. We look to scientific research as a means towards full employment, continuing prosperity and a higher standard of living for all with a resulting increased population.

GOVERNOR OF NEBRASKA

GOVERNOR OF IOWA

GOVERNOR OF KANSAS

GOVERNOR OF MISSOURI

GOVERNOR OF OKLAHOMA

GOVERNOR OF ARKANSAS

The following statistics are from the U.S. Bureau of Census "Population —Special Reports, Series P-46, No. 3" and testify why the civic leadership of Mid-America was gravely concerned over the then existing trends in national population. Far more people were leaving the midwestern states to settle elsewhere than were coming to make their homes in that region. Taking the six states to which Midwest Research Institute was basically dedicated, the picture was as follows.

• Arkansas—262,609 more people had migrated from the state than had migrated into Arkansas during the period from April 1940 to July 1945. That was equivalent to the combined population of Little Rock and the 12 next most populous cities of the state, based upon the official U.S. Census of 1940.

• Iowa—224,693 more people had migrated out of the state than those who came to make their homes there. This represented the equivalent of the entire population of Des Moines and Cedar Rapids in 1940.

• Kansas—61,678 more people had left Kansas to live elsewhere than had migrated into Kansas. That was equal to the entire 1940 population of Topeka.

• Missouri—130,946 more people had sought homes elsewhere than had come to Missouri to live, a number very closely approximating the combined official 1940 population of Springfield and St. Joseph.

• Nebraska—112,543 more people migrated out of the state than settled in it. Otherwise expressed, more than the combined population of Lincoln, Hastings, and Beatrice.

• Oklahoma—353,802 more people sought employment and homes elsewhere than settled in the state. Equivalent to more than the combined population of Oklahoma City and Tulsa on the official U.S. Census of 1940.

Eleven of the 12 states bordering on the foregoing six likewise had more people migrating elsewhere than were immigrating into them.

The map which follows may serve to give an even better picture of what was happening in Middle America . . . and the statistical table following the map, the situation nationally for the same period, April 1, 1940 to July 1, 1945.

It is worthy of note that 2,100,450 or nearly 47 percent of this redistributed population was to the Pacific Coast states of California, Washington, and Oregon—or practically 54 percent of the total net loss of the 30 states which were losing.

CIVILIAN MIGRATION IS REDUCING THE POPULATION OF MID-AMERICA

FIGURE IN EACH STATE INDICATE NET LOSS...OR NET GAIN...
BETWEEN APRIL 1, 1940 AND JULY 1, 1945...
BASED UPON U. S. BUREAU OF CENSUS REPORTS

MIDWEST RESEARCH INSTITUTE
KANSAS CITY 2 MISSOURI

Trends of Civilian Migration in the United States
For the Period From April 1, 1940 to July 1, 1945

(These figures deal solely with the problem of Civilian Migration and are from U.S. Bureau of Census "Population—Special Reports, Series P-46, No. 3." They constitute a special study of the problem, and should not be confused with normal U.S. Census reports.)

State	Net Loss	State	Net Gain
Alabama	-132,293	Arizona	+ 94,298
Arkansas	-262,609	California	+1,639,824
Colorado	- 23,937	Connecticut	+ 153,834
Georgia	-146,409	Delaware	+ 23,467
Idaho	- 52,216	Dist. of Columbia	+ 225,572
Iowa	-224,693	Florida	+ 226,903
Kansas	- 61,678	Illinois	+ 94,666
Kentucky	-306,266	Indiana	+ 98,563
Louisiana	- 16,493	Maryland	+ 281,924
Maine	- 34,253	Massachusetts	+ 49,832
Minnesota	-224,311	Michigan	+ 343,060
Mississippi	-227,599	Nevada	+ 32,259
Missouri	-130,946	New Jersey	+ 224,933
Montana	- 81,054	Ohio	+ 286,754
Nebraska	-112,543	Oregon	+ 166,320
New Hampshire	- 13,197	Rhode Island	+ 36,163
New Mexico	- 51,076	Utah	+ 39,573
New York	-241,407	Virginia	+ 188,788
North Carolina	-303,802	Washington	+ 294,306
North Dakota	-118,243	*19 States Gained	4,501,039
Oklahoma	-353,802		
Pennsylvania	-119,907		
South Carolina	-160,030		
South Dakota	-104,774		
Tennessee	- 76,501		
Texas	- 2,586		
Vermont	- 36,801		
West Virginia	-161,189		
Wisconsin	-116,663		
Wyoming	- 9,823		
30 States Lost	3,907,110		

*The 593,929 between the gains of 4,501,039 and losses of 3,907,110 is explained by the U.S. Census Bureau as the excess of immigrants over emigrants during the period studied.

The Indiana-Illinois-Michigan-Ohio sector gained 823,043 or 18 percent of the total redistribution—or 21 percent of the 30-state loss. The District of Columbia-Maryland-Virginia area was next with a gain of 696,284, while the East Coast states of Connecticut, Delaware, Massachusetts, New Jersey, and Rhode Island (long known as manufacturing centers) fared next best.

With the exception of Florida, it is significant that all of the Southern states lost, as did the states of Middle America, as well as all of the Southwestern states except Arizona. Civic leaders of the South and Southwest were concerned over the lack of balance of their regional economy, while similar leaders on the Pacific Coast foresaw the necessity for more industry as the base to provide gainful employment for the tidal wave of migration into their area. Those regions will be dealt with later herein, but first let us complete consideration of Middle America and its Midwest Research Institute movement, the first objective of which according to its charter was "(a) to promote pure and applied science."

In October 1945, the tenth month of Midwest Research Institute operations, the Trustees of the Herbert F. Hall Estate announced that the entire $6.5 million in that trust would be devoted to establishing in Kansas City, for the benefit of all Middle America, a free library to be known as the Linda Hall Library of Science and Technology. It was the first such public library devoted to science and technology west of Chicago, and up to that time there was none on the Pacific Coast. It is significant that some of the trustees of the Hall Estate which took this pioneering action were also trustees of Midwest Research Institute, all of whom had been inspired by and were virtually interested in the Midwest Research Institute movement dedicated to the upbuilding of Middle America through science. By February 1946, the Linda Hall Library had made an excellent start and already had more than 1500 scientific publications coming in monthly and was constantly adding to its reservoir of scientific and technological information so it would be immediately available to the scientists of Midwest Research Institute and those in the colleges, in industry, to students, and in short to everyone interested in the use of science as a tool for the upbuilding of the region.

As might be expected, these activities attracted national attention, and feature articles almost beyond number began to appear in both the popular and scientific magazines of the nation. *Chemical Engineering* for August 1946 carried a feature on-the-spot story by its assistant editor who titled it, "Midwest Research Institute Catalyzes New Industry in Mid-America," and his introduction was:

When an individual, a community, or an entire region faces economic reverses, it can follow either of two courses. It can let itself run down without a struggle, or it can fight back. Mid-America, the region between the Mississippi and the Rockies, has chosen to fight back and the Midwest Research Institute is its strong right arm. Their banner: A balanced economy through industrialization.

"Midwest Research Institute Fosters Area Development" was the title of a feature article in the September 1946 edition of *Manufacturers Record*. "Grass Roots Research" was the theme of a feature in *Science Illustrated*. Radio Station KCMO won a citation from *Variety*, which is the *Journal of Commerce* and the *Wall Street Journal* of show business, for the 13-week series of programs it produced as a public service in support of the Midwest Research Institute movement and its regional upbuilding objectives.

Midwest Research Institute regularly and consistently emphasized it was neither interested in nor trying to entice established industries from other sections of the nation because its purpose was to help develop new industries based upon the natural resources of Middle America. The region was determined to better itself, but not at the expense of other regions which likewise were vital to a sound nationwide economy.

The *Kansas City Star* of November 12, 1946 reported "Rich Farm Prize—Development of Grain Sorghums as Sugar and Starch Source a Boost to Area—a Victory for Science—Midwest Research Institute, Industry and State Agricultural Schools in Joint Experiments—Big Market for Crop—the Step Will Mean Increased Acreage and Wealth for the Middle West."

The *Star* then went on to report how the Corn Products Refining Co. had sponsored a project at Midwest Research Institute, which in turn had provided fellowships at Kansas State College, the University of Nebraska, Oklahoma Agricultural and Mechanical College, and the Texas Agricultural and Mechanical College. "Although millions of bushels of grain sorghums are produced yearly, the announcement marks the first time they have been used in the commercial processing of dextrose. A new market has been found for a common farm crop. Acreage is expected to increase greatly, just as soybean planting soared after plants for processing the oil were built," the *Star* continued. Concurrently, Corn Products Refining Co. announced the start of a new $10-million plant to be located on the Gulf Coast to process grain sorghums raised in the Middle West and the Southwest.

Midwest Research Institute was on the march and Trustee Truman took time out from his White House duties to send the message on the following page on the occasion of its second annual meeting.

WB104 NL PD GOVT=WASHINGTON DC 9

ROBERT L MEHORNAY=

        CHAIRMAN BOARD OF GOVERNORS MIDWEST RESEARCH
                INSTITUTE HOTEL MUEHLBACH KSCTY=

I WISH IT WERE POSSIBLE FOR ME TO BE WITH YOU AND MY
FELLOW TRUSTEES OF MIDWEST RESEARCH INSTITUTE TODAY.
THE INSTITUTE HAS RENDERED ADMIRABLE SERVICE IN ITS
SCIENTIFIC STUDIES DIRECTED TO THE DEVELOPMENT OF THE
RESOURCES OF MID-AMERICA AND IMPROVEMENT IN LIVING
STANDARDS IN OUR MIDWESTERN STATES. I CONGRATULATE
THE INSTITUTE ON ALL OF ITS CONSTRUCTIVE ACHIEVEMENTS
IN THE PAST AND HAVE FULL CONFIDENCE THAT IT WILL
RENDER EQUALLY HELPFUL SERVICE IN THE SOLUTION OF
THE PROBLEMS WHICH CONFRONT US TODAY. MY HEARTY
FELICITATIONS AND WARMEST PERSONAL GREETINGS TO ALL=
        HARRY S TRUMAN

The year 1947 was one of continued progress and regional service by Midwest Research Institute. One of its first acts of public service had been the compiling of a 10-state map showing the known mineral resources of the area. This was accomplished with institute funds and with the help of the several state geologists of the region. On completion, the Gas Service Company of Kansas City, already one of the largest contributors to the institute movement, despite the fact its own business interests were almost totally local, generously paid for the reproduction of several thousand copies so that it might be distributed to every school, every chamber of commerce, every college and university, and every other interested group throughout the region.

One copy came to the attention of the Arkansas Power and Light Company which serves most of the state of Arkansas. This company promptly engaged the institute to make an on-the-spot survey of Arkansas irrespective of whether the territory covered by the survey was served by Arkansas Power and Light Company, or not.

This was done county by county and, as each county survey was completed, mass meetings were called, usually at the respective county seats. The Arkansas State Resources and Development Commission, the Bureau of Research of the University of Arkansas, the Arkansas Economic Council-State Chamber of Commerce, and other public service organizations all cooperated.

Findings in each county were laid before these mass meetings, and the scientists of Midwest Research Institute explained the manufactured end uses into which such resources could be processed. Even more important, they told the local people whether such potential end products were in short or long supply, regionally, nationally, and internationally—in short, whether a new plant based upon such local resources gave promise of success or struggle.

This brought new hope to the people of a state which had been largely dependent upon an agricultural economy. Funds were subscribed in various communities which the citizens loaned at low interest or interest free to qualified firms or persons who would construct plants which would provide industrial employment. As soon as one new plant was successful and the loan repaid, the funds were extended to another which scientific investigation and study had pointed out as a roadmap to greater industrial employment. While it is not the purpose of this review to name individuals, it is only proper to note of record that Mr. C. Hamilton Moses, president of the Arkansas Power and Light Company and a trustee of Midwest Research Institute, was subsequently voted Man of the Year of the South, and that one of his many services cited as reason for that honor was his vision and the vision of his company in giving this great service to the people of the State of Arkansas.

The Public Service Company of Oklahoma added a research scientist to its staff for the first time in its history and engaged the Midwest Research Institute to make a like survey of the 47 counties it served. Midwest Research Institute again invited and obtained local cooperation. The University of Oklahoma, Oklahoma Agricultural and Mechanical College, the University of Tulsa, the state geologist, and many other organizations interested in helping develop the state participated.

Neither Arkansas nor Oklahoma has fully achieved its goals, but they both have the visible target of sufficient industry to balance their agricultural economy and to serve as insurance against depletion of the natural gas and oil reserves.

It is not the prerogative of this reviewer to indulge in conjecture, yet the feeling is inescapable that these *self-help plans in Middle America* were in fact the foundation for President Truman's Point 4 Program seeking the upbuilding of underdeveloped friendly nations. To the third annual meeting he wired the message reproduced below.

A.WA210 NL GOVT PD=THE WHITE HOUSE WASHINGTON DC 7
ROBERT L MEHORNAY CHAIRMAN=
       BOARD OF GOVERNORS MIDWEST RESEARCH INSTITUTE
          HOTEL MUEHLBACH KSC=

THERE MUST BE NO RETROGRESSION IN THE MARCH FORWARD OF
THE MIDWEST RESEARCH INSTITUTE IN ITS DETERMINATION TO
DEVLOP THE RESOURCES OF THE MIDWESTERN STATES. GREAT AS
OUR WEALTH BOTH AGRICULTURE AND MINERALS WE NEED TO
DEVELOP THOSE RESOURCES THROUGH EXPANDING INDUSTRIES.
ONLY THEN SHALL WE ACHIEVE A BALANCED ECONOMY. ONLY
THEN SHALL WE BRING GREATER PROSPERITY. HAPPINESS AND
SECURITY TO ALL OF THE PEOPLE ON THE RICH MIDWEST. MY
MESSAGE TO THE THIRD ANNUAL MEETING OF THE BOARD OF
TRUSTEES. OF WHICH I AM PROUD TO BE A MEMBER IS TO GO
FORWARD WITH PROGRESS UNTIL MID-AMERICA IS IN A
POSITION TO MAKE TO THE NATIONAL ECONOMY THE FULL
CONTRIBUTION OF WHICH SHE IS CAPABLE. MY HEARTY
FELICITATIONS AND WARMEST PERSONAL GREETINGS TO ALL WHO
ATTEND THE MEETINGS TODAY=
       HARRY S TRUMAN

Thus, irrespective of where the international self-help aspects of Point 4 originated, the irrefutable fact remains that the civic leadership of Middle America had conceived their own regional self-help "Point 4" and had backed it with their time, their experience, their hearts, their minds, and their contributed dollars in a concerted effort to solve through science the fundamental problems which had placed their region and their population at an economic disadvantage for generations, and had charted such a course of regional self-help long before Point 4 came into being as part of our nation's foreign policy of helping friendly nations help themselves with American science, technology, and "know how" as the major tools . . . as a practical substitute at small expense . . . instead of billion-dollar grants.

Now, let us direct our attention away from Middle America and into the south and southeastern United States. What conditions were confronting the South?

ALABAMA RESEARCH INSTITUTE (Predecessor of Southern Research Institute)

With the exception of Virginia on the north and Florida to the south, every state of this vast region was suffering a grave loss of population due to civilian migration to more highly industrialized states as previously shown on page 193 of this study. But, unlike the midwestern states, the natural growth of population in the South was not only offsetting its losses due to civilian migration . . . the South was showing a 10 percent increased population overall despite such losses occasioned by civilian migration.

When it is remembered that for decades the South had been handicapped with the lowest per capita income of all our regions, no doubt is left that the South not only was confronted with all the problems confronting Middle America, but also many problems distinct to the South itself.

• Between April 1, 1940 and July 1, 1945, **Alabama's** net loss due to civilian migration had been 132,293 which was equal to about half of Birmingham's official 1940 population of 267,583, or more than Mobile's 129,009 on the official census of 1950.

• **Georgia's** net loss during the same period due to civilian migration was 146,409 which closely approximated one-half of Atlanta's official total of 302,288 on the 1940 official census, or far more than Savannah's entire population of 119,638 on the United States census of 1950.

• For the same April 1, 1940-July 1, 1945 period, civilian migration net loss of **Mississippi** was 227,599 . . . more than the combined official 1940 populations of Jackson (62,107), Meridan (35,481), Vicksburg (24,460), Hattiesburg (21,026), Greenville (20,892), Laurel (20,598), Biloxi (17,475), and Gulfport (15,195).

• **North Carolina's** loss during the same period and for the same reason —civilian migration—was 303,802 which otherwise expressed was equal to the combined 1940 population of Charlotte (112,986), Winston-Salem (79,815), Durham (60,195), Greensboro (59,319), and Raleigh (46,897).

• **South Carolina's** comparable loss was 160,030, in excess of Columbia (62,396), and Charleston (71,275) combined on the official census of 1940.

The insidious factor about these shifts of population insofar as Middle America was concerned was the fact they were hard to believe at the time because the cities were bulging, housing was in very short supply, schools were overcrowded, and it seemed incredible that civilian migration was draining off such large segments of population. The explanation, of course, was that the rural sections were suffering the greatest losses.

In the southern states the trend could not help but be even less discernible because those states were absorbing such losses and still running well ahead of the national overall average increase in our nation's growth.

A brief review of overall population trends in the South during the 20-year period, 1930 to 1950, will serve to clarify.

Official Census—Southern States

State	1930	1940	1950
Alabama	2,646,248	2,832,961	3,061,743
Florida	1,468,211	1,897,414	2,771,305
Georgia	2,908,506	3,123,723	3,444,578
Mississippi	2,009,821	2,183,796	2,178,914
North Carolina	3,170,276	3,571,623	4,061,929
South Carolina	1,738,765	1,899,804	2,117,027
Virginia	2,421,851	2,677,773	3,318,680
Region	16,363,678	18,187,094	20,954,176

Thus, from 1930 to 1940 the southern states gained 11.1 percent in population compared with the national average gain of 8.8 percent. The next 10 years, from 1940 to 1950, the southern states gained 15.2 percent compared with average national gain of 14.4 percent.

We have already noted that the gain in the Midwest from 1930 to 1940 was less than 1 percent, and we might add that from 1940 to 1950 the Midwest gained only 1.6 percent.

These somewhat dull, but to their reviewer highly provocative statistics are brought out to emphasize the fundamental problems that confronted the civic leadership of the South and the Midwest in their respective regions, and the significant fact that both groups turned to science to solve them—the

Midwest to reverse her static and almost overall downward trend, the South to find ways of providing gainful employment for her increasing millions and the upbuilding of her lowest of all regional per capita income.

Thus, it was on October 11, 1941, that 78 totally unselfish, personally very successful community leaders from throughout the state of Alabama (the group was spearheaded by Mr. Thomas W. Martin, Chairman of the Board of Alabama Power Company), filed Certification of Incorporation of the not-for-profit Alabama Research Institute. These gentlemen constituted a cross-section of the business, banking, transportation, educational, agricultural, and industrial leadership of the state.

These leaders dedicated themselves to the following objectives and purposes.

• "**Article Two, Section 1.** Alabama Research Institute is formed to promote the general welfare of the State of Alabama and its citizens and for the promotion of other public purposes; to aid through scientific research in the utilization of the natural resources of the state of Alabama and in the development of agriculture, industry, and commerce in the state, and elsewhere, and to that end

(a)   to coordinate and utilize existing agricultural, industrial, and commercial research facilities and operations within the state, and to organize, own, operate, and utilize such research facilities within or without the state as may be found necessary or desirable;

(b)   to determine by scientific research or economic studies whether there are resources or facilities within the state which may be profitably developed, produced, manufactured, or used, and to promote the development, production, manufacture, or use of such resources;

(c)   to investigate and further the economic and scientific development, production, and manufacture within the state of new or improved agricultural, industrial, and commercial products whether such products originate within or without the state;

(d)   to cooperate with and assist agriculture, industry, and commerce within the state in economic studies and in the utilization of organized research."

• **Article Two, Section 2** specifically provides, "The institute shall not have any capital stock nor shall it pursue any of its objects or purposes for pecuniary profit to any of its members." The remainder of this article is devoted to the usual legal enabling authorization provisions necessary for such operations.

- **Article Three, Section 1** was indicative of the determination of the founders. In its entirety it reads, "The duration of the institute shall be perpetual."
- **Article Four** provides that "Any person, firm, association, or corporation interested in scientific research may become a member of the institute upon acceptance of his or its application in the manner fixed by the Board of Trustees."
- **Article Five** concludes the document and sets forth the manner provided for amendments.

Under the original plan, Alabama Research Institute started with its base in the headquarters of the Alabama State Chamber of Commerce at Montgomery. Pearl Harbor was bombed less than two months after the founders had filed a Certificate of Incorporation for the institute, and while it never ceased in its objectives of helping promote the state's upbuilding through scientific research, winning the war came first, and Alabama Research Institute, exactly as individuals or organizations throughout our country, let its own unselfish objectives become strictly secondary to the all-important job of winning the war.

During the next two years word of the purposes and objectives of Alabama Research Institute spread into other states of the South. Civic leaders throughout the region proposed that as soon as conditions permitted, the movement be broadened to include the entire South. The original founders were delighted and welcomed wholeheartedly such region-wide cooperation on the common problems of the area.

A campaign to raise the funds necessary for expanded operations was launched; public spirited, regionally minded leaders were elected to the board from all of the states of the South, and the name of the movement was changed to the *Southern Research Institute*.

In August 1944, Southern Research Institute came into physical being with the purchase of a residence and grounds adjacent to downtown Birmingham, which were suitable for initial operations and provided adequate space for the building of laboratories as required. Thus, the volunteer leadership of the South and their counterparts in the Midwest started their respective regionally dedicated research institutes almost simultaneously. The important fact is that both groups had turned to science to solve the fundamental problems of their regions and help build them for the benefit of all the people of present and future generations.

Contributions were not used to build imposing structures. Southern's first expansion was into the carriage house and stable adjacent to its residence headquarters. Midwest's first expansion was into a garage building next door. Southern next built some inexpensive one-story concrete buildings; Midwest expanded into an old fire engine house, a bungalow, and a two-story residence. Within recent months, Southern has had its first representative building constructed through generous contributions of those who wished to assist. Midwest's last expansion was into an old boat house which actually dated back to the days of Westport and the Sante Fe Trail, as did the horse-drawn fire engine headquarters.

Contributions likewise provided the funds for equipment for both institutes. These facts are recorded because they are not and cannot be reflected in the legal language of charters.

Another highly important factor not adequately reflected in any review of the operation of these regional research institutes, dedicated and operated for the economic upbuilding of their areas, is not only the enthusiasm with which civic leaders created them, but the continued interest and support accorded unflaggingly since initial operation began.

Still another factor not apparent in the legal phraseology of their respective charters is the help, counsel, and encouragement extended by the older and more firmly established research institutions of our country. Many of the directors of such institutions have given freely and willingly of their time and experience. Dr. James R. Killian, Jr., president of the Massachusetts Institute of Technology, modestly exemplified the philosophy of such leaders when he said:

> It has been said that a research laboratory should be a source of satisfaction to every citizen because in a very real sense it is an addition to his wealth. Each of the great regional areas of our country must be prosperous, and the prosperity of each will contribute to the strength of all. The goal for the South, as for the rest of the country, must be to provide the most ample possible opportunity for men and women to lead full and rewarding lives.

STANFORD RESEARCH INSTITUTE

Next let us direct our attention to the West and the Pacific Coast where California, for example, has an area of 158,693 square miles which far surpasses the 94,279-square-mile area of England. California was admitted to the Union in 1850, and 100 years later on the official census of 1950, had a population of 10,586,223 compared with England's 50,368,455.

The civic leadership of the Pacific Coast had been delighted with the steady growth of their area but it had also given them grave concern at times when it appeared that industrial development was not keeping pace with the region's natural population increase and the spectacular gains by reason of civilian migration from other sections of the country. Stanford Research Institute is interested in and dedicated to the upbuilding of the entire West, but for the purposes of this review and some degree of brevity, the three coastal states fully suffice.

From April 1, 1940 to July 1, 1945, California had a net gain of 1,639,824 due to the redistribution of national population occasioned by civilian migration; Oregon a gain of 166,320, and Washington a gain of 294,306—a total of 2,100,450 for the three states.

This trend together with natural growth of population is reflected in the official U.S. Bureau of Census statistics as follows.

State	1900	1920	1940	1950
California	1,485,053	3,426,861	6,907,387	10,586,223
Oregon	413,536	783,389	1,089,684	1,521,341
Washington	518,103	1,356,621	1,736,191	2,378,963
	2,416,692	5,566,871	9,733,262	14,486,527

The region already enjoyed the highest per capita income of any area in the United States, and it would have been easy for the civic leadership to adopt a "we have arrived" attitude, but they did not because the blood of pioneers was still dominant and their projected calculations convinced them in 1946 that their region certainly, and perhaps California alone, was destined to have a population of at least 50 million persons within the next 40 years. If such expectations look fantastic on the surface they become conservatively realistic when one observes that California multiplied seven times over between 1900 and 1950, and that growth at the same rate would give her a population of over 74 million by the time the official census of the year 2000 is taken.

In contrast, the states of Middle America which Midwest Research Institute was founded to serve had a combined population of 9,977,268 in 1900, and 13,949,397 in 1950—a 50 year gain of only 40 percent—whereas the three Pacific Coast states gained 600 percent.

The national census of 1950 brings out the fact that our farm population today must produce enough to feed approximately twice as many people today as a comparable number of farmers had to raise when the census of 1910 was taken, and government forecasts point out that each individual farmer will soon have to produce food enough for more than three times as many people as did the individual farmer of 1910. More scientific farming and the mechanization of agriculture has made this possible, and science and technology continue to reduce the number of farmers required to raise the crops necessary to feed our population. It is not inconceivable that within the next 50 years much of our own, as well as the world's food supply, will be produced in chemical plants as a result of photosynthesis research. German scientists have reached the pilot plant stage and significant developments have been made in this country. Continued progress might well bring the inroads on our farm economy that synthetic fibres have had on cotton, silk, and wool.

It was only natural, therefore, that the civic leadership of the Pacific Coast should turn to the education of more scientists and scientific research as the vehicle to help develop their region and thereby provide for the welfare of present and future generations. There had been some discussions and investigation regarding the prospects of forming a Pacific Research Institute but because of the war the movement never materialized. Early in 1946 the Board of Trustees of Stanford University was approached and asked if the University would spearhead such a movement in behalf of the entire Pacific Coast and the West in general. After study and deliberation, the trustees felt this was a reasonable and legitimate responsibility for a privately supported university to assume; that such a program of scientific research fitted well within the public service Stanford University had been founded to render; and that while the university endowment was far below the amount it should be, still the university could and should start the movement and carry it until its value to the region was established, and others would assume its financial support.

Accordingly, on October 24, 1946, representatives acting on behalf of the trustees of Stanford University filed Articles of Incorporation which provided that the members of the not-for-profit corporation should be members of the Board of Trustees of Leland Stanford Junior University as from time to time constituted. This action was taken under and in full keeping with the laws of the state of California and, more specifically, Title XII of Division One of the Civil Code of California.

Among those taking initial leadership and promising their continuing working interest and financial support were Mr. Atholl McBean of Gladding, McBean and Company; Mr. Charles R. Blyth of Blyth and Company, Inc.; and Mr. William L. Stewart, Jr., of the Union Oil Company of California. Dr. Alvin C. Eurich, then acting president of Leland Stanford Junior University, gave his wholehearted understanding, cooperation, and encouragement.

Stanford Research Institute thus came into being as a nonprofit scientific research institution when Articles of Incorporation were signed on October 24, 1946. The purposes for which it was established are clearly set forth as follows.

- "To promote the educational purposes of Leland Stanford Junior University by encouraging, fostering, and conducting scientific investigations and pure and applied research in the physical, biological, and social sciences, engineering and the mechanic arts, and to extend scientific knowledge in the several pursuits and professions of life; and to devote its resources to the advancement of scientific investigation and research and to the assistance of the Leland Stanford Junior University in the promotion of extension of learning and knowledge;

- "To provide, equip, and maintain laboratories, experimental and other facilities for general and specific scientific and industrial research and to make such facilities available to the Leland Stanford Junior University and other institutions and organizations, public or private, for the conduct of research and investigation;

- "To engage, maintain, and develop a staff of qualified educators, scientists, and research experts to carry on the investigations and research projects of the corporation; to provide for the development and improvement of research techniques; and otherwise to aid in the advancement of scientific investigation and of pure and applied research;

- "To establish a center for the accumulation of information useful to scientific and industrial research; to foster the exchange of scientific and technical information with other research and educational institutions, and to publish and disseminate such of its findings as may be deemed of general public interest;

- "To promote and foster the application of science in the development of commerce, trade, and industry, the discovery and development of methods for the beneficial utilization of natural resources, the industrialization of the western United States of America, and the improvement of the general standard of living and the peace and prosperity of mankind . . . "

In the interests of brevity, the usual legal enabling authorization to authorize the carrying out of the foregoing objectives has been omitted from this review, but it is important that the record show the following.

The directors shall serve without compensation and no director shall receive any pecuniary benefit from the corporation except reimbursement for actual expenses incurred in connection with the business of the corporation.

It is interesting to note that the original incorporators of Stanford Research Institute included a provision which authorized dues or assessments as set forth in these words:

That the members of the corporation shall be the members of the Board of Trustees of the Leland Stanford Junior University as from time to time constituted. There shall be such other members or classes of membership as may be set forth in the by-laws. The voting and other rights and privileges of the members and the liability of each or all classes of membership to dues or assessments and the method of collection thereof shall be set forth in the by-laws. Neither the members nor directors of the corporation shall be personally liable for the debts, liabilities, or obligations of the corporation.

In conclusion, the Articles of Incorporation of Stanford Research Institute specifically provide the following.

- "That the corporation is a corporation which does not contemplate pecuniary gain or profit to the members thereof. No part of the net earnings of the corporation shall be distributed to, used by or inure to the benefit of any private member or individual. The corporation shall not carry on propaganda or otherwise attempt to influence legislation. The property of the corporation shall be irrevocably dedicated to charitable and scientific purposes.

- "Upon the dissolution or winding up of the corporation, all funds and property remaining after paying or adequately providing for the debts and obligations of the corporation shall be distributed to the Board of Trustees of the Leland Stanford Junior University for the use and benefit of the Leland Stanford University."

By-laws were adopted and 35 outstanding leaders of banking, construction, education, insurance, investments, rail and water transportation, communications, public utilities, newspapers, lawyers, merchants, oil men, and industrialists were invited and accepted membership on the Board of Directors of Stanford Research Institute to guide its policies. Some of the gentlemen were trustees of Stanford University; most of them were not.

Space was scarce, the university buildings overcrowded. The institute began its operations in rented quarters which previously had been a part of a sprawling temporary government hospital but did have the very real advantage of being closely adjacent to the university.

Funds were provided first by Stanford University and later by history-making loans from six San Francisco banks which had great faith that science could solve the fundamental problems involved in keeping the West prosperous and charting the road to further industrialization which would provide the base of gainful employment of the constantly increasing millions, and finally by private contributions, to a total of approximately $1.5 million. The necessity for the bank loans was the direct result of the institute's having accepted a very considerable volume of research for federal government defense agencies and the three-month and more lag in receiving reimbursement therefor with which to pay the scientific staff and meet normal operating expenses.

SOUTHWEST RESEARCH INSTITUTE

The fourth and latest of the only four such institutions dedicated to regional upbuilding for the benefit of present and future generations was conceived before World War II but did not come into being until September 4, 1947, and for nearly a year thereafter was engaged chiefly in the remodeling of an old Texas ranch house as its first laboratories. Let us turn our study to Texas and the Southwestern United States.

Not everyone in Texas and Oklahoma owns an oil well, as is adequately shown by U.S. Department of Commerce statistics, which disclose that in 1946 the average income of all Texans was $972 compared with the national average income (in the continental United States) of $1211. For the same year in Oklahoma the figure was $895 against the $1211 national average.

By 1951, Texas had drawn closer with $1412 against the national average of $1584, but Oklahomans with an average income of $1182 not only had not kept up, but had actually fallen more behind the national average income than they had been five years previously.

Texas had broken about even in the matter of redistribution of population because of civilian migration, but Oklahoma had suffered disheartening losses as has been brought out earlier in this review. Overall, Texas was enjoying a steady and healthy growth but Oklahoma had less population in 1940 than in 1930, and seemed definitely on the road to further losses. Arkansas and Louisiana, bordering Texas on the east had even lower per capita incomes than Oklahoma. New Mexico and Arizona to the west compared favorably with that of Texas.

State	1920	1930	1940	1950
Arkansas	1,752,204	1,854,482	1,949,587	1,909,511
Arizona	334,162	435,573	499,261	749,587
Louisiana	1,798,509	2,109,593	2,363,880	2,683,516
New Mexico	360,350	423,317	531,818	681,187
Oklahoma	2,028,283	2,396,040	2,336,434	2,233,351

As early as 1941, a young native of Oklahoma still in his twenties had moved to Texas following his graduation from Yale University with a degree in science, and generously founded the Southwest Foundation for Research and Education at San Antonio. He provided all the initial funds through a trust indenture at that time, but completely divorced himself of any and all control by placing the trust in the hands of a self-perpetuating group of seven trustees. The broad objectives were set forth as research chiefly in the fields of medicine, biology, and agriculture.

When the war came, the young founder was commissioned in the U.S. Navy. The trustees were hampered with building and personnel shortages, and as a result they confined themselves to making grants to other nonprofit scientific research institutions for the duration of the war.

While in the service of his country, this young man became imbued with the conviction and determination to do even more for his fellow men when the war was over. This time he wanted it to be something which would help advance the economic position of the people of his native Oklahoma and adopted Texas, and thereby the entire Southwestern area. He was well aware of the contributions that institutions such as the Armour Research Foundation, Battelle Memorial Institute, and the Mellon Institute for Industrial Research had made to the economy of our country. Likewise, he was well acquainted with the regional upbuilding movements which had started in Birmingham and Kansas City, and he felt it would be nationally helpful to have a Southwest Research Institute to serve the Southwest and cooperate with Midwest Research Institute to the north and Southern Research Institute to the east. By the time he returned from navy service, Stanford Research Institute had been established to serve the West and made cooperation easier in states such as New Mexico and Arizona.

This young man also felt the nation needed an institution to help and encourage inventors. An institution which would be so thoroughly nonprofit and noncompetitive that it would inspire inventors with the confidence that they could ask for help and counsel without any fear that their invention would be "stolen from them," a fear those experienced in the field found to be almost universal.

The desire to stimulate and help inventors and inventions was based on the sound knowledge that at least 60 percent of all employment in this country is in jobs brought into being by inventions and discoveries since the year 1900. Automobiles, aircraft, radio, mechanical refrigerators, washing machines, nuclear energy, and radar were but a few of the many hundreds of advancements which had been developed, and which he, like all men trained in science, felt was only the beginning. In that spirit he founded the Institute of Inventive Research as an integral link in his overall plan to help give the region, our nation, and the world a new and all-inclusive family of scientific organizations dedicated to the advancement of mankind. In the few years of its existence it has processed literally thousands of inventions, and encouraged in many ways their developments. But this section primarily regards Southwest Research Institute—yet this mention is necessary to reflect his complete concept.

This young man was Tom Slick. His business interests were cattle and oil; his avocation, science and the contributions science could make to the welfare of our nation's expanding millions. With this background, the reader will be enabled to more fully understand that which was in this young man's heart and mind when he, on September 4, 1947, founded Southwest Research Institute by a trust indenture under the laws of the state of Texas. In legal language the entire purpose of Southwest Research Institute is stated in paragraph 3.01 of said indenture, as follows.

• "It is the purpose of the Donor in creating this trust and the purpose of each of the Governors in accepting the Office of Governor hereunder that this Trust shall establish, and forever during its existence maintain and operate, research facilities available to industry and the public generally and to conduct other activities and always for the public benefit for the following charitable, educational, and scientific purposes:

(a) To stimulate, encourage, and promote applied scientific, technical, and inventive thought and study and to disseminate the information thereby obtained;

(b)   To conduct scientific investigations and industrial research for industry, agriculture, and the public generally;

(c)   To foster the exchange of technical experience and research results among producers, manufacturers, agriculturists, and all others who may be benefitted by the application of pure science;

(d)   To assist manufacturers, farmers, and all others in the development of more efficient and scientific methods of production;

(e)   To advance the use of natural resources by the application of science and research;

(f)   To study, test, and develop new and useful devices, processes, projects, and materials designed for adaptation to public use and application;

(g)   To assist established educational institutions in practical mechanical and technical research and instruction;

(h)   To grant scholarships and fellowships to deserving students, scientists, and engineers desiring practical laboratory study and experience;

(i)   To foster the promotion and development of devices and projects designed to improve public health, hygiene, and well-being;

(j)   To participate in and assist the activities of other nonprofit research organizations engaged in studies and research designed to improve public health, hygiene, and well-being."

In founding Southwest Research Institute, the youngest of the four regional research institutes, Mr. Slick divorced himself completely of any and all control. A board of governors, originally seven in number but subsequently increased to 15, holds title to all property of the institute and is wholly in control at all times. The Board of Governors is self-perpetuating, and as a means of always having at hand qualified successors, has created a board of trustees comprised of 120 leaders in all walks of life. Every governor and trustee serves as a volunteer and, of course, without compensation. Such membership is centered largely in the southwestern states with sufficient members from other regions of the country to assure the mutual benefits of close liaison and cooperation. Mr. Slick is neither a governor nor a trustee, although he gives fully half of his time in volunteer activities in behalf of the institute.

INITIAL FINANCING

We have noted how Dr. Alvin C. Eurich and the trustees of Stanford University responded to the call to take leadership in founding a research institute to provide facilities dedicated to the upbuilding of the Pacific Coast and the western states. Likewise how the business, industrial, and civic leaders of the region subsequently fulfilled their pledge to obtain contributed funds to expand the movement and are giving it their continued working interest and financial support.

History is repeating itself at Southwest Research Institute where one man provided all initial funds until the institute demonstrated its region-building value in the public interest. Now the contributions from many others combine to approximately equal the founder's initial endowment.

The launching of both Stanford and Southwest Research Institutes was similar to the long-established policy of many of America's most renowned foundations which often finance movements considered valuable until such new activities demonstrate their worth and can attract the support necessary for continuance and expansion.

In the social service field, the Community Chests of our nation also follow a similar policy of making grants or extending temporary support to new services deemed essential, until such new activities can prove their worth and warrant inclusion among Chest agencies.

In contrast, Midwest Research Institute and Southern Research Institute each started with a much broader base of contributed financial support. Both procedures are in the best American tradition.

Each of these four institutes is clearly shown to have been founded primarily for the purpose of helping solve the fundamental problems confronting their respective geographic areas. It is significant that the leadership in these four widely separated regions unhesitatingly turned to scientific research to make the discoveries and chart the courses which would lead to gainful employment and career opportunities for our nation's constantly increasing millions. It is encouraging to every believer in the free enterprise system that all four were started small and operated economically solely with funds contributed by unselfish individuals and organizations possessed of the desire to help make America bigger and better for everyone. It is particularly heartening that none of the four groups either sought, or would have accepted local, state, or federal government aid.

THE FOUR REGIONAL INSTITUTES DO NOT COMPETE

There is a saying to the effect that competition is the spice of life, and it is unquestionably true in many ways under the American system. There is another saying that the exceptions prove the rule, and this is clearly exemplified by the fact that each of the four regional institutes has consistently sought to encourage the widest possible use of science in every logical segment of business and industry. The directors and key staff members all give substantially of their time in addressing public meetings and counseling students and young scientists, and follow the policy that known scientific facts are freely available without any charge whatsoever if no laboratory work is required to answer the inquiry.

Each of the four institutes has a strict rule that it will not compete with commercial testing and engineering firms. They consistently reject any and all proposals for commercial testing. They confine themselves to fundamental and applied research, with the thought always uppermost in mind of how the solving of any given problem will accrue to the benefit of the region they were founded to serve. They encourage the use and the growth of commercial facilities because they are well aware there is a vast shortage of scientific and technological personnel, and that the problems to be solved are so vast and so numerous that all existing facilities everywhere are inadequate to meet the demand. The directors and staffs of the four regional research institutes feel that science is the servant of mankind. Respectfully, your reviewer would compare their enthusiasm and sincerity to that of clergymen, for just as the men of the church know and teach how much religion means to the spiritual welfare of mankind, these scientists know how much science has done and how much it can continue to do for the physical and economic upbuilding of the peoples of the world.

Any review of the four public service not-for-profit regional research institutes would not be complete if it failed to point out that these institutions do not indulge in "cheap research." They each have a formula under which the prospective sponsor seeking their services is frankly told he will be carrying his fair share of the public service activities for which the institute was primarily founded and operated.

* * *

In Chapter IV the story of the founding of Mellon and Battelle is told; Chapter V covers IIT Research Institute; and Hugh Buhrman's treatise gives the unique background of the founding of Midwest, Southern, Stanford, and Southwest research institutes. Of the so-called "nine independents," Cornell and Franklin remain. Their stories follow.

THE BIRTH OF CORNELL AERONAUTICAL LABORATORY, INC.*

The following deals with the fortuitous wedding of a university with an industrial research laboratory, which has resulted in a pattern unique and interesting and perhaps truly significant in the framework of pure and applied science of the nation. Although the marriage was not of the shotgun variety, it was accomplished hastily and the ultimate merits of the union cannot yet be completely evaluated. (It is the author's view that, with some 20 years having since transpired, the merits of the union are abundantly evidenced by a host of technological contributions.) Be it said, however, that the relations are happy and the progeny are all healthy.

The Curtiss-Wright Airplane Division Research Laboratory came into being in 1942. It was the result of the dreams and hardheaded thinking of Burdette S. Wright, Vice President of the Curtiss-Wright Corporation, in charge of the Airplane Division. At that time, no aircraft company in the country had, or ever had had, a research laboratory. That may seem to be a strange statement since it is obvious that aviation has been able to advance only on a wave of vigorous and imaginative research. The research involved, however, had nearly always been someone else's; the aircraft companies had seldom seen the necessity or accepted the responsibility to undertake it themselves.

In this atmosphere Burdette Wright with his ideas of an autonomous research laboratory which would be in an organizational position parallel with, not subservient to, engineering, sales, and finance, and which would be expected in its own right to make contributions to aeronautical knowledge, was a bit of a dreamer! But he was also an agressive and persuasive man. So the research laboratory idea was consummated; priority battles for materials and equipment were won; and on February 11, 1943, the new Research Laboratory of the Curtiss-Wright Airplane Division at Buffalo, New York, was dedicated with Dr. Clifford C. Furnas being named as director.

This laboratory, representing an ultimate investment of approximately $4.5 million, was housed in a building of about 90,000 square feet across the street from the home plant of the Airplane Division. The largest, most expensive, and most dramatic piece of equipment in the laboratory was a large wind tunnel, to cost $3.5 million, which would be capable of testing large airplane models up to the then unheard-of speed of 750 miles per hour—approximately the speed of sound.

---

*Based on "Experiment in Research, Cornell's Aeronautical Laboratory on the Niagara Frontier," by Dr. Clifford Cook Furnas.

During the remaining war years, this laboratory grew and progressed. Admittedly, during this period its research contributions did not achieve any great significance. The effectiveness of research organizations grows— but slowly. Five years is the generally conceded minimum for a new research organization to grow to a stature to produce worthwhile results. Be it said, however, that as of V-J Day the flower of Burdette Wright's dream was flourishing nicely and bore the promise of fine fruit to come.

The joyous sounds of victory celebration were still under way when there came the inevitable flood of telegrams cancelling contracts for wartime production of aircraft. Within weeks production activities were reduced to a mere 5 percent of the wartime peak. Rightly or wrongly, Curtiss-Wright Corporation decided that it would not be financially justified in continuing to underwrite the activities of its Airplane Division Research Laboratory. To disband would not only bring serious hardships to many members of the scientific staff, it would also mean the loss of a vigorous research organization which could and should make significant contributions to the aircraft industry and to national defense. The only answer appeared to be to convert it into a public research institution, preferably as part of a recognized university, and to seek support from the aircraft industry, as a whole, and from the government.

With this decision in hand, Burdette Wright and Guy Vaughan, president of Curtiss-Wright Corporation, entered into discussions with Cornell University to see if it would be willing to accept the gift of this active and slightly obstreperous brainchild.

The potentialities of the situation captured the constructive imagination and enlisted the immediate enthusiastic support of Cornell University's president, Edmund E. Day. He and Dean S. C. Hollister, head of the College of Engineering, prepared the case for asking the Cornell Board of Trustees to accept the new, elaborate, and obviously expensive facility that an aviation company, for some reason, wished to remove from its list of assets. (It is the author's opinion that the Cornell trustees undoubtedly realized how immensely valuable such a laboratory would be to the entire aircraft industry and were therefore confident of acquiring the needed financial support from that industry's constituents.) After due consideration, the board lived up to the Cornell tradition of aggressive and constructive action and unanimously accepted the gift, with the understanding and proviso that no university funds would be used to cover operating expenses.

Thus, Cornell became the owner of the laboratory, and the appropriate amenities in the form of legal documents were exchanged. But this was only half the battle. Any business must have cash in the bank to carry on its operations, and this called for working capital, which would be used as a revolving fund to pay current bills, which the university was not in a position to supply. Dean Hollister, ably assisted by J. Carleton Ward (one of Cornell's most enthusiastic alumni and president and chairman of the board of the Fairchild Engine and Airplane Corporation) began harassing the top executives of the eastern aircraft manufacturers to give necessary working capital for the new research venture. Though the difficulties of seeing and persuading the necessary individuals and boards of directors were extreme—the ultimate response was excellent. At a memorable and final dinner meeting in New York, six of the eastern companies—Fairchild Engine and Airplane Corporation, the Grumman Aircraft Engineering Corporation, the Republic Aviation Corporation, the United Aircraft Corporation, the Bell Aircraft Corporation, and the Avco Manufacturing Corporation—pledged to match the Curtiss-Wright gift with the contribution of a $675,000 working capital fund, provided official concurrence could be obtained from their respective boards of directors, and payment could be made before the end of the calendar year 1945. All the pledges were fulfilled, but the race with the calendar was close—the last check of the pledged amount was received by the university on the afternoon of December 31, 1945. Thus, one era of the existence of this new laboratory closed dramatically.

THE BIRTH OF THE FRANKLIN INSTITUTE RESEARCH LABORATORIES

Ever since 1824, when The Franklin Institute was founded, it has been engaged in serving mankind through applied science. What started as a case of models became a major science museum; excess books donated by early members resulted in one of the largest science libraries on the east coast; and periodic experimental investigations led to the establishment of a laboratory for research and development.

The early research efforts at the institute focused on meteorology, strength of materials (for which the first tensile testing machine was designed and built in the United States), screw thread standardization, patent activities, and other technical pursuits. So widely known were these early activities that Franklin became the recipient of the first research grant ever awarded by an agency of the United States Government. The 1830 grant provided for investigative work into the causes of the dangerously frequent steam boiler explosions. One such explosion destroyed a vessel at the Philadelphia docks shortly before Andrew Jackson, the then President of the United States, was slated to inspect the ship.

While this effort was worthwhile, the resultant labors were sporadic; however, research and development activities at Franklin increased during World War II, and the attendant results proved to be very valuable to the federal government. Such success eventually led to the establishment of the Franklin Institute Research Laboratories as a separate division.

During the wartime years, the Office of Scientific Research and Development and the National Defense Research Committee (NDRC) were charged with getting classified war work accomplished. NDRC was looking for available people and space—and Franklin had both.

Preliminary contract negotiations were conducted in January 1942 by Dr. Henry B. Allen, secretary and director of the institute, with Dr. S. H. Caldwell, the then chief of Section D-2 of NDRC. Plans were discussed with the staff, and on February 1, the original work began. The first project called for the design of airborne fire control sights and director systems. Later in 1942, a second contract was started to improve ammunition and projectile design. Shortly thereafter, the latter effort was expanded into a third area of gun design.

The electrical engineering staff busily engaged themselves in the development of stabilized torpedo directors, gyroscope gun sights, bomb and rocket sights, and control systems. This effort included all of the auxiliaries, controllers, servomechanisms, radar, and fire control aids. In addition, preproduction prototypes of several sighting and computer systems were built for aircraft tests in the Franklin model shop. The many computations required were done in those days by specially designed analog computers and by the forerunner of the digital computer, namely a room full of mathematicians with desk calculators.

In the chemical engineering field, propellants were evaluated, and some three dozen single- and double-base powders were test fired in a special caliber 50-scale gun to learn which kind least eroded the tube. Meanwhile, the engineering group designed recoil mechanisms capable of handling the large forces of firing.

The Franklin Laboratories as they exist today are an outgrowth of this war work. The state of the world at the conclusion of hostilities was such that the government felt military research and development should be continued in the interest of national defense.

During the early postwar period, the not-for-profit research institutes were very much in the national picture. W. F. Jackson, Jr., by then an institute vice president, along with Secretary Henry B. Allen and F. W. Fulweiler, visited Harold Vagtborg at Armour to discuss the prevailing interest in establishing such a research institution directly associated with The Franklin Institute and to determine the best way of doing this. The institute had the public image of a museum and planetarium; however, leaders at Franklin were anxious to establish a more dynamic image and at the same time make a larger contribution to the public welfare. Vagtborg shared with the group the Armour experience during the previous seven years and also provided the Franklin people with copies of Armour's documents. Subsequent to this visit, Jackson and Fulweiler had called on Battelle and Mellon as well as a variety of universities which had organized applied research contracts with the government, especially the defense establishment.

All of the people consulted were most helpful and very encouraging. As a result, the board of managers voted to continue the research as an entity in the institute family—FILRAD, The Franklin Institute Laboratories for Research and Development.* The transition was informal and can best be dated by the arrival of the first full-time executive director, C. H. Greenall, who reported on April 1, 1946. As a retired colonel, he was eminently qualified to head this ordnance effort. In addition to continuing work on guns, propellants, and fire control, FILRAD's activities were immediately expanded to cover the problems of industry, since much of the accumulated knowledge could improve industrial products and methods.

Thus, 123 years after its founding, The Franklin Institute began broadening its service to the nation and the public. FILRAD's mission was, and still is, interdisciplinary in nature to serve a multiplicity of clients. With the help of its competitors, the fledgling lab was able to accept the challenge of making a name for itself as a not-for-profit organization.

---

*Shortened in 1965 to The Franklin Institute Research Laboratories and "FIRL."

CHAPTER VII

GROWTH OF THE NINE INDEPENDENTS

The story of Mellon Institute from its origins to its merger in 1967 with Carnegie Institute of Technology to form Carnegie-Mellon University has already been told in Chapter IV. Likewise, in this same chapter the founding of Battelle Memorial Institute in 1929, its vigorous growth to the present time, and its international status are related.

The demonstrated success, without endowment, of Armour Research Foundation (now IIT Research Institute) and the need for regional economic development in four regions of the nation led to the creation of Southern, Midwest, Stanford, and Southwest Research Institutes as well as Cornell Aeronautical Laboratory, Inc. and The Franklin Institute Research Laboratories. Chapter VI has given the background that brought about the establishment of these seven institutions, and following is the story of their development to the present time.

MODERN HISTORY OF IIT RESEARCH INSTITUTE

IIT Research Institute (IITRI) was established in 1936 as a not-for-profit contract research and development organization "to promote, encourage, maintain and aid scientific investigation and research in affiliation with Armour Institute of Technology by the faculty, staff, and alumni thereof, and others associated therewith." Today that excerpt from its charter still accurately defines the institution's mission, despite far-reaching changes that have evolved in the nation's research and development activity. IITRI was chartered as the Research Foundation of Armour Institute of Technology. When Armour Tech merged with Lewis Institute in 1940 to form Illinois Institute of Technology, the affiliated research arm was renamed Armour Research Foundation (ARF). In 1963, to avoid confusion with similarly named organizations and philanthropic foundations, the institution assumed its present designation, IIT Research Institute.

The story of the growth of IITRI reflects the growth of research and development activity in the United States. When Dr. Thomas C. Poulter became the first director of the Research Foundation of Armour Institute of Technology in 1936, several projects already were being pursued by a staff which numbered about 30. During that first year, the foundation conducted research involving automatic coal stokers, electrical characteristics of steel strand, and coal washability. In 1937, at the end of the first fiscal year, the foundation's receipts for research totaled about $40,000.

Dr. Harold Vagtborg, who became director of the foundation in 1938, was instrumental not only in the early growth of IITRI, but also in the founding of other research institutes. After leaving the foundation in 1944, Dr. Vagtborg went to Kansas City, Missouri, where he formed Midwest Research Institute, and later to San Antonio, Texas, to form Southwest Research Institute and other sister institutions. By 1944 ARF had grown to employ 350 staff members who conducted projects representing an annual volume of $1.7 million. With Dr. Vagtborg's departure at the end of 1944, Dr. Jesse E. Hobson was named director. During the war years, ARF had responded to the nation's military research needs. In the years directly

IITRI Administration Building, Chicago, Illinois

following World War II, Dr. Hobson guided ARF in realigning its expanding research capabilities to concentrate again on aiding the nation's peacetime industrial development. Dr. Haldon A. Leedy, a member of the IITRI staff since 1938, was named director in 1948 upon the resignation of Dr. Hobson, who became executive director of Stanford Research Institute. ARF research volume reached $4.25 million by 1949—a 250 percent increase in five years.

Under Dr. Leedy's direction, the institute maintained the position of eminence which it had achieved among the nation's independent, contract research organizations. During the postwar years, many such research organizations had been formed; however, many did not survive, as industrial firms established or expanded their own research facilities. Others prospered by successful adjustment to changing research needs.

In 1961, ARF's 25th anniversary year, a $2-million contract was awarded by the Department of Defense for technical supervision of the Electromagnetic Compatibility Analysis Center (ECAC) in Annapolis, Maryland. The contract has been subsequently renewed on an annual basis. The ECAC facility is devoted primarily to radio frequency interference research. In 1963 ARF conducted over $23 million in research, an increase of 16 percent over the previous year.

In June 1963, Dr. Elmer H. Schulz was appointed to the post of executive vice president and director of IITRI, succeeding Dr. Leedy who had recently been named president of Nuclear-Chicago Corp. Dr. Schulz had joined the ARF staff in 1946, subsequently serving as manager of the Physics and Electrical Engineering Divisions and as vice president for research operations. He was responsible for the development of the institution to national and international prominence.

The constantly changing emphasis in industry and government needs have influenced the growth and direction of growth at ARF. When military research was needed, ARF responded by developing staff and facilities to perform military research. When the space program developed, ARF became involved in space research. Environmental emphasis led the organization to develop this area of capability. Now energy, health, and transportation research have become important elements in determining the direction of growth. Thus, over the years, new divisions have been formed and old divisions have been phased out according to the emphasis being given in government and industry. The policy was adopted that no unit within the organization was sacred, recognizing that to be dynamic, the organization must change with the needs of the times. A unit is no longer useful if it cannot be self-supporting.

Representative technical achievements over the years include the following developments: design and construction of a mobile laboratory (The Snow Cruiser) for Admiral Byrd's third Antarctic expedition; the first commercially practical magnetic tape recorder; magnetic film and sound track for 8- and 16-mm movie film; titanium alloy; lightweight brick aggregate; flexible ceramic coatings; automatic revolver-type 20-mm aircraft cannon; 106-mm recoilless antitank rifle and new type ammunition; 115-mm boosted rocket launcher; fiber metal; elimination of contrails from military jet aircraft; mechanical olive harvester; computer programed optical lens design; automatic packaging and labelling machines; combustible cartridge cases; fine particle counter; technoeconomic studies of Chicago's industrial future;

surgical stapler; fiber optic ear probe; fire spread and control program; electromechanical articulated dummy to test space suits; thermal control coatings for space vehicles; economical video tape recorder for home and classroom use. IITRI also installed the first industrial research nuclear reactor and has played an important role in atomic weapons testing, cancer chemotherapy, olfactronics, microencapsulation, polymers metallic alloys, nondestructive testing, composite materials, plasma physics, space exploration planning, biomedical engineering, advance propulsion systems, and man/machine communications.

CORNELL AERONAUTICAL LABORATORY, INC.

Cornell Aeronautical Laboratory (CAL), now Calspan Corporation, came into being New Year's Day 1946 as "an instrument of service to the aircraft industry—to education—to the public at large." On January 2, 1946, the more than 500 employees who had been employed by an industrial corporation just two days before, came to work as the employees of a quasi-public research institution which had to make its own living. And, while the laboratory had a research backlog which would enable it to sustain itself for several months, in the words of Dr. Clifford C. Furnas, "not even the collective hope and enthusiasm of the employees could provide real assurance that this 'experiment in research' would be a success." When the laboratory's employees were offered aid in finding more stable employment, however, only one man left.

Two years later, in 1948, the university installed Dr. Theodore P. Wright in the new post of vice president for research. This office, exercising general cognizance over and full-time responsibility for all contract research in the university, formed the optimum link between the laboratory and the university. At the same time, CAL was incorporated as a stock corporation of the state of New York, wholly owned by the university. Because of its not-for-profit and public service objectives, CAL received a federal tax exemption. The laboratory thus achieved the status of a subsidiary with an initial capitalization of $5 million and a sufficiently autonomous position to act as an independent unit without involving the university in its business operations or financial liabilities.

Since its inception, Cornell Laboratory has performed some half billion dollars of research in the aeronautical and associated sciences, as well as in broadening areas of electronics, computers, ecology and transportation. Its

More than $25 million worth of research facilities are available at Calspan's Advanced Technology Center. Oval partly visible at upper right is the vehicle test track.

physical facilities have quadrupled and include some of the most advanced equipment for experimental research in the world.

In late 1972, the laboratory began a process of separation from Cornell University. It changed its name to Calspan, converted to a for-profit operation, and sold 32 percent of its stock to the public. While Cornell remains a majority stockholder, the university is committed to total divestiture over the years. In its new role, Calspan continues as an independent institution devoted to applied research in engineering and physical science, but has added the dimension of new product development and sale to its business objectives.

OUTSTANDING ACHIEVEMENTS OF CAL/CALSPAN RESEARCH

■ CAL conceived and developed the first hypersonic shock tunnel—a new testing device in which a wind tunnel nozzle was added to a shock tube to provide hypervelocity air flows.

■ As a follow-on to the development by NACA of the slotted throat to prevent choking of wind tunnels when testing models at the speed of sound, CAL conceived and developed a perforated throat for transonic testing, which not only deblocked the tunnel's test section, but markedly reduced the reflections of shock waves from the tunnel walls upon the model.

■ Through research in supersonic aerodynamics, CAL has produced theories, with experimental verification, of basic value to aircraft and missile designers. One of the four or five basic methods for solving general supersonic wing problems was developed at CAL in 1949 and has been widely used ever since.

■ In the field of low-speed aerodynamics relating to helicopters and V/TOL's, CAL became an international authority on dynamic loading.

■ CAL designed and developed through the prototype stage the Lacrosse guided missile, a highly accurate, close support weapon of the army.

■ To assist the navy in aircraft carrier operations, CAL conceived and initially designed the first computer-based automatic landing system designed.

■ Calspan has pioneered in the development of "the variable stability" aircraft as an in-flight simulator to study the flying qualities of advanced aircraft designs.

■ In a program begun under internal funds, CAL conceived and developed the "perceptron," an electronic device capable of brainlike recognition, perception, and memory. From that start, Calspan has become a technical leader in various areas of automatic pattern recognition.

■ Recognized as the foremost expert in terrain-following techniques for aircraft, Calspan developed techniques over the years which are now widely accepted by the military and industry and employed in operational aircraft.

■ One of the first to raise its voice to the effect that radar cross sections of missiles could be made infinitely smaller than generally believed, Calspan has pioneered in the development of techniques to measure small cross sections of our own vehicles.

■ During the course of an early missile program, CAL developed a high response hydraulic valve that was superior in performance to its contemporaries and formed the basis for a spin-off company with sales today in the $40-million range per annum.

■ Calspan has developed a major program over the years in all elements of transportation research, particularly highway safety. Its findings, including experimental evidence, of the value of seat belts helped spur adoption of this safety device by the public and automobile manufacturers. Its unique project in Automobile Crash Injury Research (ACIR) has led to important findings about the major causes of injuries during automobile accidents, many of which have influenced the industry to take remedial action. (For example, Cornell's findings that ejection was the leading cause of death in auto accidents has led the manufacturers to universally adopt a safety door latch.)

SOUTHERN RESEARCH INSTITUTE

Mellon Institute had Robert K. Duncan, with his original idea of a working partnership between science and industry; Battelle Memorial Institute had Gordon Battelle, who left a sizable endowment to breathe life into his dreams of an organization for industrial research; and Southern Research Institute (SRI) had Thomas Wesley Martin, who supplied neither the original idea nor an original endowment, but provided instead the vision, energy, influence, stamina, business acumen, and patience to transform the mere words of an incorporation paper into a living, growing, successful research organization.

A comparison might be made between the actions of SRI's Thomas W. Martin and those of the Mellon brothers—Andrew and Richard. In both instances, the enlightened pursuit of a goal—a scientific research organization —followed close on the heels of a good idea from a chemistry professor. In the case of Southern, there were actually two chemistry professors, both at the University of Alabama, who played key roles in the development of the organization. The first was Dr. Stewart J. Lloyd, who was commissioned by the Birmingham Industrial Board in the early 1930s to prepare "A Chemical Survey of the Birmingham District." His exhaustive study on natural resources of the district and the most promising avenues for their use was capped with a personal observation that perhaps "the most useful step which could be taken to promote the growth of the chemical industry locally" would be to organize a small company to "take over, patent, and exploit, or facilitate the exploitation of, the ideas and chemical discoveries of local inventors. This should be a commercial, nonaltruistic company, conducted along ordinary business lines for profit, and above all, composed of people whose main interests are in Birmingham."

Although Dr. Lloyd's report was destined to be widely distributed, and the data therein a useful reference for many years, his suggestion for a research organization had no such immediate acceptance. The idea did not die quietly, however, but remained to prick the conscience of men who were genuinely concerned with improving the economy of the South and who believed, with Lloyd, that science might chart the pathway.

Eight years after Lloyd's report was written, some of his words surfaced as part of a well-researched and forceful address by another University of Alabama chemistry professor. Dr. George D. Palmer, Jr., delivering a talk to the Alabama Academy of Science, just before stepping down as president in 1940, first described the South's economic condition. His facts documented

President Roosevelt's contention that the South was "the nation's number one economic problem." Little scientific research was being done in the region, Palmer said, and few patents were being issued. He then urged that Southerners develop some scientific fields related to utilization of the natural resources of the region and earn patents in those fields. This would, in turn, create new industries and additional jobs in the South and help solve some of its problems, he said. He suggested an approach—the development of laboratories in the South by individual businesses, colleges, and the federal government *and* the development of a scientific research organization that would assist any and all industries, as suggested earlier by Lloyd.

That address, in March 1940, attracted attention and produced results, one of which was the organization of the Southern Association of Science and Industry, an organization that for more than a decade was a common forum for men of industry, science, and finance to discuss and plan their individual and combined efforts for the advancement of the region. Another result was an invitation to Palmer to repeat the address at the annual meeting of the Alabama State Chamber of Commerce in October 1940.

It was immediately after Dr. Palmer's address to the State Chamber that Thomas W. Martin entered the picture. The leader of Alabama Power Co. through its first 40 years, Mr. Martin was a successful combination of a dreamer who saw possibilities for improved business and economic development and a hard-driving pragmatist who marshaled human and material resources to put substance into those dreams. He proposed that the State Chamber pick up Dr. Palmer's suggestion immediately and that $250,000 be raised over a period of five years to launch this industrial research organization. A committee to study the proposal was appointed under the chairmanship of Benjamin Russell, a textile industry executive. After appropriate study, the committee voted, in February 1941, to establish the Alabama Research Institute, to be incorporated as a nonprofit organization. Investigations were begun to look again at the state's economic and scientific situation and the best methods for their improvement. The study included consultations with Director Edward Weidlein of Mellon Institute, who was later to address the first and several other official functions of Mellon's counterpart in Alabama.

This study culminated in the signing of a charter by 78 leading business or industrial leaders of the state and two days later, on October 11, 1941, in the filing of incorporation papers for the Alabama Research Institute. Chapter VI provides an account of the incorporation and describes the purposes for which the organization was founded, as listed in its Constitution and By-Laws. Also mentioned there is the war-imposed hiatus between the incorporation in 1941 and the beginning of operations in 1945, the change of name to Southern Research Institute, and the purchase of an 1890s mansion and its conversion into the institute's first building. Mr. Martin, chairman of SRI as planning for operations began, remained in the position until his death in 1964, always providing his special enthusiasm and sense of urgency to get on with the job at hand.

A search committee sought the best advice available all over the nation and interviewed dozens of candidates before announcing their choice for the first director of Southern Research Institute—Dr. Wilbur A. Lazier. A Ph.D. chemist from the University of Wisconsin, Lazier was a veteran of 19 years in the Wilmington research laboratories of DuPont, where he had established himself as an expert on catalytic hydrogenation. He went to work immediately after his appointment in August 1944, recruiting scientists, looking for scientific equipment in the midst of wartime shortages, and supervising the work of carpenters as they converted drawing rooms into laboratories and bedrooms into offices.

In April of 1945, with V-J Day still five months away, research was begun. The subjects of early research projects could have been lifted intact from the founders' hopeful prospectus: peanuts, tobacco, oranges, cotton, coal, iron, wood, petroleum, potatoes, sugarcane, and other southern products and resources. The year ended with $66,000 in research completed and a total staff of 33.

The first permanent building built by Southern Research Institute, the Engineering Laboratory, was dedicated in November 1947. It was the first of an almost continuous parade of new buildings popping up as the research program grew and demanded more space. An average of one new building every two years has been maintained, with total space now in excess of 230,000 square feet.

One year after operations began, a would-be contributor placed an advance condition on his gift which was to be one of the most significant actions in the institute's early history. Ben May, a successful Mobile businessman and lumber operator, was approached for a contribution to the capital fund. His reply was an offer to contribute a sum for the operating funds if the money would be used for research for human welfare, rather than for industrial advance. This additional scope was deemed to be within the intent of the charter, and research was soon underway on experimental cancer chemotherapy—a program that was destined to become the largest single area of work within the institute. From the beginning, and continuing now through 28 years, the cancer research program has been under the direction of Dr. Howard E. Skipper, who assembled over the years a strong team of biologists, biochemists, organic chemists, pharmacologists, mathematicians, veterinarians, and others, who have blended the skills and viewpoints of their disciplines into a carefully coordinated assault on cancer through the use of drugs. Several of the drugs developed at Southern Research Institute, notably those in the nitrosourea and imidazole triazine groups, are among the best available today for treatment of certain types of cancer. Concepts and strategies of drug treatment carefully worked out in animal studies at SRI have had an impact on the national program of cancer research and treatment by suggesting the best methods and schedules of administering drugs. The American Cancer Society, the institute's oldest continuous sponsor, has supported a portion of this work almost from the beginning. The National Cancer Institute first made heavy investment in the program about 1957, and has been for the past several years the agency sponsoring the greatest amount of SRI research as measured in dollars. Other support has come from the Charles F. Kettering and Alfred P. Sloan Foundations as well as other sources.

Growth of the Southern Research Institute was steady during the first several years, with the volume figure for each year reflecting an increase of approximately $100,000. Thus, in 1948, the fourth-year volume was $406,000. A notable occurrence in that year was the appointment of a new director. Dr. Lazier accepted an offer to become Director of Chemical Research with Charles Pfizer & Co., Brooklyn, New York, early in 1948. An assistant director of SRI, Dr. William M. Murray, Jr., was appointed acting director in Lazier's place. Six months later, following a wide search for other candidates and an evaluation of the institute's performance during that period, the trustees elected Dr. Murray as director. It was a position he was to hold for 26 years, as his organization grew twentyfold, from a $400,000 volume to $8 million in 1973. The success and growth of a research organization have a simple explanation, according to Dr. Murray. It was all a matter of a sponsor having a problem or a need and believing that your research organization had the best skills and capabilities to solve the problem. He was a strong believer in "research entrepreneurs," scientists who would launch out into a certain specialized field; talk convincingly to sponsors, professional groups, and others; build a team for research;

A portion of Southern Research Institute today (1974), showing several interconnected life sciences laboratory buildings, the administrative building, and the Martin Memorial Library.

produce results in the laboratory; and grow and change with the field. It was a theory derived, at least in part, empirically, for that had been the pattern of Southern Research Institute's growth.

With life sciences research accounting for well over one-half of the annual volume today, the most obvious entrepreneur example might be Dr. Skipper, who launched his cancer chemotherapy program in 1946, when "everybody knew" that cancer was incurable, and that anticancer drugs didn't work. Unfortunately, "everybody" was largely correct at that time, and the research field was new and uncrowded. When the National Cancer Institute began significant funding for research in the mid-1950s, it found few experienced laboratories qualified to take part in its contract program. Southern, with a decade of qualification, was one. Through the years, Southern's Kettering-Meyer Laboratory, as the life sciences departments are called, has been in the forefront of cancer research.

Since Dr. Murray's retirement June 30, 1974, Dr. Skipper has been president of Southern, but he also retains his direction of the Kettering-Meyer Laboratory. Day-to-day administration is in the hands of Rollin D. Osgood, Jr., executive vice president, a 28-year veteran of the organization's business and financial positions. John A. Montgomery and Sabert Oglesby, Jr., are vice presidents; Andrew Wyper, Jr., is secretary, and Paul J. Sharbel is treasurer.

The growth of Southern to its present size and stature would surely be pleasing to its founders, and some of them are still on the board of trustees to enjoy that pleasure. Others, if transported suddenly from mid-1940s to mid-1970s, would notice some deviations from their plan. First and foremost among the ideas of the founders was the development of southern industry and agriculture through scientific research. Research for southern sponsors has been performed continually from the beginning, and is still today. But after only a few years, the institute's leadership recognized that research was a national business and that substantial growth of the institute could not be expected on the basis of sponsorship solely from within the region. The founders had in mind an organization doing research primarily for companies and for individuals, and so it was—100 percent—in the first year. By the sixth year, government contract dollars accounted for 20 percent of total volume, and a decision was made to actively seek more government contracts in order to maintain a lower overhead and to provide more stability. The percentage of government research grew steadily, and during the period 1964 through 1967, it exceeded 75 percent of the total volume. From its early emphasis on "industrial chemistry," the institute's experience over the years has realigned its emphasis until today well over half of the total volume is created in the life sciences area. Engineering has remained a strong second through the years. On one goal, the founders would find special satisfaction—that of providing job opportunities at all levels for southern young people who wished to study science and remain in their own region for a career. Today, as always, the preponderance of the Southern Research Institute staff is made up of Southerners.

Finally, the founders might be surprised at the size of the institute today. In 1945, they spoke hopefully of a facility that might eventually employ as many as 200. In 1974, 540 staff members are at work, with the volume of research expected to exceed the 1973 record of $8 million.

Comparing their 30-year-old dream with present reality, the founders would almost certainly consider their efforts worthwhile and the organization successful according to the spirit, if not the letter, of their original blueprint. They probably would regard as prophetic the words of Charles Kettering, speaking to the scientists of the two-year-old Southern Research Institute in 1947:

> Set up your laboratories, equip them. You cannot tell what is going to come out of them now, or ten or fifteen years hence.

Your achievements will be different from what you now think, but they will be wonderful. And that won't be the end—there are no terminal points in human progress.

MIDWEST RESEARCH INSTITUTE*

In Chapter VI under the Midwest Research Institute section, Hugh Buhrman related the circumstances that brought about the creation of Midwest Research Institute (MRI). It is the story of how over 100 business and professional leaders in the six states surrounding Kansas City were instrumental in the organization of a research institute designed to bring industrial development to an area of the nation where the economy was based almost entirely on agriculture.

During the year 1944, at a time when I was Director of Armour Research Foundation (now IITRI) in Chicago, I consulted with the principals who established the new institute on matters relating to organization, by-laws, procedures, fund raising, selection of initial rented quarters, and personnel, making numerous speeches throughout the six-state area to explain how science and technology bring about industrial development. On January 1, 1945, I resigned my position at Armour and became president of the new organization. During my first year, I accepted almost 200 additional invitations from numerous types of groups in the area to speak on this same subject of industrial development.

MRI's initial capital and operating fund of just over $500,000 was provided by 212 individuals and businesses. By May of 1948, Midwest had a staff of 106, an annual budget of $600,000, and a site for its permanent facilities; moreover, there was a surplus of almost $900,000 (including a special building fund of $700,000), and MRI was actually self-supporting on its research operations.

With a balanced budget and a course for the future charted, I resigned as of September 1, 1948, to accept the offer of a position that had been held open for me over a year—namely, president and director of the research institutions that were being established in San Antonio, Texas. Dr. George Ziegler of the MRI staff became executive officer until the appointment of Dr. Charles Kimball as president in 1950. Kimball, a Bostonian educated at Harvard, arrived at MRI in June 1950, having headed the Research

---

*The author's intimate involvement necessitated the use of the first person point of view in this section.

Laboratories Division of Bendix Aviation in Detroit, following wartime research in the electronics and radar fields.

In its early years, MRI's work was largely confined to clients in the six states surrounding Kansas City. This presented a major growth dilemma because the role of research in industry was recognized in only a few advanced specialties. The degree of industrialization in the Middle West was much less intensive than on the two coasts, and many regional industries did not appear to require the application of sophisticated technology, although the demands of earlier World War II production had emphasized the significance of technology to industries in Kansas City and other centers throughout the region.

Initially, three major areas of research appeared promising at MRI—all based generally on chemistry. Thus, MRI's early management team emphasized chemistry. Only a few of the initial research projects bore any semblance to those undertaken today. Many were small troubleshooting tasks posed by plant managers who had not as yet developed their own research capabilities. In some instances, sustaining arrangements were made with local firms whereby MRI, in effect, functioned as a standby research department. As companies gained in sophistication over the years, the sustaining and troubleshooting assignments gave way to larger programs.

Early projects for regional companies were typically product and process development in soluble coffee, home laundry improvements, lightweight aggregates, glass fibers, sorghum grains, and natural resources indigenous to the Midwest. An important wider spectrum of projects coming from out-of-region clients included studies in the relationship between smog in Los Angeles and automobile exhaust; the first multiclient project for Sucker Rod Pumping Research, Inc. (some 20 petroleum and supplier companies); the first activity abroad—banana head rot disease for Standard Fruit and Steamship in Honduras; extensive efforts in high energy boron type fuels; and the development of the NEAR system for civil defense.

By 1952, the institute passed two benchmarks: it was again "in the black," a record that has continued without interruption to date, and it recorded in that year the first $1-million-volume year.

A special characteristic of MRI has been its close ties with the public and private leadership of the region. This began when some 212 individuals, companies, and foundations contributed the initial $500,000 to found the institute. Throughout the years, this relationship has been continually nurtured, particularly through the MRI Board of Trustees, which has some

125 members, most of them residents of the midcontinent states; the balance have close ties to this region. The trustees have played a significant role in developing the institute's programs for regional benefit and have also served as advocates for contract research among their own businesses and other connections.

While the majority of research spending emanated from federal agencies, and still does, MRI operated for many years virtually exclusively on private sector projects; however, the corporate base of the Middle West could not alone support an institute with a set of disciplines broad enough to meet the region's research needs. As time passed, federally sponsored research helped supply the greater depth of professional capabilities upon which many regional programs have been built. Today, over half of MRI's funding is from contract research for various federal agencies, with strong emphasis on Midwest problems. For example, the institute figured quite actively in the "space age," being the first technology utilization subcontractor to NASA, as the intermediary between space developments and their commercial use in 10 Midwest states. Currently, MRI is engaged in a number of technology assessments programs of regional and national import.

Over one-third of the institute's activity today is related to environmental concerns where MRI has established widely accepted expertise in dealing with air, water, and solid waste pollution. Cancer research, traffic safety, toxicology, birth control, biofeedback, leisure recreation, and crime and criminology are also major undertakings.

MRI and its region have changed dramatically since the late 1940s when the Midwest faced the specter of returning to an agriculture-dependent depression economy after a few brief years of war-induced prosperity. Today, the region has moved away from this historic pattern and shows an increasingly diversified economy without the blight of deteriorating coastal-type industrial regions and is justifiably proud of the quality of its life. MRI has played a key role in this regional turnabout, a concept quite close to that envisioned by its founders. The institute was a dominant force in increasing the population of the scientific community in the greater Kansas City area from 500 professional people in 1944 to the present 12,000 persons. Today, they represent a wide variety of skills and boast an annual payroll in the range of $150 to $200 million.

During the early 1970s, MRI undertook its first geographic expansion, one result of a unique relationship between MRI and Battelle Memorial Institute. This was an MRI program for establishing Centers for Regional

Midwest Research Institute, Kansas City, Missouri

Progress. Dr. Sherwood Fawcett and his colleagues saw this program as a means of activating in the midcontinent states some provisions of the Battelle commitment to advance and utilize science for the benefit of mankind. The relationship was established in recognition of MRI's regional commitment, namely, its accomplishments and broad ties with community leaders and community problems throughout the Middle West. The new centers offices, while performing contract research placed appropriately, are primarily identifying unmet problems and opportunities and assisting in the process of applying research results.

Another MRI regional extension is now in progress. In mid-1974, the trustees of North Star Research Institute, founded in 1963 in the Minneapolis-St. Paul metropolitan area, were faced with increasing operational problems and came to MRI for assistance. As a result of several management- and board-level discussions, MRI undertook managerial supervision of North Star as a prelude to a possible merger of the Minnesota institute into MRI.

Midwest Research Institute is today a mature, economically viable institution. It has a staff of some 500 persons, two-thirds of whom are professionals. Research volume will exceed $10 million in 1974. Over the years, MRI has acquired extensive research facilities and equipment. The main complex is situated on 13 acres in Kansas City's Cultural Center, with some 250,000 square feet of modern buildings immediately adjacent to the William Rockhill Nelson Gallery of Art, the University of Missouri-Kansas City, Linda Hall Library of Science and Technology, Menorah Hospital, and the Kemper Performing Arts Center. A 75-acre research station in suburban Kansas City is also maintained for special purpose experimentation.

MRI is regarded as an institute of national scope and reputation, unique in the emphasis placed on the immediate midcontinent region while successfully undertaking many problems of national import.

THE FRANKLIN INSTITUTE RESEARCH LABORATORIES

The Franklin Institute Research Laboratories (FIRL) was founded in 1946 as an outgrowth of a group of people working for the OSRD/NDRC during World War II. Actually, significant but sporadic research stretched back much further. The year 1946, however, marked the establishment of a formal division of the institute to perform applied research and development. The present name dates from February 1965.

Almost all of the early effort was performed for the military to assist in problems of national defense. While contracts of this nature have continued to be a strong capability to this day, FIRL quickly applied its experience to other government agencies at all levels and to industry. Always strong in the physical sciences and engineering, FIRL has more recently established expertise in the life sciences as well, to fill the modern need in this area.

The institute's purpose, recently restated by the Board of Managers, states that "while continuing to promote inquiry at the cutting edge of basic research, the Institute will devote its resources to the synthesis of the many kinds of expertise in the natural and social sciences and in technology that are required to attack with significant impact:

- our complex and urgent socio-technological difficulties;
- the problem of improving the public understanding of science and technology; and
- fundamental questions raised in man's quest for a better understanding of nature's laws."

At the time of this writing, FIRL has a staff of 325 full-time scientists, engineers, and technicians engaged in over $7 million of contract research annually. Shops, instrument rooms, and publication facilities are all institute owned. The other divisions of the institute include a museum, technical library, and meetings management. Moreover, FIRL is affiliated with several

Main laboratory building of The Franklin Institute Research Laboratories, Philadelphia, Pennsylvania.

hospitals for specialized services. Directors have been C. H. Greenall (1946-1948), N. H. Smith (1948-1961), F. L. Jackson (1961-1964), J. R. Feldmeier (1964-1972), and W. B. Ligett (since 1972).

Over the years, FIRL has feathered its cap with many achievements. At first, contracts were related mainly to national defense. Significant efforts have included the following.

- The design of a 240-mm gun-and-carriage that were to function on the double recoil principle, the first time this concept was put to modern use. Subsequently, the institute was asked to enlarge the caliber to 280 mm, learning later that this was the atomic cannon.

- The construction of a machine to simulate the friction of projectiles in a gun. Unheard of rubbing speeds of 2000 ft/sec were achieved by spinning a disk in an evacuated chamber.

- The participation in the design of some dozen command-control centers from Washington to Kodiak, Alaska. Sophisticated communication and computer display equipment enabled the monitoring of worldwide military situations and armed forces status.

- The evaluation of the radio-frequency hazards to electroexplosive devices. In this area, FIRL has established an international reputation in contracts not only for the military but also for NASA, AEC, and industry.

- Development of a capacity gage the size of a dime, an ideal device for measuring body pressure. The Veterans Administration used it to fit stump sockets; the navy applied it to the design of crash helmets; and the Quartermaster employed it to improve the fit of boots. From there it was but a small step to an industrial use in improving mattresses.

The last two examples indicate clearly the broadening of applications for peacetime use. More recently, FIRL's programs encompassed the following examples.

▪ The operation of an AC network analog computing center that stimulated large electric power generation and distribution systems for 15 years. When built in 1953, it was the largest of its type.

▪ The design and construction of the first simulator of helicopter motion that permitted programed independent or combined motion of all six degrees of freedom. The patented device can carry a helicopter cockpit for test or training.

▪ The performance of science information services including automated information retrieval and specialized current awareness services. This large effort is aided by field offices in Munich, Tokyo, and the nation's capital.

▪ The conduct of a broad variety of energy research and development activities. This effort includes evaluation of dry cooling towers, flow loop modeling, workshops for teachers and citizens, safety analyses of nuclear plants, qualification testing of components for nuclear power plants, and introduction of solar energy.

▪ The performance of complex stress analyses through advanced computer programs written for this purpose. The programs permit the solving of difficult mathematics for stresses in such irregular shapes as piping connections, ship hulls, mine roofs, and the human thorax.

▪ The design and construction of microelectronic sensors and transmitters for the monitoring of life signs. These instrument capsules are being used for animal testing in laboratories, in space, and in the wild.

▪ The development of a porous pavement for flood control and water pollution abatement. The pavement resulted from contracts in the areas of ecology, waste disposal techniques, environmental impact studies, and water quality analyses.

The outstanding features of FIRL's accomplishments then are twofold. First, its progress reflects many features of the research history of the nation, beginning with the solution to current problems to the present emphasis for improving the quality of the human environment. Second, and more important, FIRL has enjoyed the services of gifted and energetic men, highly motivated to add to the sum total of human knowledge.

STANFORD RESEARCH INSTITUTE by Dr. Weldon B. Gibson

Although affiliated with Stanford University from the outset, Stanford Research Institute (SRI) has always operated as a separate corporation with its own staff and facilities. The original legal relationship between the two institutions was changed in 1969 when SRI became a fully independent organization. The change was made simply by designating the SRI board members also as general members in lieu of the university trustees. Although a plan calling for long-term payments to the university was adopted, the basic purposes of SRI were unchanged.

SRI's research activities grew rapidly during its formative years of the late 1940s. Its initial projects were largely for western companies and governmental agencies (on western development problems). However, the organization's pursuits soon led it to economic and technical services throughout the United States. But it still concentrated a major effort on further industrialization and economic progress in the western states. In these early days, SRI was in fact known as the "Research Center of the West."

The initial success of Stanford Research Institute—even with its recurring working capital problems—led by 1950 to a far-ranging self-examination on fundamental aims consistent with the broad statements in its charter. One reason for this review was that the federal government was turning to SRI on an ascending scale for research assistance especially on national security and military problems. In the meantime, SRI had built up a considerable research capacity in economic, management, and social science fields—this in addition to the physical and life sciences and the engineering sciences (mostly electronics). The early SRI emphasis on technoeconomic fields had indeed been contemplated by the founders in an announcement in September of 1946 that the new institute would not restrict its operations "to research in the natural sciences." The release went on to say that research programs in economics, management sciences, marketing, and the social sciences would be created.

One feature of the basic policy review in 1950 was a clear recognition that SRI "had an important obligation to the Government of the United States to assist with scientific research needed for the national defense and welfare." Also, SRI resolved in 1950 to contribute wherever it could by "training and channeling" technical and professional manpower into industry and government. The 1950 policy decision called upon the institute to do all within its power "to develop and improve methods of scientific inquiry." And of special future significance, the SRI directors both re-

affirmed responsibilities to the "western region" and called for wider participation in helping solve both national and international problems within its
fields of competence. As the 1950 decade began—and as SRI's purposes were
given new meaning—about three-fourths of the institute's research efforts
were for industry and one-fourth for government. In mid-1950, the Korean
War began and soon brought new demands on research institutions throughout the nation. Thus, the proportion of government research to the total
began a long-term rise within Stanford Research Institute. The changing
situation greatly influenced the institute's future.

SRI continued to grow rapidly during the early 1950s—sometimes at
rates of 25 percent per year or more. Within less than a decade since formation, its staff had risen by 1954 to about 1000 and gross revenues were at an
annual rate of $10 million. The earlier "red" figures on the balance sheet had
been eliminated by mid-decade. The number of active projects stood at
around 500 for a wide variety of clients. In a real sense, SRI had become a
significant "western resource."

Perhaps, again, the institute's early success contributed in many ways
to a new policy reappraisal at the end of 1954. An expanded set of purposes
was soon adopted. The new statement strongly emphasized a series of
"services and obligations" and prominently featured the "public service"
functions of a nonprofit, independent research institute affiliated with
Stanford University.

Several major thrusts for SRI—in addition to contract research for
business and government—were envisioned in the 1954 policy. They included,
among others, research aimed at strengthening the defense of the United
States, studying and developing the resources of the western states, creating
new products and processes, improving industrial efficiency, and creating
new and expanded markets. There was, of course, a clear recognition that
these and other "public service" obligations could be achieved in part
through client-sponsored research projects and in part through self-sponsored
research made possible by fees received from clients. This was the beginning
of SRI's "independent research and development program" that continues
today on a considerable scale.

The mid-1950 policy then established a new mission, i.e., to go beyond
the areas of contract research including various public service functions and
general scientific and research activities spelled out in the 1946 charter. The
new functions included, for example, financial assistance to Stanford University, area development research on western resources, research on such

public problems as air pollution and waste utilization, creating a "center of information" useful to industry and government, and participating to a much greater extent on government panels and in the advancement of professional societies.

This policy thrust had a major impact on SRI. Many new activities were generated to help achieve the new objectives. They included, among other things, a "Western Resources Handbook" issued on a continuing basis, a worldwide Chemical Information Service, and a similar multiclient program known as the Long Range Planning Service. Scores of research projects were carried out for states, counties, and cities in the western states on development potentials and plans. The theme is expressed succinctly in one of the institute's annual reports—"in the public service for the public benefit."

As SRI continued to grow and diversify, it became apparent by 1956 that special policy attention should be given to its fields of research and to the types of projects it sought and selected. This led, in 1956, to the third outline of basic philosophy to guide the organization's development along with the enabling charter. Three broad guidelines—and a long list of implementing tests—soon emerged as a basis for project selection.

One of the three policy guides was the "development of new or improved products, processes, materials, techniques, or systems." This applied particularly to research programs in the physical, life, and engineering sciences. The second, written with SRI's economics and management research programs in mind, called for projects aimed at solving "important business, industrial, or government problems." The third, applicable to all programs, covered projects dedicated to creating "fundamental knowledge underlying scientific fields of interest to the institute." These and other portions of the new "search for purpose" also have greatly influenced SRI's development to this day.

SRI was fortunate in its earlier days—especially during the first decade —in being able to invest its limited resources largely in staff and equipment rather than in buildings. One by one it was able to "take over" a large group of barracks-type structures on its Menlo Park property and convert them to research purposes. However, beginning in the late 1950s, the pendulum swung in the other direction as construction of new buildings became a necessity. The movement has since been back and forth on at least two occasions as SRI attempted to house its staff of close to 3000 people. The institute still faces a formidable building program.

One of the ways SRI pursued its special regional objectives in the 1950s

SRI, Menlo Park, California.

and part of the 1960s was through "regional offices and laboratories" in several western cities. For some time there were such offices and professional staff in Portland (Oregon), Honolulu (Hawaii), and Phoenix (Arizona), in addition to field sites in Alaska, Nevada, and several places in California. Also, a laboratory and research staff concentrating on special southern California research problems (air pollution, for example) were maintained in the vicinity of Los Angeles.

As time went by, it became more feasible—economically and professionally—to concentrate the institute's main resources at its Menlo Park headquarters. But reflecting growing research relationships with comapnies and governmental agencies in other parts of the nation, the institute moved in the late 1960s to a plan involving a substantial staff in SRI-Washington and SRI-Huntsville (Alabama) and offices in Los Angeles, Houston, Chicago, and New York—and at one time in Detroit. The movement to a similar arrangement outside the United States is outlined elsewhere along with the story of SRI's international operations.

The basic motives of the founders in creating SRI were clearly to develop a western resource that would aid in economic development of the West—and of the nation generally—and to pursue the public interest. Their major attention at the time was concentrated on business and industry. In the meantime, the role of government in research and development has increased steadily and in a diversified manner. SRI, along with several other organizations of its type, has been greatly affected by—and has responded to —this movement. The institute's research volume from governmental agencies now accounts for at least two-thirds of its total, the balance being from business, industry, and other public service organizations. This is consistent with the national pattern of research expenditures. However, as each year passes by, a growing proportion of SRI's government-sponsored research comes from civilian rather than military agencies.

One of the features of SRI's development since its formation in the mid-1940s has been a balance among the natural sciences, the engineering sciences, and the social sciences. Perhaps more than any other institute of its type, SRI has pioneered and developed research programs on a large scale in industrial economics, the management sciences, and related social sciences. The basic philosophy has always been to create a "diversified multidisciplinary research capacity" that can be applied to the problems of industry and government. A related object has been—and still is—to strengthen the purely technical research programs with economic-management skills and to provide a technical-supporting base for programs in the "soft sciences." This sort of combination is quite unique in the United States and is seldom found in research organizations abroad. In any event, SRI has pursued a policy over the years of developing "soft science" programs on a significant scale.

Although SRI benefited greatly in its earlier years by contributions to capital from more than 175 associate companies—and later in financing its International Building—the basic policy of the organization since the mid-1950s has been to "earn its own way" in the marketplace of research. This it has done with considerable success as have most of the other nonprofit, independent research institutes. SRI has no endowment and has never sought to create one. However, it did recently receive about $1 million from a private estate. The earlier Associates Plan, unveiled in 1951 at a "Million-Dollar Luncheon" in San Francisco (addressed by the late David Sarnoff), provided urgently needed working capital of some $1.5 million by the mid-1950s and another $1.5 million during the following decade. The plan is now dormant.

When SRI was created in 1956 the amount of money spent by industry in the West on research and development was very small in relation to outlays by eastern companies. Furthermore, many of the area's larger enterprises were in such fields as banking, agriculture, and engineering/construction with low spending rates for research. Thus, perhaps even more than in other parts of the country, it was necessary from the outset for SRI to aggressively promote the values of research—contract research in particular. This was done in several ways, one being the sponsorship of various conferences and seminars on topics of particular interest to western firms and civic organizations.

These events were organized in such fields as air pollution, natural resources and energy. Typically, case presentations were made by SRI people involved in the particular field and widespread distribution of research reports as well as information about SRI itself was accomplished. Also, at that time, the leaders of the institute were intently engaged in public appearances before business, industrial, and government groups. Extensive mailings were made to selected executives and governmental officials not only in the West but throughout the nation. Gradually, SRI became well known throughout the western region and then increasingly around the nation and eventually the world. In any event, these early "research promotional efforts" were instrumental in expanding the scale of R&D spending by western companies.

Several features in SRI's operations over the years have exerted a major influence on its growth and development and will affect its future. Momentum was generated in the early days and remains today as an underlying force. Great diversification in research endeavors by types of industry, geographical areas, and governmental agencies has provided an important element of strength. Early initiation of a research program in the engineering sciences, principally involving electronics, has greatly affected the directions in which SRI has developed. Also, the launching of a research program in industrial economics and the management sciences in 1947 has led over the years to new dimensions in scope, interests, and strength of the West's principal research institute. Still further, the beginning relationship between SRI and Stanford University undoubtedly sped up development of the organization.

One aspect of the institute's history is clearly dominant as a positive influence on growth and maturity. SRI has been exceedingly fortunate in the composition of its board of directors. In times of success, they have repeatedly urged the institute to "raise its sights" and more energetically pursue its purposes and potentials. During periods of stress and strain and vexing problems, they rallied to the cause of the institute and generated long-term solutions for the future. This occurred in 1949 when SRI was faced with the possibility of closing its doors for lack of sufficient capital. It occurred in 1956 and 1957 when construction of a headquarters building was vital to an organization extremely short of capital. And it occurred again in 1968 and 1969 when it became evident that in the best interests of both Stanford University and Stanford Research Institute the legal tie between the two organizations should be severed. At the time, SRI was "under fire" from various quarters because of its extensive involvement in classified research for the Department of Defense. A solution was finally worked out that both benefited the university and enabled SRI to continue its operations in line with long-established policies.

Two of SRI's original directors are still serving the organization as "founding directors." They are D. J. Russell (formerly chief executive of Southern Pacific) and Paul Davies (formerly head of the FMC Corporation). Another early director, S. D. Bechtel, Sr. (Bechtel Corporation), made a major contribution to the institute's future in his urging of greater international involvements.

Each of the nation's nonprofit, independent research organizations has featured a certain diversity in its research operations. At the same time, each has developed a few "specialties" in which it occupies a unique position. So it is with SRI. Its main "hallmarks" are probably to be found in the engineering sciences and particularly in the development of new devices and systems for high-speed processing of information involving computers, in the techno-economic field and especially the techniques of long-range business planning and corporate strategy, in electronic and radio sciences involving upper atmosphere research and satellite communications, and in the social sciences with programs in education, national welfare programs, and income maintenance concepts.

SRI's annual revenues from research operations now total some $80 million per year. This indeed represents a rapid growth in less than three decades. But growth itself has created severe problems along the way— shortages of capital, inadequate housing, and maintaining a balanced and competent staff. The institute has never imposed a rigid ceiling on the size of its operations, but by policy it has restrained growth during recent years. However, during the earlier years some confusion developed regarding growth, at least at policy levels. In attempting to expand the early organization to the "threshold" point, several targets of "optimum" size were mentioned. The first of these was 100 people. This was subsequently raised to 300 people, then 500, and again to 1000. The institute moved quickly through and beyond each of these "optimum" points to its present complement of 3000. In retrospect, this was fortuitous. Rising demand for research programs such as those provided by SRI and the other nonprofit institutes was obvious. A limit on SRI's size, particularly at that stage, probably would have been harmful in the long run.

More than two decades ago, an SRI annual report included the following statement.

> The responsibilities . . . of the public service research institute are unmistakable. It must serve industrial, governmental, regional, and scientific interests. It must contribute to scientific education and to the public welfare wherever and whenever it can . . .

These principles apply not only to SRI but in varying degrees to all independent, nonprofit research institutes. They have been guideposts to SRI—along with the principle of operating on sound business practices (articulated earlier by the eastern institutes) so as to enable the organization to pursue the purposes for which it was founded.

SOUTHWEST RESEARCH INSTITUTE

The circumstances that brought about the founding of the several research organizations in San Antonio by Tom Slick are related in Hugh Buhrman's section on Southwest Research Institute in Chapter VI.

Mr. Slick established the Foundation for Applied Research (FAR) on December 11, 1941, for the purpose of conducting basic scientific research that would benefit man. This institution was rather dormant during the World War II years, except for modest research grants that were made to universities and colleges; however, it became active with the building of its first laboratory in 1946 and the recruitment of a small staff. When it became evident in the word "applied" in the name was detrimental to securing outside research support in the basic sciences, the name was changed to Southwest Foundation for Research and Education in February 1952.

Slick founded the Institute of Inventive Research (IIR) in December 1946 for the purposes of (1) assisting inventors from all walks of life in commercializing their inventions of merit by determining the product's economic feasibility and (2) generating funds to support the basic research program in the Foundation of Applied Research—i.e., the royalty income shared with inventors. IIR was liquidated in 1953 after an investment by Mr. Slick of almost $1 million (without tax exemption). This action was necessitated after Slick's realization that the cost of processing and developing inventions sought from all sources under an "open door" policy far exceeded the royalty income produced by that "one in a thousand" that proved commercially feasible.

The Southwest Foundation has developed other sources of income and endowment over the years, having become an important contributor to new knowledge in the biomedical sciences; however, of concern in this book is Southwest Research Institute (SwRI), the institution which was founded in December 1947 by Mr. Slick and was to become one of the strong and successful organizations among the 9 independents.

In April 1947, while Harold Vagtborg was president of Midwest Research Institute, he met and spent two days with Mr. Slick in San Antonio, at the latter's request. At that time, operations of both FAR and IIR were being conducted in a restored and refurbished landmark residence (the Cable House), while the first FAR laboratory building was under construction. Vagtborg was offered the presidency of the new institutions, but declined because he felt Midwest had neither matured sufficiently to be firmly on a course for the future nor had achieved a balanced budget. However, he did agree to spend a day or two each month with Mr. Slick to help where he could in developing the project. Time passed, and by the summer of 1948, Vagtborg agreed to answer the unique challenge of directing the development of a research complex located "nowhere for no reason" as many claimed. On September 1, 1948, he moved to San Antonio to become president and director of three institutions, Southwest Research Institute having been established in the interim.

From the beginning, the mission of SwRI was to seek out the kind of projects that would be most valuable to the businesses and industries of the area as well as to undertake, as feasible, those activities on a national scale that were not already provided for at other institutions. This latter thrust provided the new institution with the opportunity to develop a few areas of distinction and specialty. During the second year of operation, an immediate need that was met was the establishment of a neutral laboratory through which automotive and petroleum industries could develop better fuels and lubricants as well as improved methods of evaluation in order to meet the requirements of rapidly changing engine design. Other early activities involved fire, construction, and petroleum technology, including new methods of exploration and offshore oil drilling.

In the early going, it was found that an institution such as SwRI was ideally suited to undertake "common denominator" problems of a given industry to the mutual advantage of all participating members, who benefited by having a common problem solved on neutral ground. Through the years, the institute has undertaken many assignments of this kind. Another activity proved to be regionally important as well as especially distinctive for SwRI—research dealing with regional mineral resources. This type of activity has been espoused by most of the independent research institutions over the years on both a regional and national basis, with support coming from utility companies, railroads, and banking institutions, as well as from funds raised by general subscription.

In its first full year of operation, SwRI's budget was $100,000, but, in its first three and one-half years of operation, the institute developed an accumulative deficit of about $250,000. However, the institution was soon able to balance the budget and in the next several years restore this deficit to capital funds. By the end of 1959, SwRI had experienced impressive

Southwest Research Institute campus, San Antonio, Texas.

growth, and Vagtborg began to concentrate his efforts in behalf of the Southwest Foundation, since at the time, a special opportunity had evolved for this institution because of the new national emphasis on research in the health sciences.

Martin Goland was elected president of SwRI in November 1959, after having become affiliated with the institute in 1955. His leadership steered SwRI toward greater heights of activity and international reputation. New specialties were introduced, and a few of them should be mentioned. Despite the fact that the institute was located well inland in a semiarid part of the country, it became a national center for the evaluation of deep-diving submersibles constructed by both corporate organizations and SwRI. This special service was made possible through the installation of large testing facilities that could exert hydrostatic pressures equivalent to a water depth of up to 30,000 feet and that provided a facility large enough to test a full-scale unit or large-scale model. This activity grew out of the institute's extensive work in nondestructive testing techniques, which in turn brought about the development of a major activity in pressure vessel testing. As a result, SwRI has served many organizations, both domestic and foreign, in safety testing nuclear power plant high pressure vessels.

By 1975, SwRI had expanded to include a staff of 1400 people and an operating budget in excess of $33 million. It is interesting to note that SwRI has reached this pinnacle while maintaining through the years one of the lowest ratios of government to industrial funding among the 9 independents.

* * *

FISCAL ASPECTS

Considering their levels of grant and contract underwritings, these institutions have made a most unique contribution to American society and industrial development. Not only have they been forerunners in the stimulation of research in industry, but they have also, as much as any other group, brought about an understanding of research and its benefits to the American public. They have trained thousands of personnel who have transferred to laboratories in industry, and their activities in friendly foreign countries have had a positive effect on increased industrial production. These institutions have had a profound impact on the American research scene, despite the fact that their combined operating budgets in any one year have never exceeded approximately 1 percent of total national R&D expenditures as shown in the following table.

Fiscal Growth of the Nine Independent Research Institutes in Five-Year Intervals

Year	Underwritings	Comments
1935	$ 600,000	Mellon only
1940	1,900,000	Mellon, Battelle, and Armour
1945	7,200,000	The above plus Southern and Midwest
1950	23,650,000	All nine
1955	64,200,000	All nine
1960	105,490,000	All nine
1965	214,220,000	All nine
1970	240,608,000	Mellon omitted*
1975	305,810,000	Mellon and Cornell omitted†

*Mellon became part of Carnegie-Mellon University in 1967.
†Cornell became Calspan, a profit-making corporation in 1972.

CHAPTER VIII

EXPLOSIVE GROWTH OF APPLIED RESEARCH INSTITUTES

World War II clearly demonstrated beyond any doubt that industrial development and national security depended to a large extent on a continuing and expanding program of research. New knowledge of natural phenomena was required on the one hand and, on the other, the application of this knowledge. Someone once said, you cannot take more water out of the well than goes into it. Astute awareness of this maxim spurred greater emphasis on both basic and applied science, with government's role growing more in the direction of basic science and that of industry directed toward the latter.

Public awareness was reflected by groups calling for more independent institutions to help in the development of certain geographical areas. Universities likewise saw an opportunity for greater service and set about to more clearly define their role in both basic and applied science—at the same time developing activities in the latter on a more formal basis. Program funding in both scientific areas was more readily available. Further, by their demonstrated success, research institutions such as Armour, Cornell, Southern, Midwest, Franklin, Stanford, and Southwest had shown that substantial endowment was not necessary. All that was essential was moderate funding (for initial capital to be used for facilities, often rented quarters, and for operating deficits for the first three or four years), a strong governing body, good administration and a sound objective.

During the late- and postwar years, there were two general types of applied research institutions being established. The greatest number by far were those established in close relationship with educational institutions; the other variety was represented by several "independents," as previously described, which functioned with their own governing bodies, staffs, and facilities, even though a loose affiliation might have existed with one or more universities.

In the case of the former, the universities realized that a clear-cut distinction had to be made between basic and applied research activity. Basic research, the results of which are fully available to the public primarily through publication, is an important part of the educational process, particularly in the graduate school. The process needs to involve students. Conversely, applied research, in order to attract industrial and certain types of governmental support, has to be conducted under controlled circumstances, wherein confidentiality is guaranteed and results and patentable developments are the exclusive rights of the sponsor. Such parameters make the use of students very questionable. In order to clearly separate the two types of research activity and to avoid legal litigation that could involve the university, the usual procedure has been to establish a separate legal entity that would nevertheless be under the full control of the university.

A partial list of this type of institution and their control affiliations follows.

Auburn Research Foundation, Alabama Polytechnic Institute
Augustana Research Foundation, Augustana College
Institute of Science and Technology, University of Arkansas
Institute of Polymer Research, Polytechnic Institute of Brooklyn
Microwave Research Institute, Polytechnic Institute of Brooklyn
Institute of Engineering Research, University of California (Berkeley)
Institute of Industrial Cooperation, University of California (Los Angeles)
Committee on Sponsored Research Projects, Carnegie Institute of Technology
Institute for the Study of Metals, University of Chicago
Institute for Nuclear Studies, University of Chicago
Division of Research and Industrial Service, Clarkson College of Technology
Division of Cooperative Research, Columbia University
Denver Research Institute, University of Denver
Georgia Tech Research Institute, Georgia Institute of Technology
Division of Applied Science, Harvard University
Johns Hopkins University Institute for Cooperative Research
Institute of Gas Technology, Illinois Institute of Technology
Institute for Atomic Research, Iowa State College
Iowa Institute of Hydraulic Research, State University of Iowa
Kentucky Research Foundation, University of Kentucky
Institute of Industrial Research, University of Louisville
Lowell Textile Institute Research Foundation, Lowell Textile Institute
Department of Industrial Cooperation, University of Maine
Institute for Fluid Dynamics and Applied Mathematics, University of Maryland
University of Miami Research Foundation
Forest Products Research Division, Michigan College of Mining and Technology
Institute of Technology, University of Minnesota

Desert Research Institute, University of Nevada
Department of Research, New York State College of Ceramics
Oregon Forest Products Laboratory, Oregon State College
Ottawa University Research Institute (Ottawa, Kansas)
Department of Engineering Research, Pennsylvania State University
Ordnance Research Laboratory, Pennsylvania State University
Office of Sponsored Research, University of Pennsylvania
Engineering Research Division, University of Pittsburgh
Forrestal Research Center, Princeton University
Rensselaer Polytechnic Institute Research Foundation
Bureau of Engineering Research, Rutgers University
School of Mines Research and Development Association, South Dakota School
    of Mines and Technology
Electronics Research Laboratory, Stanford University
Microwave Laboratory, Stanford University
Powder Metallurgy Laboratory, Stevens Institute of Technology
Syracuse University Research Institute, Syracuse University
Temple University Research Institute
Texas Technological College Foundation, Texas Technological College
Bureau of Economic Geology, University of Texas
Bureau of Engineering Research, University of Texas
Bureau of Industrial Chemistry, University of Texas
Research Laboratory in Ceramics, University of Texas
Research Foundation of the University of Toledo, University of Toledo
Utah Scientific Research Foundation, Utah State Agricultural College
Industrial Research Institute, Vanderbilt University
Virginia Polytechnic Institute Research Foundation, Virginia Polytechnic Institute
Division of Industrial Research, State College of Washington
Division of Sponsored Research, Washington University (St. Louis)
Wayne Engineering Research Institute, Wayne University
University of Wichita Foundation for Industrial Research

Some of the organizations were only proposed, never being formally organized. Nonetheless, in every case their parent institutions sent representatives to already established, operative institutions around the country to study philosophies of operation and the institutions' procedures. Of those that subsequently evolved, a few became distinguished organizations and contributed much to industry and government.

In this same vein, it must be remembered that there were a number of university-controlled applied research organizations organized many years before the so-called "war baby" group. This older group has had varying degrees of success through the years, some members having excelled sufficiently to enjoy a national reputation. This senior group of university-associated applied research organizations includes the following.

Case School of Applied Science (Cleveland, Ohio)
University of Chattanooga Industrial Research Institute (Chattanooga, Tennessee)
University of Kansas Research Foundation (Lawrence, Kansas)
Lehigh Research Institute, Lehigh University (Bethlehem, Pennsylvania)
University of Louisville Research Foundation (Louisville, Kentucky)
Division of Industrial Cooperation, Massachusette Institute of Technology
Department of Engineering Research, University of Michigan
    (Ann Arbor, Michigan)
Research Division, College of Engineering, New York University
Northwestern Technological Institute, Northwestern University (Evanston, Illinois)
Ohio State University Research Foundation (Columbus, Ohio)
Oklahoma A & M Research Foundation (Stillwater, Oklahoma)
University of Oklahoma Research Institute (Norman, Oklahoma)
Purdue Research Foundation (Lafayette, Indiana)
Stevens Research Foundation, Stevens Institute of Technology
    (Hoboken, New Jersey)
Texas A & M Research Foundation, Agricultural and Mechanical College of Texas
Carver Research Foundation of Tuskeegee Institute
Wichita University Research Foundation (Wichita, Kansas)
Alumni Research Foundation, University of Wisconsin (Madison, Wisconsin)
Natural Resources Research Institute, University of Wyoming (Laramie, Wyoming)

THE ENGINEERING EXPERIMENT STATION

A significant type of organization that was a main contributor to the development of technology, particularly in the first half of the twentieth century, was the engineering experiment station. These stations, which are associated with a large number of colleges and universities in the United States, continue to this day to make substantial contributions to the solutions of engineering problems in their states and to industrial development in general. In the 1920s and through the 1940s, their role was especially important to the national effort; however, in more recent years, they have had to share the research activities in their institutions with other forms of in-house research organizations such as institutes and foundations.

The establishment of the engineering experiment stations followed the provisions of the Morrill Act of 1862, which provided grants of land to state colleges that would emphasize the teaching of agriculture and the mechanic arts without excluding the general sciences and classical studies. By provision of the second Morrill Act of 1890, land grants were supplemented by annual monetary grants of $25,000 to all land-grant institutions. By 1915, 67 land-grant colleges were giving instruction to 69,000 students.

The typical engineering experiment station was staffed by engineering faculty members working part time with varying degrees of involvement on programs supported by state and private agencies to develop solutions related to public works and by manufacturers and often by associations of companies in a particular industry. The work was usually of a nonproprietary nature, thus enabling the employment of students who not only gained research experience but also financial assistance, which in many cases was essential to their continued education. Their contributions have been substantial and they remain an important factor in the industrial development of the United States

Since 1947 there have also evolved several "independents" that are patterned much after the original nine. These include Research Triangle Institute (1958–the largest), Spindletop Research Institute (1961), and Gulf South Research Institute (1965). The following sections of this chapter relate their circumstances of organization and their development into nationally recognized institutions.

* * *

THE RESEARCH TRIANGLE INSTITUTE

With the filing of articles of incorporation on the last working day of December 1958, the Research Triangle Institute (RTI) of North Carolina was created by its three founding universities as the first of a new generation of not-for-profit institutes. It was the newest addition to the loose-knit family of not-for-profits in a dozen years. In its multidisciplinary organization, self-supporting business operations, scope of research objectives, and national character of clients, Research Triangle Institute generally follows quite closely the patterns and methods successfully established by its predecessors. In the circumstances leading to its formation, however, Research Triangle Institute was unique and within a very few years was itself used as the pattern on which younger institutes were molded and planned.

Pervasive and deepening associations with three major universities have made Research Triangle Institute not only unique, but also probably beyond duplication.

From the moment it began active operations in the spring of 1959, Research Triangle Institute added a distinctive new characteristic to the tradition of the older institutions. While retaining the commitment of the older organizations to undertake broad research programs that would increase the nation's scientific resources and serve national purposes, Research Triangle Institute was also a new economic asset consciously created as an integral part of a larger blueprint developed in and for its state. The locations of the older institutes, spread from coast to coast, were not accidental, but location was incidental to such other considerations as convenience, the community and civic interests of institute founders, existing and potential industrial demand, or parallel but unformalized university activities. RTI was something new. Its conception and formation were entirely and exclusively within the context of North Carolina's special needs and resources. It sprang from statewide recognition of statewide problems and from a statewide determination to meet and surmount them. The Research Triangle Institute was to become the focal point and namesake for one of the most ambitious exercises in regional economic development ever undertaken.

The ideas for what is now North Carolina's internationally familiar place name, the Research Triangle, began fermenting during the mid-1950s. They sprang from a recognition that the state had been too dependent on the agricultural segment of its economy and on the important, but generally low-skill, industries of textiles, tobacco manufacturing, and wood products. As a result, per capita income was low; new investment lagged; tax revenues were insufficient to provide improved and expanded public services; and, perhaps most critical of all, large numbers of college and university graduates were forced to leave the state to find their career opportunities. Needs clearly existed for new levels of enterprise to help spur the state's economic growth and to enable it to share in the benefits of industrial advance being enjoyed in other regions of the United States.

Leaders from industry, the university community, and state government recognized the needs and knew they could best be met by diversifying and expanding the industrial sector of the economy. Looking at the other regions of the country which had benefited from the growth of technology-based industry in the preceding decade, they identified the crucial relationships which existed between universities and research centers and, in turn, between research centers and new industrial activity. Those concerned observed further that North Carolina possessed a unique and pivotal asset which could open the way toward industrial diversification and growth. This asset was, simply, the existence of three major universities at the points of a compact geographic triangle near the center of the state, each in its own community and each with its own distinct character, but in such close proximity that they combined to create a total area environment comparable to that in which successful research centers had started and thrived in other parts of the country. The triangle they form consists of the University of North Carolina at Chapel Hill, Duke University at Durham, and North Carolina State University at Raleigh. Viewed not as separate campuses, but as a single educational and scientific resource, the three schools represented a solid foundation to undergird the dream of building a major new center of research enterprise and industrial technology in North Carolina.

Research Triangle Institute campus and buildings, center, and several neighboring organizations in the Research Triangle Park.

Clockwise from upper left are Beaunit Corporation's fibers and textiles technical center, Monsanto Company's Chemstrand Research Center, International Business Machines Corporation, the North Carolina Science and Technology Research Center, and Triangle Universities Computation Center occupying the same building below RTI's campus, Hercules Incorporated, the National Center for Health Statistics, and the Becton, Dickinson and Company's research center.

Hidden in the trees or just out of camera range are the National Institute of Environmental Health Sciences, EPA's National Environmental Research Center, the American Association of Textile Chemists and Colorists, the U.S. Forest Service Southeastern Experiment Station, Troxler Electronics, and the building sites for the Army Research Office and the National Driving Center.

As a reality, the Research Triangle Park fulfills the dream in every way. Lying at the center of the university-anchored triangle, the park is a tract of 5200 formerly empty acres of meadowland and rolling hills. Scrupulously maintained to preserve its natural parklike atmosphere, the Research Triangle Park at the end of 1974 listed two dozen industrial and governmental research occupants with combined payrolls of more than 10,000 persons and 50 laboratory and office buildings.

Planning for the Research Triangle Park proceeded during the late 1950s, and a decision was reached to have as its focal point a separate, not-for-profit contract research institute closely tied to the universities. By the end of 1958, most of the land had been assembled, and private and corporate citizens of North Carolina had contributed $2 million in initial funding to the Research Triangle Foundation—a separate, independent, nonprofit trusteeship responsible for developing the park. In December, RTI was created by the joint action of the presidents and trustees of the three universities, and George R. Herbert, selected as president, became the new institute's first employee. (During the formative years of Stanford Research Institute, Herbert had served that organization in a variety of positions ranging from assistant to the director to executive associate director.) A start-up grant of $500,000 was awarded to RTI by the foundation and 180 acres set aside for the institute campus.

Physical development of the Research Triangle Park, in which RTI's campus is centered, had not yet started, and early operations were housed in leased office and laboratory space in nearby Durham. The first permanent building was occupied in January 1961, but it was not until 1971 that all of the institute's staff was assembled in facilities on the park campus. By 1974, RTI had grown to a permanent, full-time staff of 550, nine buildings, and approximately 200,000 square feet of laboratory and office space. Contract revenues were at the annual rate of $13 million.

Close ties with its parent universities are RTI's most distinctive feature. The institute's place in the university family, from the corporate level to the laboratory bench, exists by design and has been carefully nurtured through the years. Although RTI management, staff, and programs are separate from the schools, academic officials at Duke, the University of North Carolina, and North Carolina State University exercise an important influence in institute affairs. Thirteen of RTI's 27-member Board of Governors represent the universities, including the presidents and chancellors. Thirteen more are named from the business, industrial, and professional communities, and the institute president is an *ex officio* board member.

Institute-university relationships are most productive in terms of co-operative effort, and mutual support and cooperation among the four institutions are evident in many activities. Some joint contracts call for a portion of the work to be performed by a university group and a portion within RTI, and for the larger number of projects conducted exclusively at the institute, the range of consulting expertise available in university departments is a tremendous resource for extending institute capabilities. In any one year, a hundred or more faculty members may be active as consultants assisting with RTI contract work. RTI senior scientists frequently hold adjunct faculty appointments in their fields of specialty, and many others of RTI's professional research staff continue with postgraduate studies for advanced degrees while employed at the institute. This degree of institute-university involvement assures that RTI research complements and strengthens university programs, and that it in turn draws maximum benefit from academic resources.

RTI research operations are organized into four major groups that are multidisciplinary in nature and interdisciplinary in performance. The four groups cover: statistical and survey research, social and economic systems and human resources, physical and life sciences, and environmental and engineering sciences.

A decisive influence in shaping RTI's character and stimulating its relatively rapid growth (in its first 12 years RTI became the fifth largest of the not-for-profits) has been the shifting emphasis among national priorities. In RTI's formative years, the major concerns engaging many of the not-for-profits, as well as other elements of the applied research community, included

The Robert M. Hanes Memorial Building, headquarters of Research Triangle Institute.

defense and weapons, nuclear physics, electronic communication, information systems design, industrial processes, materials, and the all-out space effort. These were areas to which the fledgling Research Triangle Institute had to address itself, but in which it was handicapped by lack of any established track record. However, an early decision had already been made by the institute's board and management that, although RTI sprang from regional origin and was to have a clear regional identity, it should take its place with the older institutes through research serving national purposes, building programs and staff that encompassed a broad scientific spectrum, and attracting a widely diversified sponsorship. Under this policy, RTI research managers were able to garner secure footholds of contract support in statistical studies, natural products chemistry, solid-state electronics, civil defense preparedness, and polymer physics and chemistry. Within three years, in 1962, these programs achieved operating break-even for RTI on an annual contract volume of approximately $1.3 million.

While RTI was building staff and programs and attaining a solid, in-the-black status as a business operation, perceptible shifts were becoming apparent both in the variety and direction of the institute's research interests and in the nation's societal goals. As a newer member of what is perhaps the most innovative and dynamic of industries, RTI's youth and flexibility enabled it to gear staffing and program development to rapidly emerging new research missions. RTI's research emphasis turned to meet them. Moving into young maturity with completion of its sixteenth year, a distinguishing mark of Research Triangle Institute's operations was its degree of involvement in programs aimed at improvements in the quality of life. By the end of 1974, three-quarters of RTI's research effort was in areas directly concerned with education, health, environment, transportation safety, state planning, and regional economics as well as with behavioral subjects such as drug abuse, alcoholism, crime, and problems of special concern to the young and the aging. These areas, combined with a continuation of strong programs in laboratory and engineering sciences, mark the course of future growth and service for RTI.

SPINDLETOP RESEARCH, INC.

Spindletop Research, Inc. was established as an independent, not-for-profit applied research corporation on December 15, 1961. It was established primarily to stimulate the economic and industrial development of Kentucky and its region. Spindletop's creation was part of an extensive effort by governmental and industrial leaders in Kentucky to reverse the economic trends of the 1950s. Spindletop's initial funds were appropriated by the Commonwealth of Kentucky; thus, Spindletop was the first applied research institute in the nation to receive substantial funding directly from a state government.

The founders and incorporators of Spindletop Research* were the leaders of the largest industries in Kentucky, the highest elected officials of the state, and the leaders of the major universities.

One of the early questions was the legality of the state's granting funds to an independent, not-for-profit corporation. Kentucky's Attorney-General wrote the opinion that the state could make grants to such corporations if they served the public broadly. This opinion paved the way for an initial $3.2-million grant to the new corporation to acquire land, construct and furnish a facility, and to build its staff.

The original concept of Spindletop was that it would be a part of the University of Kentucky. This was the main reason for locating Spindletop in Lexington, rather than in Kentucky's largest city, Louisville. In the early days, however, disagreements developed between the university and some of the industrial and political leaders. These disagreements were apparently severe enough to cause the incorporators to establish Spindletop as an independent entity separate from the university. Furthermore, little consideration was given to making Spindletop a part of state government. The principal reasons were that the new organization was designed to serve industry as well as government, and that the salary scales and political vagaries of state government would hamper the new organization's growth.

Many of Spindletop's incorporators expected that this new research institute, with heavy emphasis on physical sciences and engineering, would attract technology-based industry to Kentucky. Some saw spin-off companies forming to exploit Spindletop-developed products and processes. Few, if any, envisioned the transformations in research programs that would occur five years later.

Although the initial $3.2-million grant from the state was most generous (representing about $1 per capita in 1960), approximately $2.2

---

*Spindletop was the name given to a salt-dome near Beaumont, Texas, which was the site of two of the nation's greatest oil strikes. Later, the Spindletop name was given to a famous show horse farm north of Lexington, in Kentucky's Bluegrass region. The farm is the present site of Spindletop Development Center, which contains the facilities of Spindletop Research, the Council of State Governments, and the Interstate Mining Compact.

Spindletop Research, Inc., Lexington, Kentucky.

million had been committed to land and building before the staffing was begun. The founding fathers were determined to launch Spindletop in a deluxe structure (the result of a statewide architectural competition) that expressed a degree of stability. It was expected that industry would join with the state in sharing the early financing. Some of the leading industries did make grants, but these did not compare with the amount of state funds. Very few industries sponsored research work, even when the research program emphasis was on physical sciences and engineering. There was also a belief that vast sums of federal contract research funds could be obtained readily.

The board chose Beardsley Graham to be Spindletop's first president. Graham had both industrial and research institute experience, having been with Lockheed Missiles and Space Corporation and Bendix Corporation and also had been an assistant director of Stanford Research Institute.

Early in 1967, Graham resigned as president, and the board of directors appointed Theodore R. Broida as executive vice president and chief operating officer. A year later, in May 1968, Broida was elected president. Broida had come to Spindletop in August 1962 to establish a technoeconomics research group. Prior to joining Spindletop, Broida was on the corporate staff of

United Research Services (now URS Systems Corp.), and previously with Stanford Research Institute. He resigned in early 1974 and D. W. Rogers was made chief executive.

Since its inception, Spindletop has been strongly dependent on the Commonwealth of Kentucky. In recent years this dependence has diminished somewhat; nevertheless, annual operating budgets widely fluctuate because in some years there were commonwealth grants and in other years there were none.

Spindletop reached its highest level of operation in 1971 with an annual budget of $3 million. Since then its problems have worsened, and in March 1975, the board of directors voted to dissolve the institution.

This is a case where, in spite of capable management, erratic funding procedures established at the initiation of the institution caused failure.

GULF SOUTH RESEARCH INSTITUTE

The Gulf South Research Institute (GSRI) was incorporated in 1964 under Louisiana's nonprofit corporation law and began operations in late 1965. It was chartered to stimulate the growth and prosperity of Louisiana and the Gulf South region through applied economic and scientific research as well as help stop Louisiana's "brain drain" by providing employment for the science graduates of its universities. The institute is governed by a council of trustees, composed of approximately 180 prominent citizens throughout the state, and policies are formulated by a 16-member board of directors elected to staggered 6-year terms by the trustees. Five of the directors are selected from nominations made by Louisiana State University, Tulane University, state colleges and universities, smaller private colleges, and the State Board of Commerce and Industry. Ten are chosen at large. If GSRI terminated operations, any assets remaining after satisfaction of indebtedness would be distributed to Louisiana's institutions of higher learning as determined by the trustees.

In 1964, legislation was passed creating the Louisiana State Science Foundation, the primary mission of which was to provide start-up assistance to GSRI. The institute realized assistance in the form of $1.25 million in laboratory facilities constructed in New Orleans; $1.5 million in revenue bonds purchased by the foundation, which are being repaid at the rate of 3 percent per year (without interest); and an additional $2.2 million in research funds over a several-year period. The research monies were matched

New Orleans Research Park (Physical and Engineering Sciences).

Baton Rouge Research Park
(Resources Planning and Management Division and Corporate Headquarters).

New Iberia Research Park (Life Sciences).

three or four to one by federal support of the programs undertaken. GSRI's New Orleans facilities consist of 20,000 square feet of modern laboratory space, a 20,000-square foot unfinished shell building, and 30,000 square feet of barracks-type structures converted to laboratories, machine shops, X-ray facilities, and "wet labs" for polymer spinning and casting.

At the time of its formation, GSRI also received some $2.5 million in private contributions, principally from industry, business, and foundations, including 200 acres of land donated by the Baton Route Area Foundation for a research park. In 1971, facilities and land in the Baton Rouge tract, appraised at $1.5 million, were exchanged for the GSRI bonds, and a lease-purchase arrangement for occupancy of the Baton Rouge facilities similar to that in New Orleans was entered into with the State Science Foundation. During fiscal year 1974, the institute's research facilities and 85 acres of contiguous land in the Baton Rouge Research Park were sold to Ethyl Corporation for $2.250 million cash. This transaction allowed the institute to satisfy all outstanding mortgage indebtedness and meet its needs for working capital for a period of at least one year. New facilities are being constructed in Baton Rouge for lease back from the State Science Foundation, under the same terms as before.

From its inception, the Gulf South Research Institute has been a three-site undertaking, with operations in Baton Rouge (corporate headquarters; Resources Planning and Management Division), New Orleans (Physical and Engineering Sciences Division), and New Iberia (Life Sciences Division). In New Iberia at the former U.S. Naval Auxiliary Air Station, the institute occupies four buildings, with 85,000 square feet of floor space containing offices, laboratories, operating rooms, clinics, animal quarters, a library, and various outside structures. Also located there is a 35,000-square foot building housing primates for the National Institute for Neurological Disease and Stroke. The property to which GSRI holds title, represents a federal government contribution of buildings and land appraised at more than $1 million. The title will be perfected by the conduct of R&D activities for 30 years.

GSRI began operating in the black in its eighth year (fiscal year 1973), after incurring expenses in excess of revenues for its three-site research effort of $1.7 million. This was in line with projected start-up expenses of $1.4 million for a single-site undertaking. The institute conducted $4.2 million of research in the fiscal year ending June 30, 1974. Of this amount, $2 million was derived from its Life Sciences Division, $1.4 million from the Physical and Engineering Sciences Division, and $.8 million from the Resources Planning and Management Division.

Specialty areas within the institute include land use and water re-sources planning, systems analysis, environmental assessments (involving teams of archaeologists and anthropologists among others), polymer research (including production of hollow fiber and flat sheet membranes), chemical process studies (emphasizing effluent treatment), analytical and clinical chemistry, carcinogenesis and toxicology studies, operation of experimental animal colonies (including over 1000 primates, 200 of which are adult chimpanzees), and infectious disease research with armadillos.

For fiscal year 1975, the Gulf South Research Institute projects revenues of $5.3 million, and it is anticipated that this rate of growth will be maintained for the next several years.

CHAPTER IX

THE FRESH APPROACH

The organizational/operational characteristics of the independent research institutes are such that some of the results achieved there probably would not have been possible in any other type of laboratory and certainly not as early.

As individuals, research institute staff members are distinctive. They have a special preference for the unique environment that is somewhere between what prevails at the university and that of industry. In the main, these people are very innovative and like to work in "practical" research, but do not feel comfortable in a limited process of an industrial product-oriented research department. They like the nonindustrial, campuslike grounds of the independent research institution. They are likewise attracted by the distinctively broad multidisciplinary expertise.

When the large majority of research institutions were organized, their statement of purpose emphasized service to (1) a particular geographical region where economic development was essential and (2) the tens of thousands of small manufacturing companies that had no research department or, as a matter of fact, not even a technically trained man in the organization. At first it was believed that the major activity would be service to small companies, but shortly it became apparent that it was also the large corporations that were bringing their problems to these institutions, either to avail themselves of special staff expertise and equipment or in search of a "fresh approach." In numerous instances, it was only at these institutions where the neutral ground existed for competitive companies in an industry to jointly sponsor a project or seek a solution to a common problem.

These nonprofit research institutions have also provided the birthplace for new industries or spin-off activities.

MELLON INSTITUTE*

Mr. Andrew Mellon, in his address at the dedication of the present Mellon Institute Building in 1937, stated that it was Robert K. Duncan's book entitled *The Chemistry of Commerce* that caught his interest. Mr. Mellon said,

> . . . the part which particularly enlisted my attention was the last chapter in which Dr. Duncan described his plan for industrial fellowships, by means of which industry could utilize the services of qualified scientists to solve its problems, in much the same way as is being done here today. It seemed to me that an institution based on Dr. Duncan's ideas could help in this advanced movement; and, as my brother (R. B. Mellon) was keenly interested in the project, we lost no time in persuading Dr. Duncan to come to Pittsburgh (from the University of Kansas) and organize (in 1911) for us here at the University of Pittsburgh, this Institute of Research.

The early activities of Mellon Institute so surpassed any general use of science in industrial development that this institution not only solved problems for its sponsors, but also spawned many new industries and provided numerous trained personnel. The training prepared individuals to fill key positions in new research departments started by industrial companies as well as enter the highest echelon of management.

Over 650 novel processes and products have been invented or developed by Fellows of the Institute. In a number of instances, fellowship inventions have created new industries such as the Visking Corporation, Plaskon Company, Inc., and Dow-Corning Corporation. In other cases, new branches have been added to existing manufacturers, the most outstanding example of which is the chemicals division (now Union Carbide Chemicals Company) of the Union Carbide Corporation. This organization was the pioneer of the present great petrochemical industry that embraces chemicals derived from petroleum.

The extensive research facilities of the Gulf Oil Corporation originated with Mellon Institute. Likewise, the institute concept served to inspire and encourage the beginnings and growth of many similar research institutes and

---

*This section excerpted from and based upon "Fifty Years of Science and Human Progress," by Dr. E. R. Weidlein, in *50th Annual Report, Mellon Institute, Science for Human Progress*, February 1963.

foundations as separate organizations, or within universities to serve their particular areas.

Functionally, the institute, a center for both pure and applied research, is also a training school for advanced scientists and a clearinghouse for specific scientific information to the public. Through cooperation with the University of Pittsburgh and the Carnegie Institute of Technology, 232 men and women have received their advanced degrees while employed in scientific research at Mellon. The average stay of the scientists has been short, most personnel moving from the institute to the sponsor organizations to continue their scientific contributions. In this way, the institute has been an important manpower reservoir of scientifically and technically trained individuals moving in increasing numbers to responsible positions elsewhere. They have become presidents, vice presidents, and research directors of organizations, as well as professors and department heads in our universities. The people, as well as the industries, have faith in the use of the scientific method when its value is demonstrated again and again.

Contributions by Mellon staff members to scientific literature have been numerous. The total number of publications over the past 50 years adds up to 60 books, 369 bulletins, 3909 research papers, 1574 patents, and many miscellaneous articles in professional and trade journals. It has always been the belief of the institute that only part of its responsibility is discharged when a research project has been completed successfully. The more critical duties are those of making the resultant knowledge available through the scientific literature and translating the results to the people in terms of modern industrial evolution.

Besides their many contributions to literature, Mellon Institute's members have taken a very active part in many scientific and engineering societies. They have been presidents, directors, and editors of the scientific journals and have served on numerous important committees. The institute is a center for the regularly scheduled meetings of Pittsburgh's scientific, medical, and engineering societies. Also, many symposia and conferences of national scope are held at Mellon. The building was designed to render this service without interference with the normal activities of the institute staff.

Mellon Institute has carried out a number of specific research projects for the benefit of the public, and all the results of this work have been published and given wide distribution. Such studies usually relate to public health, addressing areas such as smoke abatement, industrial and urban dusts, dental caries, nutrition, sleep, diagnosis of tuberculosis in its early stages, and new compounds valuable in treating pneumonia and cancer.

The institute most effectively served the government during World Wars I and II, when its scientific resources were placed at the disposal of the federal government. The first gas mask for use in World War I was invented at Mellon, which subsequently played an important part in developing the synthetic rubber program in World War II.

In a period of 50 years, Mellon has accomplished many tangible results which have won the esteem of science and industry. Yet, when one pauses to ponder the accumulated evidence of accomplishment, it does not seem enough to put one's finger at any point and say "This is what it has done." Often, no matter how dramatic or distinguished the definite results may be, it is the imponderable achievements that make an organization great. For instance, the fact that some industries have been aided to evolve better products may prove to be ultimately less important than the profound influence the Mellon point of view on scientific research has exerted on industry. Likewise, the contribution of men trained to follow their researches successfully in industrial plants may pale in comparison to the elevation the general concept of the value of scientific research achieved as the objectives and methods of Mellon Institute became understood and evoked trust. One may also consider that the institute through its research in pure science has laid the basis for fundamentally new services to man.

BATTELLE MEMORIAL INSTITUTE

▪ As a young patent attorney, Chester F. Carlson became annoyed and frustrated by some of the tedious copying work (contracts, pleadings, briefs, etc.) inherent to his job. It is typical enough for an employee to become irritated by such mundane aspects of his work, but most accept these chores as unavoidable . . . perform them as quickly as possible . . . and then proceed with more important business. Carlson was a remarkable exception to this cycle; he decided to do something about this time-consuming albatross. The idea that he conceived was electrostatic printing or photography, the fundamental principles of which he worked out in the kitchen of his New York apartment.

Carlson began with the idea that a photographic plate could be formed from a very thin layer of photoconductive material and that electrostatic charges on the plate could be controlled by the light pattern or image on the object being reproduced. By combining electrostatics with photoconductivity, he had discovered the basic concept of xerography. All that remained was to reduce the invention to practice in a laboratory. On October 18, 1937, he applied for a patent for a process he called electrophotography, exemplifying the combination of electrostatics and photography. Because his idea was completely innovative, he was able to get quite broad patent protection. After this milestone, he continued his personal efforts to develop the invention, but he realized he needed help in its perfection and marketing. In that regard, he contacted 20 or more organizations, including several major corporations and the National Inventors Council. He received what he termed "an enthusiastic lack of interest."

Circumstances were on the verge of reversing in Carlson's favor, however, with Russell Dayton, Battelle metallurgist, filling the role of catalyst. Early in 1944, Dayton went to New York to see Chester Carlson, a patent attorney for P. R. Mallory and Company. The reason for Dayton's trip was that Mallory's request for a patent on a project undertaken by Battelle was rejected, and Dayton was needed to testify on the matter. After that business was taken care of, Carlson, probably with little or no hope, approached Dayton about his invention. He asked if Battelle ever developed ideas for other people and, although the answer was "No, we never have," Dayton was interested enough in Carlson's process and the previously granted patent that he took a copy of the patent back with him to Columbus. By this time, Dayton was indeed excited and far past the interested stage. Once at home, he spilled his excitement to John Crout, at the time director of the Battelle Development Corporation (BDC), a not-for-profit subsidiary of Battelle. Then it was Crout's turn to become excited, and he arranged for immediate conferences with Carlson. BDC was indeed interested. In fact, it envisioned a great potential for the invention. In the 1944 annual report, the following statement appears: "It is felt that this process has an excellent chance of succeeding in the majority of possible applications." The following year, BDC officials reported, "Electrophotography may be the most fundamental development which BDC has undertaken." Battelle Development Corporation subsequently negotiated a contract with Chester Carlson in which BDC received control of the invention in return for a financial investment and sharing of future income. Carlson was to receive 40 percent of the proceeds.

With money from BDC, research was conducted at the Battelle Laboratories in Columbus. The basic principles of the process were worked out in fuller detail, and a better understanding of the whole innovation was slowly obtained. In addition, a number of significant developments basic to the success of xerography were accomplished. Among them were the fully automatic mechanism for charging the plate by means of corona-spray discharge; the idea of transference of the powdered image to paper by using the charging mechanism to effect an electrostatic transfer; the improvement of powders for use in developing the latent electrostatic image; and the two-component powder-carrier material which, when used in cascade development resulted in cleaner backgrounds. Also, metal, glass, and paper surfaces were successfully coated with various photoconductors by evaporation under a partial vacuum. With these advancement efforts accomplished, it was then necessary to find a manufacturer who would be willing to pay further development costs and to manufacture a device that would be marketable. Early attempts in this regard were as futile as Carlson's frustrating beginnings. Finally, the Haloid Company, a producer of photographic and photocopy papers and machines in Rochester, New York, agreed to sponsor further research on the project at Battelle. The name XeroX was decided upon because of (1) the discarding of "electrophotography" as too cumbersome and unimaginative a name for a commercial product; (2) the selecting of the term *xerography* based on the Greek words *xeros*, "dry," and *graphos*, "writing"; and (3) the shortening of the Greek to XeroX, with an admitted influence of "Kodak" in the choice of the name for the product.

The first public disclosure of the new process was at a Detroit meeting of the American Optical Society on October 22, 1948, 10 years to the day after Carlson made his first successful image with his remarkable innovation. In that year, xerography was cited as one of the 10 most noteworthy technological accomplishments of 1948. Developing the copier proved a great strain on Haloid's resources, eventually requiring the company to go outside to raise $4.3 million. After many years of extensive development, improvement, and refinement, as well as negotiation after negotiation regarding patent rights, shares of stock, and royalties among Carlson, Battelle, BDC, and Haloid, the "914 Office Copier" was ready to be manufactured and marketed. The machine was so named because it could reproduce on paper that measured up to 9 by 14 inches. A desk-sized, fully automatic machine, it could reproduce the first copy in 30 seconds and additional copies at the rate of one every 8 seconds. The 914 became an immediate success, and the term Xerox® quickly invaded the language of some as a noun and adjective, and "to xerox" became a verb—usages to which Xerox Corporation staunchly objects as improper since it is their brand name. (The trade name XeroX had long since been changed in favor of Xerox®.) Haloid changed its name to

Haloid Xerox® in 1958, and then to Xerox® Corporation in 1961.

The 1960 appearance of the Automatic 914 Xerox® Copying Machine marked the emergence of a whole new industry, and those involved in its development—Carlson, Battelle, BDC, and Haloid—were just beginning to reap the rewards of the long, difficult, and continuing labor to refine a brilliant idea of a poor struggling inventor. As for Battelle's multimillion-dollar share of the endeavor, the money has been used to expand and enhance their basic objective—"the utilization of science for the benefit of mankind."*

■ While the story of the successful development of xerography is in a class by itself in terms of its impact on society—the jobs and wealth created and new ease and speed in copying—there are many other developments carried forward by Battelle that have been of benefit to people.

Two of the more recent of these, of which Battelle is particularly proud, are the result of its research on materials that can be implanted in the human body. Such research is a natural extension of Battelle's strength in industrial materials research. In a sense Battelle's involvement in biomaterials research dates back more than 30 years, and it is an interesting sidelight on history that a metal alloy it developed for watch springs was found to be the best material available at the time for artificial valves. Today, this same material is being used in the electrodes of heart pacemakers because of its biocompatibility and its resistance to fatigue and corrosion.

Indicative of the significance of these two developments is the fact that both of them have been singled out for the award given annually by the publisher of *Industrial Research* magazine for the most significant technical developments. One of these is a void-metal composite; the other is a treatment for plastics to make them compatible with blood.

The void-metal composite, prepared from titanium or stainless steel, contains a network of precise interconnected pores or voids that permit ingrowth of living tissue. Solid bonding of the prosthetic devices made from this material, including posts for permanent dental anchors, have been demonstrated in laboratory animals. Experiments to date have been encouraging, suggesting use of dental anchors to support clinical crowns and bridges.

The award-winning treatment for plastics makes it possible to bond an anticoagulant substance known as heparin to the surface of a variety of

*"Resource" (newsletter of Battelle Development Corporation, Battelle Memorial Institute), vol. 1, no. 2, January 1970.

plastics to prevent them from causing blood clotting. Once treated, plastics can be sterilized. Treated devices have been used successfully in humans in limited clinical trials by surgeons. The process is applicable to a wide range of devices for use in the body, including artificial hearts and lungs.

The process has proved extremely useful in providing a blood bypass needed in surgical repair of an aortic aneurysm. A number of surgical procedures for repair of aortic aneurysms have been carried out utilizing a length of tubing treated with the anticoagulant to shunt the patient's blood around the section of vessel under repair. This allows the surgeon to repair the vessel while maintaining a blood supply to vital organs. The clinical trials using coated bypass tubes have been very successful, and the future for applications of this type appears to be promising.

IIT RESEARCH INSTITUTE

■ In 1940, when Vagtborg was director of the Armour Research Foundation in Chicago, he interviewed for a position as technician in electronics, a young man by the name of Marvin Camras, who had just graduated from the Armour Institute of Technology (now called Illinois Institute of Technology). When asked to demonstrate his ability to work with his hands, he produced a black box containing two spools connected to gears in the box and joined by a fine wire. He called it a magnetic wire recorder and demonstrated it, explaining that he had put the device together so that he could record music for his cousin who was practicing singing and wanted to hear his voice. Vagtborg was intrigued by his homemade device and hired Camras, stipulating that he would like to have the inventor's authorization to explore the commercial potentials of the device on a basis that he would share in any proceeds that might come from inventions developed from it. This proposition was completely unexpected by Camras, but he agreed to cooperate in every way. Vagtborg proceeded with his plans and set up an immediate meeting with the patent attorneys. Much to his amazement, he found out that Camras had employed two distinct and different applications in the development of his device which, the attorneys said, were "flashes of genius" and could undoubtedly be patented.

In due course, two basic patents were assigned to Armour Foundation, the first of many more to come. This patent pool became an important source of magnetic wire, tape, and disc recording developments, and Armour found itself in the licensing business.

The earliest Armour wire recorders were designed to be low-cost home recorders, the idea being that they would appeal to the same people who used movie cameras, etc. Business and education would be served by slight modifications of the basic design.

World War II interrupted all plans for domestic use; however, various military agencies needed recorders that were portable and durable. During the war, recorders were used in pilot training activities, submarine sonar recording, operational data, news gathering, and sound decoys. Airborne, pocket, and cartridge loading models were developed.

The General Electric Company, Armour's first licensee, foresaw a large domestic market after the war. They did not want exclusive rights to the patents but encouraged Armour to license others, because in that way a broader market would develop. With an eye toward postwar production, major manufacturers signed up. As it turned out, the giant companies, including G.E., were never major producers of equipment compared to specialists such as Ampex, Webcor, Peirce, Magnecord, and V.M.

When the production needs of the military were satisfied, Armour turned again to its proper role of research. Magnetic tape offered intriguing possibilities, but the low coercivity tapes, used by the Germans, required high speed (30 inches per second) for high fidelity reproduction or gave limited fidelity at lower speeds as used by Brush Development Company. In the search of a better tape material, Armour hit upon an iron oxide consisting of extremely fine needles, less than a micron long. This oxide is the basic material still used by the tape industry which is now a multibillion-dollar operation.

Immediately after the war, there was a race to get into the production of magnetic recorders. Wire recording was well established, thus overshadowing the uncertain tape recording, which would have to wait. One of the first postwar designs was made by St. George Recording Equipment Company for Sears Roebuck. It utilized a phonograph turntable which reeled the wire, allowing recordings to be made from a disc record, a microphone, or a built-in radio. The most popular wire recorder was made by the Webster-Chicago, and to this day, Armour (now IITRI) receives requests to transcribe wire recordings made on this unit. However, by 1950, interest in wire recorders had waned, and reel-to-reel tape recorders were in their heyday.

After introducing the two-track tape recorders in 1945, Armour explored other aspects of magnetic recording. One of the most interesting was magnetic sound tracks for motion pictures demonstrated in 1946 to the society of Motion Picture Engineers in Hollywood, California. The result was rapid adoption of the magnetic system by movie studios. Within three years, this system was used almost exclusively.

Stereophonic sound was simple to achieve on multi-track tape, and Armour had no competition in this field in the 1940s and 1950s. In fact, ARF was the first to demonstrate the advantages of stereo tapes, urging recording companies to make their master recordings, at the very least, on stereo so that the artistry of Toscanini, for example, could be preserved for future generations. The recording industry saw no possibilities in this new-fangled gimmick in 1948, however, and so these opportunities were lost. Fifteen years later they were adding pseudo (fake) stereo to their old mono-phonic recordings. Stereo discs were subsequently inspired by the success of stereo tapes which loomed as a threat to the phonograph industry.

For the more mundane applications such as office dictation, the advantage of erasability was shown in the earliest days by Armour's director, Harold Vagtborg, who could change a single word in an incorrect sentence on a wire recorder. Postwar dictation machines included a magnetic belt unit by Peirce, who later sold his design to IBM. Very popular, also, was the reel type, the DeJur Stenorette.

In the late 1940s, Armour was trying to record television signals with a rotating head machine using a vacuum cleaner motor turning at about 22,000 rpm, so fast that the friction could melt the coating of early tapes. Ampex liked the idea, set up a development team, and in 1957 announced a video-tape recorder that revolutionized the broadcasting industry. Armour has envisioned a low-cost version of the broadcast model, which, at a cost of about $100,000, is too expensive for general use. Shown below (next to a TV set) is an early sample of the economy model, which is estimated to cost

no more than a sound recorder. It uses a fixed head (nonrotating), ¼-inch tape, and 10 tracks for one or two hours of playing time. At each end of the reel, the tape direction reverses while the head moves to the next track. Later designs are cartridge loading and much smaller in size. Eventually such television recorders will be used just like phonographs and tape recorders to give you the program you want in color pictures and stereo sound.

■ In May 1973, IIT Research Institute worked around the clock to prepare the thermal coating (S-13G) for the curtains to be installed by the astronauts on *Skylab 1* that had just gone into orbit.

A specially prepared thermal control coating which reflects 80 percent of the sun's energy was to be sprayed on a mylar film to form the heat curtain being built to protect the space laboratory from the sun's heat.

Ordinary pigments such as zinc oxide catalyze the decomposition of the pigments in the paint brought about by intense ultraviolet light radiation to which space vehicles are exposed. The degradation results in a change in the absorption-emission characteristics of the paint, and the coating loses its ability to reflect the light allowing the space cabins to heat up. Under a previous contract with NASA, Gene Zerlaut, manager of polymer research at IITRI, found that encapsulation of the zinc oxide pigment in potassium silicate prevents the decomposition of the pigment and stabilizes the absorption-emission characteristics of the coating. The encapsulated pigment is blended into General Electric's ATV Silicone.

IITRI produced six gallons of paint a day to provide the 30 gallons ordered by NASA to coat the curtains to be carried to *Skylab 1* by the astronauts on May 25. The paint costing $550 per gallon, was sent to Marshall Space Flight Center in Huntsville, where it was sprayed on the mylar curtains in time to meet the flight deadline.

The thermal control coating was developed for use on the Apollo flights to the moon. Ninety percent of the paint that reached the moon on the space ships was the S-13G developed and made in IIT Research Institute's Laboratories.

CORNELL AERONAUTICAL LABORATORY
■ **Advances in Automotive Safety Research**—The modern automobile and its associated safety systems did not come into being as the invention of a single man or even that of a closely knit group of individuals. Indeed, it is the

child of an evolutionary process of development in which many uncommon individuals have devoted their talents.

Calspan Corporation—when it was known as Cornell Aeronautical Laboratory—entered the field of automotive safety research back in 1947, at a time when little attention was being devoted to the problems of protecting motorists involved in crashes. But even then, the company's engineers were convinced that monumental payoffs could result from protecting the human body from severe levels of deceleration.

By the early 1950s, the company's engineering analysis was providing a strong recommendation for the use of seat belts, as well as documented criteria for their design and installation. Recommendations also included interior car padding and "delethalization" of such objects as knobs and door handles. Early strength requirements for seat belts and their anchors were established, and a seat-belt kit was designed for the Hickok Manufacturing Company of Rochester, New York, which manufactured and marketed the kit.

It was in 1952 that the world-renowned Cornell Automotive Crash Injury Research (ACIR) project was formed at the Cornell University Medical College in New York City. (ACIR became the responsibility of Cornell Aeronautical Laboratory in 1960 and was reorganized and relocated in Buffalo, in 1962.)

What happens when automobiles of unequal weight collide? As part of Calspan's safety research, the crash-resistance of many types of vehicles is measured on the company's extensive testing facility.

During its nearly 20 years in operation, ACIR made substantial contributions toward a sounder knowledge of injury-causing elements in highway accidents and subsequently identified a number of injury-reducing means. For example, at its very beginning, ACIR revealed a most significant finding: Ejection from a car in an accident is a serious problem, and those who are ejected fare, on an average, much worse than those who are retained inside the car. Ejection subsequently was pinpointed by ACIR as the leading contributor to death and serious injury, and a preliminary ranking of the 10 leading causes of injury in auto accidents was issued. In response, the auto industry developed several generations of improved, interlocking safety door latches to keep doors closed in accidents. ACIR studies then showed that lethal ejection had been substantially reduced. For the first time in transportation history, engineers in the 1950s were getting precisely documented information on how the automobile could be improved as a "package" for safer transport of human beings.

The ACIR program was succeeded in the fall of 1969 by a more comprehensive effort, the primary thrust of which is to pinpoint the precise causes of injury in highway accidents and the causes of accidents themselves. Also being determined is how human failure, highway features, and car design may have contributed to accidents involving late-model cars. This multi-level program also evaluates the effectiveness of new safety features on cars as well as that of federal motor vehicle and traffic safety standards. It also provides an "early warning" of any design or functional problems of vehicles and highways.

Among the components of the automobile that received early attention by Cornell Laboratory, as well as by ACIR, was the padding of instrument panels. As a result of this research, new padding techniques were brought into being, and a new type of energy-absorbing material was developed in conjunction with a major rubber company.

In 1955, the company and the Liberty Mutual Insurance Company combined on a project to apply accrued knowledge to the design and construction of a safety concept car as a showcase of feasible, engineered safety innovations. The unpowered car, unveiled in 1957, contained more than 60 new safety concepts, some of which have since been introduced in various forms on production cars. The car was displayed at many places around the nation, including the Smithsonian Institution, and attracted enormous public interest, as well as attention from the auto industry.

In 1960, the company turned its attention to the formulating and programing for computer use a mathematical model simulating the dynamic action of an impact against a roadside guardrail. With the use of applied-mechanics theory, a computer simulation technique of guardrail and vehicle dynamics was developed by Raymond R. McHenry of the company's technical staff. Using this analysis, a new design called the Box Beam concept for median barriers and road-shoulder guardrail and bridge railing was conceived. The company received a U.S. patent on the new design and granted all states royalty-free licenses for its use. The safety Box Beam design is now in widespread use.

Also in the 1960s, the company developed a mathematical model, or numerical description, of an auto crash victim and subsequently conceived a three-dimensional representation of a crash victim and car striking an obstacle in a violent evasive maneuver. The 3-D vehicle computer simulation subsequently was supplied by the company to over 50 companies and organizations for such uses as vehicle design, vehicle handling properties investigations, and design of the roadside and roadside structures, as well as in accident reconstruction.

In the area of transportation safety as it applies to the automobile, the company's largest basic research program has been the development of cars with new crashworthiness features to give motorists a better chance of surviving high-speed crashes. This research program, begun in 1968, has shown that the new crashworthy structures, as well as other new energy-managing systems, could provide a dramatic improvement in motorist protection in high-speed crashes.

Research, development, and engineering related to automotive safety and associated fields over the years at Calspan have encompassed a broad panorama of investigations. Among others, they have included: sophisticated tire research, utilizing one of the world's most advanced tire research facilities; continuing broadened accident research; vehicle safety improvement; crash testing of cars to determine their compliance with federal safety standards; vehicle handling qualities research; development of advanced passive restraint systems; vehicle exhaust emissions research; automobile bumper testing and evaluation; driver research; highway design criteria; and conceptualization of future transportation systems. Calspan has also applied its computer simulation techniques to programs involving improved safety for bicycles and motorcycles.

Calspan operates extensive facilities in support of its transportation research programs. These include a large proving ground for vehicle crash testing, driver research, and various car handling and other programs; a high-energy indoor impact sled for simulation of crashes; an advanced computer-controlled tire research facility; a large vehicle crushing machine; a bumper pendulum test facility; a linear accelerator for simulating crash conditions; and various machine shops. Extensive large-scale computing facilities also are available at Calspan.

▪ Following World War II, military aircraft began probing deep into the sound barrier. The age of spaceflight and intercontinental missilery lay just ahead. For design and operational purposes, it became essential to develop a precise scientific understanding of the interaction between the atmosphere and vehicles moving faster—often many times faster—than the speed of sound.

To make the simulation of such conditions possible in the laboratory, two major technologies were conceived at Calspan (which was then Cornell Aeronautical Laboratory) during the late 1940s and 1950s. In each case, the company used its own funds to develop and test the concept. Once validity had been demonstrated, sponsors joined in to finance the hardware necessary for full-scale utilization.

Both concepts—the perforated throat for transonic wind tunnels and the shock tunnel for hypersonic airflows—are now in wide use in the aerospace industry.

The need for improved wind tunnel technology evolved from two limitations inherent in the design of the conventional tunnel. These limitations took on greater significance as airflow was pushed to higher speeds. The engineers found that the increas-

Model of advanced military aircraft is prepared for aerodynamic testing in Calspan's continuous-flow transonic wind tunnel. During airflow, a bulkhead seals the front of the access port.

ing friction between the airflow and the tunnel's walls, was acting as a blockage to the flow, and the "brute force" method of increasing velocity simply by applying more and more power to the tunnel fans required expensive, single-flow-condition replaceable nozzles. In addition, as transonic speeds were achieved, shock waves propagating from the model aircraft mounted in the test section were being reflected off the walls and back onto the model, causing erroneous readings from the instruments.

To partially offset the problem of wall friction, some wind tunnel engineers installed slots in the walls of their tunnel's test section in an effort to bleed off the slowed-down boundary-layer air. Cornell Aeronautical Laboratory's engineers, however, came up with a better solution. Their studies showed that perforations would be more efficient than slots, so they cut thousands of dime-sized holes in the test section's walls. At the same time, they designed a suction system, driven by motors totaling 14,250 horsepower, to pull the boundary-layer air through the perforations and out the tunnel. The evenly spaced perforations also performed a second function: they provided multiple exit paths through which most of the energy from the shock waves could escape from the test section, rather than being reflected back toward the model.

The $2 million perforated transonic throat and pumping system in the company's tunnel was installed under air force contract, and it proved so successful that the perforated-throat concept was adopted by the air force for its central tunnel facility at Arnold Engineering Development Center. Both this air force tunnel and Calspan's original tunnel have logged thousands of hours of transonic testing since then; at times the company's facility has been the busiest wind tunnel in the nation, carrying out aerodynamic testing of virtually all of the nation's military and commercial aircraft as well as many missiles.

For the speeds and conditions encountered during reentry from space, however, a totally new type of testing facility was required. To meet this emerging need, in 1950 and 1951, CAL conceived and developed the first shock tunnel, described as a "hypersonic" tunnel because it is capable of producing steady airflows at five times the speed of sound or faster. The shock tunnel has since become an accepted research tool and is currently in wide use by universities, government, and industrial laboratories in this country and abroad. Some of these tunnels now provide flows as high as 30 times the velocity of sound, making them valuable devices for investigating the aerodynamic-high temperature problems of missiles and spacecraft during reentry.

SOUTHERN RESEARCH INSTITUTE

▪ Many leaders in the field of cancer chemotherapy have insisted for years that "the cure," to be suddenly announced in large headlines, is probably an unfortunate myth. Progress is more likely to take the form of step-by-step advances in knowledge about the many diseases called cancer, and in steady improvement in the effectiveness of drugs used to treat them. The slow but steady pace of this type of development is well illustrated in the history of two drugs, or more precisely, two drug families, that are products of research at Southern Research Institute (SRI). Both were first synthesized about 15 years ago, but are only now becoming generally available, after exhaustive evaluations in animal tumors, pharmacology studies to determine toxicity, and carefully monitored clinical trials in man.

One of these drugs is BCNU, the acronym for 1,3-bis (2-chloroethyl)-1-nitrosourea, which is being used increasingly today in the clinic. It is a member of a family of drugs called nitrosoureas, which includes several other compounds that may also prove to be useful.

The institute's interest in this type of compound was sparked by a 1959 report that MNNG (1-methyl-1-nitroso-3-nitroguanidine) had some rather weak activity against a mouse leukemia. (It moderately increased the lifespan of mice inoculated with the L1210 type of leukemia.) This observation came out of the random screening program of the National Cancer Institute (NCI). MNNG was not active in man, but its activity in animals led SRI to begin evaluating compounds that were structurally related to MNNG, including one called MNU (1-methyl-1-nitrosourea). The initial trials were disappointing because it was effective only in a very narrow range of doses and was also quite toxic. With a careful selection of dosage, however, the drug was found to be effective not only against L1210 leukemia in the peritoneal (stomach) cavity, but also against L1210 implanted in the brain, a model disease for human meningeal leukemia. Thus, the drug must have crossed the "blood-brain barrier," the natural mechanism that pervents certain foreign substances (such as drugs) from entering the brain and its sheathing membranes, the spinal cord, and the spinal fluid. This activity was unique. Previously, when cancer cells spread from some other part of the body into the brain or spinal cord and began to multiply, they were considered beyond the reach of drugs, protected by the "blood-brain barrier."

Excited by these findings, SRI organic chemists began synthesizing structural variations of MNU—attempting to maintain the desirable activity while minimizing toxicity and instability problems. The twenty-third drug in this series, BCNU, was highly active, giving a good percentage of cures in both the peritoneal leukemia and in the brain. Extensive animal evaluations were begun, and then initial clinical trials were started in 1963. In clinical trials at the investigational stage, BCNU has been helpful in the treatment of glioma, a type of brain tumor; advanced Hodgkin's disease and reticulum cell sarcoma, cancers of the lymph system; multiple myeloma, cancer of bone marrow cells, melanoma, an uncommon and often fatal type of skin cancer; leukemia; and to a lesser extent, in cancers of the breast, colon, and lung. More than 200 nitrosoureas have been synthesized at SRI, and at least two others, in addition to BCNU, appear to be especially promising. The clinical trials of CCNU are less complete than those of BCNU, but it may prove to be superior to BCNU. A third compound, methyl-CCNU, is the best single agent known against a variety of solid tumors in rodents.

All three of these compounds were developed in drug programs sponsored by the National Cancer Institute and were the subject of the first formal agreement between NCI and a pharmaceutical firm for manufacture and eventual marketing of NCI-developed anticancer drugs.

The development at SRI of a second family of drugs, the imidazole triazines, was the result of a successful attempt to modify a toxic compound to give it selective toxicity against cancer cells (but not against normal cells). Several dozen compounds of this class have been synthesized at SRI, and a number of them have shown promising results in trials against cancer in animals, but only two, called DIC and BIC, have reached the stage of clinical trials in man. The story of this "family" began more than 30 years ago, when AIC (5-aminoimidazole-4-carboxamide) was found in cultures of bacteria inhibited by sulfa drugs. Profiting from this information, biochemists discovered that a derivative of AIC, its ribonucleotide, is an intermediate stage in the biosynthesis of nucleic acids in living cells. SRI's studies on the chemical transformations of AIC resulted in the isolation of diazo-IC (5-diazoimidazole-4-carboxamide). This compound proved to be very toxic to cancer cells growing in culture, but in animals it was found to be toxic to normal cells. When the dose was lowered enough to be nontoxic, it was also ineffective against the cancers. The drug lacked not only selectivity but also stability. Diazo-IC was then converted to DIC (5-[3-dimethyl-triazenol imidazone-4-carboxamide), a potentially latent form of the toxic diazo-IC having a structure that was similar to the metabolically important AIC. The new compound, DIC, proved to be very active against three different types of mouse tumors. Clinical trials followed, and DIC has gained acceptance as a useful agent for treatment of malignant melanoma. DIC, like BCNU, is now the subject of an NCI agreement with a pharmaceutical firm for manufacture and marketing.

The success of DIC led to the synthesis of several related compounds, including BIC (5-[3,3-bis (2-chloroethyl)-1-triazeno] imidazole-4-carboxamide), which proved more effective than DIC against leukemia and is still undergoing clinical trials.

The development of these drug families, which is still continuing, is a combined effort of organic chemists who design and synthesize the compounds, biochemists who study their mechanism, experimental oncologists who evaluate the compounds in animals, pharmacologists who study their toxicity, and clinicians who administer the drug to man.

■ Air pollution research had been a familiar subject at Southern Research Institute for many years, but it was not a significant contributor to total operations until the institute entered the field of electrostatic precipitation research. Many of the earlier projects were analytical in nature, such as the development of techniques for sample collection and instruments for counting fine particles. So it was not unusual that the subject of air pollution should come up in periodic discussions at SRI on emerging fields in which the competence and experience of the research staff might be complementary to increasing public and scientific interest. In the mid-1960s, a decision was made to move more aggressively into the field of research on air pollution.

The first few projects followed the earlier pattern of analytical work, but one of them was to have a special significance. At the request of an electrical utility, the institute attacked the problem of buildup of a material on the plates of an electrostatic precipitator used to control particulate emissions from coal-burning power boilers. The project provided the institute with its first specific background on the electrostatic precipitator, which is the most widely used type of equipment for the control of particulate emissions.

Soon after the utility project, a group of SRI engineers made a project development call on the National Air Pollution Control Administration (NAPCA) (which was later to become a major part of today's Environmental Protection Agency). They found that proposals were being sought for broad "systems studies" on the three major classes of particulate control equipment—electrostatic precipitators, fabric filters, and scrubbers. The institute's engineering group decided that it would submit a proposal on the precipitator study. SRI was awarded the contract in mid-1969 and began work to define the current state of electrostatic precipitator technology to determine the state-of-the-art in application of this type of equipment and to identify areas where research might be beneficial in improving or expanding the application of the equipment.

The proposal for the NAPCA contract had not been limited to not-for-profit research institutes; however, the work required a critical analysis of control devices produced by many different companies, and the impartiality of the opinions of any one manufacturer on his own equipment, or that of his competitors, might be suspect. The project required some theoretical work, to be sure, but it also required field studies, surveys, and analysis of operating problems in various industries—much more applied work than university researchers are generally accustomed to or capable of handling. Finally, the timing was critical requiring an immediate start by researchers in place and ready to begin, with no time for the gradual buildup of a research team. At a research institute, it was not difficult to assemble a group that included physicists, electrical engineers, chemical engineers, chemists, metallurgists, ceramics engineers, and scientists of other disciplines.

One major product of the year-and-a-half NAPCA systems study was an 875-page, two-volume *Manual of Electrostatic Precipitator Technology*, which represented the current state of that technology as of December 1970, and which quickly became a basic reference on the subject. Another major product was a preliminary mathematical model of precipitator performance, relating the electrical charge on the dust particles and the probability of collection to the precipitator current, particle size, dust concentration, and other factors known to influence performance. The model has been continuously refined and further developed to include effects and phenomena not taken into account by the preliminary model.

There have been numerous follow-on programs supported by NAPCA, now EPA, exploring those areas of both theory and application where information was needed. Information from the original study and from the later projects has been picked up and put to use by manufacturers and users of the equipment.

There has also been a steady flow of studies on all phases of electrostatic precipitator operation from industrial firms in many fields, particularly electric utilities, the largest users of this equipment. Many of these research programs have involved measurements of the capability of existing precipitators to meet emission standards, while others have required the sizing of new precipitators. Other subjects have included conditioning the dust by addition of chemical agents to reduce dust resistivity, and general troubleshooting.

What has Southern Research Institute accomplished in this field? In general, the institute group has applied a greater degree of engineering and scientific technique to the analysis of electrostatic precipitators and to the sizing of this equipment than had been done in the past. The practical, tangible result of this new knowledge is a considerable reduction in some of the costs of air pollution control. An electrostatic precipitator, which can represent an investment of several million dollars, can be tailored to the needs of the specific situation—not expensively overbuilt or inefficiently underbuilt.

MIDWEST RESEARCH INSTITUTE

■ In 1945, the first year of operation of MRI, Dr. Ernest Reid, president of the Corn Products Refining Company, visited the institute and asked the staff to undertake a major program that he judged the institute to be ideally suited to. He explained that corn for commercial use would ultimately become in short supply because the areas in which it was grown in the United States were limited. In the northern United States the growing season was too short. Eastern United States was too industrially congested and hilly for extensive corn-growing areas. The southern part of the country had too great a rainfall. The southwest and western parts of the country had inadequate rainfall for corn. He pointed out that there were several alternative crops that his firm had considered as a commercial source of starch and the numerous derivatives it produces. Corn was producing over 100 such products. Cowpeas produced in the northwest and sweet potatoes in the deep South were ruled out because they were too unstable to store in quantity to assure year-around refining. The only remaining possibility was grain sorghum that was grown extensively in the low rainfall Southwest and was suited to long-term storage. However, all of the grain sorghum varieties grown had objectionable tannic acid, color, and fiber. He suggested that the institute undertake the coordination of an intensive plant breeding program by utilizing plant breeders in central and southwest state agricultural experiment stations (MRI selected those in Nebraska, Kansas, Oklahoma, and Texas) and by use of its own laboratories determine if suitable new varieties of grain sorghums could be developed. A normal 12-year breeding program was telescoped into three years, and two new and satisfactory varieties resulted. As the plant breeding program began to show promise, the Corn Products Refining Company started construction of a grain sorghum processing plant in Corpus Christi, Texas, and started to make arrangements with farmers in the Southwest to grow the new varieties. Four years after the beginning of the project the plant was in successful operation.

■ Forty years ago there was particularly keen competition between the manufacturers of burned clay sewer pipe and the producers of concrete pipe. The concrete pipe association advertised extensively that "if it is good enough for the pipe it should be good enough for the joint." This comment evolved because it was standard practice to use cement mortar for the sealing of joints in a clay pipeline. The clay pipe manufacturers incessantly tried to develop an inorganic or organic material to replace cement joints. By the late 1950s, the W. S. Dickey Manufacturing Company had successfully developed a castable compression seal for vitrified clay pipe but the plastic material was too expensive. The development of material program at satisfactory cost was given to MRI in January 1963, and by September of that year the institute had developed a castable polyurethane material that solved the problem.

Following completion of the development program, the company built a facility at its Pittsburg, Kansas, site for manufacturing the major components of the urethane elastomer formulation. The present production of over 10 million pounds per year of elastomer by Dickey or their licensee makes them the largest producer and user of solid urethane elastomers in the United States.

STANFORD RESEARCH INSTITUTE

■ One of the outstanding research accomplishments in SRI history was ERMA, the first electronic check handler and forerunner of the automated systems in major banks in the United States. This project, undertaken for Bank of America, involved the development of a prototype system for automated checking account bookkeeping (Electronic Recording Method of Accounting).

Work began in 1950 and was completed in 1956. At times the project required the full-time efforts of a staff of 100 engineers, technicians, and supporting personnel. The result was a prototype automatic bookkeeping system that proved to be a major influence in establishing automated systems in virtually every bank of more than $50 million in assets in the United States. It also brought about a system of machine-readable numbers on checks adopted by the American Bankers Association for use by banks throughout the United States. Other countries, including Canada, England,

and Australia, have adopted these standards. And finally, it established banking as a major new market for electronic equipment manufacturers and provided an important stimulus to the printing industry.

The problem, as originally presented by Bank of America to the SRI engineers, was to develop a system that would physically handle paper checks, extract the essential information from them with a minimum of manual handling, perform the necessary bookkeeping functions, and finally, sort the checks by customer. The bank felt the need for such a tool to cope with the increasing volume of paper work flowing in and out of the branches each day.

Engineers concentrated their efforts in two major areas: the development of a means for sorting and reading checks at high speed, and the development of an electronic bookkeeping system.

The key to the sorting problem was the development of a method for the machine to read bank and customer account numbers printed on the checks—checks that had to be conventional in appearance and would not require a change of style. Optical reading was abandoned early in the project because of overstamping, pencil and ink marks, smears, and dirt.

The engineers then developed an ink containing magnetic particles (MICR—Magnetic Ink Character Recognition). When specially shaped, but visually readable numbers, are printed on the checks, they can be read by an electronic system that distinguishes between the wave shapes of the 10 digits.

Development of the sorter itself was based on electropneumatic principles. Checks could be machine read and sorted at a rate of 600 checks per minute. This device was the forerunner of high-speed check sorters now in use in hundreds of banks.

For the bookkeeping function, the engineers built a special-purpose, digital computer equipped with input stations having the ability to read magnetically encoded account number data. This computer was based on vacuum-tube technology inasmuch as transistors were still very new and of unproven reliability.

ERMA was built and tested at SRI and it clearly demonstrated the practicability of automatic bookkeeping. It remained for the manufacturer chosen by the bank to redesign ERMA into a solid-state, general-purpose, digital computer.

The first production ERMA system was installed at Bank of America in

1959. The units included a sorter/reader, a computer, magnetic-tape units, and a high-speed printer. By 1966, 12 regional ERMA centers served all but 21 of the bank's 900 branches. These centers handled more than 750 million pieces of paper a year—about the number predicted for 1970 at the time of the ERMA development.

Since that time, of course, the regional ERMA centers have been replaced by solid-state computers manufactured largely by IBM. But the impact of the ERMA project on banking automation remains a significant one. MICR continues as the common machine language for check processing in the United States and elsewhere.

▪ Anyone traveling in a modern airplane can see the rodlike elements on the trailing edge of the wings and tail. These play an important role in the pilot's radio communication system. They are precipitation-static suppressors.

When an airplane flies at high speed through a high-altitude cloud, the ice crystals beating on the aircraft's metal surfaces cause electrical charges to accumulate on the metal surfaces, just as charges develop when a person walks across a rug on a dry day. The charges on the airplane build up to the point where sparklike discharges (Saint Elmo's fire) occur from the wing and tail tips. These discharges produce radio noise called precipitation static that is picked up by the aircraft radio and makes communication difficult or even impossible.

At the request of the U.S. Air Force, SRI radio engineers made a study of the problem—and particularly how to overcome it. Prevention of the static charging seemed impossible. The approach taken, therefore, was to devise techniques for dissipating the charge so as to produce the least possible noise in the radio communication and navigation systems. By combining fundamental theory and data from experimentation both in the laboratory and on a Boeing 707, discharger devices were developed that are capable of dissipating all of the charging current normally generated on an aircraft flying through a cloud without generating appreciable noise. Both their construction and placement are critical.

A typical discharge device consists of a nylon rod about the size of a lead pencil, with a tungsten pin crosswise through it at a very carefully determined location (about an inch) from the outer end. The nylon rod is coated with paint having the proper electrical resistance.

By choice of element shape and resistance, the device virtually eliminates the coupling between the discharges and the radio receiving antennas on the aircraft. The characteristics of the resistive rod are such that a point of minimum coupling to the antennas exists at a point about an inch from the aft end of the rod. The discharge points are placed at this point so that the noise generated by discharges occurring from the points is decoupled from the antennas. These have proved to be fully effective in reducing the precipitation-static noise to such low levels that the interference to the communication system is not troublesome.

These suppressors are now made commercially by Granger Associates of Palo Alto. Most commercial, U.S.-built, jet airplanes now flying are equipped with these precipitation static suppressors. Several types of U.S. military aircraft, as well as many British and French aircraft, are likewise so equipped.

SOUTHWEST RESEARCH INSTITUTE

▪ In 1952, a group of gas transmission companies presented to SwRI a problem that was common to all of them, and that was the continuing damage to gas transmission systems caused by pulsations, particularly in and around the pumping stations.

After all possible solutions to the problem had been explored, it was agreed that the development of a special type of analog computer offered the most promise. In due course, such a computer was designed, built, and implemented at SwRI, with most satisfactory results. Other companies soon began participating in the program, and eventually, since most of the transmission companies were members of the Southern Gas Association, sponsorship of the program was transferred to the association.

Early use of the computer system involved the redesign and modification of existing pumping stations and resulted in successful reduction in breakage problems. Soon the demand for service developed to the point that additional computers were constructed and implemented at SwRI and at companies that designed equipment for pumping stations.

Through the years, this program has continued to grow, to the extent that now almost all designs for new pipeline compressor stations throughout the United States and in many foreign countries are checked out with the computer system before construction.

▪ A major problem in the operation of internal combustion engines has been the need to use fuels and lubricants that provide optimum performance. All

Analog computer for design of compressor stations.

fuels and lubricants vary in their chemical composition and physical characteristics depending on the particular petroleum reservoir source. In addition, engines are constantly being redesigned, a situation that necessitates modification of the chemical and physical characteristics of the liquids as engine changes are made. These circumstances, therefore, require continuing laboratory and engine operations to relate optimum fuel and lubricant characteristics to specific engines.

The staff of SwRI recognized the need for a neutral laboratory to serve the petroleum and automotive companies in resolving this problem. Several companies in each industry were brought together, and in 1949, the first independent fuels and lubricants research laboratory at SwRI was established with three engine installations. Ten years later, in 1959, the operation utilized 75 engine test installations in its evaluation of engine components, fuels, and lubricants.

Today, more than 150 installations are operated by the department 24 hours a day, 364 days a year, shutting down only on Christmas Day. Recently, a new engine laboratory (the fifth major engine test building) has been completed wherein a unique method of central control over 32 of the 54 engines in two wings is employed. With this method, the test procedures are automated so that the operators merely record the test data. In the principal Caterpillar engine complex, the reverse procedure is used, whereby operators are responsible for conducting procedures while all data are automatically recorded by a digital computer. This computer system has 800 analog input channels, disc storage capacity of 2.5 million words, a tele-type for operator control and system output, a high-speed paper tape reader, a communications line to the software development system, and a keyboard display for on-line monitoring. An unusual feature of the system is the closed

Neutral Fuels and Lubricants Laboratory

circuit television system with monitors in the laboratory which permits operators to evaluate the performance of the engines at any given time.

These two SwRI case histories are indicative of many efforts that have served groups of companies with common problems. In this way, the cost of expensive programs were shared by many, and the results of the programs were available to all. Such efforts cannot be undertaken in the laboratories of a particular company because of the danger of exposing confidential works in other fields to competitors. Hence, the need exists for a "neutral" laboratory, the type of facility a research institute alone can provide.

CHAPTER X

TECHNOLOGY AS A COMMODITY IN INTERNATIONAL TRADE*

In previous chapters we have explored research and development efforts in the United States, their roots and origins, how various major industrial firms utilized technology in one form or another to achieve new horizons in growth, and how the independent research institute fits into the picture in delivering technology to the nation's industry.

Another facet of the role of research and development—*technology*—in the national well-being has been identified and quantified by Dr. Michael Boretsky, Senior Policy Analyst, Office of the Secretary, U.S. Department of Commerce. It is Dr. Boretsky's thesis that technology can, in effect, be considered an extremely important commodity in world trade. He has made the point that highly technical (technology-oriented) goods or commodities sold abroad produce a far better balance of trade than do basic less-technology-oriented items. Thus, computer equipment sales abroad will produce a much higher proportion of return to the United States than will agricultural goods or minerals.

The implications of this concept with respect to national policy are important and obvious. Dr. Boretsky delivered a paper, "The Role of Technology in U.S. Trade and International Competitiveness of U.S. Companies," at the 1974 spring meeting of the Western Economics Association in which he brought together a great deal of statistical evidence to support his view. It is the purpose of this chapter to draw on the wealth of his background and present the arguments succinctly for the reader's benefit. The following has been entirely derived from Dr. Boretsky's learned paper, quoting directly in many cases, and paraphrasing in others. All the thoughts are his.

---

*The material in this chapter has been assembled from Dr. Michael Boretsky's work by W. Lawrence Prehn, principal consultant in Applied Economics to Southwest Research Institute.

INTRODUCTION TO THE CONCEPT

Man's curiosity about what makes a country successful or unsuccessful in its foreign trade is probably as old as the practice of international trade itself, which goes back several millennia. Dr. Boretsky believes that people who had serious reasons to be curious about it always managed to provide an explanation. In the discipline of modern economics, some recognized economists have explained successes and failures in terms of comparative cost. To others it was comparative advantage, or differential factor endowment, or, in the current established theory, it would seem to be total factor productivity. Each of these principles has some advantage and some disadvantage in explaining success or failure in international trade.

The question of what role technology plays in a country's foreign trade might not be as old as the larger question of what in general makes the country successful or unsuccessful, but some of the old masters in economics such as David Ricardo, T. R. Malthus, John Stewart Mill, and many others pondered this question.

An intensive attempt to analyze the question, however, was not undertaken until the 1960s. Dissatisfied with the seemingly growing discrepancy between the established theory and the observed patterns of international trade and investment, a number of economists set out to find out to what extent technology might explain the phenomenon. It has been observed that there was a persistence in large United States trade surpluses and a rapid growth in the United States company investments abroad despite a much slower rate of growth of productivity in the United States than in most other industrialized countries. The new analysis has been especially interesting in view of the fact that technology is not explicitly recognized as the factor affecting trade in the established theory. Several modern-day economists began their studies by equating technology with current expenditures on corporate research and development. Their studies concluded in unison that technology was *indeed* the explanation for the increase in the balance of trade beyond the productivity growth in the United States. Incidentally, these studies also yielded what is now known as the product-cycle "theorum" which purports to describe three things: (1) the source of United States companies' strength in international competitiveness, (2) the reason for their moving abroad, and (3) the consequences of this movement for the United States.

In the most recent and seemingly most comprehensive formulation that Dr. Boretsky has found, this "theorum" (proposed by Dr. Robert B.

Stobough for the National Science Foundation in 1973) goes as follows:

> . . . high-income U.S. market induces innovation in the United States of certain types of new products—those that save labor or appeal to high incomes—especially when scale economies are involved in production. Technology is embodied to a substantial degree in many of these products. Later, the United States then becomes an exporter of the product as a market develops abroad. Exports are followed by production abroad, initially in developed countries and later in less-developed countries. U.S. firms are involved in some of this production in two ways: initially through wholly-owned plants or joint ventures with foreign companies, and later by sales of know-how, usually through licensing to unaffiliated foreign companies . . . [and] There are reasons to believe that the export of U.S. technology through U.S. foreign direct investment and licensing generally is good for U.S. economic welfare and hence should not be discouraged. On the other hand, there might be cases in which such activities reduce U.S. economic welfare, but we do not know what the characteristics of such cases are. . . .

Dr. Boretsky's paper represents a reasonably coherent set of excerpts of his work covering essentially the same territory as the studies that yielded the product-cycle "theorum." But his work relies on a novel and more comprehensive approach. The approach is technology-policy oriented, one of the products of his last 10 years or so of official work as Senior Policy Analyst in the Office of the Secretary at the Department of Commerce. Some of the conclusions he reaches in his analysis are similar to those arrived at by the proponents of the product-cycle theorum, but some are not. The policy implications for the United States arising out of his study are drastically different.

THEORETICAL FRAMEWORK

As an alternative in United States international trade policy, Dr. Boretsky starts with an assumption that a country's trade is primarily determined by three factors:

- First, *the country's endowment with natural resources relative to its own need.* Other things being equal, the more abundant the country's resources are, relative to its needs, the more likely to export and the less it will import.

- Second, *the price levels of the country's products relative to such price levels in other countries*, all valued in commonly used international currency. Other things being equal, the lower the country's relative price levels the more products it will be able to export and the fewer it will be likely to import.
- Third, *the comparative quality and scope of the country's technological know-how embodied in its manufactured products* (other than that working through relative productivity and relative prices). For the kind of know-how he has in mind, he refers specifically to the Boeing 747 aircraft in which the United States enjoys substantial surpluses in trade because of the quality of U.S. know-how in this particular product line as compared to the know-how possessed by other countries. It is proposed that the *scope* (that is, how many product lines have superior technological know-how) is probably equally or perhaps even more than its quality.

Perhaps it would be well to define the term "technology" as *the way we do things*. If reference is made to "production technology," this would mean *the method of processing raw materials into semifinished or final products*. Technological innovations then may be defined as improvements in technology permitting either (1) the production of products or services at a lower cost than before, or (2) the production of products and services that were impossible or impractical to produce before.

Technological innovations might carry a price tag such as the communications satellite which opens an entirely new horizon in communications around the world but at a new cost, or the technological innovation may be noneconomic or price-free such as the wide bodied transcontinental commercial aircraft (exemplified by the Boeing 747) whose operating efficiency is 20 to 30 percent higher than the earlier jet aircraft with regular bodies.

Consistent with these definitions of technology and technological innovations, Dr. Boretsky equates the relative quality of technological know-how with the relative economic or utilitarian advantage which uses the products embodying the know-how in question derived from using the products. To this should be added the important factor of the relative satisfaction on the part of consumers in the use of the product in question. The technological progress can thus affect the country's foreign trade in two ways: (1) new or better production techniques which improve productivity and reduce costs of products render a country's products more competitive with respect to price; and (2) new or better equipment, synthetic raw materials, or even new hybrids of grain for seed, which tend to place a nation in a better position for export.

One disadvantage of the first effect is that its technological improvements work through costs and prices only. The advantage a country derives from them can thus be nullified not only by similar improvements in other countries but also by any development affecting relative prices. Accordingly, such technological improvements are not considered to be a distinct determinant in foreign trade, although they might be crucial in maintaining or improving a country's *price* competitiveness.

For technological improvements which result in better equipment there can also be a price tag or price-free improvement as previously discussed. In the areas of seeming international parity of know-how, the noneconomic or price-free improvements tend to be decisive factors of competitiveness since such improvements represent a sort of surplus value to the product's users, and this surplus value frequently outweighs even substantial price and cost disadvantages which a country might have. With respect to this latter point, it is a generally known fact among U.S. manufacturers of capital equipment that in competing for sales in the world markets, the greater reliability alone of U.S. products in use frequently offsets the price disadvantage by as much as 20 percent. Foreign trade advantages that a country derives from comparatively higher quality of technological know-how (other than that working through productivity and relative prices) is obviously of a monopolistic nature because it can rarely be nullified by measures of similar know-how. Hence, it is considered as a distinct determinant in world trade.

Frequently, a specific technological innovation can benefit a country's foreign trade in two ways, either in increasing exports or in use at home to improve production efficiencies. However, to be a distinct factor in international trade, technological innovations must be embodied in manufactured products. That is, the technology must be built in and thus exportable. Other things being equal, the higher the level and the broader the scope of the country's know-how of this type relative to other countries, the stronger will be its technological competitiveness and hence the more products it will be able to export and the fewer it will need to import.

An example of the importance of this type of know-how for a country's foreign trade might best be illustrated by Japan's experience since the middle of the 1950s. At that time, its know-how in shipbuilding and the manufacture of automobiles, electronic products, and optical devices was hardly outstanding. But today it appears that Japan is second to none (or second only to the United States) both in regard to relative quality as well as to the scope of its technological know-how. This change has been the essence of most if not all of the gains which Japan has scored in foreign trade since that time, and these gains have been simply immense.

Happily this type of know-how has also been immense in U.S. trade. For example, based on a recent study by the National Bureau of Economics Research, looking at machinery other than electrical, we know that although prices of United States internationally traded machinery products in the 1960s were at least 10 percent higher than those in Europe and at least 25 percent higher than those in Japan, the United States had an overall trade surplus for this product group amounting to $4.1 billion in 1965, $5.5 billion in 1970, and about $5.3 billion in 1971 and 1972. In the face of the stated price disadvantages, the only thing that could have produced these surpluses for the United States is the unique or superior know-how embodied in U.S. made products. The quality in the scope of a country's technological know-how is a function of four contributing sources: (1) a gradual improvement in technology, introduced over time, by technical people such as production engineers, technicians and skilled workers or craftsmen; (2) formal or organized research and development efforts; (3) innovative activities of individuals or small groups; and (4) even the importation of advanced technology from abroad.

One further note on the export of technology. It is apparent that technological innovation or know-how can be exported either as the embodiment of an improvement in a commodity being traded, or in its "naked" form via the sale of patents and licenses. In the real economic world, the demand abroad for products embodying know-how is hardly infinite. Accordingly, the more this know-how is exported in the naked form, the fewer products embodying this know-how will a country be able to support and, conversely, the more of such products it might import. An example of this can be found in the licensing for the production of transistors in Japan which is thus afforded both a technological and a price advantage because of lower labor costs.

So much for the theoretical framework. It is now appropriate to take a look at trends in U.S. trade since the early 1950s in order to demonstrate, from actual world trade facts, the soundness of the principal that technology is indeed a commodity in international trade.

TRENDS IN U.S. TRADE SINCE THE EARLY 1950s

Consistent with the theoretical framework set forth in the preceding paragraphs, Dr. Boretsky's statistical analysis of trends in U.S. trade uses a four-way classification of commodities traded (with a fifth classification consisting of the summation of all):

- Agricultural products
- Minerals and raw materials
- Nontechnology intensive manufactured products
- Technology intensive manufactured products

Trade in agricultural products is naturally presumed to be a function of a nation's relative endowment with agricultural land and climate combined with the relative prices of these products as placed on the market. In the international trade of agricultural products, relative technological know-how rarely affects the quality of the exported product; it only affects the cost. This is not true in such examples as the introduction of new hybrids of grain for seed. But these exceptions are rarely important in terms of the overall value of trade; consequently, Dr. Boretsky does not consider the quality of technology (as he defines it) a distinct factor in trade of agricultural products.

Trade in minerals and unprocessed and other raw materials (products of nature other than agricultural land and climate) is again largely a function of a nation's relative endowment with natural resources as well as the relative prices of these commodities. The quality of technology, as in agricultural products, is not an independent factor because it rarely affects the quality of the products.

The most important commodities in the nontechnology intensive product group are textiles and apparel, steel, nonferrous metals, paper products, furniture, glass products, and the like. Trade in these products is most probably largely a function of relative prices. The quality of technological know-how embodied in these products (other than that working through comparative prices) might be of importance, but this effect is regarded more as potential than actual. This is true because with some exception, such technological know-how is the result of worldwide evolution of industrial art over a very long period of time rather than the result of advanced engineering or concerted R&D effort.

The technology intensive manufactured product group includes ordnance, chemicals, nonelectrical machinery, electrical machinery and apparatus (including electronics), all types of transportation equipment including aircraft and automobiles, and scientific and professional instruments and controls. The chief criterion in designating these products as technology intensive is the relative intensive of the new technology generating inputs used in their production—that is, the application of research and development. Also important are the degree of use of scientific and engineering manpower in functions other than research and development (design, production supervision, customer services) and the relative level of skill or craftsmanship of the workers.

An "all-commodities fifth group" would consist of the sum of the four groups plus other commodities not classified by kind and, in the case of U.S. exports, reexports of foreign merchandise. Incidentally, these reexports include all types of commodities and ideally they should be accounted for. But data are not available in sufficient detail for such accounting. However, such inaccuracies will be small because the overall value of reexports is actually quite small—1.0 to 1.5 percent of total export value.

While pure statistics may sometimes be dull and lifeless, it is frequently necessary to give some number relationships so as to illustrate, dramatize, or emphasize a point. Accordingly, with the reader's indulgence, we will use a few statistical tables (condensed from those presented in Dr. Boretsky's paper) to provide the proper perspective for understanding his points. All tables are derived from papers and publications from the private sector as well as such government departments and agencies as the Department of Commerce, including the Bureau of the Census and the Bureau of Economic Analysis; the Organization for Economic Cooperation and Development (OECD); the Department of Labor, including the Bureau of Labor Statistics; the National Science Foundation; the U.S. Department of Agriculture; and others. While all sources are given in complete detail in Dr. Boretsky's paper, they will only be quoted here in general terms for brevity but to provide at the same time the proper authoritarian background for sources.

Our main interest, of course, is with the fourth category of commodity, the technology intensive manufactured products. For the United States, the relative intensity of technology input used in the production of selected manufactured products is shown in Table 1. Manufacturing industries are grouped into three groups: ordnance; chemicals and engineering products (including electronics and transportation equipment, including aircraft and parts and motor vehicles and equipment; instruments, and related products); and the rest of manufacturing not included in the first two groups.

TABLE 1
Relative Intensity of Technology Application in U.S. Industry

	1960/1961	1970
A. *Expenditures on R&D, Percent of Value Added*		
Ordnance	75.9	37.7
Chemicals and Engineering Products	14.8	12.2
All Other Manufacturing	1.2	1.1
Average, All Industry	6.6	5.8
B. *R&D Employment as Percent of Production Workers*		
Ordnance	28.1	24.1
Chemicals and Engineering Products	7.9	7.4
All Other Manufacturing	0.9	1.0
Average, All Industry	3.0	3.0
C. *Scientist and Technician Employment in Functions Other than R&D Percent of Production Workers*		
Ordnance	23.9	28.2
Chemicals and Engineering Products	9.1	11.2
All Other Manufacturing	2.3	2.3
Average, All Industry	4.4	5.9
D. *Employment of Craftsmen as Percent of "Operatives and Laborers"*		
Ordnance	NA	46.6
Chemicals and Engineering Products	55.7	49.2
All Other Manufacturing	32.2	34.9
Average, All Industry	39.0	39.3

On the average, the industries manufacturing technology-intensive products spend about 11 or 12 times as great a proportion of their value added on R&D compared to the "all other manufacturing" group. This is shown in item A of Table 1, expenditures on R&D as percent of value added for 1960/1961 and 1970. Chemicals and engineering products spend 12.2 to 14.8 percent on R&D as compared to 1.1 to 1.2 percent for all other manufacturing. Three other methods for evaluating relative intensity of technology application are shown in Table 1: item B gives R&D employment as percent of production workers showing that there is an equal disparity between the technology-oriented industries and all other manufacturing; item C gives scientist and technician employment in functions other than R&D as a percent of production workers and shows again a disparity between technology-oriented manufacturing industries and all other manufacturing; and item D gives the employment of craftsmen as percent of "operatives and laborers"— again a disparity is seen between technology-oriented manufacturing industries and all others.

In all probability, the relative intensity of technical inputs used in the manufacture of technology intensive products is not unique to the United States. To show this quantitatively there are not sufficient data, at least readily available. However, in an international survey by the Organization for Economic Cooperation and Development (OECD) of the resources devoted to R&D in 1969, the following statistics were released on the proportion of all research and development expenditures for all purposes that were spent in technology-oriented industries in various countries: France, 78 percent; West Germany, 87 percent; Italy, 76 percent; United Kingdom, 79 percent; Canada, 62 percent; and Japan, 71 percent; all compared with 86 percent for the United States.

The industries manufacturing technology intensive products are, however, not the only users of new technology-generating inputs. They are unquestionably the primary domestic originators of technology innovations which are not only for their own use but for other sectors of the economy through the provision of new equipment, instruments, and synthetic materials embodying innovations. Internationally, disparities in technological prowess among industrialized countries is largely concentrated in these technology-intensive industries already identified by category. International trade in products produced by technology-intensive industries is largely a function of the quality of technological know-how embodied in the products, scope of this know-how, and the relative prices of the products. The quality and the scope of the technology know-how are undoubtedly far more important than the relative prices of the products.

Data on what occurred in total U.S. trade in each of the four commodity groups are shown in Table 2, which gives the average export-import balances, by commodity group, for the 1951-1955 and the 1971-1973 periods. Three important points should be taken into account in understanding the stability of the data shown. First, the data start in a period after the time when the European countries and Japan had completed their reconstruction of war-ravaged economies and after the United States had

TABLE 2
U.S. Export/Import Balances By Commodity Group ($Billions)

Commodity Group		Annual Averages	
		1951-1955	1971-1973
Agriculture:	Exports	$3.2	11.6
	Imports	4.4	6.8
	Balance	-1.2	+4.8
Minerals:	Exports	1.3	4.7
	Imports	3.3	10.7
	Balance	-2.0	-6.0
Nontechnology Mfg.:	Exports	3.7	7.8
	Imports	1.9	17.7
	Balance	+1.8	-9.9
Technology Mfg.:	Exports	6.6	28.5
	Imports	0.9	20.0
	Balance	+5.7	+8.5
All Commodities:	Exports	15.5	55.1
	Imports	10.9	56.8
	Balance	+4.6	-1.7

ended the Korean War. Therefore, the implications in the data are not distorted by atypical economic circumstances. Second, inflation in terms of average annual increases in priced indices (irrespective of the index used), has been substantially lower in the United States than in any other industrialized country. The only exception to this lies in wholesale prices of manufactured goods in Japan. The third point to take into account in viewing statistics in Table 2 is the fact that data on U.S. exports, both total and by commodity group, include noncommercial transactions such as shipments of grants-in-aid (both military and nonmilitary) and sales of agricultural products for nonconvertible currencies under Public Law 480. Imports, on the other hand, generally reflect only commercial transactions. Hence, the trade services shown in the table generally overstate the U.S. commercial trade performance and the deficits understate the true state of affairs by as much as $2.5 to $3.5 billion, depending on the year and what is counted as a noncommercial transaction.

Bearing these points in mind, and proceeding with the analysis, it can be seen that trade in agricultural products produced deficits in the 1951-1955 era but produced in the 1970s trade surpluses averaging $4.8 billion for the 1971-1973 period. The 1973 trade surplus in agricultural products was actually $9.3 billion, but it should be taken into account that these surpluses have been derived from noncommercial exports—largely sales for nonconvertible currencies, outright donations, and long-term dollar credits under Public Law 480. In 1972, the large surplus was attributed to extraordinary purchases by the Soviet Union and stockpiling by some other countries.

Now look at the data for minerals, raw ores, mineral products, fuels, and other nonagricultural raw materials. The United States had deficits in the 1951-1955 era and larger deficits in the 1971-1973 period. As a matter of fact, the United States has had deficits in most years between 1910 and 1920, and in every year since 1921 in minerals. The growth in the deficit has been almost proportionate to the real growth of the gross national product in the United States, and it is clearly attributable to the inadequacy of natural resources relative to the economy's need. This is especially true of petroleum in the United States. The dependence on imports of raw materials is common to all Western industrial countries (except Canada) and it is increasing rapidly. All are substantially more dependent than the United States. It is estimated that in 1970, France's relative dependence on imports of extractive raw materials and fuels was over four times as great as that of the U.S., while West Germany's about five, Italy's about five, and the United Kingdom's in excess of five times as great. In the years ahead, therefore, because of the rising level of economies in other nations, we must expect a tremendous worldwide scramble for minerals and other raw materials on the part of all industrialized countries (except, perhaps, Canada and the Soviet Union) and a tremendous intensification of competition for export markets of manufactured goods to secure "hard" currency in order to pay for the imports of raw material.

In the nontechnology manufacturing group in Table 2, it is seen that the United States had a slight positive trade balance in the 1951-1955 era which disappeared resulting in a $9.9 billion average trade deficit for the 1971-1973 period. On the other hand, U.S. trade in technology intensive manufactured products shows, first, the highest dollar value of all trade and, second, produced a positive balance in both the 1951-1955 and the 1971-1973 study periods. This technology intensive commodity group is the only one that has consistently yielded surpluses. These surpluses have heretofore been sufficient to offset deficits in trade in other commodity groups as well as deficits arising from other U.S. financial transactions with foreign countries.

The figures in Table 2 for All Commodities is largely made up of the four major commodity groups plus a few others. The data reflect a dramatic deterioration in the U.S. trade position from a surplus of $4.6 billion in the 1951-1955 period to a deficit in the later period of $1.7 billion. The actual total deficit in 1972 was $5.8 billion. Part of this turnaround is attributable to a more than doubling of the deficit of trade in minerals, fuels, and other raw materials. The bulk of the turnaround in trade deficiency occurred in manufactured goods, both nontechnology and technology-intensive where the overall U.S. trade balance turned from the surplus of $7.5 billion in the 1951-1955 period to a deficit of $1.4 billion in the 1971-1973 period. A 1973 deficit of nearly $9 billion gives even more dramatic evidence of the deterioration in the balance of trade.

Data given for individual years in the various periods covered in Table 2, as well as in other information sources, show that the deterioration has not occurred suddenly but *has been in the making since the early 1950s.* This long-term deterioration has been taking place despite much lower rates of inflation in the U.S. (as it is usually defined) throughout the period than in other industrialized countries. Within the framework of Dr. Boretsky's theory, this could have happened only because the levels of foreign prices had been lower than U.S. prices. This was true because the industrial and technological capabilities abroad have grown faster than those in the United States. Perhaps the reason for growing deficits lies in a combination of both effects. Of some importance in understanding the relationships of data shown in Table 2 and in emphasis of the absolute statistical conclusions to be drawn therefrom with regard to relative price levels, is a recent study released by the National Bureau of Economic Research. This study deals with the comparative productivity and dollar costs for production in 1970 and 1973 in the United States and abroad, based on the experience reported by 298 U.S. based multinational firms. The apparent cost-per-unit produced *in every foreign country* was lower than that in the United States. The change in this relationship between 1970 and 1973 shows the costs of production in foreign countries are increasing, compared to costs in the United States.

It is important to note that the statistics presented so far refer to relative *rates* of growth of the capabilities in question and not to their levels.
There is no evidence yet that the level of technological capability in foreign
countries has surpassed that in the United States in any important product
line. On the other hand, there is no question whatever that the differences
between the United States and foreign levels that have existed in the past
have narrowed, and in many product lines they have essentially disappeared.
It is the narrowing of this gap that has caused the deterioration in U.S. trade.
The fact of the narrowing of the gap can be readily demonstrated by a number of direct indicators given in a paper by Dr. Boretsky in October of 1973.

One factor is the rapid and practically one-way growth in exportation of
advanced U.S. technology in a naked form, that is, the selling of licenses and
patents rather than the technology-intensive commodity itself. Another
factor to be taken into account is the slowing of the rate of growth in productivity and the growing gap in civilian economy of relevant R&D efforts
in the United States compared with most other industrialized countries.

Despite the overwhelming evidence that U.S. inflation, or even the
deterioration in the relative price level, could hardly have been the major
force that caused the deterioration in the U.S. trade position, the federal
government chose the devaluation of the dollar as the tool to correct the
situation. From May of 1971 until February of 1973, the dollar was devalued
(against the average value of 67 foreign currencies) by 8.1 to 10.7 percent
(the figure depends on whether U.S. exports or imports are used in weight-
ing individual changes). In February of 1973 the dollar was devalued further
by a nominal 10 percent and set "afloat." Through the middle of May 1974,
the second devaluation and the floating resulted in additional effective devaluation of 1.6 to 2.5 percent from the time just prior to the initial runs on
the dollar in 1971 (April) until the middle of May 1974. The dollar was devalued against all 67 foreign currencies of the world by some 9 to 14 percent,
but even more against the average of industrialized countries. What all this
really means is that the primary effect of the devaluation was the further
deterioration in the trade balance largely because of the worsening in the
U.S. terms of trade by just about the amount of actual worldwide devaluation. In fact, the U.S. trade situation in 1973 might best be described as
having been in a state of "aggravated disequilibrium," even though the overall trade deficit actually vanished as a result of unusually high activity in
grain shipments.

Bear in mind another devaluation-generated problem: because it has caused price disparities resulting in considerable demand abroad for U.S. products and a competition for raw materials in world markets, the volume of exports of products in question has risen to a magnitude well above the nation's ability to sustain it without causing serious shortages in supply to domestic markets. This is evident in the virtually uncontrollable inflationary pressures in the economies at large. The greatest demand can be expected from continental Europe and Japan, those countries which revalued their currencies when compared to the dollar by the greatest margins. In response to these inflationary pressures, restrictions had to be temporarily imposed on certain commodities. All of this, of course, is rather disappointing because it indicates that the U.S. agricultural sector does not have as great a potential for the expansion of exports and thus was unable to make up for losses in industry's technological advantage as many had hoped. The key determinants of farm output are *acreage* of planted or otherwise cultivated cropland, and the *yield per cultivated acre* resulting from the combination of weather conditions and technology (largely the use of fertilizers and insecticides). These determinants are true both for the demand for grain foods as such and for livestock, dairy products, and poultry requiring grain for feeding. The U.S. Department of Agriculture estimates show that about 70 percent of the readily usable idle acreage had been brought under cultivation in 1973 and the reserve of such land was reduced to about 19 million acres—a mere 6 percent of the harvested cropland for that year. Historically, at least since 1950, the yield per acre has grown on the average at about 2.2 percent per year while the use of fertilizer and liming materials (reflecting productivity) has grown by about 6.5 percent per year. Thus, given the strong market demand that currently prevails and average weather conditions, we might, therefore, expect in farm output in 1974 an increase in real terms by a maximum of about 8 percent or so over 1973. The 8 percent growth of farm output for 1974 would only suffice to eliminate the 1973 type shortages in the supply to the domestic market including a provision for the combination of growth in population and growth in demand. Eight percent growth would *not* allow for any growth in exports without continued rise in prices (unless, of course, there is a substantial increase in imports of the products in question).

The growth in exports of manufactured products, both technology-intensive and nontechnology-intensive, reflected in Table 2 is generally of the magnitude which, if sustained over some time to come, would markedly improve the U.S. trade position and make the devaluation of the dollar pay off. But it seems highly improbable that this growth will continue for very long. Current growth in exports can be attributed to five factors: first, the devaluation of the dollar; second, an appreciably faster-than-usual economic growth abroad induced largely by recovery from recessions in the 1971-1972 period; third, increased inflationary pressures all over the world which, if continued, might easily lead to a worldwide depression; fourth, apparent attempts by Japan and West Germany to deliberately reduce their trade surpluses with the United States by importing more than normal levels of our commodities; and fifth, exceptional U.S. initiatives with the Soviet Union and China, the outcome of which (apart from grain transactions) will heavily depend on the availability of long-term credits in the United States and the Soviet Union's rate and volume of progress in producing the kind of exportable products which could be competitively sold in our own markets.

While some changes have been experienced and noted, manufacturing costs in practically all foreign countries remain lower than those in the United States despite devaluation of the dollar. On top of this, there is a good reason to believe that the rate of growth in technological and industrial capability will continue to be faster in most other industrialized countries for some time to come—whether the United States initiates policies that would counter this trend or not. This is not to say that the actual growth in total dollars will be higher in foreign countries than in the United States.

In summary, even a casual inspection of the figures given in Table 2 will show that the greatest positive balance of trade potential lies in the technology-oriented manufactured commodities, and encouragement of export of these can only lead to a betterment of the balance of payments situation in the United States. Having used actual export and import information to demonstrate this fact, it is now appropriate to look at policy as it might affect future technology application in the United States, policy which would be for the benefit of balance of trade here.

TECHNOLOGY TRANSFERS

The complexity, sensitivity, and the importance of the issue of international transfer of advanced U.S. technology as it affects the national well-being of the United States, coupled with the almost unbelievable confusion about the matter, make it important that this subject be addressed in considerable detail. While the international flow of advanced technological know-how might take place in a great variety of ways, the most important two channels which will be discussed are (1) transfer of advanced technology embodied in products produced in the United States and (2) transfer of licenses and patents, the so-called "naked" transfer of technology.

Briefly restated, data contained in the previous section of this chapter have generally shown that if companies have products embodying advanced technology when compared to those produced abroad, the very embodiment of this technology makes the products in question either totally new or superior to similar products embodying conventional technology produced in other countries. Other things being equal, foreign demand for such products with respect to price tends to be either inelastic or, at most, to have a fairly low elasticity thus assuring companies trying to market such products in international markets a stronger competitiveness and a general tendency to make overall sales and profits greater than otherwise would be the case. From the foreign market point of view, the advantage gained through buying these products lies in the obtaining of products enabling the user either to do things that were heretofore impossible or impractical or to obtain products, the use of which yields an economic or utilitarian surplus value such as increased efficiency. For the United States, finally, the transfer of technology embodied in the product represents practically the only means for overcoming the disadvantage of high wages and high prices in U.S. trade with other countries. Further, the foreign trade advantage derived by the United States (or any other country) from a comparatively higher quality of technical know-how embodied in its products is generally of a monopolistic nature since it can rarely be nullified by measures other than similar know-how. The point of emphasis is that for a *high-wage and high-price country such as the United States, the advantage of superior technology is the absolute essential factor in its international competitiveness.*

But what about the transfer of technology in the naked form? The consequences of such U.S. exports of advanced technology depend on the nature of economic activity abroad in which the technology in question is used and whose interests are considered. According to Dr. Paul B. Simpson of the University of Oregon, in a paper published over 10 years ago, this is also largely true of the export of capital.

Exports of advanced technology in the naked form tend to benefit the importing country, the companies exporting it and, in the long run, the United States at-large only when usable in areas of foreign economic activity supplementary or noncompetitive with U.S. economic activities (such as the extractive industries, utilities, and retail trade). The reason for the benefit to the importing country is that these imports tend, by the definition of "advanced technology," to enhance the productivity and hence the real income of the importing nation. The reason for U.S. benefits lies in the fact that such exports of technology command fees that otherwise would not be forthcoming. If the technology is used in the production of products which the United States needs, this technology tends to keep the cost of these products down and thus secure better terms of trade for the United States than might otherwise be the case.

On the other hand, exports of advanced technology in the naked form, usable in areas of foreign economic activity competitive to the United States (such as those in the manufacture of internationally traded goods) may tend to be advantageous to the importing country and to the exporting companies involved, but detrimental to the well-being of the United States at-large.

The reasons for the importing country's advantages are obvious. The transfer of technological know-how frequently allows a marked increase within the importing country in technology advancement and represents an almost immediate substitute for imports. It also implies at least a potential base for export expansion and an overall "blessing" to its balance of payments. From 1950 through 1972, for example, Japan was spending about $158 million per year on purchases of foreign technology from all sources, merely 0.2 percent of their gross national product. In the aggregate, Japanese total outlays for *purchased technology during the 22-year period* amounted to about $3.6 billion, *not quite 3 percent of what U.S. industry spent, in its own funds, on research and development,* and only slightly more than 1 percent of what the U.S. total expenditures on research and development were for the same period.

The reasons for U.S. companies' advantages in the naked transfer of technology are simply the enhanced profitability and a potentially larger piece of the action abroad than they could get by exporting from the United States. But the reason why the United States at-large gets the short end of such deals is that, the technology in question being new and thoroughly market tested, the demand for products embodying this technology tends to be highly or at least fairly inelastic by the definition of new and market tested technology. U.S. technology export in the naked form, though commanding fees and, in many instances, conducive to some exports of products from the United States (such as capital goods and components impractical to produce abroad), tends not only to be a substitute for export of products from the United States but is also a promotion of competitive imports. In

TABLE 3
Relative Use of Naked Technology Compared to Growth in International Trade

	West Germany	Italy	France	Japan	United Kingdom	United States
License, Patent, and Royalty Fees: Ratio of Payments to Receipts						
1963-1965	2.43	4.17	2.53	22.0	1.05	0.14
1968	2.39	3.36	2.32	10.0	0.84	0.15
Technology-Oriented Products: Average Annual Growth, Percent Per Year						
1955-1967	7.7%	10.1%	5.1%	19.7%	3.7%	4.9%
Share of World Exports Among 14 Nations in Technology-Oriented Products						
1954	17.6%	2.4%	6.4%	1.8%	19.0%	35.5%
1970	21.0	6.0	7.8	9.7	10.3	23.0
Gain or (Loss)	3.4	3.6	1.4	7.9	(8.7)	(12.5)

order to illustrate this point, information is shown in Table 3 for five foreign competitive countries and the United States. Data cover three factors relating to share of international markets. The first group shows the ratio of payments to receipts within the country for licenses, patents, and other technology-oriented fees. In the period 1963 to 1965, European countries paid two to four times as much for external fees as they received in their own licensing arrangements; Japan paid 22 times as much; the United Kingdom was about even; and the United States received seven times as much for their licensing arrangements as they paid. These relationships changed somewhat for 1968 mainly in the reduction in Japan of their expenditures for fees.

The second set of figures shows the average annual growth of technology-oriented products between 1955 and 1967. Growth in the United States was about 5 percent per year; more than in the United Kingdom, about equal to that in France, but less than that in the other countries and considerably less than growth experienced in Japan.

The third set of figures shows the share of world exports of technology-oriented products among 14 nations. It can be seen that the United States, while still enjoying a large share of world markets, lost 12.5 percent while all of the European countries (except the United Kingdom) and Japan gained significantly in their shares of the market. It would be naive to assume that the only thing that made Japan, West Germany, Italy and even France perform so much better in domestic output and exports than the United States was simply the import of naked technology, but it would be equally naive to assume that these countries would have done even nearly as well as they did without these imports, *and most of the technology came from the United States.*

The Bureau of Economic Analysis released a study dealing with a comparison of the relative intensity of the United States multinational companies' transfer of technology to manufacturing subsidiaries abroad and their return on capital investments in these subsidiaries in 1963 and 1970. The figures were based on data covering Canada, all of Europe, Australia, New Zealand, South Africa, and Japan, and developing countries. Results did not vary significantly between 1963 and 1970. The payments by foreign subsidiaries to parent companies for royalties, licenses, and rentals, figured as a percent of total operating cost, ran from 0.5 to 0.7 percent, while the net income for the year as a percent of the book value of investments (or of net worth) ran about 11 percent for both years. The correlation between the two variables is quite strong, and the implication is that the transfer of advance technology to their subsidiaries abroad not only tends to be more profitable for the U.S. company exporting such technology than the production of materials and commodities in the United States, but also the higher the subsidiary's saturation with new technology, the higher the U.S. company's profit in the transfer of naked technology.

When we talk about "new technology," we really mean, knowingly or unknowingly, a relative few but radical advances made or introduced since World War II or thereabouts. These advances are in electronics, communications, jet aircraft, synthetic fibers, and a few others. Advances in electronics, however, have been almost the absolute basis for progress in most, if not all, innovations, and this is not only true in the United States but throughout the world. The country in which most of the post-World War II advances in electronics have been made (and much of this with taxpayer money) is the United States. In fact, out of 16 innovations in electronics which OECD and other organization studies of the subject matter consider as pivotal in the post-World War II progress, 12 originated exclusively in the United States including transistors, microcircuitry systems, and other types of circuits; *one* originated independently in the United States, Great Britain, and the Netherlands (a diffusion process); *one* originated in the United States and Great Britain (integrated circuitry); *one* solely in West Germany; and *one* (the tunnel diode) solely in Japan.

The worldwide diffusion of these U.S. innovations *and mostly in the naked form* have been, by historical standards, almost instantaneous. The U.S. trade situation in electronics (and communication equipment, the product group in which progress is most closely related to progress in electronics) furnishes, therefore, as specific and as meaningful a test of the impact of the technology transfers on U.S. economy as one can devise. The situation is illustrated by a steady decline in the balance of trade from 1965 to 1972 in the United States in electronics and communications equipment. In 1965, the balance of trade was a positive $206 million. This declined rather steadily to a 1972 trade deficit of $953 million—a total decline of nearly $1.2 billion! Calculating domestic consumption and figuring imports as percent of consumption with price adjustments, we find that in 1965, imports were 4.8 percent of total demand; whereas in 1972, imports amounted to 19.4 percent, a dramatic change. According to figures released by the Bureau of Economic Analysis, receipts by manufacturers in the United States during the period 1960 to 1972 for royalties from foreign countries rose from $275 million to $1.4 billion, an average annual increase of 14.7 percent. During this same period, payments to foreign nations for licenses and royalties rose from $38 million to $166 million, an increase of 13.1 percent.

The primary analytical value of these estimates, however, is not what the companies in the United States receive or pay for technology, but what the information implies regarding the minimum value of sales of products abroad based on transferred U.S. technology and without which the aggregate impact of the transfers in question on the U.S. economy cannot be assessed. In order to produce some kind of aggregate analytical calculations, we have to know or have a good reason to assume with a fair degree of certainty the following five questions:

- What have been the values of sales of manufactured products produced abroad at various points in time on the basis of technology know-how transferred from the United States?
- What is the probable elasticity of foreign demand with respect to price for the products embodying the kind of technological know-

how that U.S. companies are exporting in a naked form?

- How much more expensive would have been the products in question abroad had they been produced in and exported from the United States?
- To what extent were the transfers of naked technology conducive to exports of products made in the United States?
- To what extent were the transfers of naked technology in question conducive to imports of competitive products to the United States?

Of the five questions, by far the most important is the first question relating to the values of sales of manufactured products produced abroad relative to the transfer of U.S. technological know-how in the naked form. Studies based on average experiences of 141 United States multinational companies made in the Department of Commerce show that the bulk of royalty payments average about 4 percent of relevant sales. Assuming this ratio to have been constant from 1960 through 1972, the implication is that manufactured products produced abroad resulting from the transfer of naked technology amounted to a minimum of $6.9 billion in 1960, $13.1 billion in 1965, $27.4 billion in 1970, and $36 billion in 1972. These values are considered by Dr. Boretsky as minimums, not only because the estimates exclude the acquisition of equity rights in foreign companies (in exchange for technology transferred to them), but also because they refer only to the values of products based strictly on the protected know-how for which the companies receive royalties and license fees.

A series of alternative calculations based on examination of import and export of licensing fees and other information emanating from the Bureau of Economic Analysis strongly implies that had the United States done nothing more than it did in promoting new technology at home (but without engaging in any kind of export of such technology), the kind of deterioration of U.S. trade balance of payments as we have been witnessing since the early 1970s might have come in the twenty-first century rather than in 1971.

A Hypothetical Example. Dr. Boretsky gives two illustrative operations research-type calculations concerning the implications of export of advanced U.S. technology to a foreign country. Each example is compared to the would-be production and export from the United States of the same commodity in question. In the example, this would be the production of an aircraft such as the Boeing 747. The first comparison is between the licensing of a foreign company to produce the plane versus the production of the same plane in the United States. The second illustration compares the setting up of a U.S. company subsidiary in a foreign country versus U.S. production.

The assumption has been made that a foreign country would need 25 to 30 highly competitive aircraft: 25 at U.S. prices (about $25 million per plane), or 30 if the unit price were some 30 percent lower. The price could be assumed to be 30 percent lower if the airplane were produced in the foreign country in question. In order to achieve this lower cost, the foreign country offers to buy the complete package of know-how from the U.S. company manufacturing the plane at a royalty of $1 million-per-unit produced. Inasmuch as the price for the know-how represents a greater percentage of the company's earnings relative to their sales than the average in the last 10 years (about 3 percent), the U.S. company accepts the offer. The company reached this conclusion by comparing the $30-million licensing profit versus $18.8-million production profit which represents 3 percent on 25 units at $25 million apiece. However, there are other implications to the United States. In terms of receipts of the U.S. Treasury, the corporate tax on the $30-million profit from licensing would be $14.4 million (42 percent) versus $56 million had the company produced the planes in the United States (figured as taxes on payroll plus corporate income tax on profits). In terms of balance of payments, the net to the United States from licensing to foreign countries would be $30 million versus $625 million for production in the United States. In terms of employment, licensing produces essentially none, while U.S. production implies a total of 36,500 man-years of jobs.

In the second illustration, suppose that, instead of selling the licenses to an external country, the United States company in question is permitted to set up a wholly owned manufacturing subsidiary in the foreign country. In line with the common practice of U.S. based multinational companies in developed countries, the subsidiary would probably service not only the country in question but also part of the adjoining geographic area, and a small portion of its output would be exported to the United States. These assumptions lead to the following data. For the subsidiary operating in a foreign country, the assumption is that there would be (a) $630 million in sales in the foreign country, plus (b) $132 million in exports to a neighboring countries, and (c) an additional $65 million in exports to the United States. On the other hand, and under similar market circumstances, production in the United States would include (a) $625 million (the 25 planes at $25 million each) exported to the foreign country in question, plus (b) $112 million of exports to third countries, plus (c) $55 million of production of imports substitutes (that is, 85 percent of the $65 million assumed of reexport into the United States from the foreign country). These ratios and relationships are based on data developed in the Department of Commerce. Using these assumptions, the implications for U.S. companies and the United States would probably be as follows. Total earnings to the companies from foreign sources of a subsidiary would be about $80 million. The earnings (3 percent) from U.S. production would only be about $24 million. Receipts by the U.S. Treasury for the company producing through a foreign subsidiary would be about $31 million versus $71 million for U.S. production. If we take into account a capital transfer of $135 million per year (an assumed requirement of capital assets for the subsidiary based on the experience of 298 multinational companies in 1970), then the U.S. balance of payments would amount to a *deficit* of $45.4 million per year, including capital transfer versus a $774 million *positive balance in trade* if the production is achieved in the United States. From the company's standpoint, the attraction is the $80 million in total earnings versus $24 million in U.S. production. From the nation's standpoint, of course, not only is there an employment deficit of considerable magnitude (some 40,800 man-years), but a very marked change in the balance of payments ($819 million!).

POLICY IMPLICATIONS

It is clear from Dr. Boretsky's work, and the illustrations which he has provided in his paper, that technology-concentrated industries are far more important to the United States economy than are the low-technology- or nontechnology-oriented industries. Further, it is clear that the exportation of naked technology in the form of licenses and royalties can eventually be detrimental to the balance of trade in the United States. Accordingly, it is apparent that the United States has some concerted thinking to do concerning its attitudes toward both the application of technology and the exportation of technology in the naked form.

Once the mechanism or mechanisms for long-term economic policy making and a focal point of responsibility for the state of such policy making in the civilian technology are established, it is envisioned that it would formulate a comprehensive national technological policy which would correct the situation as quickly as possible. In broad terms, the definition of the concept of national technological policy is simply *the sum of deliberate actions on the part of government aimed at the increase and improvement of technological option* and alternatives for all productive units in the economy for the furtherance of national objectives within the constraints of available and/or accessible resources.

At this time we have bits and pieces that might fall into the scope of this definition, but the country does not have a coherent policy, per se. In the real world of today's markets and governmental institutions which we want to preserve as intact as possible, the kind of comprehensive national technological policy needed would have to include such strategic elements as the following nine.

- A continuous review and some sort of long-range planning of the country's level of effort in R&D combined with the enhancement or encouragement of technological development.
- Development and institution of policy measures which would assure an optimum supply of appropriately trained scientific and technological manpower.
- Development and institution of general and meaningful incentives for an optimum level of private investment in research and development.
- Securing an optimum public investment in R&D in the social infrastructure, including those relevant for society's quality of life and in market-oriented technological opportunities where, for various reasons, the market forces and general incentives cannot assure an optimum level of effort.
- Securing the proper industrial environment for an optimum utilization of new technology especially in adequate availability of venture capital.
- Securing the proper governmental, legal, regulatory, and procurement posture with respect to the development and utilization of new technology.
- Development and institution of policies that would assure optimum benefits of the country's technological effort for foreign trade and balance of payments.
- Development of adequate and rational safeguards against the use of new technology.
- Institution of a system of publications which would inform the public of the social consequences of major technological changes, both beneficial and not so beneficial and the available alternatives.

It might be anticipated that some feel that the policies suggested are really selfishly U.S. national interest oriented. However, this is only an attempt to optimize the taxpayer welfare and not an attempt to provide for worldwide equilibrium. Moreover, it is believed that the kind of lopsided international business deals as have been referred to in this chapter cannot be sustained indefinitely, or, even if they were sustained, the world would soon be elevated to the kind of standard of living that the United States has already attained.

So there you have it: Dr. Boretsky has not only demonstrated conclusively that importance of research and development-oriented technology applications in the balance of payments in U.S. trade but has, at the same time, provided the basis for national policy, one important aspect of which would be the marked encouragement of the use of research and development by American industry. The role of the private research and development institutions in provision of technology application to industry is clear and obvious.

CHAPTER XI

THE RESEARCH INSTITUTES ABROAD*

It is difficult to determine which of the "independent research institutes" was the first to go abroad; however, it is known that it was not until after World War II that most international activities took place—*most*, but not all. There were some earlier instances of foreign activity involving Armour Research Foundation (now IITRI) in which I participated. These incidents are worth relating because they indicate the awareness foreign groups had of the high level of technology in the United States and their keen desire to likewise reach such a plane.

SOUTH AMERICAN INTERESTS

In 1941, the National Research Council sponsored a 7-week tour of 7 countries in South America, under the direction of Maurice Holland. These 7 countries had urged that such a mission be undertaken to enable their industrial leaders, business leaders, and bankers to explore with an American group ways and means by which they could develop their industries and thus become less dependent on imports. I served as an R&D administrator on the American team, which was made up of 21 *U.S.* business and industrial leaders as well as bankers. The group was limited to 21 because this was the capacity of the DC3, the largest available passenger aircraft at that time.

Shortly after the return of the group to the United States, the Argentine Trade Promotion Corporation, a quasi-government organization, asked the Armour Research Foundation to make a study of the potential of certain industries in the Argentine as well as the possible diversification of the agricultural economy. A team was ultimately assembled, but two of the members were not from the ARF staff and thus were obliged to take a one-year leave of absence from their institutions. A team of this kind was difficult to assemble for two reasons. First, it is not easy for any institution,

---

*The author's intimate involvement has necessitated the use of the first person point of view at various points in this chapter.

including ARF, to give up the services of a key person for a year; and second, such a person must leave his family behind because of the need to be completely mobile. Once organized, the team traveled 25,000 miles in the Argentine and produced a report containing many recommendations regarding industrial development in that country. One recommendation was to emphasize applied research in existing institutions and to create new organizations for this expressed purpose.

MEXICO BECKONS

In 1945, on the recommendation of the National City Bank of New York, the Banco de Mexico engaged ARF to study the technology of 17 specific Mexican industries and develop techniques for their technological improvement. The study and report, which were completed in about a year, included strong recommendation that an applied research institute be established in Mexico City. It was to be funded initially by national funding agencies until such time as its effectiveness had been demonstrated, whereupon industry would take over as prime support. This recommendation was implemented, and ARF was commissioned to design and equip the laboratories, recruit the first staff members, and manage the operation until a qualified Mexican national could be located to serve as director. Today, this institution—Instituto Mexicano de Investigaciones Technologico—flourishes in Mexico City under the direction of Ing. Ignacio Deschamps.

Since that time ARF has played a major role in the establishment of industrial research institutes in other foreign countries including Burma, Columbia, Afghanistan, Libya, Venezuela, the Argentine, India, and the Philippines.

POSTWAR ACTIVITY

By 1950, I had become president of Southwest Research Institute and at that time was the recipient of numerous requests from various U.S. federal agencies as well as foreign governments to form scientific missions that would stimulate applied research in such countries. The motivation to undertake these assignments was that a properly assembled team could make an important contribution to a friendly nation and at the same time profit from a most valuable experience. The difficulty of staffing such teams, however, necessitated the formation of a consortium of three of the independents—Armour, Stanford, and Southwest—that were to act jointly in providing the teams and to rotate the contractual responsibility and direction of each program.

The first program under this arrangement was one in Cuba, under Batista, for the International Bank for Reconstruction and Development, aimed at determining the rate at which the Cuban government could repay a substantial loan that depended on the country's industrial and agricultural economy. A program in Brazil for the establishment of an applied research institution followed, after which Battelle joined the group, and a series of missions sponsored by the Mutual Security Agency of the U.S. government was undertaken during the early 1950s. Matching funds were supplied by participating countries that were visited by teams consisting of six or seven individuals. Each mission lasted an average of 7 weeks, and the sequence in which they occurred was determined by the Organization for European Economic Cooperation (OEEC) in Paris. Germany was first, then France, Austria, Italy, and others.

The year 1950 was also the year in which Southwest Research Institute, acting jointly with the Instituto Technologico de Monterrey (Mexico), created the Instituto de Investigaciones Industriales (III) to operate in Monterrey in affiliation with both parents. As the years went on, Southwest was to be involved in many foreign assignments where its special competencies were desired, including programs in Mexico (other than III), Spain, Venezuela, Columbia, Peru, the Argentine, Jamaica, West Germany, Japan, Canada, Sweden, Guatamala, and elsewhere.

LEADERS IN RESEARCH ACTIVITIES ABROAD

Of the independents, Battelle has undoubtedly been the most active abroad, with Stanford running a close second, particularly in technoeconomics. Following their lead have been Armour and Southwest and, to a lesser degree, the other five independents. Because of their eminence in this area, special attention should be given to Battelle and Stanford.

BATTELLE ABROAD*

A review of Battelle's beginnings in Europe can be presented more clearly

---

*Abstract of the paper (1971) by Frank C. Croxton.

if the setting, at the time, is described. Of course, such an undertaking does not begin suddenly. Rather, there is a gradual development from the elements of an idea to an eventual implementation as a functioning research organization. We can say, then, that Battelle in Europe began in or shortly after 1950.

With the conclusion of World War II, strenuous efforts to restore normal political and economic relations with Europe began. An important direction was toward rapid reestablishment of agriculture and industry, as well as housing, in all of the free nations of Europe. It has been estimated that between 1939 and 1945, 40 million people of the warring nations had been killed. Property damage was believed to have been $4 trillion. The ability of the survivors to live as normal human beings at all had been interfered with very seriously.

Meanwhile, back in the United States, the voices of doom had not been entirely correct. The wartime expansion of industrial production, even after the headaches of reconversion to civilian-oriented operation, did not lead to excessive inventories, oversupplies of goods, and layoffs of production personnel. Industrial activity in this country expanded rapidly and so did research and development.

Although Battelle had been conducting research for overseas industries since only a few years after its founding, a new interest in and enthusiasm for international activity took hold. Participation in international scientific congresses increased and research for foreign firms and governments expanded.

During 1951, several Battelle individuals and teams were in Europe, some for the specific purpose of exploring the climate for contract research, others for studying the question in the course of other Battelle work there. These investigations covered essentially all of the nations of Free Europe and sought the views of both industry and government.

The consensus of the several studies of the climate for a Battelle laboratory in Europe was favorable. It appeared that a laboratory in an international location would have ample opportunity to be of service to European industry, particularly after a short period of becoming acquainted and becoming convinced of Battelle's confidential treatment of proprietary information. One thing was very clear in Europe, that was that Battelle's technical ability was well known. It remained, then, to decide at the top-management and board-of-trustees level whether the money and the manpower would be well invested in such an undertaking.

During these discussions, the question arose, "Why should Battelle do research outside the United States?" Perhaps the question is phrased better in the negative sense: "Why shouldn't Battelle do research outside the United States?" After all, let us remember that the wills of Gordon Battelle and his mother provided what seemed to be a liberal endowment, one which it was thought, even in 1940, could carry the staff of 200 through any depression yet experienced. When research was begun in 1929, it would have been possible to adhere to a policy of using only income from the endowment for scientific investigations. Fortunately, Battelle's management and trustees were sufficiently foresighted and public spirited to welcome and encourage research capabilities of a technical staff having more than the usual entrepreneurial sense. The question at that time might have been, "Why should Battelle undertake research by contract for industry instead of adhering to a conservative program of in-house research?" It has been good for industry, good for Battelle, and since about 1940, good for government that Battelle has proceeded as if the question more than 30 years ago had been, "Why *shouldn't* Battelle do contract research in addition to in-house research?"

What then was to be thought of as an international location in Europe? In 1951, this meant pretty unequivocally, Switzerland. If that was to be the country, then which city was to be chosen? Basle was a center of chemical, particularly pharmaceutical and dye chemicals, manufacturing. Research and development were important to Basle and environs. Zurich was the commercial and financial center of the country. The truly international city of Switzerland, however, was Geneva. After serious study and discussion, it was concluded that a Battelle laboratory should be established in Geneva, Switzerland.

Battelle Geneva Research Centre, Geneva, Switzerland.

With Geneva selected as the site, the many essential planning and formalizing steps were begun. Offices were occupied in rented space in the very center of Geneva. An excellent piece of land, amounting to 20 acres, was purchased in the suburb of Carouge. Concomitant with design of a laboratory building was a program of acquainting the Swiss government and industry, as well as the industry of surrounding countries, with the research abilities which would soon be available.

Meanwhile, it was possible to inform European industry and government that contract research services would soon be available in laboratories of Battelle, an organization well known to them for its accomplishments during the preceding 23 years. Let us understand at this point that there was not the slightest thought that Battelle could tell Europeans how to do research. Was it not the technical developments of Europe before and during World War I which had awakened the United States to the need for research in its own industry? The concept taken to Europe by Battelle was that of the independent, not-for-profit research institute conducting research under contract for the benefit of the sponsor, client if you will. Two small institutes patterned after Battelle existed in England. One was Fulmer Research Institute at Stoke Poges, Buckinghamshire. The other was Sondes Place Research Institute at Dorking, Surrey. Neither was truly independent. Neither became large enough nor was sufficiently versatile to serve sponsors to the extent that Battelle and others like it in the United States could. There was an additional feature of Battelle which added to the impressiveness of its services to European industry. This was its affiliate, Battelle Development Corporation. Just as the United States was an attractive market to commodity exporters, it could be an attractive market for licensors of technical developments. A knowledgeable organization such as BDC could aid both the licensor and the licensee, sometimes, as with Bavonizing, finding the licensees more numerous in Europe than in the United States.

As word of the new laboratory in Geneva spread, an extraordinary reaction occurred in Germany, the Federal Republic, of course. It amounted to enthusiastic approval of the idea of contract research but with the added, extremely emphatic statement that there had to be a Battelle laboratory in Germany for German industry. No amount of protesting that only one laboratory could be swung at a time and that the Geneva Laboratory would be available for German-sponsored research would satisfy the Germans. Soon, Stuttgart and Frankfurt am Main were vying with each other to encourage Battelle to build there. Both offered land without cost and extension of utilities. Finally, it was decided that a laboratory would be built at Frankfurt, on 13 acres of land contributed by the city to be followed later by an additional 13 acres.

It was not quite so simple to organize Battelle in Germany as it was to organize Battelle in Switzerland 7 years after the close of World War II. Although no blocks were put in the way, the concept of a not-for-profit organization was a difficult one. In time, however, Battelle became, in Germany, an *eingetregener Verein*, which can be translated literally as a registered association.

Articles about Battelle appeared in the European press as well as in trade journals. Talks were given to industry associations. It soon became evident that offices in metropolitan centers would be advantageous both to make contact with the nation's industry and to negotiate currency exchange as needed. Representation was established in London, Paris, Milan, and Madrid. It was surprising how receptive industry was to presentations of facts and plans for Battelle in Europe. There had been predictions, however, that the Norwegians and probably the French would never agree to sponsoring research at Battelle-Frankfurt. Actually, one of the bureaus of the French government was a very early sponsor at Frankfurt on the stated principle, "If I can have the study made in Germany more advantageously for France than elsewhere, I will."

The Frankfurt Laboratories of Battelle Memorial Institute.

The new building of the Geneva Laboratories was completed during the latter part of 1954. On November 26, it was dedicated in conjunction with a conference at which Denis de Rougemont, Director of the European Cultural Center, was the principal speaker.

By the beginning of 1955, both laboratories were actively conducting research in the typical Battelle manner for industry and for a few governmental agencies of several of the nations of Europe. The research staffs performed admirably showing ingenuity, resourcefulness, and an enthusiasm for "teamwork." That term and others such as "weekend" and "up to date" were adopted without change into the German and French languages as succinct and useful additions. A few firms of the United States sponsored research at the Battelle Laboratories in Europe. Even those first projects, however, appeared to be for the purpose of obtaining fresh points of view rather than finding cheaper research, i.e., more man-hours of research personnel per thousand dollars. Gradually, research sponsorship from the United States declined to a constant low level based on the need for special studies provided only, or best, by the Geneva or Frankfurt Laboratories. Concurrently, both laboratories were finding their services to be of special value to sponsoring firms and governments in various parts of the world, particularly Africa and South America.

It had already been proved that research at both laboratories would find sponsorship from essentially all nations of Free Europe. In fact, for a considerable period, excluding Germany for obvious reasons, sponsorship was greatest from the United Kingdom. This naturally led to thoughts about a Battelle laboratory in England. Although there were several good reasons for such an undertaking, two, in opposition, were sufficient. The London County Council was quite properly guarding with zeal the area bounded by the so-called green belt. Further, London appeared to be the only suitable location for a laboratory serving the United Kingdom in much the same way as the Frankfurt Laboratory was serving primarily the German Federal Republic. The second evolved from a principle on which Battelle grew, i.e., a single large, interdisciplinary laboratory with maximized capabilities for the benefit of its sponsors. A single additional laboratory in Europe, or even two, did not stretch this idea too far, but stretching this to three laboratories for the European economy might easily leave one or all below the critical size necessary for effective contract research. Accordingly, there is no Battelle-United Kingdom Laboratory but there is an active office in London.

Nearly 20 years have passed since the first explorations of possibilities for Battelle research in Europe. Where do we stand now? The two laboratories have established an enviable record of research for their sponsors. Aside from many publications and patents, the size of the staff in Europe and the volume of research performed provide measures of success. Together, the two laboratories have staff numbering 1600, which is equal to all of Battelle in 1951, 22 years after its founding. This is a better measure of research volume than annual expenditures since conversion according to official rates of exchange still leaves questions of research productivity in such a different ambiance. However, the combined research effort of the Frankfurt and Geneva Laboratories in 1970 corresponds to $17 million, calculated according to currently accepted rates of exchange.

Was it a good decision in 1951 to proceed with research in Europe? There is not the slightest doubt whatever that it was. Much has been done to benefit the economies of European nations. One can be quite certain that the Battelle laboratory staffs have profited as they have performed research according to the independent-institute method. We in the United States have learned from our counterparts in Europe. We have been gratified in the extreme to see ruined cities and industries rise again and to see people in despair become—through their own efforts—happy, healthy, and prosperous citizens. Modern technology, intelligently and humanely applied, has been a major factor in this evolutionary process. To one who has worked intimately with the Europeans, especially in Switzerland and Germany, the power of science in dissolving international barriers is evident. May it continue to be so for many years to come.

STANFORD RESEARCH INSTITUTE ABROAD by Dr. Wendell B. Gibson*

SRI's move abroad began in 1950 as a member of a triumvirate with Armour and Southwest on a study for the World Bank dealing with possible economic development programs in Cuba. Almost immediately thereafter the three institutions staffed a series of projects for the Mutual Security Agency on future development of scientific research problems and facilities on a national scale in Germany, France, Austria, and Italy. At about the same time, SRI undertook a major project in Italy on post-World War II recovery problems of the nation's heavy mechanical industries.

---

*The story of Stanford's activities around the world can best be told by the man primarily responsible for that institution's development worldwide: Dr. Wendell Gibson, Executive Vice President. and President SRI International, Stanford Research Institute.

These two activities outside the United States launched SRI on a slow but continuing spiral of its operations throughout the world. The basic approach differed from that followed by Battelle, particularly in Europe. While Battelle was able to create laboratories and other facilities abroad, SRI decided to concentrate its investments at home but to extend its research scope to business, industry, and governments in other nations with initial emphasis in the management services and industrial economics.

Even in the early 1950s, an initial objective was established—"to acquire skills, experience, and information . . . that can ultimately be of value to . . . domestic research programs and at the same time contribute to the solution of important international and foreign problems."

SRI International Building, Menlo Park, California.

Some of the more specific aims at the time were to widen SRI's sphere of knowledge and capabilities so as to serve industry and government (at home and abroad) more effectively, assist in solving some of the world's economic development problems, strengthen the security of the Western world, enhance professional development of the staff, contribute to an international exchange of scientific information, and increase prestige and influence of the organization.

An early impetus to SRI's move abroad was provided in a most energetic manner by one of its directors, S. D. Bechtel, Sr., of the San Francisco-based Bechtel Corporation. Beginning in 1951, he urged the institute to expand into the international field by predicting that "the next two decades will surely bring many opportunities for the advancement of private enterprise around the world." He then added, "The move to further internationalization of business is unmistakable," and also "in its own interests and in keeping with the times, SRI should extend its operations in a major way into the international field."

Following the first European projects with Armour and Southwest in the early 1950s, SRI decided to establish an office in Zurich, Switzerland, and thus to be in a position to serve some of the research interests of recovering economics in Western Europe. As the years went by, similar offices—primarily for liaison purposes—were opened in London, Milan,

Madrid, Stockholm, and Paris. Research projects for European companies—mainly in technoeconomic fields—grew steadily throughout the 1950s and 1960s. A professional staff was gradually built up in England and on the continent.

This trend of events led SRI in 1973 to rearrange its organization so as to serve the European market more fully. A full-fledged division called SRI-Europe was created with headquarters in London (Croydon).

One of the major areas of SRI activity in Western Europe—during the 1960s especially—has been Scandinavia. Early in 1968, Marcus Wallenberg of Stockholm's Enskilda Bank (and also chairman of SAS) asked SRI to assist the airline on some of its management and economic problems. This launched a relationship with SAS that continues to this day. And it led to many other projects with leading Swedish, Danish, and Finnish companies in their efforts to modernize both production and marketing operations.

Having gained a position on the European scene by the late 1950s, SRI turned its attention in the opposite direction—across the Pacific to Japan. Believing that Japan was launched on a sustained industrial expansion, SRI was searching for a way to enter the picture consistent with its basic policy on moves abroad. An avenue was opened in 1960 when the Nomura Securities Company decided to create a Nomura Research Institute (NRI) in the U.S. pattern of independent, nonprofit research organizations.

SRI quickly accepted an invitation to assist in this initiative, and on a consulting basis established a "sister institute" relationship. At the same time, an SRI-Japan office was opened in Tokyo. Both the SRI-NRI relationship and the SRI office have continued and grown over the years. Today, NRI is a large multidisciplinary research organization, and with NRI and separately, SRI works with most of the leading Japanese companies.

As indicated earlier, SRI's first venture into the developing world began on a cooperative effort in Cuba. Then in 1954, the Ford Foundation asked SRI to send a group of economists in succession to India to assist in that country's development program. This project was later expanded to both East and West Pakistan, especially in the field of small industries. There then followed during the next two decades an unbroken involvement by SRI in the Third World—such countries as Brazil, Ecuador, Mexico, Ethiopia, Morocco, Tanzania, the Cameroons, Egypt, Cyprus, the Philippines, Taiwan, Thailand, Malaysia, Turkey, Iran, the Congo, Peru, Nicaragua, Honduras, Bolivia, Korea, and indeed most of the developing nations.

SRI's research operations also spread during the 1960s and early 1970s to all of the industrialized nations in addition to Japan and those in Western Europe. These included especially Canada, Australia, South Africa, New Zealand, and semi-industrialized Brazil. For about three years beginning in 1970, an SRI-Australia office was maintained in Sydney to help on research relationships with Australian companies. Then in 1974, an SRI-Brazil office was opened in Sao Paulo.

Another significant event in SRI's expanding international operations occurred in 1969. The Kingdom of Saudi Arabia asked for an SRI team to be sent to Riyadh on a long-term basis. The task was to assist the Kingdom in creating its First Development Plan. The team remains there today, having helped Saudi Arabia in preparing the Second Development Plan to guide the nation in spending billions of dollars of newfound oil revenue on a rapid industrialization program.

SRI has also given considerable attention to the growing East-West business movement. During the 1960s, its Strategic Studies Center in Washington, D.C., initiated a cooperative research program with agencies of the Academy of Sciences in the USSR. This program has continued in full force and today is one of the principal avenues of joint study between the U.S. and the USSR on basic economic, political, and strategic problems. Then in September of 1973, SRI signed a Cooperation Agreement with the Soviet's State Committee for Science and Technology. The main aim—was and still is—to stimulate greater economic, industrial, scientific, and economic cooperation between the USSR and western companies. The first activity under this agreement was a major SRI-sponsored conference in Moscow in June 1974, attended by some 200 senior western executives (from 30 countries) and an equal number of high Soviet officials.

One of the early features of SRI's international movement was an International Fellowship Program under which promising young scientists, engineers, and economists from abroad are given opportunities (under sponsorship by their companies or governments) to spend up to one year working at SRI. The program has been successful and continues today. More than 75 people from 20 countries have participated and returned to various pursuits in their homelands. One later became president of the University of Mexico; another rose to a high economic post in the Philippines; still another is a key member of SRI's present European staff.

Throughout most of 1962, SRI and many of its directors devoted much time and effort to developing a basic policy for SRI's future in the international field. Several trends in a rapidly developing world were held to have special meaning to the institution. These included; for example, the industrial reemergence of Western Europe and Japan, rapid economic development in other industrialized nations (e.g., Canada and Australia), expanding activities by American and foreign companies, the thrust toward economic development in the emerging nations, and rising economic and political interdependence among the countries. Also, SRI and its board took note of rapid developments in science and technology with impacts around the world on business, government, and military security.

They came to the conclusion that these trends, separately and collectively, would bring further opportunities to, and demands upon, SRI in the international field. A few years later, in 1967, this thrust was recognized further by creation of an internal entity known as SRI International. Its purpose was to accelerate SRI's internationalization so as to make the organization "a truly significant international institution." In keeping with SRI's long-standing policy of closely integrating its international operations with domestic programs, the SRI International staff has from the outset been rather small—operating in close cooperation with other parts of the institute, especially an International Development Center devoted largely to work in developing nations.

As part of the spreading involvement by SRI around the world, its board of directors decided in 1957 that a special International Building should be provided at the Menlo Park headquarters site. Not having the necessary capital, a decision was made to seek participation in financing from companies and individuals around the world. On September 2, 1969, a magnificent 60,000 square foot SRI International Building was dedicated at a ceremony attended by senior business executives from 40 countries. Housing artifacts from more than 50 nations and being financed by companies in as many countries, the building has been called "A House of All the Lands." It is now the center of SRI's far-flung international activities.

One special feature of SRI's international program over the years has been a series of five major worldwide conferences of senior business executives held in San Francisco. The first in 1957 was cosponsored with Time-Life International. Succeeding ones have been cosponsored with The Conference Board of New York. Each of these week-long events (known as the International Industrial Conference) has been dedicated to advancing economic and industrial development, and particularly private enterprise. Each was attended by some 500 senior executives and high government officials from more than 60 countries. Whatever their success may be in a philosophical sense—and it is considerable—the events portray SRI's dedication to economic and industrial development on a global scale. Plans are already being developed for similar events in 1977 and 1981.

A related SRI international exchange program also has grown to substantial proportions. As part of the new SRI International entity, an International Associates Plan was adopted in 1966. It features a series of world business reports and world conferences held in cities abroad. All this is made possible by a group of 500 companies in 60 countries that are affiliated with SRI as International Associates. So far, some 30 meetings of senior executives involving more than 50 countries have been held in such places as Sydney, Tokyo, Manila, Sao Paulo, Seville, Lima, and Beirut. More than 3500 executives at these events have heard presentations on world business prospects and exchanged views on international economic problems.

On many occasions since SRI began its movement abroad, questions have been raised about "why" the organization should pursue such a wide variety of research projects—economic, scientific, and technical—in other countries. The questions have always been resolved in terms of "research knowing no geographical boundaries" and that the domestic and international interests of both government and business (which SRI and other institutes serve) are intermingled. Thus, SRI and its directors have long believed that the institution must be global in outlook and in service to its clients.

The extent of this involvement abroad is considerable; more than a third of SRI's commercial, industrial, and public service volume is "international"—and in due course the proportion probably will reach the 50 percent point.

CHAPTER XII

THE FEDERAL GOVERNMENT'S ROLE IN RESEARCH SUPPORT

To define the part the federal government has played in the advancement of industrial research in the United States is a challenging task . . . primarily because through the years, the nature of the role has undergone considerable change. In this country, the pendulum has hit both extremes swinging from the "famine-like" days of the 1787 Constitutional Convention, at which many suggestions regarding the government's role in the promotion of science were offered, studied, debated, but then abandoned because of a lack of agreement among representatives . . . to the bountiful years in the mid-1960s when almost $5.5 billion was appropriated for space research and development alone. Opinions differ as to where the perfect middle ground exists. It is the belief of one "man of science" that the government's role in the area of research is to support (1) "fundamental science, especially when it is closely connected with higher education," and (2) "science that directly contributes to public purposes, such as defense, public health, weather forecasting, environmental improvement, or primary food production."* Another perspective can be seen in the following section taken from a report† compiled and published by a group of National Research Council members who toured Europe in 1937 to "look behind the scenes of industrial research."

RESEARCH CONSCIOUSNESS AMONG LEADING INDUSTRIAL NATIONS
Edward R. Alexander

One of the vital questions of this age is how far national governments are what we may call research-conscious in scientific and industrial fields.

Those in closest touch with the trend of events in our modern world have become convinced that the extent to which each nation is alive to the

---

*Brooks, Harvey, *The Government of Science*, Cambridge, Massachusetts: The M.I.T. Press, 1968.
†"What We Found Behind the Scenes in European Research–1937."

importance of scientific research and its practical application will determine largely the degree of its economic security. And—the degree of its economic security will, in turn, determine the measure of its good-will with the rest of the world.

Let us see, then, what the history of the last few decades has to show us of the attitude of four of the world powers on this vital question of scientific and industrial research, namely, the United States, England, France and Germany.

It was not until the World War that the United States government began to consider the importance to the nation of scientific and industrial research. Just before we became involved in that war, President Wilson took under consideration what our government might do to assist or encourage research in industry. Various industries of this country, on their own initiative, had already developed their own research laboratories. Research divisions were operating in a number of our universities with gratifying success, usually assisted in their enterprises by industry itself, while several important independent research laboratories had been created and financed by interested individuals.

The Bureau of Standards at Washington prior to the War was one of the few government-fostered institutions contributing directly or indirectly to scientific research, and this without broad contact with industry generally. Thus it will be seen that practically all of the research work in the United States up to that time must be credited to private initiative and foresight.

During the Civil War, President Lincoln, recognizing the growing importance of applied science in industry, had encouraged Congress to create by Congressional Charter the National Academy of Sciences. This Academy is largely of honorary nature, consisting of distinguished American scientists elected by their colleagues and limited to two hundred and fifty in number. It serves in an advisory capacity to the United States government upon request of department and bureau chiefs.

President Wilson's active interest gave impetus to the establishment of the National Research Council, which is a cooperative organization of scientific and technical men of America. Its members include also businessmen interested in engineering and industry. Established under the auspices of the National Academy of Sciences, it enjoys the cooperation of most of the major scientific and technical societies. Its membership is largely composed of representatives of eighty of these societies. The Council was organized in 1916 to coordinate the research facilities of the country for work on war problems. In 1918, by executive order of the President of the United States, it was reorganized as a permanent body, for the promotion of scientific research and of the application and dissemination of scientific knowledge for the benefit of the national strength and well-being. Its administrative expenses are largely paid from an endowment provided by the Carnegie Foundation. In most cases actual research work must be financed by interested industries or from other than government sources.

The United States government has not provided and does not now provide funds for the carrying on of this important work. So we begin to see that we have a government that is not research-conscious.

England during the War found itself short of many important goods which it had been relying essentially on Germany to supply, such, for example, as magnetos for igniting internal combustion engines, optical glass of various characteristics and dye-stuffs. The War over, England's government, by then definitely aware of the importance of the application of science to industry, began to create and subsidize numerous research institutes whose work it considered would be of vital importance to the future of the nation. Among these were the Cotton Research Institute at Manchester and ones for fuel, rubber, leather and building research, near London.

Prior to this, about 1900, at Teddington, outside of London, the National Physical Laboratory was formed under the control of the Royal Society. Its purpose was to carry out research especially required for the determination of physical constants and to establish and maintain precise standards of measurement and to make tests of instruments and materials. Until 1918 its activities largely corresponded with those of our Bureau of Standards, then it was made a part of the newly established Department of Scientific and Industrial Research, whereupon it became more actively engaged directly than theretofore with various industries of the Empire in the solution of important scientific and research problems. England had had for many years large research operations undertaken by certain of her industries on their own initiative, such, for example, as the chemical, electrical and metal industries having close operating relations with corresponding industries of Germany and the United States and has, through some of her university laboratories, like Cavendish at Cambridge, reached the very pinnacle of pure research achievement. When, however, the British government after the War began the creation and maintenance of state-subsidized research laboratories for certain industries, it cannot be truthfully be said that industry in general in England was research-conscious, and undoubtedly some of the State Research Institutes experienced difficulty at the start in getting industry cooperation, particularly among the older industries, largely family controlled and quite self-satisfied as was to be humanly expected with empirical formulas of manufacture upon which their respective experiences, knowledges and judgment acquired through the years, were largely based. But England has had an outstanding good fortune. She succeeded in selecting for the directors of her state-created laboratories men of great foresight, executive and organizing ability, inspirational force and personal charm. They were able quickly to surround themselves with loyal, hardworking and competent staffs of associates, and today they have the wholehearted cooperation and support of the industries in which they are so effectively helping to point the way. Visiting one or all of these laboratories, you come away with one idea uppermost in your mind, having to do with a save-the-nation incentive which motivates every man and woman of each laboratory staff. England grows less than fifteen percent of her foodstuffs necessary for national sustenance. For the balance thereof she must exchange goods in the international markets. With France, Germany, Japan, and the United States among others, competing with her in those markets England must rely on efficiently directed and applied research *to live*.

In France an entirely different situation prevails. She is practically self-sustaining so far as food is concerned. It is a question if the French government, other than from time to time, is definitely research-conscious. Undoubtedly ex-Premier Blum was, for French scientists are his friends and they have in him a sympathetic listener. And who would not always be glad to listen to a French scientist, a man completely inspired by his devotion to the seeking out of the laws of nature, a fervent disciple of Pasteur in his devotion to work, and such a brilliant conversationalist that he completely enraptures you with his sheer exuberance of spirit and happiness resulting from his scientific contributions to mankind. But, alas, is he really appreciated in his own country? Apparently the French industrialist does not know of or believe in constructive cooperation in industry in any such measure as we know it in this country. Only recently the French government has felt called upon for national safety's sake to buy up all of the principal airplane manufacturing companies in France. The inspirational director of one of the outstanding government laboratories in France advised us that French industry did not freely cooperate with his institution and that he did not have free access to any of the industrial laboratories in his country. We came away from France in love with the French scientist and deeply grateful to him and to the French government for the many things they did to make our visit there so interesting and instructive.

Of the four governments abovementioned, the German alone recognized the importance of research in science and industry before the World War. In the early part of the nineteenth century, Von Humboldt had laid down the necessity of encouraging research in Germany free of restraint of any sort. About 1870, almost coincident with the Franco-Prussian War and the creation of the German Empire, the open-hearth process of making steel was invented. Germany's iron ores were of too low grade for successful use commercially in earlier steel-making processes. Her major industrial progress dates from the invention of the open-hearth process, which gave her good, cheap steel. Her scientists henceforth were encouraged by the application of their discoveries and inventions to the up-building of her great steel, electrical and chemical industries, the latter including dye-stuffs.

The government of Germany, however, apparently did not begin to appreciate the true value of scientific and industrial research until Von Harnack, a disciple of Von Humboldt, succeeded about 1910 in getting the ear and financial backing of Kaiser Wilhelm II. Then Germany, as a government, began to become really research-conscious with the result that a number of research institutes were created, of which the earliest, established in 1911, were those for chemistry, physical and electro-chemistry and biology at Dahlem in the outskirts of Berlin. Since then, upwards of thirty such institutes have been started, fostered and maintained by the government and industry jointly.

In Germany today, we find a government which is, above all, work-conscious, and which is successfully teaching the nation that the real rewards of life come through *work*. And, consequently practically everybody in Germany is at work. The present government is distinctly research-conscious. Within the past year it has promulgated what is commonly referred to as the "New Thought Movement." This comprehends the idea that the cultural future of Germany lies in the application of science to industry and the arts of life. The German scientist has become completely re-inspired. When he addresses you, you feel that his innermost soul has been released, that hope again springs eternal from his mind and that he looks to the future with confidence reassured. The German people is being shown what the nation has accomplished through the application of science to industry by means of inspiring expositions most carefully planned to appeal to the mind through the eye. So that not only are the people being taught the vital importance to the nation of *work*, but also that the cultural future of the nation resides in mass cooperation with industry and science in the application of science to industry. And why, under such conditions, should not the people become research-conscious, with artificial rubber, artificial leather and gasoline and oil from coal now available to it and artificial wool from beech trees and artificial silk from pine roots and synthetic fats practically ready for the market? Germany grows upward of eighty percent of the foodstuffs necessary for national sustenance. She only has to exchange goods in the international markets for about seventeen percent of such foodstuffs in order to live, and she is rapidly gaining confidence in the ability of her scientists and industrialists to insure any such exchange that may be necessary.

To sum up, in England, today, the government is research-conscious, and industry is increasingly so. For the nation as a whole—which lives so much in the past and which has placed so much of a social handicap on work throughout its history—it would be difficult to estimate or prophesy in regard to the people's attitude toward research. In France, you see the pure scientist at his scintillating best, and he is seen very clearly indeed—outstandingly so, in fact, for the very reason that he appears quite alone, receiving apparently touch-and-go encouragement from government and little cooperation from industry. In Germany, both government and industry are research-conscious, and the nation is rapidly becoming so.

As for the picture in the United States, only industrial organizations, scientists, engineers and those constituting the staffs of university, government and private laboratories are essentially research-conscious. The government is not; the mass of the people is not. Will it require another World War to make our government research-conscious?

If it desires to become so before such another catastrophe, it might well profit by a study of England's government-created research institutes—the cotton and the fuel, for example, and in mentioning these two specifically no reflection in the slightest degree upon any of the others is intended. It might examine the work of the institutes of optics and welding in Paris, the only ones we saw in France where the government and industry cooperated directly with scientists. And—it might look into the many outstanding government-created institutes in Germany, notably the Iron and Steel at Düsseldorf, which insures Germany's future in steel; the Silicate Institute at Dahlem, responsible for keeping Germany in advance in optical glasses and automobile roads, among other things, the Wood Research at Elberswald, which keeps the nation in a dominating position with products from forestry —and last but by no means least, the Diesel Engine Laboratory at Dresden, where apparently real history is in the making.

* * *

It is interesting to note Mr. Alexander's ironic, indeed prophetic, question about the United States—"Will it require another World War to make our government research-conscious?" Now, 37 years later, that question can be answered with a resounding, *YES*; that's exactly what it took. Indeed, the threat of war imposed by a neighboring, more technologically advanced European country was the catalyst responsible for the intense degree of research consciousness prevalent in England, France, and Germany prior to World War II. Unfortunately, for the United States, such consciousness did not take root until the bitter experience of a second world war was recorded.

EARLY ATTITUDES

In general the attitude of the federal government toward sponsoring research and development activities was indifferent, at best, from the eighteenth-century days of the Constitutional Convention through the nineteenth century. Only isolated incidents, such as the following, offer any evidence of a government predisposed at all toward advancing scientific research.

- In 1862, the first and largest permanent scientific agency was established by Congress—the Department of Agriculture. It was given cabinet status in 1889.
- The National Academy of Sciences (NAS) was founded by congressional act in 1863. Surviving an onslaught of objections, the Academy grew out of recognition by President Lincoln of the increasing importance of science to industry.
- Before the turn of the century, several other agencies were fostered as part of the rather weak national effort to promote science. Among them were the U.S. Coast and Geodetic Survey, the Military Academy, and the Corps of Engineers. The beginning of the twentieth century offered a little more hope to the advancement of the scientific front.
- In 1915, the Department of Invention and Development was established within the Department of the Navy. A name familiar on the U.S. scientific scene belonged to the head of the department—Thomas A. Edison.
- The National Research Council (NRC) evolved in 1916 in a move to foster greater cooperation among existing governmental, educational, industrial, and other research organizations to provide a unified effort in strengthening the national defense.

- The 1920s saw little development of government-sponsored scientific activities, but Franklin D. Roosevelt did his part to accelerate such endeavors in the 1930s. The influential National Institutes of Health (NIH) was born in 1930 out of a trend toward more basic research—the impetus which promoted the Public Health Service to broaden its outlook and move its Hygienic Laboratory to Bethesda, Maryland. Once moved, the laboratory was renamed the NIH. The same trend accounted for the congressional ratification in 1937 of the National Cancer Institute, a step that heralded a new era of research in the Public Health Service. In 1933, the Presidential Science Advisory Board was created, and from 1938 to 1941, a survey of scientific activity in government, industry, and universities was published under the name *Research—A National Resource*.

Nonetheless, such evidence of scientific awareness was meager. Perhaps the best barometer was that of funding for, in 1940, prior to the U.S. entry into World War II, only $75 million in the federal budget was allocated for science and technology. The years that followed brought more than just another world war, however, and the United States came out of that ordeal awakened to the critical interdependence of national defense and scientific advancement.

AN AWARENESS TAKES SHAPE

By 1950, the time was ripe for the establishment within the federal government of an organization to provide leadership in the assessment of national scientific needs and in the promotion of activities aimed at fulfilling those requirements. The National Science Foundation (NSF) was established by Congress to perform those functions. The realm of authority of the NSF was clearly delineated from its inception, namely, cultivation and not control. One of the first notable projects undertaken by the NSF was a survey conducted in 1953 of federal research expenditures at universities and other nonprofit institutions, including federal research centers funded in full by the government. Established during and immediately after the war, these centers included the AEC laboratories at Ames, Argonne, Los Alamos, and Hanford; the Navy's Applied Physics Laboratories in Maryland and Washington and its Center for Naval Analyses and Ordnance Research Laboratory, all founded in 1941-1943; the AEC's Brookhaven National Laboratory, the Air Force's RAND, and the Army's Operations Research Office, evolving in the immediate postwar years 1946-1948. A number of wartime centers, as well as those of earlier origin, were initially managed for the most part by universities and industrial firms. However, as independent research institutes have grown in strength, they have undertaken the management of several Federally Funded Research and Development Centers (FFRDCs) as they have become known. The extent to which these centers have become entrenched in the scientific research program of the federal government is evidenced by these fiscal facts: "In 1951, the 23 centers managed by universities or other nonprofit organizations received $122 million, or an average of $5.3 million each from the federal government; in 1969, 67 such centers received $1,164 million, or an average of $17.4 million each from the government."[*] By 1973, these FFRDCs were expected to spend approximately $1.6 billion, with the college-administered centers accounting for the spending of one-half of the R&D dollars; the industry-administered centers, one-third; and the nonprofit institution-administered, the remaining 15 percent.

By 1954, the movement to advance science in the United States—from all outward appearances—was taking hold; the president, issuing an executive order directed toward bolstering the effectiveness of federal participation in scientific activities, stated that, in 1940, the federal government spent only $75 million in support of research and development, whereas, in 1954, he transmitted to Congress a budget calling for expenditures over $2 billion for these purposes. Among the government agencies most intensely involved in R&D were the Atomic Energy Commission, the Defense Department research agencies, the National Institutes of Health, the Department of Agriculture, and the National Advisory Committee for Aeronautics.

An increase in scientific activity naturally demanded more technically trained personnel. By looking at the ratio of scientific and technical workers to the total labor force, it is possible to gain a broader understanding of how scant the U.S. involvement in scientific pursuits was before 1950. In 1870, when the population of the United States totaled nearly 40 million persons, only one in every 1100 workers (about 12,000 individuals in all) was employed in science and technology. By 1950, the population had exceeded 150 million, and the number of scientific and technical workers had passed the million mark, reflecting that one in every 60 workers was a scientist, engineer, or other type of technologist. In 1951, the Bureau of Labor

---

[*]Orlans, Harold, *The Nonprofit Research Institute*, New York: McGraw-Hill Book Company, 1972, pp. 10 and 11.

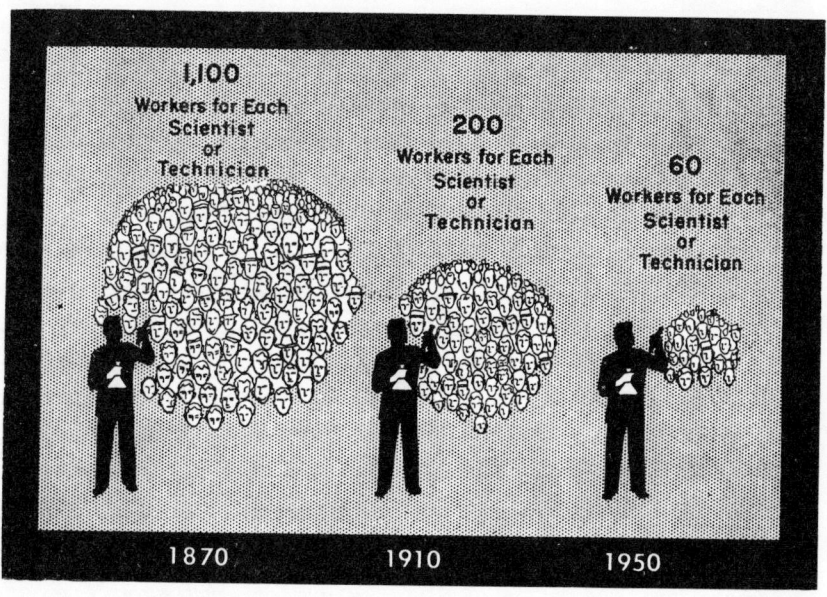

Ratio of scientific and technical workers to total labor force in 1870, 1910, and 1950.

Statistics estimated that approximately 48 percent of the scientists in the United States were employed in private industry, 26 percent in government, and 26 percent in education. For engineers, the percentages were 75, 22, and 3 for private industry, government, and education, respectively.

The responsibility within the federal government for encouraging professions in the sciences logically fell to the NSF. It responded by fostering $1,850 million in support for graduate fellowships during the academic year 1955-1956. By this time, a full decade had passed since the end of World War II; for the United States, these ten years produced a remarkable reshuffling of priorities. The importance of progress in science and technology as it relates to economic and military strength had garnered new limelight. Nowhere was this more dramatically reflected than in the *funds* appropriated for scientific research and development. While the $75 million appropriated in 1940 represented only 1 percent of the federal government's total budget, by 1955, the sum had climbed to $2.1 billion or 3 percent. This amount takes on greater significance in light of the fact that the total expenditures for scientific research and development in the United States from its beginnings to 1953 were only $5 billion, of which $3.7 billion was provided by private industry. During fiscal year 1956, the Department of Defense accounted for approximately 70 percent of the administered

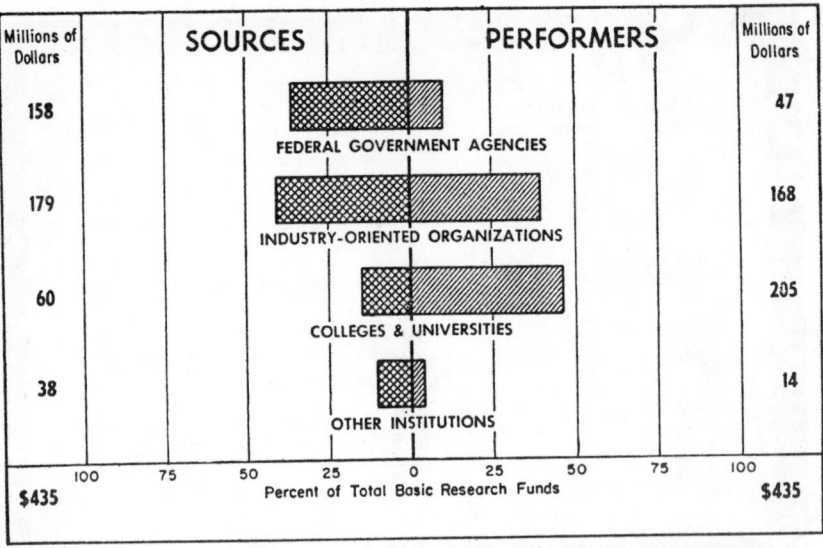

Funds for basic research by sources and performers for various sectors of the economy in the United States, 1953-1954.

funds or $1.5 billion. Moreover, a large percentage of these funds went for applied research and development as opposed to basic research.

The consideration of adequate numbers of scientific personnel continued to be an important one through 1956. For the federal government, the problem of acquiring qualified scientific and technical personnel was especially acute because salaries and other benefits offered in government employment simply did not measure up to those of industry. Though numerous legislative measures were enacted to ease this governmental handicap, it took many years before the federal government could operate on a competitive part with industry in the field of personnel recruitment.

During the late 1950s, NSF undertook a series of studies to determine just what the complexion of scientific activity in the United States had become. Such questions as what fields of science were being explored and to what extent, who was performing the work, who was paying the costs, and what was the ratio of basic to applied research were addressed. For purposes of the survey, the following denotations were given to the sectors of the economy: industry-oriented organizations; colleges and universities; the federal government; and miscellaneous institutions, including philanthropic foundations, health agencies, academies of science, and certain professional societies. As shown in the chart, the federal government was primarily a source of funds while industry combined the two functions, spending slightly more in performance than it contributed from its own funds.

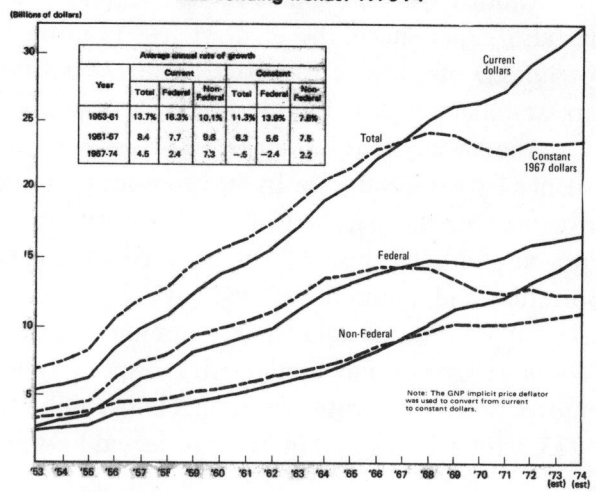

R&D funding trends: 1973-74

(Billions of dollars)

Year	Current			Constant		
	Total	Federal	Non-Federal	Total	Federal	Non-Federal
1953-61	13.7%	16.3%	10.1%	11.3%	13.9%	7.8%
1961-67	8.4	7.7	9.6	6.3	5.6	7.5
1967-74	4.5	2.4	7.3	-.5	-2.4	2.2

Average annual rate of growth

Current dollars

Constant 1967 dollars

Total

Federal

Non-Federal

Note: The GNP implicit price deflator was used to convert from current to constant dollars.

Source: National Science Foundation

Total R&D spending within the United States continues to increase. In 1974 it is anticipated that $32.1 billion will be spent on R&D activities by all sectors of the economy. This is 5 percent above the 1973 level and more than six times the 1953 amount. In constant dollars, however, a drop of 2 percent is expected between 1973 and 1974. A marked change has been underway in recent years in patterns of support. Between the late fifties and late sixties, the Federal Government supported over 60 percent of the Nation's R&D investment. Since 1967, however, this support has dropped to just over one-half. With the increased emphasis on health and energy, it is possible that this trend will be reversed in the near future. In 1974 Federal R&D support is expected to amount to $17.1 billion, up from $16.6 billion in 1973.

THE SPACE FRONTIER

It was also during the late 1950s that a scientific pursuit of enormous proportions first raised its head showing potentially vast influence on the direction of U.S. scientific activity. This was the launching by the USSR of the first earth satellite in October 1957. A sense of urgency subsequently pervaded every level of the federal government of the United States, the culmination of much self-examination and debate coming with the enactment of Public Law 85-568 on July 29, 1958. This law created the National Aeronautics and Space Administration "to provide for research into problems of flight within and outside the earth's atmosphere," as well as to serve many other purposes.

The sense of urgency that prevailed in 1957 manifested itself in greatly intensified governmental activity in defense- and space-related programs. These endeavors so dominated R&D activities from 1957 to 1966 that they claimed over one-half of all funds devoted to scientific research and development; moreover, during 1963 through 1965, 90 percent of the total government R&D expenditures was in these same areas of space and defense. Despite trends in the late 1960s and early 1970s away from such concentrated funding, these security and space functions currently remain atop the list, the former accounting for more than one-half of the overall R&D effort in recent years. For 1974, the national security share of the federal R&D total is estimated to be 54.2 percent.

Though space programs remain second in amount of funding, this area has also experienced the greatest loss in priority. From 1973 to 1974, the total R&D obligations for space are expected to drop by $234 million, the largest dollar decrease for any function.

The deemphasis in space activities has been understandably counterbalanced to some degree by growing interest and funds in other areas. For instance, for the period 1969 to 1974, support for the following programs grew substantially: health, which received the greatest relative increase; transportation and communications; environment; energy development and conversion; education; area and community development and housing; and economic growth and productivity. Especially noteworthy here is that R&D expenditures for health show an almost unbroken rise from 1963 through 1973, with a 17 percent increase reflected between 1972 and 1973.

GOVERNMENT SPENDING DURING THE PAST DECADE

A study of the overall government funding for R&D activities during the years 1969 through 1974 shows a budget increase from $16.3 billion to an estimated $18.6 billion. A slight decline occurred in 1970—the low point for the six-year period—when the total dipped to $15.7 billion. Although overall R&D expenditures in the United States *increased* by 16 percent between 1967 and 1971, such a pattern did not exist in government spending because of decreased emphasis on defense and space research. However, this 16 percent rise pales by comparison with those gains registered in the major R&D-performing countries. For this same period of time, France, the United Kingdom, Japan, and Germany experienced gains in total R&D funding of 27, 21, 150, and 90 percent, respectively.

To display graphically the involvement by the government sector in U.S. scientific research and development programs, the following chart is presented as a record of funding by the federal government from 1940 to the present. In this way, the effects of various influences can be readily seen: the surge of scientific interest during and after World War II, the *Sputnik* spell of the late fifties, the space and defense domination through 1971, and the broadening of programs in areas outside space/defense from 1972 on. It is also interesting to note that, in the separate areas of basic research, applied research, and development, most recent figures credit the federal government with the 1973 financing of 58 percent of the total basic research, 24 percent of the applied, and 52 percent of all development. Truly this is testimony to the prominence the federal government has taken since the science and technology awakening in the late forties.

Federal R&D Expenditures, Fiscal Years 1940-1975*
(Dollars in millions)

Fiscal Year	Expenditures	Fiscal Year	Expenditures
1940	$ 74	1958	$ 4,991
1941	198	1959	5,806
1942	280	1960	7,744
1943	602	1961	9,287
1944	1,377	1962	10,387
1945	1,591	1963	12,012
1946	918	1964	14,707
1947	900	1965	14,889
1948	855	1966	16,018
1949	1,082	1967	16,859
1950	1,083	1968	17,049
1951	1,301	1969	16,348
1952	1,816	1970	15,736
1953	3,101	1971	15,992
1954	3,148	1972	16,743
1955	3,808	1973	17,510
1956	3,446	1974 (est)†	18,562
1957	4,462	1975 (est)†	20,154

*Total R&D spending in the United States in 1974 has been estimated at $32.1 billion. This amount includes expenditures by the federal government, industry, universities and colleges, and other non-profit institutions. According to recent NSF information, that figure is estimated to reach $34.3 billion in 1975.

†These estimates are based on amounts shown in *The Budget, 1975*, and do not reflect congressional appropriations or changes made by Executive action subsequent to budget submission at the midpoint of fiscal 1974.

SOURCES: Office of Management and Budget and Bureau of the Budget. *The Budget of the United States Government*, fiscal years 1940 through 1975; National Science Foundation, annual surveys of R&D programs of federal agencies.

As published in *Federal Funds for Research, Development, and Other Scientific Activities, Fiscal Years 1973, 1974, and 1975*, GPO, Washington, D.C., 1974

STATUS, SCOPE OF NSF SOARS

Understandably, the growth of the National Science Foundation through the years since its 1950 origin has closely paralleled the nation's intensified activities in scientific research. As reported in the foundation's twenty-third annual report, financial support by the government agency has climbed impressively. In 1973, 6138 grants totaling $268 million were awarded by NSF, with comparable support in 1972 and 1971 of 5800 and 4461 grants for totals of $248.6 and $180.3 million, respectively. The distribution, number, and amount of grants according to the field of science for these three fiscal years are shown in the following table.

Scientific Research Projects, Fiscal Years 1971, 1972, 1973
(Dollars in millions)

	Fiscal Year 1971		Fiscal Year 1972		Fiscal Year 1973	
	Number	Amount	Number	Amount	Number	Amount
Astronomy:						
Solar System Astronomy		$ .45		$ .50		$ .66
Stars and Stellar Evolution		1.59		1.97		2.20
Stellar Systems & Motions		.52		.57		.56
Galactic & Extragalactic Astronomy		3.17		4.02		4.50
Astronomical Instrumentation and						
Development		.94		.95		.88
Subtotal	138	6.67	135	8.01	170	8.80
Atmospheric Sciences:						
Aeronomy		2.35		3.23		2.92
Meteorology		4.73		5.50		5.68
Solar Terrestrial		2.37		2.98		3.33
Subtotal	148	9.45	218	11.71	232	11.93
Biological Sciences:						
Cellular Biology		8.92		11.90		11.90
Ecology & Systematic Biology		8.86		10.28		12.42
Molecular Biology		10.02		12.65		12.50
Physiological Processes		8.89		10.63		10.92
Neurobiology		4.05		4.47		4.46
Psychobiology		3.60		4.07		4.02
Subtotal	1,391	44.34	1,644	54.00	1,584	56.22
Chemistry:						
Synthetic Chemistry		4.27		5.17		5.14
Structural Chemistry		3.11		3.71		3.60
Quantum Chemistry		3.54		4.15		4.02
Chemical Dynamics		3.56		4.37		4.74
Chemical Analysis		2.00		2.99		2.63
Chemical Thermodynamics		2.39		2.44		2.57
Chemical Instrumentation		1.70		1.69		2.38
Subtotal	546	20.57	633	24.52	675	25.08

Scientific Research Projects, Fiscal Years 1971, 1972, 1973 (continued)
(Dollars in millions)

	Fiscal Year 1971		Fiscal Year 1972		Fiscal Year 1973	
	Number	Amount	Number	Amount	Number	Amount
Earth Sciences:						
Geology		1.64		1.78		1.95
Geochemistry		3.05		3.79		3.86
Geophysics		3.43		3.91		3.95
Subtotal	227	8.12	257	9.48	296	9.76
Engineering:						
Engineering Chemistry and Energetics		5.83		8.37		8.42
Engineering Materials*		4.00		–		–
Engineering Mechanics		5.77		10.17		10.30
Electrical Sciences & Analysis		1.48		6.89		7.44
Special Engineering		1.02		-0-		-0-
Subtotal	455	18.10	665	25.43	663	26.16
Physics:						
Elementary Particle Physics		11.60		13.74		13.98
Intermediate Energy Physics		-0-		-0-		3.00
Nuclear Physics		9.42		11.27		8.90
Atomic, Molecular & Plasma Physics		2.75		3.32		3.70
Theoretical Physics		2.72		3.70		3.90
Solid State & Low Temperature Physics*		5.72		–		–
Gravitational Physics		-0-		1.25		1.40
National Magnet Laboratory*		.40		–		–
Subtotal	295	32.61	271	33.28	298	34.88
Social Sciences:						
Anthropology		3.56		3.85		3.84
Economics		4.56		5.21		5.46
Sociology, Social Psychology & Social Indicators		4.57		6.39		6.14
Political Science, Law & Social Science		1.46		2.39		2.62
Special Projects, Geography, History and Philosophy of Science		3.51		4.61		5.18
Science Policy Research		–		–		.39
Subtotal	490	17.66	619	22.45	635	23.63

Scientific Research Projects, Fiscal Years 1971, 1972, 1973 (continued)
(Dollars in millions)

	Fiscal Year 1971		Fiscal Year 1972		Fiscal Year 1973	
	Number	Amount	Number	Amount	Number	Amount
Materials Research†						
Engineering Materials	–			6.58		6.79
Solid State and Low						
Temperature Physics	–			9.66		9.76
Solid State Chemistry and						
Polymer Science	–			2.07		2.06
Materials Research Laboratories	–			12.80		13.11
National Magnet Laboratory...........	–			2.28		2.50
Synchrotron Radiation Facility	–			–		.75
Subtotal	–	–	392	33.39	409	34.97
Materials Sciences:						
Classical Analysis & Geometry		2.23		2.61		3.18
Modern Analysis & Probability		2.36		2.62		2.57
Algebra..		2.46		2.98		2.78
Topology & Foundations		2.22		2.27		2.22
Applied Mathematics and						
Statistics		3.07		3.27		3.31
Special Projects		.59		-0-		-0-
Subtotal	535	12.93	693	13.75	758	14.06
Oceanography:						
Physical and Chemical						
Oceanography		2.69		4.01		4.06
Submarine Geology and						
Geophysics		3.35		4.15		4.33
Biological Oceanography.................		3.88		4.39		4.27
Subtotal	236	9.92	273	12.55	287	12.66
Computing Activities‡						
Computer Science &						
Engineering						6.32
Computer Applications in						
Research						3.25
Special Projects						.33
Subtotal					131	9.90
Total	4,461	$180.37	5,800	$248.57	6,138	$268.05

---

*Included under Material Research for FY 1972 and FY 1973.
†Included under programs in Chemistry, Engineering, and Physics in FY 1971 at a total of $11.06 million.
‡Included in National and Special Research Programs for FY 1971 and FY 1972.

The spectrum of NSF activities has also broadened significantly since 1950, especially in recent years as NSF has led the way in our national and international scientific programs. Within the NSF, the National and Special Research Programs element has been responsible for those research efforts so far-reaching in scope as to involve "international cooperation, coordination with other agencies of government, a relationship to a specific geographic region, or interdisciplinary scientific investigations." Among the specific programs belonging in this category, according to the 1973 NSF Annual Report, are the following: International Biological Program—to investigate how ecosystems function and determine man's relation to them; Global Atmosphere Research Program—to extend knowledge of the meteorology of the equatorial belt; International Decade of Ocean Exploration—to design and implement projects concerning marine environmental quality; and Ocean Sediment Coring Program—to increase knowledge of origins and dynamics of the oceanic basins and the continents. In the realm of astronomy and atmospheric sciences, the NSF supports five National Research Centers where highly specialized instrumentation facilities and operational support are available to U.S. scientists for the conduct of advanced research in these disciplines.

Showing adherence to the philosophy that the conduct of cooperative scientific programs among nations is a practical means of improving foreign relations, the NSF supported various international projects in 1973. Funds were allocated by NSF to the National Academy of Sciences for the exchange of scientific delegations with the People's Republic of China, while exchange programs originating in previous years continued to receive support, namely, those with the Academies of Science of the USSR, Bulgaria, Czechoslovakia, Hungary, Poland, Romania, and Yugoslavia. Such foundation support of cooperative international activities has led to the formation of various offspring organizations peculiar to specific projects. Among them are the U.S.-USSR Agreement on Cooperation in the Fields of Science and Technology, the United States-Israel Binational Science Foundation, the International Institute for Applied Systems Analysis, and the United States-Yugoslav Joint Board on Scientific and Technical Cooperation. Agencies such as these truly reflect a spirit of international cooperation in certain areas of science and technology . . . an achievement made possible through the judicious guidance and leadership of the National Science Foundation.

A RECAP

On March 20, 1974, Dr. Edward E. David, Jr., executive vice-president of Gould, Inc., and previously scientific advisor to the President of the United States, delivered before the Western Society of Engineers a very timely address entitled, "Engineering, the Nation, and the World—The Next Chapter." He included some very appropriate statements recapitulating the federal government's role in scientific research in the United States, at the same time offering his own assessment of the government's position today. The salient points of this speech are given on the following pages and provide the conclusion to this chapter.

. . . In the middle 1960s, space and military [R&D Funding] were predominant. A figure which always startles me is that during the 1960s, 40 percent of all federal R&D funding went into space activities. Even including industrial funding of R&D, yearly some 65 percent went to space and military. Civilian technology was advised to depend on fall-out—indirect results from space and military technology. There was some such fall-out; the now-infamous transfer of Teflon from the space programs to cooking utensils is an example. Now, the funding pattern has reversed. R&D funding by all sources yields 40 percent for military and space and 60 percent for civilian technology. The actual projected figures for FY 1975 are as follows:

Civilian technology:

Federal funding	$ 6.8 billion
Industry funding	$13.7 billion
Total:	$33 billion (space and military make up the difference)

The contributions by industry rose from 31 percent in 1964 to 42 percent in 1974. There has been real but slow growth in the total R&D funding level during the past five or so years.

These figures, of course, represent resources—they are inputs to the R&D machine. But there are similar trends on the output side. There we see much less emphasis on pure performance; that is, on higher, faster, further and more on reliability, serviceability, repairability, and safety. Even the Pentagon is beginning to adopt a "build-to-cost" philosophy rather than "build-to-performance specifications." In the cost realm, too, we are seeing more output orientation—more emphasis on operating and maintenance costs and less on first cost. This trend has been accelerated by shortages and increasing prices of both materials and energy. In addition, of course, there is the powerful influence of trained manpower, particularly its increasing price and decreasing availability. These factors are strong incentives to cut the labor content of maintenance and operations. All of this means that fall-out from military and space technologies is on the wane (if it ever was on the wax!). Fall-out is less credible now. We as a nation are coming to a more direct approach to producing acceptable technologies for society.

. . . This output motivation has been called *market pull* as contrasted to *technology push*. While I believe this trend is long overdue, it does bring with it dangers. Obviously there is danger to basic research. That has and should continue to be opportunity (input)-oriented. The long-term effectiveness of new knowledge to provide new options and create new worlds for society has been amply demonstrated. We must maintain and expand imaginative exploratory activity. Yet, it is well to note that basic research today represents only about 10-15 percent of the nation's technical effort. That percentage is not likely to change very much. However, there will be a change in the 1950-1960's philosophy that new technology is spawned exclusively by new science. The 1970's view is that new technological needs often spawn new science. We can confidently say that in the coming era engineering will be no more applied science than science is purified engineering. Each will stimulate the other . . .

. . . The National Science Board has recently issued a report on indicators of the health and vigor of the (technological) enterprise. Unfortunately, as the report says, most of these indicators are input measures, not output.

For example, the report points out that the number of scientists and engineers engaged in R&D in the U.S. has declined since 1969, but continued to increase in the USSR, Japan, West Germany, and France. In 1971, the number per 10^5 of population was 37 for the USSR, 25 for the U.S. and Japan, 15 for West Germany, and 12 for France. But this recital says nothing about the output from these workers. In fact, those of you who have visited the USSR know that R&D productivity per capita is less there because of lack of instrumentation and facilities in many fields. The Soviets tend to substitute manpower for facilities. This tactic means less output despite the large number of people involved.

The National Science Board does examine some crude measures of scientific and technical output. These tend to confirm the above conclusion. For example, a simple count indicates that the U.S. leads the Soviets in seven of eight fields in number of publications (we don't in chemistry and metallurgy). Further, U.S. publications are of higher quality as judged by the number of citations to them in the world's literature. (This is not quite fair, for more people read English than Russian in the world.)

This same situation exists with most other nations. Notably, however, Britain outdoes us in systematic biology and mathematics. The U.S. has an increasing favorable position in sale of technical "know-how"—patents, techniques, chemical formulas, franchises, and manufacturing rights. We are preeminent in world trade in high-technology products; that is, aircraft, computers, chemicals, pharmaceuticals and drugs, machine tools, and instruments. This is not to say that we will be able to maintain these advantages, but they have been relatively stable over the past decade.

However, the patent balance has deteriorated. U.S. inventors continue to win more patents abroad than foreign nations do here. But the difference declined by 40 percent between 1966-1970. What this means is open to interpretation. One thing is clear, however; we are faced with increasing competition in R&D on the world scene. That is the inevitable consequent of the "generation-of-peace" that is being pursued in Washington, Moscow, Peking, and European capitals. It is the kind of competition which provides profound engineering challenges, and can produce immense benefits for world societies. So, though competition is on the increase, I believe the U.S. technical community is in a leadership position and can stay there.

What could intervene? How could we snatch defeat from the jaws of victory? Let me mention two possibilities. First and foremost would be a shortage of excellent manpower—scientists, engineers, and technicians. The trends here have been very disturbing over the past few years. The over-advertised lack of jobs, attacks on technology, and indeed even the rational basis of life and behavior are evidence of a profound disenchantment in many elements of our society. This will take years to repair, but fortunately we see signs of a turnaround. This is the result, less of evangelism by the technical community, and more of an obviously increasing demand for engineers. In my view, this is a sound start. Also, many elements are rallying to technology's defense . . .

. . . So, hopefully, lack of excellent people will not be a fatal handicap in the coming decade.

The other possibility for failure arises from the natural tendency to model future R&D on past successful patterns. "If we can put a man on the moon, why can't we . . . ?" The NASA approach and DOD techniques are well suited to their needs. But they would court failure in civilian technology. I can tell you that the Washington bureaucracy is fallible if you're not already convinced. Successful science and technology programs for the private civilian sector cannot be masterminded from Washington. That is why I have anxieties about the newly announced, five-year, $10-billion energy R&D program, as I do about the Cancer Crusade. However, I do not mean that the government should not play a role in civilian technology. But, in my view, the predominant mode of action should be the creation of incentives for private investment rather than direct funding. As I said earlier, the creation of markets has a profound influence and brings forward numbers of technologies which compete for a place in the sun. Incentives can be created by tax credits, by federally guaranteed markets, and other well-known mechanisms. The objective should be to stimulate numerous technological options which rise or fall on their merits as judged in the marketplace, domestic and foreign. Thereby, less expensive, more innovative and effective technology will result.

The government has another role as well. It is to support the long-range, high-risk ventures which the private sector won't or can't support. Efforts such as controlled-thermonuclear fusion and much basic biomedical research fall principally in this category. There is, too, the support of education, which is a subject in its own right. Here again I favor a market approach, aiding the student and allowing him to choose his institution to attend, rather than subsidizing the institution directly. The point is that the government must play a very different role in the seventies and eighties than it did in the fifties and sixties. There are signs that this approach is oozing into place.

There are demands from societies for effective engineering animated by national problems, national goals made concrete in government standards, regulations, and rules, and by international ambitions for increased living standards in this age of peaceful if uneasy living. U.S. science and technology are healthy but under increasing competition from abroad. Yet we are in a fine position to meet that competition. There are dangers, dangers that science and engineering cannot attract the excellent students that are required, and dangers that we will look to governments for direction rather than for stimulation, incentives, and statements of needs and goals. Yet, I believe we can avoid the pitfalls and remain preeminent on the international scene. Too, we will be able to meet the challenge at home.

* * *

Bibliography

An Analysis of Federal R&D Funding By Function, 1963-1973, Washington, D.C.: U.S. Government Printing Office, 1972.

An Analysis of Federal R&D Funding By Function, FY 1963-73, National Science Foundation, Washington, D.C.: U.S. Government Printing Office, 1973.

Brooks, Harvey, *The Government of Science*, Cambridge, Massachusetts: The M.I.T. Press, 1968.

Dearborn, De Witt C., Rose W. Kneznek, and Robert N. Anthony, *Spending for Industrial Research 1951-1952*, Boston: Division of Research, Graduate School of Business Administration, Harvard University, 1953.

Dupree, A. Hunter, *Science in the Federal Government—A History of Policies and Activities to 1940*, Cambridge, Massachusetts: The Belknap Press of Harvard University Press, 1957.

Fifth Annual Report of the National Science Foundation, Washington, D.C.: U.S. Government Printing Office, 1955.

Fourth Annual Report of the National Science Foundation, Washington, D.C.: U.S. Government Printing Office, 1954.

National Patterns of R&D Resources, National Science Foundation, Washington, D.C.: U.S. Government Printing Office, 1970.

National Patterns of R&D Resources, National Science Foundation, Washington, D.C.: U.S. Government Printing Office, 1973.

National Patterns of R&D Resources, Funds and Manpower in the United States, 1953-1973, Washington, D.C.: U.S. Government Printing Office, 1973.

National Science Foundation Annual Report, 1973, Washington, D.C.: U.S. Government Printing Office, 1973.

Ninth Annual Report of the National Science Foundation, Washington, D.C.: U.S. Government Printing Office, 1959.

Orlans, Harold, *The Nonprofit Research Institute*, New York: McGraw-Hill Book Company, 1972.

Seventh Annual Report of the National Science Foundation, Washington, D.C.: U.S. Government Printing Office, 1957.

Sixth Annual Report of the National Science Foundation, Washington, D.C.: U.S. Government Printing Office, 1956.

CHAPTER XIII

IN RETROSPECT AND A PROJECTION OF THE FUTURE

The phenomenal development of science and technology in the United States over the past 200 years has been unequalled at any time in any nation, ancient or modern. As a new nation comprised of settlers from all over the world, America was not handicapped by the obstacles of tradition. Rather, there was a will on the part of the people to acquire a better life in an environment of free enterprise and vast natural resources.

Progress was slow during the first 75 years, but rapid advances began around 1850—the time often referred to as the beginning of the Industrial Revolution—and the United States was impressively on its way to becoming the strongest industrial nation the world has ever known. Many segments of society have contributed to this ascension. First, there were excellent crafts-men who passed their skills onto their successors. These were joined by inventors and innovators, whose numbers grew as did the importance of their contributions. In time, the universities became part of the parade by initiating and then progressively giving greater and greater emphasis to basic research. Then, in the early 1900s, a few industries began to realize that applied research was *not* an expensive frill, but an investment. As a result, growing numbers of individuals and groups knowledgeable in science and technology found their places as consultants to industry. As research became more accepted year by year, groups of individuals in various parts of the country became convinced that a special kind of organization devoted to both basic and applied research in a given region would not only assist in the economic development of that region, but would, at the same time, offer a service to the local small industries that could not afford research depart-ments on their own. Thus there evolved a new kind of vehicle to assist in the industrial and economic development of the country—the independent research institution.

THE NICHE THAT HAS BEEN CARVED

In tracing the birth and evolution of this vehicle, several hypotheses surface. If we consider the very early years of both Mellon and Battelle to be years of giving birth to a new concept of enhancing technological growth and the years of World War II and shortly thereafter to be the years when the accepting of the concept became real, then we can say that the independent applied research institute is a 35-year phenomenon. The basic concept was that in a research organization founded on philosophies and operational techniques that were about midway between the commercial bustle of the industrial laboratory and the academic nature of the university laboratory, a unique environment would be created. Such an environment would offer great potential in solving technical problems of both industry and government.

Emphasis in this book has been given to what has been termed the "nine independents," mostly because these institutions worked cooperatively as a group during the war years as well as during the years thereafter. They were all organized as not-for-profit institutions to serve the public good and were competitive only to the extent that such competition was desirable. As each one was organized, the institute leaders sought out those areas of specialization that were not generally practiced by existing institutions. Today, there is little overlapping in their respective "hallmarks" despite a similarity of modus operandi. They operate on the basis of contracts with or grants from sponsors. Such an agreement covers a specific program deemed not in conflict with that of another active sponsor. A customary agreement assures that the work will be conducted in the degree of confidence requested by the sponsor; that publication of any results of the work will be done only by authorization of the sponsor; that the results of the work and any patents that result therefrom will be the exclusive property of the sponsor if he wishes; that results beneficial to the sponsor are not guaranteed; and that the sponsor will reimburse the institution its direct and indirect costs plus a small margin to enable the conduct of modest amounts of in-house research at the institution to generate professional growth of staff members and likewise a small margin to provide for other institutional growth. The governing board members of these institutions receive no compensation, and staff members receive no salary bonuses or stock options. There are no stock issues—the institutions belong to the public. These same basic operational policies have been followed by the several additional applied research institutes organized after 1946.

What is particularly significant about all of these institutions is the tremendous amount of free service they have given the public. Collectively they have handled tens of thousands of inquiries from industry, the government, and the public on a wide variety of technical matters. If laboratory work or a literature search was not required and the answer was known by the scientific community, the counsel was given on a free-advice basis.

Because of the highly specialized staff of each institution, higher education has been greatly strengthened throughout the nation by virtue of these staff members engaging in part-time teaching, thus supplementing the faculties of the college and university system. In addition, these experts have appeared before innumerable audiences throughout the country to interpret for the public the developments in technology. They have also contributed many thousands of papers on their research findings to the nation's scientific literature.

The research institutes themselves have also spawned numerous profit-making companies engaged in research and development. In addition, they have operated special government research facilities on a contract-management basis with an efficiency and effectiveness that government agencies felt they could not otherwise attain. Considering their small number, they also have an impressive record of sponsoring local, regional, national, and international symposia and conferences on advancing technology and science in the service to mankind.

Despite these and other "credits," in no year in the past 35 years has the combined research underwritings of the independent nonprofit research institutions exceeded 1.5 percent of the nation's total R&D expenditures for the corresponding year. Without question, the institutions' contributions to the public have far exceeded this small proportion of the nation's R&D effort. The federal government has so well recognized the advantages of this form of institution that it has assisted in the founding of many similar not-for-profit institutions throughout the Free World. Currently, this seems to be a continuing policy.

SURVIVAL OF THE NONPROFIT RESEARCH INSTITUTES

A penetrating look at the present-day operations of these "independents" reveals a disturbing dilemma with regard to their nonprofit status. For a number of reasons, not the least of which is pressure on the Internal Revenue Service by the profit-oriented companies engaged in R&D services—many of them having been organized by former staff members of the nonprofit research institutes—the IRS is taxing the unrelated business income of the nonprofit institutes under Section 511 of the Internal Revenue Code of 1954. Currently, the IRS seems satisfied to treat all income derived from commercial sponsors as unrelated and therefore taxable, leaving income from other sources such as federal, state, and local governments untouched tax-wise. Whether this attitude will prevail in the future or whether an effort will be made to revoke the institute's tax exemptions altogether is a matter of pure conjecture.

Reasons other than those represented by the IRS and the pressuring profit-making R&D companies may well be the deciding factors, however, in whether or not the institutes give up their not-for-profit tax exemptions and go "for profit." One such "pressure" candidate is the Tax Reform Act of 1969, which introduced into the law the concept of the private foundation. Without delving into technical details, suffice it to say that avoidance of private foundation status by the institutes can be achieved only by main-taining a more than 1:3 ratio between the kind and magnitude of sources of income and total support. Under the terms of the 1969 Reform Act, it would be difficult, if not impossible, for a broad-based, technological institute to operate successfully as a private foundation. The institutes must therefore warily watch this critical ratio, lest they inadvertently slip over into the private foundation category. Once a private foundation, always a private foundation, and it is impossible to give up private foundation status volun-tarily without incurring substantial penalties in the form of confiscatory taxes. Hence, it may come to pass that because of the constraints of the mechanical formula of the Tax Reform Act, the institutes will find it to their advantage to give up their tax-exempt status while there is still time before they are caught in the private foundation trap.

Another pressure at work on the institutes in their tax struggle is fiscal in nature. As long as the institutes operate as not-for-profit, tax-exempt organizations, their sole sources of expansion financing for buildings, equip-ment, and new areas of research are cash flow and secured and unsecured loans, both long- and short-term. In what appears to be an economy of consistently upward spiraling costs, such sources may be inadequate for the future. Bonded indebtedness and equity financing as sources of capital, both of which are available only to stockholder business corporations, must be tapped. If this is the only option, then giving up tax exemption and going taxable is the only alternative. One alternate to the equity-financing- and cash-flow procedure is contribution; however, the danger here is that large contributions might jeopardize the ratio that must be maintained to avoid the private foundation classification.

WHAT THE FUTURE HOLDS

Now, after almost 200 years, our country is faced with the need for new national priorities. Crises have resulted from our growing dependence on foreign nations for fuel and many other mineral resources. Pollution of the environment and attendant health hazards have reached levels causing grievous concern to everyone. Improved levels of health for all citizens have become mandatory. Productivity in relationship to labor costs must be substantially increased to check inflation. All these and more are areas suited to sound programs in research and development. If R&D could get us to the moon, it *can* solve these problems, but R&D funding must be substantially increased, and every unit engaged in this activity must be given every incentive and stimulation to expand.

The independent research institutes have been much more effective in the past in meeting such national challenges than is reflected by the fact that their combined budgets in any one year have never exceeded 1.5 percent of the national R&D total in the corresponding year. They have an excellent track record in conducting research where it counts and in recent years have been asked on numerous occasions to take responsibility for the operation of government-owned laboratories in order to gain better efficiency and greater productivity. A big plus is the fact that their environment and modus operandi tend to attract very imaginative and innovative personnel who shun the laboratories of a process- or product-oriented corporation or the academe of a university. In a time of new priorities, these independent research institutes are more essential than ever before; however, changing tax laws have worked a hardship on them, mostly because of confusion in interpretation. The independents have reacted in various ways: one (Mellon) has become part of a university; another (Cornell) has become a profit-making corporation (Calspan); a third (Stanford) has cut its umbilical cord with a university; and the other six are either paying taxes or are in the tax courts. Since these organizations, as independent institutions, have not had stockholders, in lieu of paying dividends, they have been able to flow income over expenses back into the activity in the form of better laboratory facilities, equipment, and staffs—a far better way for the nation to stimulate and expand research activity than by tax support. Congress may in time see the wisdom of granting institutions of this kind federal charters as it has in other instances where the activity is of great value to the public.

It is not the purpose of this book to plead the cause of any segment of the nation's R&D organizational pattern, but rather to emphasize the great gains that were made over the past 200 years when there existed a relative free reign on organizational types and procedures. We can do as well in the next 200 years if we encourage in every way, including tax incentives to industry and institutions, a greater emphasis on R&D as a means of solving the nation's problems.

APPENDIX

HISTORY OF TECHNOLOGY TABLES*

These tables show the time-relations of selected events in technological history both to each other and to named events in general history. In the earlier tables the dating is often only approximate; in the last three, where exact information is usually available, the date and place attributed to a process are—unless otherwise stated—those of its first invention.

*These tables are from Derry, T.K., and Trevor I. Williams, *A Short History of Technology*, Oxford University Press, © 1960, and reproduced here by permission of the Clarendon Press, Oxford.

I. PREHISTORY OF EUROPE

B.C.	Stage or Period	Events
	PALAEOLITHIC	Intermittent periods of comparative warmth, enabling precursors of man and man himself in very small numbers to move into Europe from the south and southeast.
c. 20000	UPPER OR LATE PALAEOLITHIC	Retreat of Scandinavian and Alpine ice-sheets, uncovering large areas of cold grass-land and swamp, where man flourished as a hunter.
c. 9000	MESOLITHIC	Further retreat of ice-sheets, with changes in sea-level, in average temperature, and in rainfall, resulting in the spread of thick forest and restriction of man's habitat to shores, hilltops, and forest edges, while he for the first time colonized the arctic north: in some respects (e.g., pictorial art) a period of retrogression and impoverishment.
c. 3200	NEOLITHIC	Spread of stock keeping and agriculture overland from southeast; sea-borne movement north from Mediterranean associated with megalithic structures; opening-up of communications by traders characterized by superior pottery.
c. 2000	BRONZE	The use of copper, followed by that of bronze, introduced from east Mediterranean lands by sea traders in search of metal ores or forest products; overland trade also important between the middle Danubian and the Baltic region.
c. 1000	EARLY IRON	Knowledge of iron-working brought from Greece via Italy to the Hallstatt area of Austria, and spread particularly by the Celts, pressing southward in a period of worsened climate, and by Iranian (Scythian) invaders of south-eastern Europe.

NORTH OF THE ALPS

Characteristic Economic Activities (*existing side by side with the more primitive*)	Characteristic Tools or Weapons (*slowly superseding the more primitive*)
Food-gathering, with some use of fire but no settled abodes; some practice of hunting by cave-dwellers.	Flaked hand-axes and other implements of flint and stone, supplementing those of wood, horn, ivory, or bone; wooden spears; heavy stone missiles.
Hunting of mammoth, bison, wild horse, deer, etc.; preparation of skins for clothing; cooking; inhabitation of caves, often embellished with hunting scenes, and of more temporary tented dwellings.	Improved flint knife-blades, awls, and gravers; barbs, bone needles, harpoons; composite tools; flint-tipped javelins and bone spear-throwers; bows and arrows.
Food-gathering, small-scale hunting (probably helped by domestication of the dog), and increased reliance on fishing, including sea-fishing from boats.	Microliths, used in composite tools of wood or bone; elaboration of fishing-tackle (net, hook and line, fish-spear, trap); stone adzes and chisels.
Stock-keeping and cultivation of wheat and barley; wood-working; making of baskets, simple textiles, and pottery. Flint-mining and growth of trade; common use of sledges and, in far north, skis; villages of mainly rectangular hut dwellings; some reduction of forest area by burning and felling of trees.	Ground, polished, and occasionally drilled implements of flint and other hard stone, the design sometimes influenced by metal prototypes; hoes and sickles; spindles and looms; flint daggers; the wheel used for transport.
Spread of west Asiatic types of sheep and cattle; use of woollen textiles; construction of clinker-built boats. Trade in manufactured metal goods, ceramics, amber; growing importance of luxury goods.	Small ploughs (*unci*); hammered axes, etc., of copper and bronze; superior implements of cast bronze; smiths' and carpenters' tools; copper and bronze spears; bronze sword evolved from dagger.
Increase of arable area, with oats and rye in north; timber frame-houses and earthworks constructed with timber and stone; larger plank-boats, some carvel-built; horse-riding (with horse-shoes) and use of wheeled vehicles became common, culminating in the Celtic war-chariot.	Large ploughs with share, etc., of iron; scythes; improved saws, chisels, and files for carpentry; wood-turning; the potter's wheel in common use; the first strong swords.

II. THE ANCIENT CIVILIZATIONS OF THE

B.C.	Mesopotamia (and Persia)	Egypt	Palestine, Syria, and Asia Minor
3500	Sumerian city states in existence; copper used and alloyed First evidence of wheeled vehicle First records (cuneiform)	Copper tools in use	Walled town at Jericho
3250			
3000	Pottery made on the wheel	Beginning of hieroglyphics	
2750		365-day calendar *Zoser*: First (Step) Pyramid	
2500	Royal tombs of Ur	*Cheops*: Great Pyramid Sea-going sailing ships	
2250	*Sargon I—Akkadian Empire (Semitic language)*	Oldest surviving irrigation dam *Middle Kingdom*	
2000	Ziggurats	Bronze came into use Horse-drawn chariots	*Hittites invade Asia Minor* Hittite capital at Hattushash (Bogazköy) with first known Processional Way
1750	*Hammurabi— Babylonian (Amoritic) Empire* *Kassite rule begins*	*Hyksos kings* *The New Empire*	

NEAR EAST, GREECE, AND THE ROMAN REPUBLIC

Eastern Mediterranean	Western Mediterranean	Central and Northern Europe
'Minoan' palaces built at Knossos and Phaestos		*Bronze Age*
Knossos at its zenith		
		Stonehenge erected

II. The Ancient Civilizations of the Near East, Greece, and the Roman Republic (continued)

B.C.	Mesopotamia (and Persia)	Egypt	Palestine, Syria, and Asia Minor
1500		Shadow-clock Great Hall of Karnak *Egyptian empire at its zenith*	
			Cementation steel made by Chalybes
	First rise of Assyrians		
		Tutankhamen Glass vessels in common use	
			Alphabet used at Ugarit
1250			*Rise of Phoenician kingdoms* *Collapse of Hittite power* *Siege of Troy*
			Reigns of David and Solomon; *Hiram, king of Tyre*
1000	*Assyrian revival* Iron equipment		Iron ploughshare
750	*Sargon II—Assyrian Empire*		*Ten tribes of Israel deported by the Assyrians*
	Sennacherib's stone canal and aqueduct	*Egypt under Assyrian rule*	*Decline of Phoenician power* Coinage introduced (Lydia) *Lydians dominant in Asia Minor*
	Nineveh destroyed by Medes and Chaldeans *Nebuchadnezzar: Neo-Babylonian (Chaldean) Empire* Euphrates bridge and Ishtar gate, Babylon		*586 Babylonian captivity of Jews*
	538 Babylon included in Persian Empire by Cyrus	*Persian conquest*	*Persian conquest*

Eastern Mediterranean	Western Mediterranean	Central and Northern Europe
Linear writing of Greek *Knossos destroyed* (acc. to Evans)		
Mycenean palaces *Achaeans in Greece*		
Dorians in Greece		Iron industry in Austria (Hall- statt)
	Etruscans in Italy *Carthage founded*	
Greek colonial expansion		
Silver mined at Laurion		
	Republic established at Rome	

II. The Ancient Civilizations of the Near East, Greece, and the Roman Republic (continued)

B.C.	Mesopotamia (and Persia)	Egypt	Palestine, Syria, and Asia Minor
500	Darius's inscription at Behistun		
	Alexander destroys Persian Empire	*Conquest by Alexander*	
		Red Sea canal renewed by Ptolemy Philadelphus *Great Age of Alexandria* Lighthouse at Alexandria (Pharos)	Colossus of Rhodes
250			Parchment made at Pergamum
		Eratosthenes' world map	
	Rise of the Parthians *Victory of Parthians over Romans (Carrhae)*		
		Egypt a Roman province; deaths of Mark Antony and Cleopatra	Glass-blowing began in Syria

Eastern Mediterranean	Western Mediterannean	Central and Northern Europe
Aqueduct of Samos Fine Athenian pottery Lathe in common use for wood-turning *Greeks defeat Persians* Hippodamus laid out Piraeus Parthenon completed *Death of Pericles*		

	405-367 *Dionysius, ruler of
	    Syracuse*
		*Celtic expansion in western
		    and central Europe*
		Iron Age in Britain

336-323 *Alexander, king of Macedon* *Death of Aristotle*		
	Romans supreme in Italy *Death of Archimedes* Catalan furnace in Spain	
Romans destroy Corinth	*Romans destroy Carthage*	
	Julian Calendar *Augustus establishes Empire*	*Caesar's conquest of Gaul*

III. EUROPE FROM THE REIGN OF

A.D.	The East	Eastern Mediterranean and Constantinople	Italy (with Spain and Portugal)
14			Use of brass
			Death of Augustus
			Drainage of Lake Fucinus
			Great Fire of Rome
			69-79 *Vespasian*
			Corn ground by water-mills
		Heron's *Mechanics*	*Pompeii destroyed*
			81-96 *Domitian*
100			Pantheon built
			138-92 *Antonine emperors (Pius, Marcus Aurelius, Commodus)*
		Ptolemy's *Almagest* and *Geography*	Baths of Caracalla
200	*Sassanian Persian empire established*		Use of shafts for wagons
300			284-305 *Diocletian reorganizes empire*
			Large Vitruvian water-mills
			312-37 *Constantine*
		330 *Constantinople founded*	
400		*Death of St. Jerome*	
	Huns advance into western Europe		
			Odoacer ends Roman Empire in West
			493-526 *Rule of Theodric in Italy*
500	Avars introduce metal stirrups	527-65 *Justinian*	*Benedictine Order founded*
		Production of raw silk attempted	
		St. Sophia built	*Siege of Rome by the Ostrogoths; Byzantine rule established in Italy*
			Mausoleum of Theodoric, Ravenna
			Lombards enter Italy
			Emergence of Venice

AUGUSTUS TO THE FIRST CRUSADE

Central and Northern Europe	France and the Low Countries	Britain/England
		Roman conquest
Trajan extends empire north of lower Danube		Hadrian's wall
	458-81 *Childeric, king of (Salian) Franks*	
	Merovingian rule in France	
		Conversion of England begun

III. Europe From the Reign of Augustus to the First Crusade (continued)

A.D.	The East	Eastern Mediterranean and Constantinople	Italy (with Spain and Portugal)
600	Windmill in Persia 622 *Birth of Islam*	*Persians and Avars besiege Constantinople* 'Greek fire'	
700	Alchemical works of Jabir Chinese paper-makers captured at Smarkand *Baghdad founded*		*Moorish conquest of Spain* *Charles Martel's victory over Moors*
800	Arabic translation of Ptolemy Chinese porcelain received and imitated in western Asia	Lateen sail	800 *Charlemagne crowned Roman emperor*
900	*Rise of Bokhara*		Cotton and silk established by Moors in Spain *Cordova at its zenith*
1000	Alhazen's writings on optics, etc. Baghdad potters migrate to Cairo	*Seljuk Turks occupy Asia Minor*	First use of magnetic compass Rebuilding of St. Mark's, Venice First translations from Arabic science

Central and Northern Europe	France and the Low Countries	Britain/England
	Fair of St. Denis in existence	
		Sutton Hoo ship-burial *Death of St. Cuthbert*
	Church organs introduced from Constantinople	
Rhineland stoneware Aachen cathedral Gokstad ship *Viking expansion*		
		871-99 *Alfred, king of Wessex*
Magyar incursions		
936-73 *Otto the Great, emperor* Mining in Harz mountains *Eastward expansion of Germany*		960-88 *Dunstan, archbishop of Canterbury*
1024-39 *Conrad II, emperor*	Norman abbeys	1042-66 *Edward the Confessor* Westminster Abbey
	Fulling mills	1066-87 *William the Conqueror* *Domesday Book*

IV. EUROPE IN THE

A.D.	The East	Eastern Mediterranean and Constantinople	Italy (with Spain and Portugal)
1100	1096-9 *Ist Crusade*		
	Venetian traders in Levant		Paper-making by Moors
1150		*Last great age of Byzantium*	Stamp-mill used in paper-making
	Saladin captures Jerusalem 3rd Crusade		
1200		*4th Crusade captures Constantinople*	Venetian glass-making
		Hinged rudder	Italian silk-throwing mills
	Mongols invade eastern Europe		
	Mongol invasion of Mesopotamia, etc.		
			Florin coined (gold)
1250			Naviglio Grande (Grand Canal of Lombardy)
	Travels of Marco Polo		
			Plate armour (Milan)
1300	*Ottoman Turks first enter Byzantine territory in Asia Minor*		Spectacle-making (Venice)
			Genoese ships enter English Channel
			Catalan Atlas
			Majolica ware

LATER MIDDLE AGES

Central and Northern Europe	France and the Low Countries	England
Mould-board added to plough	*Champagne fairs at their zenith* *Growth of the Cistercian Order* Abbey church of St. Denis, Paris (gothic)	Gloucester candlestick (*cire perdue*)
Big German expansion east of Elbe		
1152-90 *Frederick Barbarossa, emperor*		
	Foundation of University of Paris	
	Bridge of Avignon	Old London Bridge
	Windmills	
Cogs built for northern trade	Fulling mills in wide use	1216-72 *Henry III* Westminster Abbey rebuilt: Portland stone Roger Bacon's experiments
St. Gotthard Pass open to traffic		
Rise of Hanse towns and League	Beauvais choir built	
	Great age of stained glass	
	Zuider Zee at its maximum extent	Salisbury Cathedral
		1272-1307 *Edward I* *Conquest of Wales completed* *Death of Eleanor of Castile*
Use of open-sea route round Skaw	Flax-breaker	Units of length and area standardized Navigation weir on Thames
Salt-glazing of pottery		1337-1453 *Hundred Years War*
	Crecy	

IV. Europe in the Later Middle Ages (continued)

A.D.	The East	Eastern Mediterranean and Constantinople	Italy (with Spain and Portugal)
1350		*Power of Ottoman Turks expands from Asia Minor into Europe*	*Italian renaissance begins*
1400			*Portuguese voyages organized by Prince Henry the Navigator* Caravels Duomo, Florence

Central and Northern Europe	France and the Low Countries	England
1348 *Black Death*	1348 *Black Death*	1348 *Black Death*
Brandenburg an Electorate		
	Windmill-driven scoop-wheel	
	Canals with sluices	1377-99 *Richard II*
First summit-level canal, Germany		Salisbury cathedral clock
Cast-iron cannon, Germany		
	Modern lock (Damme)	
	Dutch drift-nets	
	Hollow-post mills in Holland	Tattershall castle (brick)
		King's College Chapel, Cambridge, begun

V. EUROPE IN EARLY

A.D.	World Relationships of Europe	Italy, Spain, and Portugal	Central and Northern Europe
1450	1453 *Ottoman Turks capture Constantinople*		Gutenberg's printing-press (Mainz)
			Intensive silver-mining
			Blast-furnace introduced
			Jakob Fugger II, 'the Rich'
		1471-84 *Pope Sixtus IV*	
		Patents introduced at Venice	Instrument-making at Nuremberg (Regiomontanus)
	Diaz reaches Cape of Good Hope	Vitruvius's *De architectura* printed	
	Columbus's first voyage Papal line of demarcation	*Christian reconquest of Spain completed*	
	da Gama reaches India Cabot's first voyage to Newfoundland	1494-1559 *Italian wars of France and Spain*	
1500		Mitre-gate pound-locks	
	Aztecs of Mexico and Incas of Peru conquered by Spain		1519-56 *Charles V, emperor*
	1522 *First circumnavigation of the world (begun by Magellan)*	Wheel-lock invented in Italy	
			Tinplate
			Iatrochemistry (Paracelsus)
			Death of Erasmus
		Dome of St. Peter's designed by Michelangelo	Rail-way used in mining
1550			*De Re Metallica* (Agricola)
		Potato introduced into Europe	
	Frobisher seeks North-West Passage	1572-85 *Pope Gregory XIII*	
		Portugal annexed to Spain	
		Gregorian calendar	
		Galileo's discovery of the principle of the pendulum	
		1585-90 *Pope Sixtus V*	

MODERN TIMES (1450-1750)

The Low Countries	France	England
	Earliest surviving illustration of a carrack	1455-85 *Wars of the Roses*
'Laying-dry' of drowned lands		
		1509-47 *Henry VIII*
	1515-47 *Francis I*	
		Dissolution of monasteries
		Casting of iron cannon
Brussels canal completed		1558-1603 *Elizabeth I*
		Recoinage
		Increased use of coal
Mercator's map of the world 1572-1609 *Revolt of the Netherlands*		Brass manufacture established by Mineral and Battery Works
		Royal Exchange founded
		Spanish Armada defeated
		Lee's stocking-frame
Windmill-driven saw	1589-1610 *Henry IV*	Log and back-staff
Fly-boat	*Edict of Nantes granting*	*Steelyard finally closed*
Delft ware	*toleration to Huguenots*	Rails first mentioned in colliery

V. Europe in Early Modern Times (1450-1750) (continued)

A.D.	World Relationships of Europe	Italy, Spain, and Portugal	Central and Northern Europe
1600	*Foundation of East India Companies, England and Holland*	Accademia dei Lincei Galileo's telescope	Ribbon-loom (Danzig)
			1618-48 *Thirty Years War* Sulphuric acid made at Nordhausen
			Gustavus Adolphus intervenes in Germany *Siege of Magdeburg*
			1640-88 *Frederick William, Elector of Brandenburg*
1650			
		Piazza of St. Peter's, Rome, completed	Order-Spree canal
			Peter of Russia's first visit to western Europe
1700			Polhem's cast-iron rolling process
			Porcelain (Meissen)
		1740-58 *Pope Benedict XIV*	1740-86 *Frederick II, king of Prussia; attack on Silesia*

The Low Countries	France	England
	Dangon's improved draw-loom	1603-25 *James I* (*Union of Crowns*)
Twelve Years Truce		Coal used in glass-making
First known shipment of tea to Europe		Inigo Jones's buildings
Bruges-Dunkirk canal		*Statue of Monopolies*
		1625-49 *Charles I*
		Vermuyden's fenland drainage
	Briare canal completed	*Civil War begun*
	Flint-lock perfected	
Mezzotint		*First Dutch War*
		Pepys's diary
	1661-1715 *Personal rule of Louis XIV*	1660 Royal Society founded
		Boyle's *Sceptical Chymist*
	Rise of Colbert	*Fire of London*
	Elaboration of furniture	
	Cast plate glass	Flint glass
		Greenwich Observatory founded
	Languedoc canal opened	
	Vauban's fortifications	
	Versailles completed	
	1685 *Edict of Nantes revoked*; *flight of Huguenots from France*	Dome of St. Paul's Cathedral begun
	Pont Royal built	*The Revolution*
	Papin's steam-engine	Savery's 'fire-engine'
Dutch press introduced by Blacuw		*Campaigns of Marlborough*
		Tull's seed-drill
		Act of Union with Scotland
		Coke-smelting of iron by Darby
	Treaty of Utrecht	Newcomen engine
		Lombe's silk-throwing mill
	Iron-making processes analysed by Réumur	Zinc-smelting at Swansea
		Hadley's octant
		Kay's flying-shuttle
Musschenbrock's 'Leyden jar'	Mapping of France by tri-angulation begun	*Jacobite rebellion*
	École des Ponts et Chaussées	Carding-machine for wool
		Roebuck's lead-chamber processes for sulphuric acid

VI. THE INDUSTRIAL

A.D.	Britain		Continent
1750		50 Westminister bridge completed	
		51 Crucible steel commercially established	51 The Encyclopedia *commences publication*
	54 *Royal Society of Arts founded*		
	56 *Outbreak of Seven Years War*		56-63 *Seven Years War*
	57 *Clive's conquest of Bengal*	57 Sankey Navigation	
		58 Strutt's ribbed hosiery	
1760	60 *Accession of George III*	60 Smeaton's Eddystone lighthouse completed	
		60 Carron Iron Works	
		61 Worsley-Manchester canal opened	
		62 Harrison's chronometer No. 4 tested	
	63 *Peace of Paris*	62 Wedgwood's 'Queen's ware'	62-96 *Catherine II, empress of Russia*
		64 Hargraves's jenny invented	65-90 *Joseph II, Habsburg emperor*
		67 Rails cast at Coalbrookdale	
	68 *Cook's first voyage to the Pacific*		
		69 Arkwright's spinning-machine patented	
		69 Wedgwood established at Etruria	
1770	71 *Smeatonian Club founded*	70 Ramsden's screw-cutting lathe	
	74 *Excise on calico halved*	74 Wilkinson's boring-mill	74-92 *Louis XVI, king of France*
	75-83 *War of American Independence*		
	76 *Adam Smith's* Wealth of Nations	76 Watt's steam-engine in use	
	78-83 *War with France* (the *Maritime War*)	78 Bramah's water-closet	
		79 Iron bridge at Coalbrookdale	
		79 Crompton's mule perfected	

REVOLUTION, 1750-1800

of Europe	America
50 Thiout's lathe	
	52 Franklin's lightning con- ductor
57 Rhine bridge at Schaffhausen	
	59 *British capture Quebec*
64 Trésaguet's method of road-making	
69 Cugnot's steam road- carriage	
	75-83 *War of Independence*
	76 *Declaration of Independence*

VI. The Industrial Revolution, 1750-1800 (continued)

A.D.	Britain		Continent
1780			80 *Intervention of Holland in Maritime War*
	83 *Peace of Versailles*		
		84 Meikle's threshing-machine	
		84 Cort's introduction of puddling	
		85 Steam introduced in cotton industry	
	86 *Anglo-French commercial treaty*		86 *Death of Frederick II of Prussia*
		87 Cartwright's power-loom in factory	
	88 *Colonization of Australia begun*		89 *French Declaration of the Rights of Man*
1790	91 *Ordnance Survey established*		91 *Patent law in France*
	93-1815 *French Wars*	93 S. Bentham's patent for wood-working machinery	93 *Reign of Terror*
	93 *Board of Agriculture established*		
			94 *Lavoisier executed*
			94 *French conquest of Belgium*
			95 *École Polytechnique established*
	99 *Royal Institution founded*		
	99 *Trade unions made illegal*		

of Europe	America
83 Steam-boat *Pyroscaphe* on r. Sâone	83 *British settlement of Upper Canada*
83 First balloon ascents (France)	
84 Christian VII of Denmark's Eider canal	
85 Berthollet's use of chlorine in bleaching	85 *Jefferson, U.S. minister in Paris*
	86 'Sea-island' cotton planted
87 Leblanc's soda-making process	89-97 *Washington, President*
	90 *First patent law*
91 Metre defined by French Academy of Sciences	
93 Chappe's semaphore	93 Whitney's cotton-gin
94 Balloon used for observation at battle of Fleurus	
98 Senefelder's invention of lithography	
98 Guinand's glass-stirrer	
98 Robert's paper-making machine	
99 Lebon's coal-gas patent	

VII. THE INDUSTRIAL

A.D.	Britain		Continent
1800		00 Stanhope's iron printing-press	00 *Napoleon Bonaparte in power*
		00 Trevithick's high-pressure steam-engine	00 *Treaty of San Ildefonso*
		01 Trevithick's steam road-carriage	
	02 *Peace of Amiens*	02 Mechanized manufacture of pulley-blocks for navy	
		02 Steam tug-boat *Charlotte Dundas*	
		02 West India docks constructed	
		04 Telford's Caledonian canal begun	
		04 Trevithick's railway locomotive	
		05 Surrey Iron Railway opened	
	06 *Orders in Council (trade blockade)*	06 Gas-lighting of cotton-mills begun	06 *Continental System (trade blockade)*
		07 Maudslay's table-engine	07 *Serfdom abolished in Prussia*
			07 *French invade Portugal*
		08 Dalton's atomic theory	08-14 *Peninsular War*
		09 Heathcoat's lace-making machine	
1810	11-20 *Regency period*	11 Bell Rock lighthouse	10 *French frontiers extended to Rome and Lübeck*
	11-16 *Luddite riots*	11 Standedge canal tunnel	
	12-15 *American War*	12 Steamship *Comet*	
	13 *Sunderland Society for preventing accidents in coal mines founded*	14 Steam cylinder-press printing of *The Times*	14 *First overthrow of Napoleon*
		14 Stephenson's *Blucher*	
	15 *Battle of Waterloo; Corn Law*		15 *Second overthrow of Napoleon*
			15-48 *The Age of Metternich in Central Europe and Italy*
	16 *Bombardment of Algiers*	16 Davy lamp	
	18 *Institution of Civil Engineers founded*		18 *Beginning of Prussian customs union (Zollverein)*
	19 *Gold standard established*	19 McAdam's *Practical Essay on Roads*	

REVOLUTION, 1800-1850

of Europe	America
00 Voltaic pile	00 Whitney makes muskets with interchangeable parts
01 Jacquard loom 01 Achard's sugar-beet factory	01 Finley's patent chain-bridge, Pennsylvania
	04 Evans's high-pressure steam-engine
	07 Steamship *Clermont* on r. Hudson
10 Appert's meat preservation 10 St. Quentin canal opened	11 Steamship *Orleans* on r. Ohio
12 *War against Britain* 12 *Invasion of Canada*	
15 Edward's compound steam-engine patented in France	
18 'Draisine' (patented dandy-horse)	18 Blanchard's copying-lathe for gunstocks

VII. The Industrial Revolution 1800-1850 (continued)

A.D.	Britain		Continent
1820	20 *Accession of George IV*	20 Hancock's rubber masticator	
		22 Roberts's power-loom	
	23 *Salt excise abolished*		
	24 *Trade unions legalized*	24 Aspdin's Portland cement	
		24 Manufacture of 'mackintoshes'	
	25 *Emigration of artisans legalized*	25 Stockton-Darlington railway opened	
		26 Paris's thaumatrope	
		26 Telford's Menai bridge	
		27 First friction matches	
		29 Neilson's hot-blast	
		29 Stephenson's *Rocket*	
1830		30 Roberts's self-acting mule perfected	30-48 *Orleans monarchy in France*
		30 Liverpool-Manchester railway opened	30 *Independence of Belgium*
			30 *Cholera epidemic in Russia*
		31 Gurney's steam-carriage	
	31 *British Association founded*	31 Faraday demonstrates electromagnetic induction	
		31 Bickford's safety fuse	
		31 Phillips's contact process for sulphyric acid patented	
	32 *Cholera epidemic reaches London*		
	33 *Emancipation of slaves in British Empire*	33 Pattinson's process for silver-extraction	
	33 *First successful Factory Act*		
	33 *China trade thrown open*		
			34 Zollverein *became widely established*

of Europe	America
	20 Ithiel Town's truss-bridge patented
22 Iron paddle-steamer *Aaron Manby* on r. Seine	
	24 Erie canal completed
25 Seguin's wire-suspension road-bridge	
26 Nicéphore Niepce's first photograph	
27 Fourneyron's water-turbine	
27 Ghent ship canal	
28 Seguin's multi-tubular boiler patented	28 Danforth's throstle and Thorp's ring-spinning frame invented
	30 Stevens's inverted-T rail
	31 Morris canal completed
32 de Girard's flax-heckling machine	32 First horse-tramway in New York
32 Gotha canal completed in Sweden	
	33 Iron-smelting with anthracite patented
35 Brussels-Malines railway	35 Colt revolver patented

VII. The Industrial Revolution, 1800-1850 (continued)

A.D.	Britain		Continent
	37 *Accession of Queen Victoria*		
	38 *Royal Agricultural Society founded*	38 S.S. *Great Western* initiates regular Atlantic crossings	
	38 *Typhus epidemic in London*	38 Screw propeller	
	38 *Chartist movement begins*	38 London-Birmingham railway opened	
		38 Telegraph installed on railway	
		39 Nasmyth's steam-hammer	
1840	40 *Penny post instituted*	40 Elkington's electro-plating	40 *Liebig's* Chemistry in Relation to Agriculture
	40 *Colonization of New Zealand*		
	40 *Bombardment of Acre*	41 Fox Talbot's calotype	
	42 *Shaftesbury's Coal Mines Act*		42 Zollverein *patent convention*
	43 *Export of machinery legalized*	43 Brunel's Thames tunnel opened	
		43 Lawes's superphosphate factory	
	44 *Bank Charter Act*		
	45 *Royal College of Chemistry founded*	45 McNaught's compound steam-engine	
	45 *Excise duties on glass repealed*		
	46 *Corn Laws repealed*		
	46 *Standard railway-guage introduced*		
	48 *Mill's* Political Economy		48 *The Year of Revolution*
	49 *Navigation Acts repealed*		

of Europe	America
36 Sorel's galvanized iron	36 *Patent Office established*
37 Paixhans's shell-gun adopted in France	
	38 Bruce's type-setting machine
39 Daguerreotype	
39 Tunnel-kiln (Denmark)	
40 Roller-milling of grain begun in Hungary	
41 Dreyse's needle-gun	41 Goodyear invents vulcanization
43 Zola arched dam	
45 Schönbein's discovery of gun-cotton	45 Bigelow's Brussels power-loom
45 Rifled breech-loading artillery, Piedmont	
45 Heilmann's comb	45-49 *Presidency of Polk*
	46 *Mexican War*
	46 Deare's steel mould-boards
	46 Hoe's rotary press, Philadelphia
	46 Ether established as anaesthetic in operation
	47 St. Lawrence improvements completed, Lake Ontario-Montreal
	48 *California gold-rush*
	48 McCormick reaper factory-produced, Chicago
49 Krupp's steel gun tested	
49 Minié bullet	
49 Monier's reinforced concrete	

VIII. THE INDUSTRIAL

A.D.	Britain		Continent
1850	50 *Public Libraries Act*	50 R. Stephenson's Britannia bridge	
	51 *Great Exhibition (Crystal Palace)*	51 Dover-Calais cable successfully established	
	51 *Discovery of gold in Australia*	51 Lister-Donisthorpe machine-comb	
			52 *Napoleon III, emperor of the French*
	53 *Gladstone's first Free Trade Budget*		
	54-55 *Siege of Sebastopol*		
	54-56 *Crimean War*		
	55 *Newspaper stamp duty repealed*		
	55 *Metropolitan Board of Works established*		
		56 Bessemer steel	
		56 Perkin's discovery of mauve	
	57 *Indian Mutiny*		
		58 Arc light, S. Foreland lighthouse	
		59 *Great Eastern* completed	59 *Franco-Austrian war in Italy*
1860	60 *Anglo-French Commercial Treaty*		60 *Italy united (except Venetia and Rome)*
	61 *Paper Duties repealed*	61 First all-iron warship, *Warrior*	61 *Emancipation of serfs in Russia*
	62 *International Exhibition*	62 Steel rails	62-90 *Bismarck in power in Prussia and (71-90) Germany*
	63 *Alkali Act*		
			64 *German war against Denmark*
	65 *'Red Flag' Act*	65 Electrolytic refining of copper	
	65 *Last severe epidemic of cholera*	65 Atlantic cable finally successful	
	66 *Cattle Diseases Prevention Act*		66 *Austro-Prussian war*

REVOLUTION, 1850-1900

of Europe		America
		51 Bogardus's cast-iron frame-buildings
		51 Kelly's steel-making converter
		51 Singer's sewing-machine
53 Vienna-Trieste railway through Alps		53 Colt's armory (inter-changeable system)
	54 *First trade treaty with Japan*	54 Gesner manufactures kerosene (paraffin oil)
55 Deville's aluminum	55 *Maury's* Physical Geography of the Sea	55 Turret lathe
55 Bunsen burner		55 Roebling's wire-cable bridge, Niagara
55 Köller's tungsten steel (Austria)		
56 Three-high steel mill, Motala		
		57 Otis's safety elevators installed
58 Bessemer steel perfected by Goransson		
59 French ironclad, *La Gloire*		59 Drake's oil-well, Pennsylvania
59 Steam-roller invented in France		
60 Exploitation of Stassfurt potassium deposits	61-65 *Lincoln, President*	
61 Solvay's soda-making process patented in Belgium	61-65 *Civil War*	
	62 *Land-grant colleges*	62 Brown's universal milling-machine
	62 Monitor *in action*	62 Gatling gun patented
64 Whitehead's torpedo designed in Austria	65 *Massachusetts Institute of Technology*	
	65 *Abolition of slavery completed by 13th Amendment*	65 Atlantic cable finally successful
66 Chassepot rifle introduced in France		
66 Furens arch dam completed		
66 Nobel invents dynamite		
66 Siemens-Martin open-hearth steel		

VIII. THE INDUSTRIAL REVOLUTION, 1850-1900 (continued)

A.D.	Britain		Continent
			67 *Paris Exhibition*
1870	70 *Education Act*	70 Weldon's process for bleaching powder	70 *Franco-Prussian war*
			71 *German Empire established*
		72-76 World oceanographic survey by *The Challenger*	
	74-80 *Disraeli's second government; imperial expansion*		
	75 *Explosives Act*	75 London main drainage system completed	
		76 Contract process for sulphuric acid brought into use at Silvertown	77 *Full protection for patents in Germany*
		77 Rubber plants successfully established in Ceylon	
		78 Swan's carbon-filament lamp	
	79 *Board of Trade authorizes steel in bridges*	79 Gilchrist-Thomas basic steel	79 *Bismarck's first tariff increases*
1880			
		82 Kynoch's brass cartridge-case	82 *The Triple Alliance of Germany, Austria-Hungary, and Italy*
			83 *International patents convention*
		84 Maxim gun	84 *Charlottenburg Technical High School completed, Germany*
		84 Parsons' steam-turbine	
		85 Rover 'safety' bicycle	

of Europe	America	
67 Michaux manufactured velocipedes	67 *Dominion constitution of Canada established*	68 Armour's meat-packing, Chicago
		68 Westinghouse brake
69 Suez Canal opened		69 First trans-continental railway
69 Alizarin synthesized, Germany		
70 Gramme's ring dynamo		
71 Mont Cenis tunnel opened	71 *Chicago fire*	
73 Baku oil industry		73 Remington Company's typewriter
		73 Brayton's oil-engine
		74 Eads's St. Louis bridge
76 Otto gas-engine	76 *Centennial Exhibition, Philadelphia*	76 Bell's telephone
		76 Edison's phonograph
77 Reinforced concrete beams patented by Monier		
77 Frozen mutton shipped (Argentine-Le Havre)		
77 Laval's cream-separator		
79 Electric railway exhibited, Berlin	79 *War of the Pacific* (*Chile* v. *Boliva and Peru*)	79 Edison's carbon-filament lamp
		80 Half-tone block used in *New York Daily Graphic*
		80 Carnegie's first big steel furnace
82 St. Gotthard tunnel completed		82 Edison's Pearl Street generating station
		83 Completion of Brooklyn bridge
84 Magazine rifle adopted in Germany		84 Koller uses cocaine as anaesthetic
84 Electric trams in Germany		
85 Mannesmann's seamless steel tubes patented		85 Stephenson's rail-gauge standardized
85 Welsbach's gas-mantle		

VIII. The Industrial Revolution, 1850-1900 (continued)

A.D.	Britain		Continent
	86 *Nobel Dynamite Trust*	86 Severn tunnel opened	86 *Optical glass made at Zeiss works, Jena*
	87 *Golden Jubilee*	87 Cyanide process for gold and silver	
		88 Dunlop's pneumatic tyre	
		89 Ferranti's Deptford power station	
1890		90 First 'tube' railway	
		90 *Daily Graphic*, fully illustrated	
		90 Forth bridge completed	
			92 *Witte Finance Minister in Russia*
			92 *Meline tariff in France*
		94 Castner's electrolytic process for caustic soda	
	96 *Repeal of 'Red Flag' Act*		
	97 *Diamond Jubilee*	97 Parsons' *Turbina*	
	98 *Battle of Omdurman*		
1900	99-1902 *South African War*		
	01 *Death of Victoria*		

of Europe	America	
85 Daimler's first petrol-engine		
85 Benz's first motor-car		
86 Vieille's *Poudre B*		86 Linotype first used by *New York Tribune*
		86 Niagara Falls hydroelectric installation begun
87 Aluminum produced electro-lytically, Schaffhausen		
87 Steam-tricycle, France		
87 Laval's turbine		
88 Marey's *chambre chrono-photographique*		88 Eastman's Kodak camera
89 Eiffel Tower		
	90 *McKinley tariff*	90 First completely steel-framed building, Chicago
91 Trans-Siberian railway begun		
93 Benz's four-wheeled car	93 *World Exhibition, Chicago*	93 New Croton aqueduct tun-nel completed, New York
94 Kiel canal		94 Edison's Kinetoscope Parlor, New York
95 Cinema set up by the Lumières, Paris		95 First main-line railway electrified
		95 Northrop's automatic loom
97 Synthetic indigo made by Badische Fabrik	96 *Bimetallist election campaign*	96 Ford's first automobile
		97 Monotype printing established
97 Diesel engine successfully manufactured in Germany		
98 French '75' quick-firing gun	98 *Spanish-American War (in Cuba, etc.)*	98 Owens's automatic bottle-making machine
99 Dortmund-Ems Canal		
00 First Zeppelin launched		
01 Marconi begins transatlan-tic wireless telegraphy		
		03 Orville Wright achieves heavier-than-air, powered flight

"Highlights of 50 Years in R&D Management"

A Personal View

by

Maurice Holland

Maurice Holland

Present Position
Retired
436 Love Lane
E. Greenwich, Rhode Island 02818

Originator of Industrial Research Institute

Education
Lowell Institute   Mass. Institute of Technology   1916

Former Affiliations
1923-41:
National Research Council, Division of Engineering and Industrial Research Director, which included
the following activities:
    National Research Endowment, Special Assistant to Secretary of Commerce Hoover 1925-27
    World Engineering Congress, Tokyo
        Secretary American Committee 1927-29
    Chicago Century of Progress Exposition
        Director Science Advisory Comm. 1929-33
    Science Advisory Board, Liaison Officer with Department of Commerce 1933-36
    European Laboratory Tour for American Executives—Organizer and Director 1937
    New York World's Fair
        Advisory Committee Member 1938-39
    Industrial Research Institute, Promoter, Organizer, Executive Officer, 1938-40
    Research Advisory Service, Liberty Bank of Buffalo, Chairman, Science Committee 1939
    National Roster Scientific and Specialized Personnel 1940, Chairman, Evaluation Committee
        in Engineering
    South American Tour of Industrial Exploration (at request of Secretary of Commerce Jesse Jones),
        Organizer and Director 1940-41
1941-58
Industrial Research Adviser
Scandinavian Research and Industry Tour, Organizer and Director 1946
Silver Medal, Royal Academy of Engineering Sciences, Stockholm
Member, ECA German Mission 1951
Member, ECA French Mission 1951
Member, ECA Italian Mission 1952

Executive Assistant, Associates Program
Communications Research Institute
3908 Main Highway, Miami 33, Florida

Founders Award, Industrial Research Institute, 1955
Fellow, New York Academy of Sciences
Fellow, American Association for the Advancement of Science
Honorary Fellow, Industrial Research Institute
Fellow, American Institute of Management
Member, American Institute of Consulting Engineers
OX 5 Club of America (Fliers of Jennies in 1917)

Author
"Industrial Transition of Japan" (1927)
"Industrial Explorers" (Harper 1928)
"Profitable Practice in Industrial Research" (Harper 1932)
"Architects of Aviation" (Duell, Sloan & Pearce, Inc. 1951)
"Managements Stake in Research" (Harper 1958)
"Helpful Hints for Shell Hunters" Hawaiian Malacological Society

Specialization—Industrial Research Adviser on the Management level on matters of research policies,
organization, administration and "research audits."

Gearing technical research to sales and sales promotion.

FOREWORD

Maurice Holland is in the unique position of having observed at first hand and been deeply involved in the development of industrial research in the United States and abroad over the past half century. Few other men have had this experience.

Mr. Holland has undoubtedly done as much as anyone to induce American industry and financial institutions on a broad scale to invest in the process of converting basic scientific knowledge into profitable industrial usefulness. He coined many terse and applicable phrases now well known in the industry. In this case it was the process of making basic science "ring up in the cash register."

Mr. Holland's many contributions to the development of industry through the use of scientific research are referred to in other chapters in the book because his "Highlights of 50 Years in R&D Management" tells only part of his story.

Harold Vagtborg–March 1975

* * *

"Highlights of 50 Years in R&D Management"
A Personal View
by Maurice Holland

BACKGROUND

I have been living the history of industrial research growth and development for the last 50 years. That's quite a long span in anyone's mortality table. My vantage point to review the parade of progress was the high bench of the national center in Washington. While serving as Director, Division of Engineering and Industrial Research, National Research Council, we kept a close watch on significant trends in the national R&D structure. In fact I gave a paper on this subject, "The National Structure of Pure and Applied Science in the U.S.A.," at the first International Management Congress in Prague in 1924.

The Research Council, the operating arm of the National Academy of Sciences, was composed of about 400 men divided into 12 divisions covering all fields of science, engineering, and technology. This was a working, "shirt sleeve" group of dedicated men, selected by their respective science and engineering societies to represent their sector of national interest at the policy making level. The council was just what its name implies, a council with no authority to order any organization to do anything. Their only power was that of persuasion and self-interest.

The executive board of the council met once a month in the boardroom of the National Academy at 2101 Constitution Avenue. The monthly meeting of all chairmen of divisions met to report the current activities to the chairman of NRC, who was also a senior member of National Academy. In the early days our chairman was Gano Dunn, President, J. G. White Construction Company of New York. Incidentally, he was one of the Selection Committee of NRC to find a director for the Engineering Division, headquartered in the National Engineering Societies Building on West 39th Street, the location of most of the national engineers societies. We were the only division located in New York, all others were housed in the "NRC-Academy" building in Washington. They still are, as far as I know.

The primary reason for the New York location was to maintain continuous contact with research activities of about 30 engineering societies, their national secretaries, presidents, and prominent active leaders.

Our mission was to coordinate research activities of the engineering societies when two or more were involved on current projects. As I write, I can remember Gano Dunn's instructions to me as clearly as if he were sitting here now. "Holland," he said, "Dr. Frank Jewett, President of Bell Laboratories, one of our most distinguished members of the Academy, has agreed to serve as Chairman of Engineering Division, if Dr. Robert Milliken, Secretary of Commerce, Herbert Hoover, and myself can find a suitable candidate for the Director of the Division. We have agreed on you to meet with Dr. Jewett and if you pass muster with him, *you are in*! We will now go over to Jewett's office at the AT&T building for your inspection, and getting to know each other. You will hit it off with Jewett, I'm confident. General J. J. Carty, Chief Engineer at AT&T, tells me Dr. Jewett is one of the best picker of men in American technical industry.

"One or two points of briefing before we go," said Mr. Dunn in a kindly avuncular manner:

"One—low-key approach. Answer questions in short crisp sentences. Think before you speak.

"Two—no details on any subject he brings up, *unless he asks for them*. In five minutes he will be away ahead of you, getting ready for the next question.

"Three—he's a kindly, considerate man, this future boss of yours. His only criteria of measuring his close associates *is performance*. He would not be impressed if your father was Chairman of the Board of AT&T. What can you do in the specific job—now?

"Four—in NRC we have a saying, 'To act is easy—to think is difficult.'

"Five—also in NRC, we have 'a passion for anonymity'; let the other fellow take the credit for a job 'well done.' We will get our reward in the history books and records of NRC. They are the finest, most dedicated men in one group, in the country. I love them all.

"Six—finally, in the Engineering Division, you are the Director of Operations. Jewett is Chairman and he sets the policy and program. *Your job is to get it done*. General Carty remembers that you came to him last year, when you were making a survey of management methods at Bell Laboratories, DuPont, General Electric, Aluminum Company, and Edison's Laboratory at Menlo Park. Carty was impressed with your report to Colonel Bane, Commanding Officer at Engineering Division of Air Corps at Dayton. Carty, being a General in Reserve, checked up on it with Bane. Bane gave him a real good report; that's why you are here. Carty is Jewett's boss and his 'mentor.'

"Well, let's go over to see Jewett and if you pass, which I am confident you will, maybe Frank will take us to lunch!"

To telescope this long-winded story, the only justification for it is to indicate the background and authority with which I approach my task of putting on paper a personal view of the emergence of applied research institutes in the late 1930s and early 1940s, as one significant feature of "50 Years in R&D Management." In fact, their breakthrough of the crust of American industry surface *was almost volcanic*.

THE DEPRESSION ERA

In the closing days of the depression era, the early war years of the 1940s, the institutes sprang up like mushrooms, 50 of them in every cow pasture in Middle America, extending from Chicago through Kansas to San Antonio. This area was emerging from an agricultural economy to an "industrial incubator," where small, technically based companies were being developed to put the veterans of World War II to work. They came home assured that there would be new industrial companies—more than when they left to serve their country to save France singing the *Marseilles*. They went to war as their fathers did, in "the war to end all wars," said President Wilson. But this is Hugh Buhrman's story of "The Four Regional Institutes"—so expertly told and documented (a chapter in this book) by my old friend and colleague of the pioneering days, that it would be presumptuous of me to dot an "i" or cross a "t."

Hugh, with whom I worked in the institutional development of Midwest, Southwest, Stanford research institutes—and at the college of Engineering at New York University, is highly regarded as a consultant in management and institutional development by Harold Vagtborg, Tom Slick, Jesse Hobson, and Dean Thorndike Saville.

He should be; for years he was *senior staff member* of a New York professional fund raising firm, whose clients included many big name organizations from "GOP" Headquarters in New York to Yale University to Catholic Charities. I served for a time as member of the "Cardinal's Committee of the Laity." Al Smith was chairman in my time. He called himself "Sales Manager." We checked on Buhrman's firm. Its record was good! Why the diversion from our story of the research institute's development? We had used Hugh's firm, in money raising, *to compare our methods and results* with the best in the field of universities, hospitals, charities, and science institutions.

Science and religion have common roots—"faith in results." Who said that? One of my first bosses in NRC, Dr. Robert Milliken, Nobel Laureate. Milliken was research associate of my division chairman, Frank Jewett, when they were both working at the University of Chicago under Dr. Michelson, the first American Nobel Prize winner, in 1912.

To get back on the track of our story, if you are still with me, I want you to share with me the dramatic experience and fascination of history unwinding on the spool of life in the 1930s, 1940s . . . the most interesting period of what my friends called "a colorful career" in the world of R&D on the move.

The backdrop of our motion picture screen is American industry, emerging from the nightmare of the Depression years. Also, industry now was coming into the first phase of the American Dream of prosperity. War had brought with it high wages, full employment, and factories working night and day.

I visited a Chrysler plant in Detroit, which was turning out tanks with Liberty engines, on a location outside of town—where one year before only *a cornfield* stood. The American industrial machine was geared up, running high, turning out sophisticated mechanical monsters, similar to Henry Ford's automatic assembly line turning out Model T's in the pioneer days.

The manager of the Chrysler plant told the visiting committee from NRC Engineering Division, "That lunatic Hitler; he challenges American industry to a war on wheels and wings? We will beat the Jerries to the ground, when General Patton gets enough of these tanks and Jimmy Doolittle gets enough planes. Hitler, who burned the books, better reach for a bible, that's all I got to say." That was a prophetic mouthful, I say. Don't you agree?

We have had enough background, maybe more than you need, to become acquainted with the national environment in industry. Management's attitude toward R&D was negative. Negative, except for the "Big Four Hundred" of industry. In the late 1920s and early 1930s, the NRC's Directory of Industrial Research Laboratories in the United States was referred to by those in the R&D profession as the "Blue Book." The directory listed 300 laboratories with an estimated annual expenditure of $2 million.

That small base was the launching pad for the R&D rocket, put in orbit in pre-World War II days.

The success of the "Manhattan Project" as evidence of American industry's potential, followed by the explosion of the atomic bomb over

Hiroshima, which rattled the windows in every industrial executive office in the country, was the detonator on the R&D "bomb." This dramatic demonstration of applied science power blasted the theory of our smug complacency and propelled American industry into world supremacy. Were we ready for it?

The mobilization of basic science talent, mostly from our universities, was assisted by "European imports" Fermi, Szilard, Bohr, Hahn, and many more, who were on the American team. Hitler lost the war when he burned the books in front of the Reichstag in Berlin, books that once were men! The army of science, engineering, and industrial technology, which General Groves put together and lead with superb management skill, convinced top management that using good organization, planning, and modern techniques of R&D management was the most effective form of insurance for the growth and development of an industrial company. Also, the most offensive weapon was not only to win wars but to beat off competition, both from within the U.S. and from abroad.

In those early days of the 1930s, we were paying Germany $50 million annually for "imported technology," as I reported to the Secretary of Commerce on my return from the NRC tour of R&D in France, England, and Germany. Our report was titled "Behind the Scene in Industrial Europe." Each man on the mission (25 in number—industrial executives and five bankers from New York, Buffalo, Chicago, and San Francisco) wrote his own impression of the *current trends* in his industry field and made educated guesses of future trends,* trends which might affect American industry when World War II came along. The volunteer executives and bankers, including some presidents, vice presidents, and a few research executives, were selected by invitation by the Chairman of NRC. They spent six weeks in Europe, paying their own expenses as a public service to industry.

BIRTH OF THE INSTITUTES

As we said earlier, what we need now is a look at the "management climate" when the research institutes were born: their leaders; the regional needs for an institute with "research for hire," located in their own city, and sponsored by a hard core of community-oriented, dedicated men . . . men of imagination, vision, intestinal fortitude—sometimes called "guts"—and mon-

---

*Their report may still be available from NRC, Washington, D.C.

ey. These men who became trustees, such as J. C. Nichols in Kansas City, Athol McBean in Menlo Park, and Tom Slick in San Antonio, filled the prescription for a trustee—"one who must donate money, work, or political power," such as President Harry Truman, Trustee of Midwest and "proud of it!"*

I was invited to speak at that meeting by my old friend and colleague in the field of R&D management, the author of this book. The title of my talk was "Research, the Turbine of Progress." As an indication of the caliber of the men I met at our social hour preceding the dinner at Muehlbach Hotel, I was talking to a man I met casually, who was wearing a badge marked "trustee." I politely inquired with a side glance at his badge, "What is your interest in R&D as the owner of men's clothing stores in Kansas City, Chicago, and other cities, Mr. Rothchild?"

"Call me Louis, Mr. Holland," he said, with a firm, warm welcoming handshake. "Anything that helps Kansas City helps me and my stores. Research is people, is it not? Mostly men, I'm told. Men wear clothes, don't they? But seriously, R&D people bring 'class" to this town, a form of culture, a boost in the economy. Their children grow up here, they buy homes from J. C. Nichols—I hope. It's a two-way street. This R&D thing is the wave of the future. My son tells me, 'Get aboard, Dad. This is a fast-moving train, and research is the "GM" deisel locomotive pulling the train.' "

Mr. Louis Rothchild became Assistant Secretary of Commerce later, a move up in recognition of his "public service" to his native city. He was called to the national capital, where he further distinguished himself in the big league, "World of Business, U.S.A."

I told Dr. Vagtborg, sitting at the speakers' table, of this impressive episode and about several other VIPs I had met. I remember saying to him, "Harold, I never, in my long experience in Chicago, New York, Detroit, or Pittsburgh meetings, saw so much concentrated industrial management 'horspower-on-the-hoof' at one meeting—anywhere."

Harold observed with a broad smile, "Not many research institutes have a President of the United States on their boards and active in his responsibility. Truman is on a first-name-calling basis with most every man in this room. Harry never lets one of the hometown boys down," he said with justifiable pride.

---

*See Buhrman Report, pp. 183-218, telegrams of congratulations to his fellow trustees on the historic occasion of their first and second annual trustee meetings; addressed to Robert Mahornoy, Chairman of the Board of Governors.

If I were pushed to name some of the major factors which brought most of the research institutes to the surface as the fourth cornerstone in the national structure (the other three* being in place at the time), I would include these (drawn from the memory bank of M.H., as I am writing this in a southern retreat, far from it all, and feeling the need of a good reference library and some knowledgeable staff researchers).

Here they are as I see them:

- Industry location—present and potential. Two-thirds of all industrial laboratories listed in the NRC Blue Book were within a 50-mile radius of New York and New Jersey. The next largest concentrations were around Pittsburgh and Chicago.

    Then there were the wide open spaces. On the five-by-seven-foot map we had in our office, showing the exact locations, every laboratory was identified with a different colored pin to indicate the industry classification. Classifications of industries were taken from Department of Commerce official statistics, one girl in our office was charged with responsibility to keep it currently up to date. It proved very useful to certain government departments and agencies, especially in the war years.

- Availability of trained professional R&D people, resident or nearby.
- Aggressive management environment.
- Adjacent educational facilities for institute staff; while working at the institute toward earning advanced degrees.
- Men, money, and management.
- An "angel" such as Dick Mellon, Gordon Battelle, Tom Slick, J. C. Nichols, Athol McBean, and a few others.
- An experienced director, as they were called in those days, to conform to the code of the science community—such as Director of Bureau of Standards, etc.
- Or, a syndicate of devoted, enlightened community leaders, mostly businessmen and bankers, who had a stake in the economic growth of their city and their children's future.
- Men who were willing to stick their necks out and put their local reputations on the line!

Businessmen and bankers were beginning to learn that a well-planned R&D program operated by leaders with demonstrated performance records

---

*Industry, government, and trade associations . . . 50 of them then.

was the balanced investment mutual fund. An R&D mutual investment fund, in which the one-year projects were bonds; three-year projects, preferred stocks, and five-year projects were common stocks. Some stocks are as speculative as a roulette wheel when you pick a number. The odds are 36 to 1 in R&D roulette; even for DuPont, a table of return on investment in DuPont projects, as a *Fortune* article clearly demonstrates.

Their nylon project, for instance, cost $18 million, 12 years of work, and put the foundation of the modern textile industry in a test tube; replacing the shabby, antiquated, windowless mills which now blight the landscape of so many New England towns.

On preferred stocks, the three-year projects, the yield is higher and the risk less. It's called "defensive research," protecting present products and process with continuing improvements—"keeping up with the Joneses"—in competition.

Finally, the short term, "run-of-the-mill," one-year projects—the bonds—have the lowest yield of all. That type is the "storm cellar" for conservative players, fixed income for long pull. The New England textile tycoons are still sitting on their bonds and posing as gentlemen farmers and their sons go through the cycle of third generation—"from shirt sleeves to shirt sleeves!"

We have shared with you some of our personal impressions of the research institute movement, with a few specific examples, as I saw it happen.

There is a broad R&D highway of institutes—a Middle America "Route 128"—now running from Armour Research Institute (now IITRI) in Chicago through Midwest at Kansas City and down to Southwest Research Center in San Antonio, which is now spilling into the Gulf of Mexico at Corpus Christi, with ocean engineering projects for industry and government. "Applied science, engineering, and technology now begins at the water's edge." "The Endless Frontier of Science,"* as my M.I.T. classmate, "Van" Bush, so aptly called it some years ago. The earlier days of promoting research and development in industry could be called the "glacial period" on land.

SELLING INTANGIBLES

How to convince and persuade the small- and medium-size manufacturing company that R&D was the best form of insurance for orderly growth of the company, and to prove to them that through the use of R&D as a four-sided

---

*"Science: The Endless Frontier," a Report to the President by Vannevar Bush, GPO, Washington, D.C., 1945.

cutting tool, they could produce new and improved products, cut production costs, expand the markets through application engineers, and improve service to their customers. This was the problem I had to solve as Director of the Division of Engineering and Industrial Research of NRC.

I discussed the problem with our chairman, Dr. Jewett, and asked, "How can we use the example of big company research laboratories (Bell Laboratories, General Electric, DuPont, Aluminum Co., Gulf Oil, Goodyear) to *demonstrate* that R&D is as important to a small- or medium-size company as it is to a big one?"

Jewett said, "There are no road maps and there never have been. This was true, even in Boston, when Dr. Alexander Bell started the small laboratory of AT&T, which now serves as the technical foundation for 26 operating Bell Telephone companies; all of them are partners in the Bell system. We, in effect, are subsidized by an assessment of what amounts to royalties on the new products, new processes, and new materials developed in our laboratories. These laboratory results are then turned over to the Western Electric Company to manufacture in production quantities and field test the component parts under actual operating conditions."

There you have a basic outline of the formula for the organization and management of R&D operations, which was then followed by many of the leaders in the country. There are some minor variations in the *order of procedure* in DuPont operations; to serve the specific needs of the chemical industry or the Aluminum Company in supplying the raw material of powdered aluminum and other nonferrous alloy materials to the fabricators of kitchen utensils, airplanes, boats. Aluminum is now being used in structural beams of a bridge built in Pittsburgh, the steel manufacturing capital of the world.

AN ANALYSIS OF THE TECHNICAL ANATOMY OF INDUSTRY

Before undertaking the task of putting together a "How To Do Industrial Research" book, authored by the nation's leading R&D administrators, whose names are well known in business and industry, we made a searching analysis of the *patterns of success* in well-managed, technological-based companies. Conversely, we learned why old and tradition-bound industries had missed the technology boat. Here are some of the common denominators of case history experience accumulated through the years 1927-1937.

- The leaders in R&D were the applied science, technology-based industries (chemical, electrical, pharmaceutical, petroleum, non-ferrous metals, rubber, and aircraft).

- The tradition-bound industries were textiles, lumber, food products, iron and steel, railroads, fisheries, meat-packers, and paper products.
- Attitude of top management in the technical-based industries. Scientists and engineers were sitting in on all management meetings where policy was developed, where money was appropriated, and where long-range technical growth planning was dominated by the "Vice President of the Future." He was the man with facts and figures, who could persuade management to put their money into a new product then in a test tube in the laboratory, which would be rolling out of the plant in tank cars or trucks in three to five years.
- Management's evaluation of their V.P. in charge of R&D was based on "faith" in the "systems approach" of science to industrial problems and to the demonstrated past performance of their R&D team. *Give them the men and the money and leave them alone!*—that was the key to success.
- Many of the early R&D leaders in American industry had earned their advanced degrees in German universities. They had great respect for the country which had produced more Nobel Prize winners than all the leading industrial nations in the world.
- Our office used this information in a "war of nerves" technique and in speeches to American industry. Ammunition was accumulated through periodic inspection trips to Germany, France, and England. Reports, surveys, and industrial press articles were directed at specific industries in the U.S., which were lagging behind Germany—the world leader, until the late 1930s.
- It was typical of American industrial companies, when first getting their feet wet in R&D, to begin their operations with "strip mining." In other words, skimming the surface of the technological mine for the visible ore, which lay on top. Year by year, as they dug deeper and deeper from layer to layer, they would get down to the hard granite core of the technological mine. This was where the "diamond drill of basic science" bored deep and brought up the gold nuggets of major breakthroughs.
- Geographic location of industry and management's attitude varied considerably, from East Coast to West Coast; also from North to South. For instance, management engineers in New York charac-

terized New York's top management as "balance sheet operators," while Chicago's top management were "production oriented." New England lost the title of "Textile Capital of U.S.A." primarily because of poor management; poor marketing and blindness in the area of obsolete plants, equipment, and labor relations.

- The national map of industrial research centers first concentrated on the East Coast, moved to Pittsburgh and Chicago, then leaped the Plains states to the West Coast in 1937. I spoke that year to 30 directors of industrial research at the San Francisco Chamber of Commerce; the next day to 45 directors of research in Los Angeles. Today, there are more members of the National Academy of Sciences on the West Coast than on the East Coast. More important for basic science—the wellspring of all applied science and technology—there are more Nobel Laureates on the West Coast now than on the "Ivy League" sheltered East Coast. There are more technology-based companies on the "Peninsula" from San Francisco to San Jose than on Route 128, Boston's "Research Row."

- Finally, as a few specific examples of getting R&D started in small business, I will illustrate with three case histories extracted from the report of a seminar at the *Graduate School of Management, University of Hawaii*, at which I exchanged experiences with 60 R&D administrators from several countries around the Pacific Basin.

CASE NUMBER ONE

The Hudson Pulp & Paper Co., a small, family-owned and diversified company having plants in Maine and Florida, was considered by executives in the industry as very good in the management areas of merchandising and efficient, low-cost production. But according to a vice president in charge of sales, "The three brothers who are the owners and managers know nothing about research. It's a problem of education. I have tried it for some time, but with no success. Maybe an outside consultant is the answer."

The first step was to organize a research policy and planning committee, with the president as chairman. The committee met on a scheduled day each month, with representation from production, sales, finance, marketing, and engineering. The committee was set up with these objectives: On what are we going to do research? Do we want to be twice as big in five years in the same product fields we are now in, or do we want more diversification? Who is going to do the technical work? Shall we do R&D ourselves or farm it out?

What facilities do we have for doing technical work? How many technical men do we have in the company?

The personnel department made an inventory of all technical men, control laboratory people, and process engineers. In our Southern plant we discovered Ray S. Hatch, formerly Director of Research for Weyerhaeuser Timber Company. Hatch, who had retired to Florida, became bored with no technical activity and took a part-time job with Hudson to do some experimental work on his own.

He completed several experiments that yielded results which he thought looked most promising, but they became somehow misplaced after being sent to the New York office. He then submitted a report of an experiment which had showed real promise of an improved process for making tall oil, a product for which there was a ready market with prices rising. He had also applied for a patent on a process to substitute Manioca (made from maize) flour adhesive for animal glue, which was used in large quantities on gummed paper tape.

After several Hatch reports were received finally by top management, he was brought to the New York office as Director and Technical Advisor to Management. A small R&D staff was recruited from control laboratory and production engineering personnel. The R&D program was started with the sympathetic understanding of top management, which laid out major guideposts for future technical effort. At the end of the first year, Hatch submitted his first annual report, showing a return of $530,000 on an expenditure of about $150,000. His report was checked and audited by the accounting department.

In the second year, an additional laboratory was established at the plant in Maine to deal with mechanical problems of automatic machine napkin folding and packaging. Several new and improved products were brought out during this year. The Research Policy and Planning Committee continuously reviewed the company's major product lines and made comparative tests against competitors' products. Hatch, who sat in on every management meeting, was made Vice President in Charge of Research and Technical Advisor to the President.

Recommendations arising from this "case history" might include such items as: (1) mesh management thinking with technological potential; (2) select an experienced research executive with demonstrated performance, give him the money and men to do the job and leave him alone; and (3) insist upon establishment of a research policy committee with functions specified in writing, such as review progress monthly, establish project priorities, authorize appropriations, and approve annual budget, also supply R&D with "commercial intelligence reports" on product markets and trends.

CASE NUMBER TWO

The Vermont Marble Company, a family-owned New England business, was limited to a single product—marble—although there were many variations in color and natural design. The best illustration of use of this product was Colorado Yule marble, which the company used in designing and making the Tomb of the Unknown Soldier at Arlington Cemetery. A literature search by the Engineering Societies Library of all the references to marble down through the ages indicated that the only word that was synonymous with marble was cold—"cold as marble"—a familiar phrase which makes one think of cemeteries, marble slabs in morgues, and Grecian temples. One of the executives of the company summed up the primary problem: "Take marble out of the cemetery and bring it back into the home. We must find some way to warm it up!"

Some effort had also been made to use improved technical methods for cutting the cost of sawing and polishing. A professor from a New England university was retained as a consultant. He made magnified photographs showing crystal size, orientation, and light transmission. The company decided to make 20 sample sheets, each about 20 inches long, 10 inches wide, and ½ inch thick, of various kinds and colors of marble. These were sent to Dr. Matthew Luckiesh, Director of the Lighting Research Laboratory of the General Electric Company at Nela Park, Cleveland. When the scientists at Nela Park put high-watt electric lamps behind the sheets of marble, beautiful effects of natural color and design were developed, some resembling seashore scenes, some mountainous landscapes, and an infinite variety of decorative effects. The Nela Park staff arranged an exhibit for some of the leading industrial designers in the country. They were impressed with the great potential for illuminated marble panels in church altars, store fronts, motion picture ticket booths, and lobbies. The work at Nela Park was followed up by our "one-man research department," the university professor, who took samples to Mellon Institute to make further studies of crystal orientation and light transmission. Finally, under the trade name LUMAR, a nationwide advertising and sales promotion campaign opened up large-volume markets and a variety of new fields of application.

The next problem the company tackled was how to cut the cost of sawing large blocks of marble. The traditional method was to use smooth-edge steel saw blades and sand, which would gradually chew through the marble blocks. The company enlisted the technical assistance of their supplier of steel saw bands and worked with the Norton Company on the development of improved abrasive material. After some months of tests, supervised by the combined research laboratory staff of the steel and abrasive companies, a circular saw running at 13,000 rpm was developed that literally cut through blocks of marble as if they were butter. Research had performed two of its traditional functions: (1) it had developed new fields of application, and (2) it had cut production costs, making it possible to lower price against the competition of other stone products and thereby to open new mass markets.

CASE NUMBER THREE

The case of the National Blank Book Company, manufacturer of office supplies, loose-leaf notebooks, ledgers, and visual index files, was essentially the problem of a one-man research department in which the technical director was an inventive genius who had more than a hundred patents to his credit. Could his inventive technical talents be used as the core of a small organized R&D activity? A research policy and planning committee was formed to select technical projects which would wrap the research program around one inventive personality.

The owner-managers were technology-minded. They did not lock their lone-wolf inventor in a laboratory. Instead, they made him Director of Research, told him to classify the technical projects by fields of applied science and technology, and authorized him to hire a small staff—a chemist, a metallurgist, a mechanical engineer, and a couple of designers. The Research Policy and Planning Committee set out to explore every resource, to screen ideas from customers, suppliers, university laboratories, commercial and testing groups, as well as from independent inventors. Setting aside 2 percent of company net worth for research activities each year, the company took the lead in new products in a tough, competitive field. A dramatic, new method of making loose-leaf book bindings and rings was developed that cut costs so drastically that competition was forced to take a license or a licking. Formerly, the ring clasps had to be individually spot-welded in position by hand. With the new process, the back frame of parallel wires and clasps move through a machine where they are welded and formed in a continuous strip—in other words, made by the mile and cut off to size by the foot.

For more than two decades National Blank Book had brought hundreds of thousands of dollars worth of light green bond paper to be used in ledger and account books under the trade name of "Eye-Ease" paper. A market survey of user preferences and practices indicated that considerable improvement could be made with a "technical assist" from the large staff of the research laboratory of the principal paper supplier.

The research director, sales manager, and production supervisor of National Blank Book visited the executives and technical staff of the paper company and presented specific improvements required by customers, such as better opacity; improved erasureproof quality; improved color to ease eye strain in ledger, account, and stenographer notebooks. The delegation from National indicated that they were visiting the research laboratories of several leading paper companies to see what new products were being offered from their technical laboratory shelves. "Our customers," they said, "have been reasonably satisfied with the high quality of our products, but our line next year must demonstrate the fact that the office-supply business has now joined the parade of technological progress." As a result, the company received some new and much improved raw materials for their product from a technically alert supplier.

* * *

PROFITABLE PRACTICE IN R&D IN INDUSTRY

In the mid-1930s, it was decided at a board meeting of the NRC to collect all the speeches, reports, and all related material on profitable practice in R&D in industry,* as applied in actual practice to the organization and management of the nation's leading and most successful industrial laboratories. Since some of the vice presidents in charge of R&D were members of NRC's various divisions and some were members of the Engineering Division of the National Academy of Sciences, we had no difficulty in persuading these public-spirited men to share their experience and expertise with all who were willing to listen and learn from the "Voices of Experience," the name of a popular radio program at that time which indicated that our timing was right.

"Mike" Ross, a professional editor, was employed by NRC to edit, condense, and write the "case history story" of the philosophy of R&D in industry; the organization of a laboratory; selection of personnel; how much to spend annually; building a budget; gearing research and development to

---

*Holland, Maurice, and Malcolm Harrison Ross (ed.), *Profitable Practices in Industrial Research*, New York and London: Harper and Brothers, 1932.

sales and service; the university as a partner of industry for doing basic research; and the place of the trade association in the national R&D structure. Ross asked me to contribute a chapter on industrial research abroad as I had, some years before, spent a summer visiting research centers in England, France, Germany, and Czechoslovakia under NRC auspices.

We had much to learn from Europe in those days. In 1937, I reported to the Secretary of Commerce, as mentioned earlier, that I had documentary proof that certain nationally known companies were *paying annual royalties* to German, French, and Swiss companies to the tune of $50 million for "imported technology." I'd estimate now (1970) we *export* about $1.4 billion in technology annually, in earnings from licenses and royalties arrangements. We pay out about $100 million for imports. These figures are based on recent Department of Commerce reports. They are a significant item in the much-discussed international balance of payments today.

The technology gap between Europe and the U.S.A. then and now has more substance to it than meets the eye. In many fields of technology we lead the rest of the world in commercial, salable technology. In a few restricted areas of basic and applied research, I can think of some specific technology areas where England, France, Germany, Japan, or Sweden are leading our best efforts.

In the completed chapter, "Research Abroad," I rated R&D capability of the principal industrial nations in this order: Germany, United States, England, and France. I predicted that in 15 or 20 years there would be two changes in the list. In the forties and fifties, the list would read: United States, Germany, Japan, and England. I also remarked, "No tariff wall is a barrier to keep out commercial technology; science recognizes no geographic boundaries. Someday international meetings of scientists will succeed in 'One World of Cooperation . . . Not Competition,' where diplomats and politicians have failed." When that day comes, it will prove that President Lincoln, founder of the National Academy of Sciences in 1864, was prophetic when he said, "A nation or a house divided against itself will fall."

* * *

INDUSTRIAL RESEARCH ABROAD

In 1937, NRC organized the first tour of research centers in England, France, and Germany for executives and bankers. Limited membership was restricted to 35-40 as requested by our sponsors, the Department of Scientific and Industrial Research in England and the Ministry for Science in France, headed up by Jean Perrin. France was the first government in Europe to give cabinet rank "under Secretary of State" to national science affairs. Perrin was a distinguished scientist and a member of the French Academy, established by Napoleon—"The Immortals," as they were called. In Germany, our sponsor was the Verein Deutscher Engineers Society, headed up by an old friend and colleague at many international conferences, Dr. Matchoss. Matchoss was, for some 20-odd years, the perennial representative of Germany at all science and engineering meetings around the world. He was the author of *The History of Invention*, the classic reference book used in engineering colleges.

Our report of the NRC tour for industrial executives and bankers was published under the title "Behind the Scenes in Industrial Europe—1937,"* in which each member of the tour recorded his impressions of what he saw in the 60-odd research centers we visited in the three countries during our six-week journey. It might be noted in passing that all members of the tour were volunteers, who answered the call from NRC to contribute their time and money to this public service project.

As John Green, the then Director of the "Technical Assistance Section" of the Commerce Department, stated in the "Foreword" of "An Industrial Explorer Abroad,"† "this was the pioneering prototype of 'technical assistance' programs of the 'Marshall Plan' program—*in reverse*." The industries of the United States were the beneficiaries in those early days. Much of our highly publicized "modern miracles" of some big-name laboratories, were in fact, based on imported technology; for which we paid millions of dollars annually. The Germans, for instance, were willing to invest huge sums of what I call "patient money" and time in basic research during the 1930s, the applications of which appeared on the American scene, in the form of bright-colored U.S. postage stamps, printed with German synthetic dyes during the war years; synthetic rubber, produced before "Neoprene" was developed by Father Newland of Notre Dame University, who sold his patents to DuPont. The demand for synthetic rubber for tires on tanks, trucks, and planes were our number one R&D priority in the war years.

Dr. Fischer, who developed the "Fischer-Thrope" process for hydrogenation of coal, in a lecture which I attended at the International Coal Conference in Pittsburgh, remarked, "The least intelligent thing to do with coal is *to burn it*! First put your scientists to work in the laboratory and then extract every possible chemical component from it by physical and

---

*Available from NRC on request.
†Published by Southwest Research Institute in 1967. Limited Edition.

chemical means—use and sell them at high prices—*then* burn the residue in the form of briquettes; as the Ford Motor Company is now doing in Detroit."

The NRC sponsored book, "Profitable Practice in Industrial Research," was the first "Operations Manual" or "How To Do Research" book for many new technically based companies. Many groups of science-cooperative companies were being formed by highly specialized R&D men who preferred to own their own business rather than rely on the slow research progress controlled by an "organization man" within a large company. With the rumors of war and "crash programs" mentioned in the headlines almost daily, potential government contracts looked like a bonanza.

Some of these "war babies" survived on the business merry-go-round. When their operations became large enough, their stocks hit the "Big Board" on Wall Street. A few stayed the course and were referred to by the security analysts and market letter writers as the "Go-Go" boys of performance. One highly respected Wall Street firm brought out one of the *first technical mutual funds* "Science Preferred Securities," which included 30 or 40 companies. Their publicized laboratories were well known to the public and included such giants as the "House of Magic," where Dr. Willis R. Whitney and his associate directors Langmuir and Coolidge pulled many rabbits out of the hat; and DuPont, whose laboratories under the direction of Charles Stine, "beat the chemical swords of World War I into metal plowshares."

The research laboratories of General Electric, which geared its new product development to sales from the "House of Magic," used the familiar slogan, "Progress Is Our Most Important Product," on Floyd Gibbons's radio program, coast to coast. That phrase prompted me to seek advice from some Madison Avenue advertising friends on the successful technique of selling and marketing an intangible item such as R&D.

"How can we create an image comparative to General Electric or Du Pont, where research is the 'royal road to riches?' " I asked.

Their answer was, "Scare them! Make them realize that if they don't use research, their business will lose its markets, its volume, and could 'go down the drain,' unless they catch up with and surpass the products and processes used by their competitors both here and from abroad."

With some modifications of format and subject matter, I used both the "scare 'em" technique, as well as the "success image" in our selling and promotion campaigns.

My opening "ho-hum" crasher, in hundreds of speeches before business, bankers, and trade association groups went something like this: "You carry insurance on your factory buildings against fire and flood; you depreciate your obsolescent machinery; you pension off your employees; but you have *not insured your future business*, unless you have some form of R&D in which you invest 2 percent of net worth of the business—*in good times and in bad*.

"Figure out your total insurance premiums for one year, take the total amount and spend it each year on continuous development of new and improved products and processes to stay even with your toughest competitor. If you do not—your business is dead—put a lily on it; call in an undertaker, buy a black suit, you are on your way to the cemetery."

Who said that? "Ket" Kettering, Vice President of General Motors, the greatest salesman of science this country ever produced. I know—I worked with him for 20 years in NRC and on the Science Advisory Committee of the Chicago Century of Progress.

At the first International Exposition in which science was the central theme (Chicago, 1933), "Ket" sold Ralph Budd, Chairman of Union Pacific Railroad, the GM diesel locomotive—then on display at the "Expo" in Chicago.

"Ket" said to Budd, "That diesel will pull a train faster and cheaper with less turnaround time at the terminals in Chicago and San Francisco than those old 'tea kettles' you are now using. Mr. Budd, it's time to put the 'Iron Horse' in the barn and lock the door. You might have a chance to compete with the airlines, which now cross the country in hours, while your Pullman trains now take days."

Two or three years later, at a meeting of the board of directors in the GM building in Detroit, the vice president in charge of sales announced: "Gentlemen, our projections indicate we will sell $50 million worth of diesels to the railroads *this year!*"

"Ket," sitting in one of the back rows of the room, nodded his owl-like head. His eyes were beaming like headlights through his thick tortoise shell glasses. "Ket" made a single rejoinder: "Well, Mr. Sloan, I think our boys in the laboratory have answered your question on postwar planning. What are we going to make after the war is over, when we can't go on selling what we make now? I made a note then in my little black book, *'The vice president in charge of R&D in a company is the vice president of the future of his company.'*"

* * *

CHICAGO CENTURY OF PROGRESS

The Chicago Century of Progress Exposition demonstrated in the dramatic form of moving exhibits not only the wonders of the world of science and technology which benefited the man in the street and convinced him that science contributed to his daily life in the things he was eating, the clothes on his back, the house he lived in, even the utensils in his kitchen. New and improved products were being born in a test tube or on a bench in a laboratory every day by white-coated scientists seen bending over a microscope and peering at the "modern miracles of tomorrow," as Paul De Kruif so aptly titled his best-seller books of those times—*Microbe Hunters, Hunger Fighters*, and *Modern Miracle Makers*—a series of word portraits of great men of science, who were first in their fields.

THE TRADE ASSOCIATION FIELD IN R&D

The Trade Association field in R&D organization was in its infancy at the time of the "Chicago Exposition." Mr. Rufus Dawes, President of the Board of Trustees, was much interested in expanding the cooperative group R&D for specific industries. "Instead of 50 trade association laboratories in the leading industrial nation in the world, we should have 500 laboratories," he said. He urged the members of the Science Advisory Committee to use the experiment of public exposure (of both basic and applied science exhibits) to arouse the interest of businessmen and bankers, who were beginning to feel the effects of imported technology in the pocket nerve—their *"profit and loss statements."*

Mr. Dawes was a highly respected international banker. The "Dawes Plan" for rehabilitation of industrial Germany after World War I made several references to the fact that American dollars had rebuilt in Germany some of the most modern, best equipped and staffed laboratories in the world. "They are taking the bread out of our mouths, cutting down our exports, beefing up their international balance of payments, and they are *the world leaders in selling technology* to most of the major industrial nations. Gentlemen, it is your duty and your responsibility as members of the National Academy of Sciences and advisors to our government to reverse the flow of the tide of technology from the U.S.A. to the world.

"Our businessmen and bankers here in Chicago, who met the challenge of organizing and promoting this International Exposition with the pledges of support, not only with money on the line in the form of bond issues of many millions of dollars, but they are working every day in shirt sleeves in my office, to serve notice on American businessmen that 'Research is a paying investment, the best form of insurance for growth and development of a nation.' It was invented here in the U.S.A., by 'Yankee Genius.'

"Look through the history of earlier Expositions and read the names of the 'Great Innovators' in our industrial development. Who were they? Mc Cormick, with the reaper; Edison, with electric light and power; Sperry, with his 'Metal Mike'; and Kettering, a member of our committee who put the 'Iron Horse' of railroad fame in the barn of our Science Museum. His General Motors diesel will soon be streaking across the Kansas plains, traveling from Chicago to San Francisco in about 50 to 60 hours. The farsighted Chairman of the Board of Union Pacific, Averill Harriman, and the aggressive President, Ralph Budd, convinced some of us at the bank with this statement: 'We will soon have the equipment on our railroad to compete with the fast-coming airlines—they have speed, we have safety.' "

He made his point with a resounding slap on the boardroom table, that brought nodding members to attention. The Union Pacific Streamliners were the giant step forward for the railroad industry.

Mr. Dawes also had the answer to his plea for a trade association R&D laboratory, when the American Association of Railroads dedicated their cooperative industry laboratory as an integral unit of Technology Center along with the ever expanding Armour Research Foundation (now IITRI) in Chicago.

Speeches, articles, textbooks, and tours were all used in selling and promoting research in industry. I wanted to learn something more about marketing research and its potential for use in concentrating our fire power on the best markets.

In our continuous attempt to identify the major factors which "made friends and influenced" businessmen and bankers to stop talking about R&D in industry and to "put their money where their mouth was," I went down to C. C. Parlin in Philadelphia, the acknowledged "father of economic market research," for his advice and counsel.

Several of my advertising friends on Madison Avenue said, "Parlin knows *more* about *markets*, in *every city* and *county* in the United States, than all the agencies in New York. He can tell you, with maps and survey figures, the family annual income and buying power in any city in the country."

We know when he comes in to our office and sells our agency a two-color spread in the *Saturday Evening Post* for *$50,000 per issue*, that we had met a master salesman of intangibles. Past experience taught us that he *can deliver* the buying power of Mr. and Mrs. America families, the consumer. Go down to Philadelphia and see the 'Ole Man,' ask his advice," they urged.

"Mr. Parlin," I said as I handed him my card with the National Research Council title. I then stated my mission briefly. "Mr. Parlin," I repeated his name, "Benjamin Franklin, the founder of your magazine, once said, 'If you want to make a friend, ask him for his advice or borrow a book from him.' I am here to get *your advice* in selling and marketing research and development to the *hardheaded executives of American manufacturing companies*. Also I hope to influence investment bankers. 'They are beginning to think of R&D as the best security for long-term investment.' I am quoting Allen Lehman, senior partner in the Wall Street firm of that name, who said it at the closing session of a 'National Research Council Tour for Executives and Bankers,' which we just completed at Bell Laboratories last week." I paused to get a reaction.

"Yes," said Parlin. "I remember reading about that NRC tour of the General Electric, Kodak, Goodrich, Westinghouse, Gulf Oil, and Bell Laboratories. From the press coverage you received, I would guess you have made a *good start*. Lead those fellows on a loose rein, take them through those laboratories, let them ask their own questions, introduce them to the men who are now developing the new products which we will be advertising in the *Post* in two or three years. I've met some of them, such as Dr. Whitney at GE, Mees at Kodak, Kettering at GM, Stine at DuPont, and Jewett at Bell Laboratories. They develop and manufacture the new products . . . we sell them. We are on your team. You have to sell the products at a profit and 'ring it up in the cash register' to have more money for *more research*," Parlin said as he reached in his desk to pull out a sheaf of city maps.

"Take Cleveland, for instance, the Shaker Heights Section," he said. "The high income family budget there means three children in college, Cadillacs in the garage, electric kitchen appliances, and fur coats in the Mrs.' closet. The other end of town," he continued pointing to numbered blocks nearer to the city, "that's Ford or Chevy territory, Sears-Roebuck merchandise, and the movies once a week."

Parlin looked up to see how much of this lesson in *commercial economics* was being absorbed by his engineer visitor from NRC. I submit this bit of evidence, that is now being dredged up from the "Memory Bank of MH," to our readers as the basic training I received from the *Saturday Post* marketing "Old Master." The C. C. Parlin Annual Award for the "Outstanding Marketing Man of the Year" was presented last year to Robert Keith, who is now Chairman of the Board of Pillsbury Mills, Inc. Keith was one of the bright and up coming young men in the marketing department of Pillsbury, when I did my stint there for 10 years, 1941 to 1951, as Research Advisor to Management.

Parlin convinced me that the NRC executive and banker tours through nationally known laboratories was the most dramatic and effective promotion technique.

* * *

BANKER INFLUENCE

A few paragraphs ago we mentioned the banker influence on building confidence in companies with well-organized and managed R&D operations. I share with the *American Bankers Association Journal* some credit for this groundswell of interest in the early days.

In the late 1920s and early 1930s, I wrote a series of articles for their monthly house organ, with such titles as "From Discovery to Dividends," "The Romance of Research," and the clincher was an article in which (for the *first time in public print*) the term "Technical Audit,"* was *coined* and *used*. I happen to remember this because Arthur D. Little of Cambridge, Massachusetts, came to me to testify as an "expert witness" in a lawsuit, which had been filed against them by a Dayton, Ohio, consulting laboratory, which was attempting to secure a copyright on the name. When authenticated copies of the *Bankers Journal* were presented in court, the case was dismissed. As far as I know, the term "Technical Audit" is still in the realm of Public Domain.

Now it's time to take some of the mystery out of management and organization of R&D in industry. Comprehensive surveys, studies, and analyses were *continuously* being made by NRC. Much of this data has since been collected and published periodically by the National Science Foundation in recent years. Our division of NRC surveys of *productivity per man* in industrial laboratories were made periodically. We collected vital statistics on every laboratory listed in the Blue Book. All data submitted by individual companies were held to be confidential, as to source. All our published reports, articles, and speeches dealt only with *industry averages*; such as the

---

American Bankers Association Journal (June 1927).

number of professional scientists and engineers; the number and title of "Technical Assistants"; the number of people in administration; and finally, the name and title of management executive in the front office to whom the R&D laboratory reported.

For instance, confidential reports from the presidents of 100 representative companies (large, medium, and small) in all fields of industry and located from coast to coast geographically, indicated quite clearly that with severe cuts in budgets and heavy personnel layoffs during the Depression 1930 to 1934, they could report, "No loss in productivity!"

My on-the-ground spot checks confirmed management's report. Their explanation was simple and made sense. One tough executive reported: "We got rid of the dead wood we had been accumulating for years. Number two, the men still with us are now working nights, on their own time. Too many men who could not 'cut the mustard' are out there on the street—with no mustard on their hot dogs!"

* * *

INDUSTRIAL RESEARCH INSTITUTE

We have now set the stage for the star performer in "Management of R&D" which was to appear in the spotlight of center stage. The backdrop scenery was sponsored by that "great producer"—*National Research Council*. The *Industrial Research Institute*, was established in 1938 by NRC for improvement in organization and management of R&D in industry. Its statement of "Purposes" was circulated to 1600 industrial laboratories and listed in the NRC Directory. Those purposes were to:

(1) promote, through the cooperative efforts of its members, improved, economical, and effective techniques of organization, administration, and operation of industrial research;

(2) develop and disseminate information as to the organization, administration, and operation of industrial research;

(3) stimulate and develop an understanding of research as a force in economic, industrial, and social activities; and

(4) promote high standards in the field of industrial research.

Vannevar Bush, of MIT, then was our fifth division chairman. He was preceded by Jewett, Elmer Sperry, Charles Kettering, and Dugal S. Jackson (Head of the MIT Electrical Engineering Department).

As a result of our survey, with an NRC invitation to join as members, about 100 companies indicated a willingness to join. Annual dues were set at $250 a year, with the condition that two years in advance dues be paid with their application. Fifty or 60 checks came in—things looked rosy—for a while. Then the steepest depression in business history was reported by the *Wall Street Journal*.

Memberships were canceled and checks reluctantly returned. At its first meeting, *only 14 loyal members of IRI* appeared at the Engineers Club in New York. Robert Colgate, VP for R&D of that highly respected family-controlled business (Colgate, Palmolive, Peet), was sitting at the head of the table—the first *chairman of IRI*.

But the story of IRI, its growth and development up to 240 member companies, was well documented and told by Tom Vaughn, Executive Vice President of Pabst Brewing Company, at the twenty-fifth anniversary meeting of the institute, held in San Francisco in 1963. It was titled "First Twenty-Five Years Are the Hardest."

I could go on with this "Horatio Alger" story from rags to riches that would include the details of the birth pains, teenage struggles, and college of "hard knocks school," attended by the 240 company members whose laboratories perform a majority of all R&D being done in the United States. Three powerful industrial science management groups tried to strangle the "baby in the cradle." Others tried the "merger syndrome" to get under NRC auspices. We were not buying. More sophisticated groups urged some of our bright young men in IRI to get out from under the old "mossbacks" in the Academy and Research Council. "Join the up-coming 'Go-Go' boys in Modern Management," they proclaimed.

Right or wrong, the men who successfully steered the ship of IRI through the shoals of rough waters in business and avoided false lighthouses tied to cow tails (an old Block Island, R.I. custom). These dedicated men who directed the course of IRI in the R&D management movement could not have done better, even if they had the benefit of Sperry's "Metal Mike" aboard.

The NRC concept and objective in organizing, promoting, and sponsoring IRI was to organize a national cooperative group of top R&D administrations in all fields of industry, in all sizes companies, and located geographically in all regions of the country. Through their cooperative efforts during three-day meetings each year, its members would derive methods to improve productivity and develop new forms of organization and operation. The prime target was to bring all companies up to the level of efficiency and productivity of the national leaders. IRI serves as a "Gallop Poll" of vital statistical trends in industry, which could be used at the policy making level in Washington.

The *potential power* of IRI, as the bridge between government sponsored and funded R&D and that sponsored and funded by industry, was in the ratio of one-dollar-government versus two-dollars-industry until the beginning of World War II. During the crash R&D programs of government, focused primarily on atomics, aircraft, space technology, and military hardware, the ratio became two-dollars-government to one of industry. Under this national policy and program, the industrial "fall-out" of by-products of R&D are reduced to slim pickings for business and the national economy, through industrial growth.

For instance, NASA mobilized a 400,000-man team for basic research from universities, applied research from industry and research institutes, and the staff facilities and know-how of 20,000 subcontractors to bring back a $25-billion bag of rocks. More important, we *tied up for 10 years* the technical talent, which could have made the earthbound taxpayers "better fed, better sheltered, and better Americans."

The IRI is still one "balance wheel in the watch on the Potomac," in combination with the National Academy of Sciences and the National Academy of Engineering. IRI is the "grandson" of the Academy of Sciences; also, the "son" of NRC; a third-generation child of an aristocratic science family. I have assurance from some optimistic old timers who are still around that they hope "IRI" will *not follow* the tragic fate of New England tycoons, in going from "shirt sleeves to shirt sleeves" in three generations—during the "shell-shocked seventies!"

Turning our attention once more to Washington, where national R&D policy is made, my service with NRC took me through the administration of six or seven presidents, from Wilson to Eisenhower.

Let me make it clear that the National Academy Council has no political bias; it does have considerable prestige and privileges under its Congressional Charter. The continuous financial support, supplied by several well-heeled science foundations, has shielded them from financial pressure.

The President of the United States is the "Commander in Chief of the Army of Science and Engineers," all of whom are at his service and that of his department heads. Assistance in science and technical matters is freely given *when requested*. Members of NAS-NRC serve their country without compensation.

* * *

INNOVATION–KEY TO TOMORROW
INDEPENDENT INVENTOR–SILENT PARTNER OF R&D

R&D has been the status symbol of American industry for the last 25 years. Research and Development is now organized, automated, and computerized in teamwork cells. Systems approach to find the solution to R&D problems is the order of the day. Charles Kettering called the R&D process "Trouble as an approach to Research." Speaking at a meeting of executives in a non-technical industry, Kettering said, "Get out a pad and put down on paper every trouble and problem you have in your business. Then go to work on them one by one. There is no use spending a nickel on research unless the management can see why it is worthwhile. All research work should reflect on the products your company makes and sells. Research is a five-sided cutting tool. It should: one, reduce cost of production; two, reduce operating costs to the user; three, increase utility of the product; four, increase its sales appearance; and five, produce new business."

It is reported that 15,000 manufacturing companies now spend $15 billion a year on R&D, according to National Research Council, National Science Foundation, and other authoritative sources. R&D is a "growth industry" in itself, with an average annual increase of 5 percent in dollar investment over the last 20 years. In the late 1920s, the National Research Council's "Directory of Industrial Research Laboratories in the United States" listed 300 laboratories and an estimated annual expenditure of $200 million. A bird's-eye view of support for the R&D industry indicates the comparative division of *source of funds* in recent years in this order: government, 60 percent; industry, 35 percent; universities, 3.6 percent; and nonprofit institutes, 1.1 percent. By *performance* of R&D the picture changes to: industry, 65 percent; government, 14 percent; universities, 13 percent; and nonprofit institutions, 3.7 percent.

Let's pause a moment for a backward glance at Thomas A. Edison, the father of industrial R&D, and look over the shoulders of his staff of 75 skilled craftsmen laboring in the laboratory at Menlo Park. One might say that Edison was the patron saint of all backyard inventors, planning what he called an "invention factory." He said, "I will have the best equipped laboratory extant and facilities, superior to any other for rapid and cheap development of inventions."

The research cost of R&D projects is conceded to be a mere 5 percent of the total cost. Edison did not underestimate the "D" factor when he made this prophecy recorded in his notebook, "Working the invention into commercial shape with models, patterns, and special machinery here in East Orange, is unique; there is no similar institution in existence."

Edison's inventions went to market as commercial products. They formed the basis of new industries: electric light, storage batteries, dictating machine, and electric power generation and distribution systems. Many industrial giants have been welded together under the control of parent companies which bear his name in New York, Boston, Detroit, and Chicago.

Robert Goddard, another silent partner of R&D, launched his first liquid fuel rocket on March 16, 1926, and fired the missile at Auburn, Massachusetts. It leaped 41 feet in the air and traveled 184 feet, with a speed of 60 miles an hour. From these small beginnings, man and science, engineering, and technology have taken giant leaps forward in our lifetime.

During World War I, I was a flying officer at McCook Field, Dayton, Ohio. I had the honor of accompanying Orville Wright on the trip from Washington to the dedication of the Wright Memorial at Kitty Hawk, North Carolina, in 1921. Ed Aldrin, father of "Buzz" Aldrin, was Director, Air Force Officer School for Management at McCook Field.

We pause briefly here in silent tribute to some of the pioneer-innovators, the garage and garrett inventors who were first. They were the giants on whose shoulders man was propelled to the moon! We can add the name of Igor Sikorsky, who pioneered rotary-wing aircraft in this country, in the roster of the elite inventor-innovators. His helicopters have born fruit from the seeds of scientific genius, both in civilian and military fields of application. The inventor-innovator is one who combines the rare talent of entrepreneurs, such as Edison, Sperry, Kettering, and Land. Inventor-innovator is the word portrait of a man who has the vision, courage, and determination to turn a pale grey thought in his mind into long green in the cash register.

Many of them are natural born showmen and supersalesmen. "Selling a new idea to the production men in the factory is the toughest endurance contest in the world," said Kettering. He should know, as "Ket" was acknowledged to be the greatest salesman of science to industry in the country, by common consent of his contemporaries.

The independent inventor is not confined to the garage, the attic, or toolshed these days. Many silent partners may be found in the Bell Telephone, DuPont, General Electric, Aluminum Co., Goodrich, Monsanto, and other leading laboratories throughout industry. They are usually segregated from formerly educated professional scientists and engineers. They work in a secluded corner of a laboratory, behind temporary plywood partition walls. They follow the "Edisonian" method of trial and error, with experiments, models, and handmade special machinery. Sometimes there is a playful sign on the entrance door—"Keep out! Genius at work. Miracles we perform daily. The impossible takes a little longer."

Sperry started experimenting in a barn at his aunt's home in Cortland, New York. She called him "Aunties Old Fusser." Today there is hardly a ship on the seas or an airplane in the sky which does not sail or fly more safely because of his innate certainty that he can improve on anything. His gyrocompass and mechanical helmsman, which he refers to as "Metal Mike," has been installed on practically all ships throughout the world and insures, with assistance of nature herself, a straight course to port.

Sperry is conceded to be the last of the old-style inventors, a man who played a lone hand, who charted unsailed seas, whose miracles were the result of his own groping and flashes of genius. "The ability to invent," Sperry said, "is something that I feel is born in one. I am not sure it can be acquired." He once said at a dinner held in his honor, "My work has been a source of the keenest joy. In the thrill of the work itself, I have always felt that I have had my share of reward." Sperry had an intuitive mind. As an engineer he had no trace of what he called "the engineer's horror of a hunch." He preferred to be known as a research worker. Today companies are operating on the basis of his patents in all parts of the world, and of many of them he had not the slightest knowledge.

The Sperry-Rand Company, known today as the "Synergistic Company" to TV viewers, flashes on the screen dramatic pictures of automated farm machinery and computerized machines, which the FBI uses to find the fingerprint of a bank robber amongst millions on file in Washington. The TV message would bring a nostalgic grin to Sperry's face when the announcer concludes his sales pitch with the intriguing challenge, "Wait till you see what we do tomorrow!" Tomorrow came for Sperry a few years ago as he was lying on a hospital bed in Brooklyn, in July, during a summer heat wave. His son, Elmer Jr., was at his bedside. "A chip off the old block" young Elmer had put a chunk of ice in a basin with an electric fan behind it to blow a cooling breeze on his father. The "old man" gave his last order. "Elmer," he croaked, "put some water in the basin, then you will have a larger cooling surface. Big improvement on first model!"

As the silent and junior partner of the $15-billion R&D program of recent years, the inventor-innovator has been credited with more than half the

60 major technological breakthroughs,* in this century. Some of these little ideas which went to market in recent years were Xerox office copy machines, the ball point pen, cellophane, tape recorder, zipper, the helicopter, and home air-conditioners.

On a cost efficiency basis, the productivity of manpower and money invested in them, five innovative companies ring up impressive records in earnings. For instance, Polaroid, 13.4 percent; 3 M (Minnesota Mining and Manufacturing), 14.9 percent; IBM, 17.5 percent; Xerox, 22.5 percent; and Texas Instrument, 28.9 percent. The significance of their *average percent growth* and their earnings was not overlooked by traders on Wall Street, where their symbols flashed on the Big Board; they lead the parade of glamour stocks. Any company name with "ionics" included were the favorites of the "in crowd."

For all the millions of dollars invested and manpower employed by the nation's research-oriented corporations, a surprisingly large percentage of new ideas has come from "little guys." A panel of distinguished R&D administrators submitted a report to the Secretary of Commerce in 1967.† The report, which was widely circulated amongst members of the Administration and Congress, has been repeatedly quoted. And its substance, "Key to Innovation: Loosening Reins on the Backyard Inventors," has provided ammunition for crusading groups; from the Smaller Business Association of New England in their "1969 Proposals for Congressional Action" to university professors—John Jewkes, R. Stillerman, and D. Sawers—whose study, *The Sources of Invention*, was cited in the "Charpie Report" to government. Their study provided documentation for some of its recommendations. The report of the panel pointed out, "While the independent inventor of a small technologically based company, typically, has a great commitment to an idea or change in general and is lean enough to capitalize on them quickly, the chief problem is first attracting venture capital, then in managing the business as it grows, and finally, in marketing the product. New ideas in large organizations," the report went on to say, "face such barriers as inbreeding, which often kills good projects. The entire entrepreneurial spark, the stressing of risks versus costs and potential antitrust problems are additional burdens the large companies carry."

---

*Jewkes, J.; R. Stillerman; and D. Sawers, *The Sources of Invention*, New York: St. Martin's Press, 1958, pp. 72-78.
†*New York Times*, May 14, 1967, section 3, p. 1.

Among other recommendations which the panel made, one which goes to the core of the matter, is as follows: "The Department of Commerce should broaden its studies of the innovative and entrepreneurial processes by initiating an integrated program in cooperation with universities to develop the latent innovative and entrepreneurial talents."

Today, men who follow the Edison and Sperry tradition and methods represent "Yankee Inventive Genius" at the grass roots. They work quietly in their "do-it-yourself" laboratories. Their progress from invention to new product development to successful growth companies is unknown to the public until their securities finally appear on the Big Board on Wall Street, then the news is out!

Speaking of Wall Street, the name Polaroid is symbolic of the glamour stocks. Its name is bandied about in discrete whispers and low-toned tips in brokers' offices. The name and the creative innovator-entrepreneur, Edwin H. Land, is seldom seen in print.

Ed Land, who developed the Polaroid Camera shortly after graduating as an "A" student in science at Harvard, bucked Eastman Kodak, General Analine Film, and several of the industrial giants in the field. He started in a modest laboratory and shop in Cambridge in the early 1930s—40 years after Edison's pioneering work in motion pictures. Land had moderate success and gradual growth until World War II came along. Then military demand for high resolution of detail for aerial reconnaissance took first priority. Much of the basic research and development connected with the production of military hardware was adapted by what is known today as "technological transfer" to new commercial products and applications. Land maintained an excellent R&D laboratory through all steps in the development of Polaroid Company.

In 1965, Land was awarded the Industrial Research Institute Gold Medal, with a citation which read: "For his exceptional success in combining creativity and entrepreneurship; his contributions to industry and the public welfare; and his scientific achievements in physical optics and chemistry."

* * *

WORLD WAR II: TECHNOLOGY EXPLOSION!

Polaroid's development from a small technical-based company before World War II, competing with the such solidly entrenched leaders in the photographic-products field as Kodak and Agfa, which was a significant illustration of hundreds of small companies supported by government contracts and crash programs providing the subsidy through which invention creativity, innovation, and entrepreneurial drive, met the high-priority demands of the military services.

"Necessity is the mother of invention" may be an old cliché . . . but there is no doubt that R&D was the "father" who led the family of free nations to victory. No less an authority on winning wars than Joseph Stalin, of the USSR, publicly acknowledged in his memoirs: "It was *not* the superior number of infantry divisions, nor planes, nor tanks of the Allied Armies that won the war; but the great American industrial machine, supported by thousands of laboratories located in every sector of that great country."

The partnership of independent inventors and organized industrial R&D during World War II was joined at the summit in Washington, where Charles Kettering, referred to earlier as the "Monkey Wrench Scientist," was appointed Chairman of the National Inventor's Council. Vannevar Bush was his "opposite number" as Director of the Office of Scientific and Research Development.* Both of these national leaders reported directly to President Roosevelt.

Vannevar Bush, '16, in the lobby of the new Center for Materials Science and Engineering, Massachusetts Institute of Technology, during its dedication (1965).

---

*Bush, Vannevar, *Pieces of the Action*, New York: Wm. Morrow Co., 1970.

Reports issued by the Inventor's Council indicate that of an estimated 300,000 inventions, which were submitted by independent inventors, 120 of them passed through review and analysis by the military services and were finally evaluated as prototypes in field tests. Four or five of these inventions included radar, amphibious-tank, proximity fuse, and inertial guidance, which were later credited with "making substantial contributions to winning the war."

Simultaneously, with Kettering's efforts, Bush was organizing, staffing, and expanding the R&D "army," the OSRD, with high-priority manpower rating. The highest quality science, engineering, and technical talent in the nation was mobilized. Early in the war, the OSRD operations were extended to Europe to draw upon the full science and technology resources of the Allies. Bush appointed Dr. James Conant as his Deputy Director in London, to maintain personal contact with the United Kingdom and our allies on the continent and, through technological intelligence, kept an eye on Germany!

The NRC European Tour for Executives and Bankers laid a foundation for an analysis of technological trends in Germany, France, and England *in 1937*. Our mission of industrial executives, bankers, and research administrators brought home a report, "Behind the Scenes in Industrial Europe," which answered the questions: What has industry in Europe achieved in advance of American industry? How? Where? When?

Waldemar Kaempffert, Science Editor, *New York Times*, sums up our objectives in the Foreword of the "Brochure-Invitation," which we sent to 400 top-management executives in a dozen industrial fields in which European industry was acknowledged to be leaders. Kaempffert, a member of the tour Advisory Committee, said in part:

"Germany has her 'buna,' we our 'neoprene.' Both are synthetic substitutes for rubber. At Leuna, Germany, and Billingham, England, chemical plants are to be found where hundreds of thousands of tons of coal a year are converted into lubricants and gasoline.

"There are great works in France where steel is cast into guns and armour plate by methods not essentially different from those with which we are familiar. There are also research laboratories in France where retorts, spectroscopes, centrifuges are to be seen which agree in general design and purpose with their counterparts in the United States, Great Britain, and Germany.

"And yet the application of science is different abroad. It is different because the problems that the laboratory technicians are called to solve are different. High tariff walls, a deliberately cultivated nationalism, the fear of an inevitable war have bred a desire for economic self-sufficiency. And it is to science that Europe turns for guidance in this new situation. New materials, new processes—it is the laboratory that must find them.

"We have here one main reason why the Division of Engineering and Industrial Research of the National Research Council has organized a tour of European university, government, and industrial laboratories. Obviously lessons are to be learned that cannot be learned at home because our industrial problems are different."

Behind the scenes here at home, the highly classified "Manhattan Project," with its orchestration in a "science symphony" of imported scientists; Fermi from Italy, Bohr from Denmark, Hahn from Germany, Szilard and Teller, and others were feverishly at work under direction of Oppenheimer as Science Director and General Groves as Manager. Together they put in place the foundation of the Atomic Age.

The bomb blast over Hiroshima stopped Japan's war machine, saved hundreds of thousands of American lives, and put an end to her plans for "Co-Prosperity Era" expansion in the Pacific—at least temporarily.

Our investment of $2 billion in the atomic bomb is still questioned by the Monday morning quarterbacks. I would remind the "Doubting Thomas" that recent estimates clearly indicate that the "fall out" from the bomb explosion, which has taken the form of industrial applications from power plants to food processing, to medical and drug technological breakthroughs, shows a 4 to 1 return in every dollar spent. Moreover, the bomb was the trump card in winning the World War II "game plan." We paid a small premium on our life insurance policy which has served as a deterrent to our enemies during a quarter of century of Cold War.

R&D is the core of our "Trillion Dollar Gross Product" on which we pay an annual premium of $25 billion. In terms of return on investment that works out to 40 to 1. Our little "black navigation box," which opens ports of trade around the world for American goods and services is R&D management.

The Atomic Age brought on the urgent necessity for a delivery system for atomic weapons in war and industrial applications in peace. President Roosevelt as Commander in Chief of the Armed Forces mobilized the aircraft industry to *Win the War Through Air Power*, to quote the title of a best-seller book by Igor Sikorsky, referred to earlier as the "Father of Rotary Aircraft."

AIRCRAFT PRODUCTION

General Arnold, Chief of Air Corps, turned to the Engineering and Industrial Research Division of National Research Council to assist in the coordination and management of the dramatic challenge to mobilize the aircraft industry. A special NRC committee on aircraft products was established and was one of our most exciting projects during the war years. A meeting was called in New York of the presidents of aircraft and engine companies, the chief engineers of the Big Four auto companies, the president of the Aircraft Mechanics Union, etc. General Arnold told us, "The President, by 'Executive Order,' wants *60,000* aircraft produced and delivered to the U.S. Air Force and our allies *this year*.

"We will divide this group of 50 to 60 leaders in task forces: Aircraft Design, Development, Testing and Production, Engines and Instruments, etc. Holland, who was at McCook Field when I was a colonel and took his course in Organization and Management in Command Officer's School, knows the industry, the test flight procedure, and *gets things done*. I have appointed him Chairman of the 'Kitchen Cabinet,' which includes Jimmy Doolittle, now a major in the air force responsible for getting out Allison engines at GM for the 'P1' fighter planes. Eric Nelson, Engineering Officer, who led the first round-the-world flight in 1924, has agreed to come out of retirement. As a brigadier general, he will be my personal representative, stationed here in New York in the NRC offices on a full-time basis. I will add two more men to the 'Kitchen Cabinet' next week. The duty of this executive group, which will meet weekly and report directly to me, will be to ride herd on you gentlemen, keep the program on target, and get those planes produced; like Ford turned out Model Ts on automated assembly lines. Any questions?"

Everyone was so stunned, we staggered from the room as if the roof had fallen on our heads. But you don't ask questions when the President gives orders—you "do or die." Some of our older veterans of World War I died on the battlefield under pressure of "Aircraft Production Committee of NRC" during 1941. I pause here briefly to pay silent tribute to my comrades-in-arms, who went down fighting. As to the historical records of the air force contributions to the winning of World War II, I leave that story to the professional air force historians. I do want to add a few personal observations on the critical elements of R&D management of the project. General Arnold cited some of them in his commendations and Certificates of Merit, awarded to several key members of the NRC Committee.

The significant techniques and tools of management and planning which appear in the "Final Report, NRC Committee on Aircraft Production" (which was stamped "Top Secret" during the war years) included these points:

(1) Diagnosis of production methods used in aircraft and engine manufacturing plants; analyzed, studied in plants coast to coast by "Task Forces." Conclusion: Aircraft industry must adopt automated assembling methods, then in use by leading automobile companies.

(2) Improved flow of material component parts—in one door of plant and finished product rolled out to "Flight Test" runway, adjacent to the factory.

(3) Wind tunnel tests are scientific, mathematically controlled; but there is no substitute for the test of an aircraft in actual flight, with a skilled test pilot at the controls.

(4) The aircraft assembly line must be broken down into 30 or 40 stations for each component sub-assembly. In front of each operator on the assembly line, there was placed an enlarged blueprint of component parts with details of operation diagram on which he or she follows the numbers, put her part on moving belt, and started on the next piece.

(5) Jimmy Doolittle who had spent some months at the Allison Engine Division of GM at Indianapolis as Air Force Inspector, was standing with me in the Curtiss-Wright plant in Buffalo, then turning out P1 fighter planes. Jimmy remarked, "Maury, about 85 percent of the operations of putting an aircraft together—the operations and the operators might as well be turning out refrigerators, washing machines or autos. The same metal fabricating machines and methods are used, until you get to the end of the line. The last 15 percent of assembly requires aircraft mechanics. That solves our trained manpower problem. We can train a man or a woman taken off the farm, for that matter, with time and motion studies prepared by your consulting management engineer friends. We can slice up this baloney that 'only skilled aircraft mechanics can build airplanes,' "* he said.

Architects of Aviation, Preface by Doolittle, New York: Duell, Sloan & Pearce, 1958.

(6)   Then we had to convince the Aircraft Manufacturers Association to tool up their factories with 50,000-ton hydraulic presses that would mold an aluminum wing of a plane *in one piece*, just as the auto companies were stamping out door frames, side panels, hoods, and trunks of cars in one operation. Then "Rosie the Riveter" clambered over the plane with handgun and explosive rivets, stitching together the plane parts with no more effort than running up a new dress on a sewing machine.

(7)   Finally, we had to convince General Arnold, "Billy" Mitchell, and his "Whiz-Kid" test pilots: "*You must freeze design if you want quantity production.*" That was the "Battle of Automobile Production of Aircraft" in U.S.A. We were producing aircraft and engines not only for our own country's defense, but also the airwar sinews for our Allies.

Our foreman friend at the Chrysler tank factory in Detroit, who we mentioned earlier, summed up the story of our victory over world-famous German aircraft designers of planes, Fokker, Messerschmidt, and Heinkel, (who put wings on Goering's Luftwaffe). "When Hitler challenged the U.S.A. in a war which was to be fought with armored tanks, led by General Patton, and with planes flown by General Doolittle and his Eighth Strategic Air Command, based in London, we will flatten Germany into a rubble-strewn cemetery where they will bury Hitler and his Nazis so deep, I don't think even the archaeologists will ever bother to dig them up!"

R&D ABROAD IN UNIFORM

During World War II, R&D went abroad in uniform in the military services, but the weapon systems and hardware were the products of industrial technology and know-how. Fifteen million Americans went overseas to every corner of the world . . . "they saw the world." They came home, not as "provincial Americans," but "world citizens." I am trying to emphasize the point that the "American Presence," in the major industrial nations in the world not only demonstrated our *military power*, but our *industrial capacity* to turn out the tools of war in mass production quantities. Even Stalin was impressed!

John Green, Director of the Office of Technical Services in the Department of Commerce during most of my service with NRC, neatly summed up the international exchange of technology between Europe and U.S.A. in the "Foreword" to *An Industrial Explorer Abroad* saying, "Maury's work as a one-man 'Technical Assistance Mission' was *in reverse*, since American industry received most of the benefit."*

Green continued in this summation of world exploration of R&D organization and management with this statement:

The 1920s and 1930s were an era of national self-satisfactions in industry. Many felt that we had learned the secret of mass production and no other nation could rival us. However, Holland saw the future more clearly. He recognized that the great scientists of Europe, the many German Nobel Prize winners, and others who were making fundamental contributions to knowledge were planting the seeds for new industries. Therefore, he began an extensive series of inspection trips to Europe, the Orient, South America, and Scandinavia to visit famous universities and to penetrate industrial research laboratories and to bring back the most advanced thinking found there. It is this third function which is the central theme of this book. It took him to London in 1924, when he participated in the World Power Conference and learned of the unique cooperative research association program, which the British government had sponsored. Maury faithfully recorded the details of this plan which has since been copied with variations in many of the leading industrial nations of the world. Two years later, Holland was off again to Tokyo this time, where he was a U.S. Delegate to the Third Pan Pacific Science

Maurice Holland,
Japan, 1926.

Congress. Maury always had a second objective up his sleeve on these trips; this time it was to learn all he could about the scientific methods in the Japanese fishing industry. Recognizing the need for reciprocity, Holland presented a paper titled 'Science Audit of the Fisheries Industry—in U.S.A.' This was a competent look at the fishing industry in our country, followed by a recognition of its deficiencies in applied science, and a courteous request for help from the Japanese who at that time

---

*Holland, Maurice, *An Industrial Explorer Abroad: A Modern Marco Polo*, San Antonio, Texas: Southwest Research Institute, 1966.

were world leaders in this field. This tactic paid off handsomely and Maury had a unique opportunity to get inside the Japanese fishing industry, to visit the Mikimoto organization which produces the cultured pearls, which rival the natural product of the oyster. And, of course, he did not forget to look at the Japanese girl divers. At this time I might mention that if I find a fault in Maury's narrative, it is the absence of reference to the social side of his travels. However, as one who occasionally shared them, I can assure you he is a convivial one, who doesn't miss an opportunity to relax in good company at the end of a busy day.

This much for background, which I hope will contribute to an understanding of the man behind the story, *An Industrial Explorer Abroad: A Modern Marco Polo*. Here you will find the many devices Holland used to promote research at a time when a scientist was considered by most to be an unworldly individual, whose investigations were of little or no practical importance. Maury used to say that he had two basic techniques, both taken from the advertising world. Many industrial advertisers, at least so it seems from the television advertisements, thrive by frightening the consumer. They threaten that one will lose teeth, hair, vision, or mate unless one purchases a certain product. Seizing on this Maury would argue that business would lose its markets, its volume, and, in fact, might go down the drain, unless it caught up and surpassed the products and processes employed by its competitors here and abroad. The other Madison Avenue technique which he borrowed, was a more positive one. Here he asked his clients if they wanted an 'image' like the leaders of industry—General Electric, DuPont, or General Motors. If so, they must take advantage of 'Research—the royal road to riches.'

Since industry in Germany was particularly research conscious, Maury paid special attention to developments there and many patent licenses between American and German firms resulted from his efforts. Also he developed broad experience concerning scientific personnel and facilities in that country. After World War II when our government instituted the Marshall Plan with the objective of restoring European industry to a competitive position, the emphasis had shifted. Now America was the world leader in industrial research and we had techniques and experience which could be imparted to those nations which had been devastated by World War II. What more natural than to call on Holland for guidance.

The Office European Economic Corporation, which was brought into being by the Marshall Plan, was looking toward the United States for the kind of industrial research experience which Maury had acquired over the years. He was asked to help out and did so including providing advice on recruiting and selecting three teams of experts—one of which went to Germany, one to France, and a third to Italy. The name of Holland was well known abroad and he served as a sort of 'elder statesman' with each team. The recognition and credit he received for this work was a logical reward for the man who in the two decades before World War II was often called a 'one-man Technical Assistance Mission.' Although at that time the 'assistance' that he was performing was directed toward U.S. industry.

Our story of activities of R&D abroad would not be complete without a passing reference to Latin America and the Good Neighbor Policy developed during World War II by President Roosevelt.

There was an urgent need to put up an umbrella over South America. First, as a component of hemisphere defense and as a reminder to the world of our obligations under the Monroe Doctrine. Second, to assist in the development of the potential industrial resources of that great continent. Preliminary studies had indicated that there was an untapped treasure house of strategic industrial materials essential to U.S. industry in war, in Brazil alone. They were said to rival the mythical, but unproved, natural wealth of the USSR.

Obviously, there was a pressing need for an independent, objective survey of South America. Twenty-five executives from all sections of the United States, representing industry, banking, and industrial research left Miami by "Pan American Clipper" in March 1941, on the first leg of a 17,000-mile all-air trip through South America. They had been appointed as a Special Committee of the National Research Council to visit Columbia, Peru, Chile, Argentina, Uruguay, and Brazil. A tour of industrial exploration was arranged with the assistance of United States Department of State, the Department of Commerce, and the Council of National Defense.*

The places to be visited had been sifted from suggestions made by local program committees, which had been appointed in each country, so as to furnish a program which would properly portray their industrial possi-

---

*"Tour of Industrial Exploration"—South America, 1941, NRC.

bilities. The final schedule consisted of conferences with North American and local industrial executives, bankers, and government officials; inspection trips to certain factories, institutions, and public works; and round-table discussions between the committee and South American government officials.

The purpose of the trip can be best stated by quoting from the contract between Dr. F. B. Jewett, President, National Academy of Sciences, and the Council of National Defense, which states: Under the terms of this contract between the National Academy of Sciences, under which the National Research Council functions, and Nelson A. Rockefeller, Coordinator of Commercial and Cultural Relations between the American Republics, Council of National Defense, it is stipulated that you are to prepare and submit to the Coordinator, not later than June 1, 1941, a report on the opportunities for cooperative industrial development between the United States and the other American republics through the application of North American technical skills and production methods to Latin American raw materials.

Mr. Holland outlined the plan originally conceived as follows:

Statement of Objectives of the Tour

(a)   To observe and study at first hand the industrial progress of South America;

(b)   To exchange ideas between tour members and representative industrial executives and government officials in the countries visited;

(c)   To give advice—*when requested* by government officials, private industry, and research workers—in matters of research, engineering, and technology;

(d)   *To establish an enduring association through this committee*, by making available to South American governments and industries the services of the National Research Council on a basis similar to that given to our own government.

Statement of Procedure

(a)   Orientation conference with North American and local executives, bankers, and government officials;

(b)   Factory and inspection visits;

(c)   Round-table discussion.

The fairly near-term industrial possibilities of the countries visited follow the itinerary of the tour, beginning with Columbia and following through Peru, Chile, Argentina, Uruguay, and to Brazil, where Sao Paulo is probably the *most industrialized and fastest growing city on the continent.* There are scattered specific industrial possibilities in Peru in textiles, in Chile in steel, in Argentina in agro-industrial products such as those from corn, sole leather, and leather products from kid skin and hides, and highly specialized strategic products like beryllium. Also, there are long-term industrial large-volume low-price possibilities in Brazil such as tung oil,* industrial diamonds, paper and pulp, rubber, minerals, and metal ores.

Four fields for observation in every country were listed:

(1)   The attitude, policy and regulations of the governments with respect to industrialization, based on their past performance—as well as the present state of mind as expressed to us by government officials;

(2)   Industrial or agro-industrial raw materials organized in volume sufficient to become the basis of an industrial operation;

(3)   The pool, present or potential, of skilled industrial operatives, the educational or training institutions now located in the country which would increase or improve the industrial or technical skills of the population;

(4)   The legal, banking, and exchange regulations which have a direct bearing upon the industrialization of the country.

Each member of the tour prepared a report conveying his observations, impressions, and recommendations. Special attention was given to industrial research and technical education. Since Harold Vagtborg was a member of the Mission and also Director of Armour Research Foundation, I have turned to him to complete the task of reporting his special fields of interest in South American industry and engineering education. (His recommendations were pertinent to the main theme and objectives of this book.)

Shortly after my return from South America, NRC decided to move the New York office to the Washington headquarters. The reason for this was to consolidate and expand the staff, facilities, and contacts to meet the increasing demands from the government in Washington.

Director Holland and staff were directed to pack up furniture and files of the Division Office in the Engineering Societies Building in New York and move to Washington. After nearly 20 years of service and record performance, reaching a dramatic climax with the completion of the South American Tour (which incidentally drew some expressions of high commendation from NRC officials, from Secretary of Commerce Jesse Jones, and

---

*Then imported from China only. Essential to paint industry.

from Nelson Rockefeller), a vital decision on the move to Washington had to be made by me and the staff.

After careful weighing of all the pros and cons, I decided that the weight of this evidence pointed to a negative decision. "It's easy to make a decision when you have all the facts pertaining to the problem in hand," my chief, Doctor Jewett, reminded me. "Sometimes we make wrong decisions when there is not enough time to collect all the facts, as in wartime." He counseled with me, as with his own son.

Finally, with the help and advice of other Academy-Research Council friends and associates, including Gano Dunn, "Van" Bush, and "Bill" Batt (then chairman of our division), I came to the conclusion to strike out on my own in private consulting business.

These were the major factors upon which the decision was based:

(1) I had put in my service to my country as a flying officer in the Air Corps in World War I.

(2) I was intrigued by the challenge of selling my services to industrial management as "Industrial Research Advisor," serving U.S. industry from coast to coast, which was essentially my role in NRC.

(3) The personal contacts I had made provided me with a library of 500 or more top management executives, with whom I was associated through tours, speeches, engineering societies, and industry associations. Many of them seemed to be promising prospects.

(4) After preliminary discussions with four nationally known companies, where I was being considered for the position of liaison officer between management and R&D operations, I definitely concluded I was not an "organization man." No time-clock puncher position seemed to offer the autonomous style of operations I had enjoyed in NRC.

Working with NRC in promoting research in the early days was somewhat like the preacher in church who gave soul inspiring sermons; but when the congregation left the church, he had no count of the number of sinners he had converted. Neither did I!

One thing past experience has taught me—sell your service to a single company and when they count the results of improved performance in terms of dollars ringing up in the cash register, they will probably retain your service for another year.

In June 1942, we opened our office in the American Radiator Building overlooking Bryant Park in New York. The view from the eleventh floor reminded me of Paris, my favorite city in Europe.

My executive assistant, E. M. Bryman, my strong right arm all through NRC days, now managed the office and kept the books and me "on the beam." *An average* of 50,000 airline miles a year, for 10 years, kept me on the road most of the time. Most of our clients had government contracts on crash programs for which Uncle Sam paid more than half the bill. As they would say on Wall Street, tax deductible R&D as a business expense caused "business to come in over the transom of our office." Factories belched smoke night and day. Automated assembly lines clanged through the night shifts, where "Rosie the Riveter" turned out planes in California, and Chrysler built tanks in Detroit suburbs. Women by the thousands were moonlighting on jobs to supplement family take-home pay under pressure of the rising costs of living.

Our clients ranged from Pillsbury in Minneapolis in the North to Southwest Research Institute in San Antonio in the Southwest. Bombs, guns, powder, and explosives were flowing from Olin Industry plants in St. Louis to the battlefields in Europe, while Anheuser-Busch beer quenched the thirst of our service men around the world. The east-west axis of our client travel extended from the Grinnell Company in Rhode Island to Stanford Research Institute in California.

* * *

RESEARCH MANAGEMENT AUDIT

In our consulting practice, we had several things going for us, such as:

- Our NRC national exposure to top management in industry through speeches, articles, tours, books, and the "Science Speaks" radio program (Chicago Century of Progress).
- *Research Rating System.* Eighty member-companies of IRI were used as testing ground for "the measurement of R&D management." This is a sample of R&D rating we made for many companies:

Check List for Tested Practices in Profitable Industrial Research

1. *Research Policies*:

   Management's attitude and understanding of function;

   Appropriations in terms of net worth, sales, net income, advertising;

   Research executive position in management, title, control;

   Organization and operation methods to provide continuous flow of new product ideas and applications.

2. *Research Program*:

   Project appraisal—economic and commercial;

Project balance—long-, medium-, short-term;
Budget;
Geared to market and industry research.
3. *Research Organization*:
Management and planning;
Personnel, selection, assignment, teamwork;
Performance evaluation;
Department cooperation.
4. *Competitive Technical Position*:
Laboratory organization, personnel, performance;
Competitive position in the industry—sales, financial, technical, public relations;
Competitive industry threats.
5. *Research Geared to Sales*:
Committee organizations;
Laboratory demonstrations;
Sample products and sales aids for field demonstrations;
Meetings, market, and technical data.
6. *Research Contacts*:
Government agencies—national trends;
Universities—fundamental trends, personnel;
Industrial associations—cooperative industry trends;
Consultants, specialists—specific problems;
Industrial, technical literature, reports, meetings.

Granting that management frequently fails in adequate communications with its research arm, and vice versa, there should be a rough yardstick for measuring the effectiveness of a research program within any one company. A survey conducted among members of the Industrial Research Institute indicated that the score sheet reproduced here can reveal a consensus of what is right and what is wrong in any company's management research relationships. A score of 95 might indicate that the company is too good to be true. Any score below 60 means trouble that needs immediate attention. Any front-office executive, any research director, can make the test and draw his own conclusions.

Several years ago, leading executives who voluntarily submitted to a similar questionnaire as a measure for self-analysis rated their companies, on the average, in the low 70s. Few claimed much above 90, and 12 percent blushed in the 50s.

PROCEDURE CHART
New Products Research and Development
ANHEUSER-BUSCH, INC.

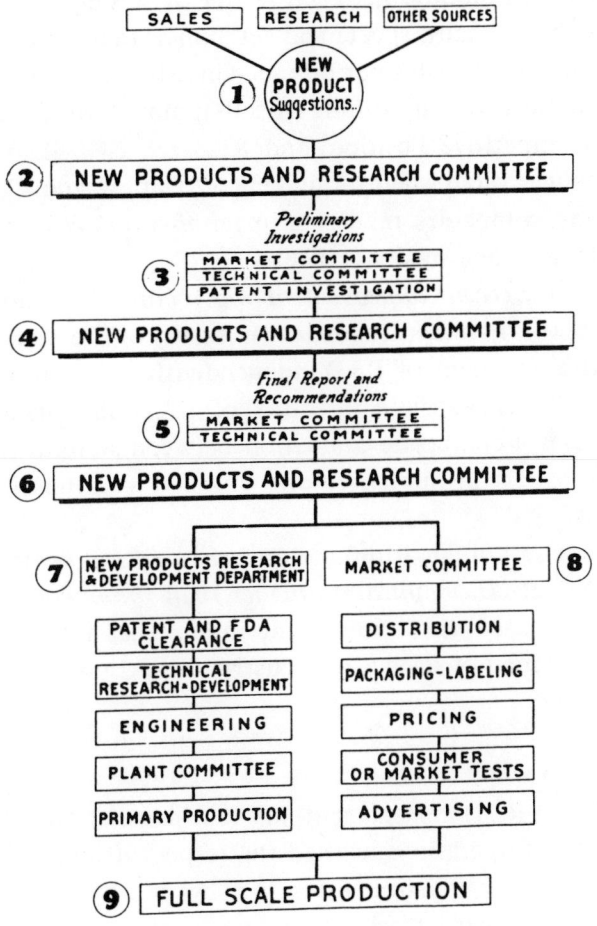

Here, then, is a collective confession of corporate guilt, without benefit of a lie detector. It could not be expected that any president, or any vice president in charge of sales, engineering, research, production, advertising, or finance, would shoulder much of the blame, or any specific part of it. But management as a whole gives itself no better than a passing mark of 70 for its performance in handling the $7 billion it was then spending on research annually. By implication management admits that it is wasting more than $2 billion of its own money. Let each reader of this book secretly score his own company on the tally sheet, and let him search his executive soul to find how he could improve his performance in using research at its full value.

The bench mark for the results of self-appraisal of Policies, Program, Organization, Competitive Position, and Research Geared to Sales and Research Contacts was established by making a "Rating Audit" two years in a row of the same companies reporting in *number values*, which were comparative in both large and small companies.

Fifteen to 20 percent improvement was recorded by most of the companies between the first and second year surveys. The first appraisal was made by the vice president of R&D independently and sent in to our office. Three or four of his associate directors of R&D also made independent ratings to arrive at a composite evaluation between administrative appraisal and the group leaders in the laboratory who had a "bench world" view of daily operations.

It may surprise you, as it did me, to learn that *top management almost always rated their R&D organization higher than the operating personnel.* I attribute that unusual observation to the intellectual honesty and integrity of the professional man of science in industry.

SPECIALIST IN R&D MANAGEMENT

Being a specialist in R&D management, my long association with NRC, while limiting my field of operations, earned the respect of older and larger consulting management engineering firms in New York. We worked closely with many of them, particularly when we needed staff engineers in our clients' plants.

Several other factors contributed to the rapid expansion of our business; for instance:

- Author of books on R&D management.
- *Profitable Practice*, the first "how-to-do" book, and *Management's*

Stake in Research, how to measure productivity.
- Long and intimate contacts with leading management engineers, both here and abroad, through attendance at international management conferences in London, Paris, Rome, Berlin, and Washington.

* * *

INVESTMENT BANKING SUPPORT

We have referred several times to the active interest and support of the investment banking community in R&D. We laid the foundation for that cooperation in articles in the *Bankers Association Journal* and *stimulated action over the years* by banker participation in laboratory tours (Lehmann Bros., Banker's Trust, Dunn & Bradstreet, Liberty Bank of Buffalo, and Harris Trust* of Chicago, to name a few representative firms).

Another facet of investment interest in R&D was our cooperative projects with Lionel Edie Associates, a highly respected econometrics advisor to many "blue chip" companies. At a meeting of the Industrial Conference Board, where Mr. Edie gave a keynote speech titled "Long Term Forecast of Industrial Securities," he predicted three major factors that would determine the future course of national economy as follows: (1) war or peace, (2) population explosion and housing, and (3) R&D in industry, *a new factor in classical economic forecasting.*

After the meeting, I gave him copies of my "Comparative Rating of R&D" of 80 member companies of IRI, with the statement that "This comparative self-appraisal by R&D executives of their operations is a '*yardstick* not a *foot-rule*, much less a micrometer.' I would like your organization to join with member companies of IRI in a continuous study to improve performance. We have digested and analyzed the results as we see them from the management viewpoint. We seek your cooperation in making an *economic evaluation* of this *representative cross-section of American business.* Many of them are clients of yours and members of the Institute, sponsored by National Research Council."

Some months later, Edie Associates published a list of "100 Preferred Growth Stocks," with this guideline for investors—"Growth in these companies which support R&D *continuously through long periods of good and bad business times, are the companies of the future!*" The gyrations of the stock market in the 1960s, when any company's name was even remotely

---

*See "Foreword," *Management's Stake in Research* by Guy Reed of Harris Trust Co.

identified with technology labels, were the "boy wonders" of Wall Street and favorites of the in-crowd of "Go-Go Performance" prophets.

It seems appropriate to introduce at this point a friend and associate of mine for many years—Ora Roehl, financial and management consultant of Boston—who has been meeting with me at the middle of the bridge, spanning the turbulent currents of economics and technology for many years. Our primary interest is our clients and is extended by periodic publication of our joint efforts to educate some of the 25 to 30 million investors on the R&D factor of investment. They now own much of American industry. Their voices are being listened to in boardrooms and in stockholders' annual meetings.

Mr. Roehl took time out from his busy schedule of meetings with professional money managers in Boston, New York, Chicago, and Hartford to summarize a belief of one of the leading authorities in the field, which was that technological change was the most powerful factor in the business environment of today.

R&D WORKS ON WALL STREET

Roehl was formerly head of investment research for Keystone Custodian Funds, Inc. of Boston, from 1946 until he retired from that company to set up his own organization as "Financial and Management Consultant," a few years ago in Boston. His writings on the subject in nationally circulated media are followed by many invitations to speak. His speeches and articles published in national media are some indication of his position of recognized authority in the field of professional security analysts, as well as in science, engineering, and educational meetings.

For 25 years or more, Ora and I have been meeting and discussing ways to improve communication and understanding of the innovative process as part of R&D in industry and to demonstrate the appraisal gap for venture capital amongst investment bankers, leaders in industry, government, and universities. Much of the financial community do not truly understand the business and the human dynamics of the "total concept" of technologically based companies, which are conceived and born through the innovative process.

Although the stock market, while I write, is presenting the spectacle of a macabre dance of death for the audience of fastbuck boys who played with "yo-yo" stocks and "go-go" funds, Roehl put on paper his "measuring stick" for evaluating the R&D factor as a *function of management*. I now present five rules in condensed form under the title, "Roehl's Rules for R&D Evaluation."

(1) Does top management really appreciate the importance of technology? Too much interest becomes harmful meddling and too little may be taken as indifference.

(2) What about management organization for research? Does management give research appropriate status in the company's organization chart? Where does the R&D executive's salary fit into the company's executive salary scale?

(3) What about research plans for the future? Is there a strong techno-economic approach? Management should have a definite idea of where its business stands today. Where it is headed, and to what areas of its scientific, research, and engineering activities are to be limited. It should have definite ideas as to product life of both old and new products. Management should determine the areas that hold high profit potential and avoid those that are overcrowded and highly competitive.

(4) What business is the company in? A company needs to continually ask: Where is it going and what research projects should it pursue to get there? The investor will pay a premium for a company that really knows where it is going. Particularly companies in technologically based industries. If management has answers to these questions, an investor will give a high evaluation of the company's R&D activities.

(5) What are the results? What does the record show? How many technological firsts has the company had? What is the reputation of the company's R&D, both amongst its competitors and other research institutions? The investor is more willing to pay a premium for stock in companies with such credentials. Is management well informed on plans for translating successful research into successful commercial practice by financing and marketing its products?

"Technological change is a most powerful factor in business environment today," says Professor James R. Bright of Harvard Business School. "The first requirement for the businessman is a keen sensitivity, awareness, and receptivity to technological change as a *major environmental force*, which he can employ and to which he must respond. In many businesses it will be far and away the most important force!"

The technological capital of American industry is undoubtedly one, if not the most valuable asset of U.S.A. business. It has been built up for half a century. The foundation stones of our national R&D structure forms a mosaic pattern of bright colors from abroad and they are cemented together by industrial management.

* * *

RETIREMENT

While I formally retired in 1958, closed the New York office, and went to Hawaii to live, I felt the urge to get back into harness after a year of golf, fishing, and shell hunting. I "retired from retirement" to serve as advisor to the Industrial Development Commission in Hawaii, Dole Pineapple Company, Honolulu Paper Company, and the Bishop Museum.

Since my return to the "Mainland," I have responded to calls from old clients on short-term assignments, on projects of current mutual interest. As I told "H.V." when I agreed to enter this "Holy Alliance" with him—little did I think I would be digging up my "life story" from the grave of memory. He asked for it!

P.S. Readers, please remember this chapter was written almost wholly from "total recall" of highlights in 50 years of R&D without benefit of "a good reference library and some knowledgeable staff researchers."

Maurice Holland (center) receiving the Founder's Award from Industrial Research Institute at its 1955 Meeting at the Shamrock Hotel in Houston, Texas. E. Duer Reeves (right), President of IRI and Executive Vice President, Esso Research & Engineering Co., and Fred Olsen (left), Vice President Olin Mathieson Chemical Corp.

INDEX